The LAST LAP

The
LAST
LAP

The Life and Times of
NASCAR's Legendary Heroes

PETER GOLENBOCK

Macmillan • USA

Macmillan
A Simon & Schuster Macmillan Company
1633 Broadway
New York, NY 10019-6785

Macmillan Publishing books may be purchased for business or sales promotional
use. For information please write: Special Markets Department, Macmillan
Publishing USA, 1633 Broadway, New York, NY 10019.

A catalogue record is available from the Library of Congress.

ISBN 0-02-862825-X

10 9 8 7 6 5 4 3 2 1

Printed in the United States of America

DEDICATION

This book is dedicated to Elmo Langley, who I'm sorry to say I spoke to briefly but didn't interview just two days before he left us too soon. Mr. Langley is remembered for driving NASCAR's pace car, but his life in racing began back in the mid-fifties. He was a fascinating man who knew everyone. Before his marriage to his wife, Nancy, he was engaged to country and western singing legend Patsy Kline.

Elmo was on his way to Japan the day we spoke. He said that as soon as he returned, I could come see him. He was behind the wheel of the pace car on a track half a world away when he drove off the track, put his head down on the steering wheel, and died. Mr. Langley was sixty-eight. Though I never knew him, I mourn his passing.

This book is also dedicated to the men who have given their lives in the service of their sport, and to their relatives, friends, and fans who have never allowed the flame of memory to be extinguished.

CONTENTS

ACKNOWLEDGMENTS   XIII

INTRODUCTION   XV

1 BOB LATFORD   1
In the Beginning

2 SLICK OWENS   7
In the Land of Cotton

3 TIM FLOCK   13
The Last of the Wild Bunch

4 RALPH MOODY   27
Curtis and Lil' Joe

5 MAX MUHLMANN   41
More Curtis and Lil' Joe

6 MAURICE PETTY   51
The Perfectionist

7 TIM FLOCK   59
Carl Kiekhaefer

8 DANNY "CHOCOLATE" MYERS 65
The Death of the Myers Brothers

9 TOM PISTONE 73
The "Converted Yankee"

10 RALPH MOODY 85
Fred Lorenzen

11 PAUL "LITTLE BUD" MOORE 89
Rough-Tough Characters

12 BUDDY BAKER 99
Buck's Boy

13 MARVIN PANCH 111
Escape from a Fiery Death

14 BOB LATFORD 127
Crash and Burn

15 RALPH MOODY 133
Death Wholesale

16 MAX MUHLMANN 139
The Death of Fireball Roberts

17 BOB LATFORD 145
Ned and Junior

18 DAVID PEARSON 151
The Reluctant Champion

19 PAUL "LITTLE BUD" MOORE 161
The Demise of Dirt

20 BOB LATFORD 173
A Small Band of Gypsies

21 MAURICE PETTY 179
Life with Richard

22 DAVID PEARSON 189
Moments Great and Not So Good

23 "SUITCASE" JAKE ELDER 199
One Great Chassis Man

24 SLICK OWENS 205
Holman and Moody's Demise

25 BUDDY BAKER 211
He Broke the 200 MPH Barrier

26 TIM FLOCK 217
Curtis Turner's Losing Gambit

27 CURTIS TURNER 223
The Day the Music Died

28 BUNNY TURNER 229
"Sweet Thang"

29 LOU LaROSA 239
Brooklyn Meets Robert Gee

30 BUDDY BAKER 249
Troubles on the Last Lap

31 WANDA LUND 259
They Were All Crazy

32 TOMMY JOHNSON 275
The Travails of Harry Hyde

33 BUDDY BAKER 285
Records at Breakneck Speed

34 LOU LaROSA 299
The Emergence of Dale Earnhardt

35 TOMMY JOHNSON 311
Harry Hyde and Tim Richmond

36 LOU LaROSA 317
Cale and More About Dale

37 DANNY "CHOCOLATE" MYERS 331
Memories of Richard Childress

38 TOMMY JOHNSON 339
The Death of Harry Hyde

39 PAUL ANDREWS 345
The Death of Alan Kulwicki

40 "SUITCASE" JAKE ELDER 363
Disturbing Memories

41 LIZ ALLISON   369
The Deaths of Clifford and Davey

42 LOU LAROSA   383
A Racer's Sad Good-bye

43 BUDDY BAKER   395
*He (and the Sport) Survives and
Flourishes*

INDEX   403

ACKNOWLEDGMENTS

To Jeanine Buceck, my crew chief and editor at Macmillan, for all your support and confidence. To Neil Reshen and Dawn Reshen-Doty, who for over a decade now have protected and nurtured me.

To Tom, Pat and Brian Cotter, Ed and Anne Carroll, Jimmy Johnson, and Cliff and Adrienne Powers, whose friendship and assistance have always been invaluable and cherished.

To Jonathan Mauk, the photo archive guru at the Daytona International Speedway, who has helped me from the beginning.

To Greg Fielden, for always being available at the other end of the phone and to Al Pierce and Al Robinson for their expertise. And to Michelle Tupper, for her diligence and care, and Natalie Chapman for her support.

My eternal gratitude to the fabled men and women of stock car racing who gave their time and memories to make this labor of love as interesting and dynamic as possible: Liz Allison, Paul Andrews, Buddy Baker, H. Clay Earles and Dick Thompson of the Martinsville Speedway, Wanda Lund Early, Jake Elder, Lou and Teresa LaRosa, Bob Latford, Tim and Frances Flock, Bunny Turner Hall, Tommy Johnson, Ralph and Mitzy Moody, Max Muhlmann, Danny Myers and Caron Pappas, Paul "Little Bud" Moore, Charles

"Slick" Owens, Marvin and Betty Panch, David Pearson, Tom and Sammy Pistone, and Maurice Petty.

And to my wonderful family, Rhonda and Charlie, and the road course hound Doris; every day you make me feel like a winner.

INTRODUCTION

THE IDEA FOR THIS BOOK AND for its title occurred at the same moment, on the afternoon of July 13, 1993, when I heard over the radio that Davey Allison had died from his injuries suffered in a freak helicopter accident. I was shocked and very upset, as were a legion of NASCAR race fans. In mid-February during the week before the 1993 Daytona 500, I had asked Donna Freismuth of the Daytona International Speedway if she would be so kind as to arrange a meeting between Davey and my son Charlie, who was then six. Davey was his favorite, and why not? He cut a dashing figure, seemed to enjoy the media and fan attention, and he sure could drive a race car. What I especially liked about him was he was serious about his work, but at the same time he knew how to laugh and have fun. Davey reminded me a lot of a co-author, former New York Yankee pitcher Ron Guidry, another great athlete with a lot of charisma.

Davey's shocking death brought tears to my eyes. I didn't know him well, but I mourned his passing. His had been the third tragic death to hit racing since August of 1992. Clifford Allison, Davey's younger brother, was killed during a practice run at Michigan that month. Then, in what seemed a cruel April Fool's hoax, but wasn't, a plane crash had killed racer Alan Kulwicki, a man I highly respected after interviewing him for my first book on racing, *American Zoom*. When Davey's helicopter crashed on July 13, 1993 the racing world grieved for Davey and for his parents, Bobby and Judy Allison.

Davey's death cast a pall over the sport the likes of which race fans hadn't seen since the deaths of Joe Weatherly and Fireball Roberts back in 1964. With Davey's death, Bobby and Judy had lost both their sons in a very short period of time. Such tragedy was, and remains, almost incomprehensible.

What sets these—and all—racers apart from less daredevilish mortals is their complete lack of fear and their joy of doing something on the edge. They love the speed *because* it's dangerous. Davey Allison was a guy who felt he could do anything. Given the opportunity, he would have grandly walked across a high-wire without a net in order to escape the mundane routine of life. Davey certainly could have chosen to drive his pickup to the racetrack that day, but that wouldn't have been any fun. Flying a jet-powered helicopter gave him that kick he needed, and flying it into an enclosed space, hey, no problem. Except that it killed him.

I said out loud to no one in particular, "What the hell did you need a turbojet helicopter for anyway, Davey? And what were you thinking trying to park it in an enclosed area?" Some witnesses said the craft Davey was flying flipped after the back rotor hit a wire fence. As the tears flowed, I thought, "You have driven your last lap." Hence the book's title.

And so I decided to write a book which would explore racers' addiction to danger and their love of doing something that seems so unsafe. But when I brought up the subject, not one of them thought racing to be either reckless or unsafe. None of them thought what they do is particularly heroic.

Whether this is a pattern of denial which makes it possible for them to perform or whether they actually deep down believe driving a race car at 190 miles an hour is really safe, there is no way of telling. But Richard Petty once told me he felt safer driving at Daytona than he did on Interstate 77, and if you look at the statistics on injuries and death on the American highways, maybe he's right.

So instead of concentrating on the element of danger—loving racing more than safety, I chose instead to celebrate and illuminate the lives of the legendary stock car drivers and mechanics who fought in the arena—current favorites like the team of Richard Childress and

Dale Earnhardt, some who have retired like Richard Petty, David Pearson, Cale Yarborough, Bobby Allison, and Buddy Baker, and especially those NASCAR legends who left us too soon—among them Bill France Sr., Curtis Turner, Billy and Bobby Myers, Joe Weatherly, Fireball Roberts, Bobby Isaac, Ralph Earnhardt, Tiny Lund, Herb Nab, Harry Hyde, Neil Bonnett, Davey Allison, and Alan Kulwicki.

These men glitter in memory. They cry out to be remembered. And in this book so shall they be, fondly recalled in all their glory by their friends in the sport and those who loved them most.

I've been told that 50 percent of all Winston Cup race fans have come to the sport in the last five years. If that is true, then everyone knows of and can appreciate the skills of Dale Earnhardt, Jeff Gordon, and Dale Jarrett among many others. But if you are to be a true fan of the sport, you ought to know something about those who came before, especially those legendary Hall of Famers about whom stories have been told through the generations. Their lives have enriched the sport. Their zest for life and for racing have given us all inspiration.

And through knowing them, we can look back and understand the sport's origins, how it came into being, who started it and why, and why the sport has been able to grow and prosper to the amazing point where it has come today.

Without the sacrifices made by these men, who literally gave their lives for the sport, NASCAR could not have become what it is today. They drove their last lap for us, and we shall always be grateful to them and remain a little bit humble having known them.

A second theme that runs throughout this book is the hold this sport has had on everyone who has ever participated in and followed it. American stock car racing has never been just a sport to the motorheads and car nuts and racing fans and small-town gas jockeys and big-city executives of oil, auto supply, and car-related companies who have made it their passion over the years. It long has been a mania, a religion even, whose origins began in the Southeast and over the years has spread throughout this nation, to the point that the popularity of stock car racing has skyrocketed. No sport, not baseball or football or basketball, has a larger following. NASCAR has grown so dramatically that today Winston Cup events have become the biggest shows of any sport in whatever state they appear.

In New York State, for example, the home of Yankee Stadium, Madison Square Garden, and War Memorial Stadium in Buffalo, the single biggest sporting event in the state takes place at out-of-the-way Watkins Glen, before 110,000 spectators. In California, the home of the Rose Bowl, Dodger Stadium, and the Fabulous Forum, no venue gets greater attendance than the NASCAR race at Sonoma. The race at the Atlanta Motor Speedway each year is the single largest gathering of sports fans in the state of Georgia, bigger than any bowl or pro game. It's like this wherever Winston Cup races are held. The NASCAR race at Indianapolis, with 250,000 fans in attendance, has become one of the largest sporting events in the world.

As NASCAR prepares to celebrate the fiftieth anniversary of its inception, be aware of yet a third theme: how the sport has changed. Today, most of big-league stock car racing is held on paved super-speedways. Once, it was mostly half-mile dirt. Today, the norm is for a hundred thousand or more to fill a track to watch a race. Used to be, a promoter was glad if five thousand fans showed up for an event. Today, sponsors as diverse as Tide, Miller beer, Kodak, and Kelloggs Corn Flakes spend millions of dollars putting their advertising on the cars. Once upon a time, a racer was lucky if he could get the local service station owner to pay him two hundred bucks to put his name on the side of the car.

The growth of the sport, the big money and the gloss has restrained its participants from engaging in much of the madcap antics. Sponsors don't want their drivers getting drunk and driving their rental cars into swimming pools anymore.

And yet, on the track, the races themselves remain as they always have been, fast, thrilling, and dangerous.

The men and women interviewed in this book have seen it all.

Some, like racers Tim Flock, Marvin Panch, David Pearson, and Buddy Baker, have left their mark on the hearts of their fans and in the record books. Others, like Ralph Moody, Maurice Petty, Jake Elder, Slick Owens, and Lou LaRosa, have built engines and chassis which allowed the greats to run up front. Others, like Bob Latford and Max Muhlmann, have covered the sport as journalists or PR men, while still others, like Danny Myers, Bunny Turner, Tommy Johnson, Wanda Lund, and Liz Allison, have rejoiced in triumph and then suffered unimaginable tragedy after the sudden deaths of their loved ones.

Remembering them, let us try to emphasize the joy they brought us and to laugh at the hijinks. These were originals who put their lives on the line and lived life to the fullest every day. As Helen Keller once said, "Life is either a daring adventure or nothing." They knew it better than anyone.

1

IN THE BEGINNING

THOUGH NASCAR STOCK CAR RAC-ing may well be the fastest-growing, most popular sport in America, part of its charm for any historian is that there are still people alive today who were around at its beginnings. Bob Latford, who grew up in Daytona Beach, went to elementary school with the son of the sport's founder, Bill France Sr. At a young age Latford sold programs, worked the concession stands, and counted laps at France's Daytona Beach and Road Course races.

Latford was there when a group of racing pioneers, led by France, met on December 14, 1947, in a meeting room of the Streamline Hotel in Daytona Beach, Florida, to organize the National Association of Stock Car Auto Racing. He watched as Red Vogt, a well-respected mechanic from Atlanta, suggested the name of the organization, NASCAR, which was incorporated in February of 1948.

France's most far-reaching, far-thinking brilliant idea was that the cars that ran in all NASCAR events would be late model cars. His theory was that race fans would be most interested in watching race cars that looked like the ones they were buying in showrooms across America. It is likely that the sport's autocratic genius even anticipated that day when the car manufacturers would back the top race teams, once they came to

1

realize that success on the track would result in bigger sales in the showrooms.

France had wanted to start his late model racing in 1948, but no new cars had been built during World War II, and he found that not enough car manufacturers were producing new vehicles yet to get his circuit off the ground. He would have to wait until 1949.

France's home base was Daytona Beach, and it is fitting to start a book about the legends of NASCAR with a discussion of both France, the founding genius and strongman, and the city of Daytona Beach, the place where it all began. And Bob Latford is the perfect witness to do it.

After high school and a stint in the army during the Korean War, Bill France Sr. hired Latford to work in the publicity department of the Daytona International Speedway. He later worked at the Atlanta Motor Speedway, then at the Charlotte Motor Speedway. While there in 1975 he designed the points system still used to determine the Winston Cup driving championship.

Today Latford is editor and publisher of a newsletter devoted to Winston Cup racing history. Since 1995 he has been the official Shell Answer Man, an expert on the sport with a font of knowledge whose job it is to supply journalists with answers to such questions as "Who was the first driver to win the 125, the pole, and the Daytona 500?" In his sixty-one years, Bob Latford has lived the entire history of NASCAR. He knows whereof he speaks. (The answer: Fireball Roberts, in 1962. According to Latford, the car, number 22, was black and silver and read "Dura Lube" on the quarterpanel.)

BOB LATFORD: "I was born in Edgeware, England, in 1935. I came to the United States in 1940, right at the start of World War II. My dad was English, my mother American. She could hear the German reconnaissance aircraft overhead from their home in England. She had been to a movie in which the heroine had some kind of a problem, and so to find the answer she opened the Bible and put her finger on a passage. My mother tried that when she got home. The passage said, 'Take your children to a foreign land.' And so she decided to return to the States. She went to Daytona because she had gone with her mother to watch Sir Malcolm Campbell make some of his early land speed record runs on the beach.

"Running on the beach of Daytona goes back to the origin of racing in this country. In the early 1900s it wasn't that different, Ford versus Chevrolet versus Olds, but at that time it was the name of the driver. Henry Ford, Louis Chevrolet, and Ransom Olds tested the new horseless carriages they had invented. The early pioneers wanted to show their dependability. The criticism was that their automobiles were always breaking down so they used the competition as a way of showing the public that the vehicles were dependable, that they could compete, and later it was more about which carmaker had the better car. At the time these guys were living in the old Gasoline Alley and eating sandwiches from a store next door, sleeping in the garage. Everything they owned was tied up in their machines. Duryea and others were down there too. And eventually Henry Ford hired Barney Oldfield to drive his cars, and Chevrolet hired its drivers, and it has evolved to where we are today with Winston Cup racing.

"Winter in Daytona has always been attractive. One of the first to come down there to winter was John D. Rockefeller. He lived in Ormond, not too far from the original Gasoline Alley. The place is called The Casements now, right at the foot of the Ormond Bridge on the mainland side. My uncle by marriage was John D. Rockefeller's bodyguard and purchasing agent. John D. used to have a big Christmas party, and he gave all the kids a dime. He built his own golf course and a big hotel, which are now condos. It was the largest wooden structure in the world.

"Rockefeller was never involved in auto racing, other than his processing of gasoline, but other people came down because of him. His partner, Henry Flagler, built the railroad from the East down to Miami.

"Bill France was the one who restarted racing after the war. He had tried a couple of races before the war with the Elks Club. When the soldiers returned from the war they had mustering-out pay, and the automobile became less a luxury and more of a necessity because of the spreading of the population. People were looking for something to do, and Bill France decided once again to hold stock car races on the beach of Daytona.

"Bill's son, Billy France, and I went to school together at Lennox Elementary School in Daytona. Billy was two years ahead of me. We are former Sandcrabs, which was our mascot at Seabreeze High

School in a much simpler time. When racing started again in 1946, Billy France asked my brothers and I if we wanted to make some money selling programs. The Frances still lived in a little house on Goodall where Bill Sr. and Annie had moved when they first came to Daytona. We were down the corner of Goodall and Peninsula when Billy asked us to work the beach race.

"I sold programs, worked the concession stands, scored, kept the lap count on the cars, even spotted for the announcers, including a character from the Smiling Jack comic strip named Flannel Mouth Don. He was called that because he talked a lot, but he was an actual person. He was the announcer in the north turn on the beach course. I worked for him, identifying the cars coming up the beach. And I worked for Sammy Bland in the south turn doing the same thing.

"A program was twenty-five cents, and I got a nickel for every one I sold. I could take two hundred of them and take off across the dunes with them. They weren't that big. We'd walk all the way up the beach side, because that's where everyone was watching the race, and I'd go from one turn to another, two miles, selling programs. I'd come back and get another stack and sell them. It was an easy way to make money and watch the cars go.

"The scoring stand was outside the south turn, down by the lighthouse. You'd sit up there, and when the cars took off to take the green flag coming into the south turn on the two-lane A1A, they'd come through the turn and take off up the beach, and as they went up the beach it looked like an invasion force coming in as the people went from the beach side to the highway side. It was a wave of people going right up the track as far as you could see.

"I grew up hanging around racing. On my way home from school I'd go by Marshall Teague's shop with the Hudsons in there. He was one of the original officers of NASCAR when it was formed at the end of '47. Matter of fact, my brothers and I were on our way home from school one day, and we stopped at the Streamline Hotel, where they were having the organizational meeting of NASCAR. We went up to the penthouse and stood in the back of the room when they called on Cannonball Baker to be NASCAR's original commissioner, or czar as they called him at the time. It was December of '47. We had no idea how significant this meeting was.

"I knew some of the people in the room. I knew Big Bill.

Everybody knew Big Bill. I knew Raymond Parks. He was a business-man out of Atlanta. He owned the first car that won a NASCAR championship. Red Byron drove for him. So did Bob Flock and Roy Hall, a convicted bootlegger who got out of the penitentiary on a Thursday and won the pole of the beach race on a Friday.

"A lot of bootleggers would come to Daytona in the winter, and racing was the way they settled the argument over who had the better car. The primary car was the '39 Ford with the huge trunks for haul-ing liquor during the week.

"Parks was very debonair, always wore a fedora, usually had a tie on, even when he was walking on the beach. I remember one year Bob Flock got there too late to qualify, so they let him start outside in the back. There were 117 cars in the race. At the time they used to send them off in waves of six across, so Bob had his crew chief, Red Vogt, stand on the dunes and signal him. When they dropped the green flag for the first wave, Bob took off from the back of the field and passed a slew of cars before the first turn. He just took off up the beach.

"Bob was my hero. I had two brothers, and we all picked various Flocks. My little brother, his champion was Tim. My older brother liked Fonty. I liked Bob because we shared the same first name. And their sister Ethel raced too. Matter of fact in the first Grand National race in 1949, the second one ever run on the beach course, all three of the Flock brothers were in the race along with Ethel, and she finished ahead of Bob and Fonty and never let them forget it. She was driving her husband's car, had it tuned to the local radio station, and was just driving around. She was one of three women in the race. Besides Ethel, there was also Sara Christian and Louise Smith. Sara Christian drove in the first Grand National race ever run in Charlotte at Brookstone Boulevard Speedway, a quarter-mile dirt track.

"The second Grand National race ever held was the beach race, and I attended that one. There were a lot of late model cars, the first time they tried it. Everyone thought it was too expensive to run late model cars, but Bill France wanted spectator identification with the car, and this is what started the Ford/Chevy rivalry, though in '49 there weren't many Fords or Chevys. The cars were mostly bigger, heavier cars like Lincolns, Chryslers, and Oldsmobiles. Those were the race cars to be run, and Red Byron in a Parks Novelty Oldsmobile won it. Tim Flock finished second in another Oldsmobile.

"The field wasn't that big, less than thirty cars, but it was an exciting show. You have to remember, there were no racing tires, just street tires. The cars were basically stock. They didn't have the exotic sheet metal we have nowadays. Aerodynamics was not a consideration. It was brute horsepower, V-8s and straight 8s. Because of the sand they put masking tape over the chrome on the front end, used parachute cord like a bungee cord to hold down the hood and the rear deck to keep them from flying up because the turns were chopped-up so badly.

"I got to meet some of the drivers, got to talk to them by selling programs down through the pits. Some of the competitors would buy them. I'd say, 'Howdy,' and ask how they were running. I was twelve, but I knew them by sight, and they knew me. They'd see me every year down there, and then in 1951 my brothers and I worked the concession stands at Darlington. I'd hang out around Marshall Teague's Hudson, or Tim and Bob and Fonty Flock, or hang around Fireball Roberts. But basically, to me they were just people. I never appreciated them like the way a fan felt, because I had grown up around them.

"When I graduated from high school, I went right into the army. I was in Korea. I was eighteen years old, the youngest guy in the company. We handled the exchange of bodies and wrapped up the armistice. I got out of the army in '56 and enrolled at the University of Florida. I worked for NASCAR during semester breaks and summer vacations in the mail room, handling distribution of entry blanks and results and anything else they wanted me to do.

"When they moved the office to the Speedway to get ready for the first Daytona 500 in '59, I was working there during Christmas break when Bill France called me aside. He said, 'What are you going to do when you graduate?' I said, 'I passed my graduate record exam and am going to graduate school. I'll get my master's degree in guidance and do that.' France said, 'What will you make doing that?' I told him a little less than five thousand a year. He said, 'We'll pay you more than that to start in the press office here.' I said I'd give it a try. There were five of us on the staff.

"Bill had watched me and his son grow up together. We had been around and knew a little something about the sport, so two days after I got my degree I went to work as assistant PR director of the Daytona International Speedway."

2

IN THE LAND OF COTTON

ANOTHER RACING VETERAN WHO HAS been around since NASCAR's beginnings is Charles "Slick" Owens. Like most of those who grew up in South Carolina in the 1940s and went on to a career in stock car racing, Owens came from a background of cotton mills and fast cars.

The first thing people who know Slick Owens will tell you about him is that he once jumped out of an airplane without a parachute and lived. The true story, while not as fantastic, is scary enough. To hear the modest Owens tell it, it was no big deal, ho hum, my chute got tangled, and I fell and landed on the side of a hill. His long hospital stay, however, gives testimony to the seriousness of his injuries.

Like two fellow Spartan Mill racing legends, driver/owner Cotton Owens (no relation) and car owner Walter "Bud" Moore, Slick Owens has a reputation for being a straight shooter, serious, hardworking, and successful. His industriousness did, in fact, lead to his acquiring his nickname.

Never a racer, Slick Owens has been part of the NASCAR scene since its very first sanctioned race on June 19, 1949, in Charlotte on a track near what was to become the city's airport. The purse at stake: $4,000. The cars were new, a novelty in American racing, but what Owens remembers most was not the cars but the conditions: dust covered everything and everyone.

Since the 1950s Owens has been a crack mechanic and parts sup-
plier to race teams. In addition to working for Cotton Owens, he has
also worked for the Ford racing factory, Holman-Moody, and today
works as parts manager for his close friend, racing legend Cale
Yarborough, who as a youngster once had worked for him. Slick knew
Bill France, and he had the opportunity to watch two of NASCAR's
legends, Curtis Turner and Joe Weatherly, in action.

SLICK OWENS: "I was born on February 14, 1933, and grew up in
Spartanburg, South Carolina. We were poor. My parents told me they
ate slingshot gravy, which was gravy made of fatback and milk, and a
lot of times they used water instead of milk.

"Most people worked in the cotton mills. When my grandmother
was nine years old, she worked in the cotton mill standing on a box.
My parents both worked there. In the early forties my parents started
making cloth for the military. A lot of people got deferred from service to work in those mills. The pay was small. When I was a child,
my father made eight or nine dollars a week.

"I grew up in Spartan Mill, the same mill village as Bud Moore and
Cotton Owens. Cotton's parents worked in the cotton mill, and later
on his father opened up a garage, and he worked on cars, and Cotton
followed in his footsteps.

"The first race I saw was in 1944 or 1945. Cotton and a guy named
Tom Arrington would take their parents' cars, meet on the weekend,
and race other drivers in this empty dirt lot. I don't think their parents knew what they were doing or where they were. I know mine
didn't know we were racing cars. I helped work on the cars because I
wasn't old enough to have a driver's license. I must have been twelve.
Cotton and Tom were older than me, and they were racing old '39
Fords and '37 Chevrolets, and they wrecked. I don't know what they
told their parents when they got home.

"When I got older I hopped cars. I worked at a drive-in, and we got
paid a cent and a half in—when we put the tray on the car—and a cent
and a half out—when we removed it.

"That was close to Bud Moore's place. His first shop that I can
remember was behind Fews' Barbeque. It was a slingshot garage, went
straight through, had dirt floors and held two cars. He had Hudson
Hornets, the first ones I remember.

"Bud's father ran a grocery store right off the mill village. He was a little better off than most, though really he was poor too, but he had more than most so Bud had more access to cars. Bud worked on cars and raced. His first driver was Joe Eubanks, who was another close friend of mine.

"At one time Joe drove Cotton Owens's Sportsman car and won something like twenty-four races in a row. Unfortunately, Joe, who was a fine person, drank, and it sort of messed up his career. As far as the drinking part, he never harmed anyone but himself.

"I went with Joe quite a bit in the late forties when he drove Cotton's car. We pulled the race car to the tracks with a chain, and someone had to ride in the race car. One time on the way to Asheville-Weaverville, which was about sixty miles away, the brakes of the car we were pulling the race car with gave out, and I had to get in the race car, and when Joe wanted to stop, he would stick his arm out, and I would brake in the race car to stop both of us. We were racing on a shoestring, but enjoyed every minute of it. It was a lot of work, but it was a lot of fun.

"I can remember one time in the late forties when Bill and Anne France and Billy Jr. came in to Bud's shop and spent the night at Bud's. France had a car on a flatbed. The Frances didn't have much. Bill France had a filling station in Daytona on South Atlantic Avenue. Bud helped Bill France, as did Joe Littlejohn, another fellow from Spartanburg. Littlejohn owned motels, and he was a bootlegger, and really, there was nothing wrong with that in this part of the country, except it was against the law. Joe Littlejohn was a very intelligent person, a good talker, and he had a little money. He had influence with other people in racing, and he knew Bud real well. Bud was involved in the early racing and helped Bill quite a bit, more than most people know. And Bill France reciprocated.

"Bill France was a good man. I liked Bill France. Other people have other ideas about him, but if he hadn't been as stern dealing with the people he was dealing with, there wouldn't be a NASCAR today.

"NASCAR began racing in 1949, and I was at the very first race here in Charlotte. As a matter of fact, Cale Yarborough's shop here is close to the site of the very first race, up here on Four Oaks and Boulevard. A driver from Gastonia, Glenn Dunnaway, won the race, but they disqualified him because it was supposed to be a Strictly

Stocks race and he had a chain holding the wheels to keep them from falling off, and they gave it to Jim Roper.

"I went to that first race with Cotton. I was fourteen. I remember I was sort of afraid, because I had never seen cars run that fast. And there was so much dust you could hardly see. I don't know how those cars were able to go through the corners and come out like they did. So what I remember more than anything else was how dusty it was.

"They had a small grandstand, so most of the people were standing around the racetrack. There were no guardrails, only markers. I don't know how it was that people didn't get killed. As a matter of fact, in the early fifties there was no barrier between pit road and the track. We would pit the cars *on* the racetrack with the race cars roaring right past. And we didn't think anything of it. It was only after Bobby Johns hit the wall at Darlington in Cotton's car and came down and unfortunately ran over three or four inspectors, killing the chief technical inspector, that they put up a wall between the racetrack and the pits. No one ever thought about the dangers. I'd fuel the cars, and the fuel would spill down my chest and down my legs right between my legs into my shoes, and it would burn like the dickens. Fortunately, I don't remember anyone getting burned early on. The drivers didn't even wear uniforms, and some didn't wear helmets.

"When the NASCAR circuit started, there was little talk about it. The purses were small. When I was working for Cotton in the early fifties, I didn't even get paid. Cotton would pay our way into the race and feed us, but we didn't get paid because he didn't make enough to pay himself and keep going.

"In the early fifties I left Spartanburg to go into the Korean War. I was sent to Stuttgart, Germany, to be a parachute jumper. All the training jumps were at 1,100 feet, and on my last jump I used the tie-down ring on the bomb bay door—we jumped out of the bomb bay door. I tied my static line, which made my parachute open faster, and this one time when I jumped the prop blast blew holes in panels of my chute. I pulled the reserve chute, and it went up and tangled with the main. I was hauling. I hit on the side of a hill and survived. It was just a freak accident. People say I landed without a parachute, but I did have *some* drag. I wasn't without a parachute. I don't remember what it felt like when I hit, but I was in the hospital quite a while. I got out of the service in March of 1954 and came back to Spartanburg.

"I went to work for Ross Building Supply, which wasn't far from Jack Purser and W. H. Watson, who owned a trucking company. W. H. and I were good friends, and I went to work for him as manager of his trucking company, and it was W. H. who bought Cotton the race car for him and Joe Eubanks to drive, and that's how I got involved making money in the racing business. I went to all the races and pitted the cars for Cotton.

"Cotton was one of the best drivers in his time. He could thread a needle with that race car. Joe Runk, a friend of mine who later worked with me at Holman-Moody, knew a racer when he saw one, and Joe said Cotton was one of the best.

"I was in the service when Cotton had a bad wreck here at Charlotte that liked to have killed him. His head swelled up to twice the size of a watermelon. He had double vision for a long time, and if you notice Cotton now, he'll look down, because he has trouble focusing if he looks right at you. After the accident Cotton kept racing. [Slick didn't think it unusual that Cotton returned to race. To him and the other racers, getting hurt was what was unusual. Driving was the natural order.] He sat on the pole at the Daytona Speedway the first race in '59.

"Cotton in his day was one of the hardest workers you'd ever want to meet, and today he's the same way. Cotton don't slow down. He still smokes cigarettes, but he still is as fast and moves and works as hard as he did when he was a young man, and he was a worker. He was an innovator. He knew a lot about race cars.

"The racers from Spartanburg were very quiet, serious people, but back then there were a couple of fellows who knew how to liven up a party, and they were two of the best drivers in racing, Curtis Turner and Joe Weatherly. Curtis drank a lot and liked to have a good time. But he was never the type to stagger, and even when he was stoned sober he looked drunk, 'cause he had curly hair and it would hang down on his forehead. Curtis was a fine person, but he liked to party. He was a womanizer. There were always a lot of women at his parties, and a lot of them were after Curtis.

"It didn't matter to Curtis if you had fifteen cents in your pocket or whether you were a millionaire, if he was having a party, he'd invite anybody coming up or down the street to his party, especially if he already had a drink or two in him. This one night this motorcycle gang came, about twenty-five of them, and Curtis wasn't going to run them off. I couldn't stand them. They were thugs, and they ran in bunches. I had fought in the service, and I asked them to leave. Darel Deiringer called the police while I held on to the lead motorcycle—I have the guy's helmet at home, and at the time I thought I was in a lot of trouble when the police came around the corner. The police said they wouldn't look.

"I said to the police, 'I'll take them one at a time, but I can't fight them all.' So it didn't happen.

"I was also good friends with Pops, Joe Weatherly. Weatherly was called the Crown Prince of Racing. He was always playing jokes on almost everybody, nothing bad. He had something going all the time for fun. Weatherly was the life of the party everywhere he went. He told jokes. And he hated snakes. He was scared to death if you put a rubber snake in his car. He'd put salt in your beer or in your drink when you weren't looking, anything to aggravate you. He loved to make comments to the other drivers: 'You can't drive a lick.' He was just that way all the time. He was full of life.

"Joe and Maurice F. 'Pop' Eargle, who was tall and weighed about 450 pounds, used to get drunk together, and Joe was the only one who could handle Pop, other than his wife, who was a little woman. Pop worked for Cotton Owens and Bud Moore, and Pop was so strong, if a car wrecked and tore the bumper up, he would just jerk off the bumper.

"One night we had a riot at the Asheville-Weaverville track. The track broke up, they stopped the race, and the people in the stands wouldn't let the cars and the people in the infield out. Right at the gate going out, they turned over a water truck. I gather they wanted the race to continue. The police were powerless to hold back the rioters. I was worried. My wife and two kids were in there, and the kids were small at the time.

"After about an hour Pop Eargle went up in the back of a truck and got a two-by-four. He and another muscle man who worked for Cotton got up on that truck and started beating the dickens out of these people so he could get out.

"I remember this other fellow who worked for Cotton cut a guy in the buttocks with his two-by-four. I saw him go out of sight jumping. After that, we were allowed to leave."

3

The Last of the Wild Bunch

THREE OF THE THIRTY-THREE racers who competed in that first NASCAR event at Charlotte on June 19, 1949, came from the same family. Fonty Flock finished second in a '49 Hudson, Tim Flock fifth in a '49 Olds 88, Bob Flock won the pole position but left the race early when the engine of his '46 Hudson blew.

Of the fabulous daredevil Flocks, the only one who survives is Tim, who won thirty-nine Grand National (now Winston Cup) races between 1949 and 1961, when he retired. In 1955 he won eighteen races, third only to Richard Petty's twenty-seven wins in 1967 and the king's twenty-one wins in 1971. He was NASCAR driving champion in 1952 and again in 1955. He might have also won in 1953 but he was injured in a bizarre accident when a truck ran over his head while he was sleeping on the ground next to his race car before a race in Darlington.

Tim today lives with his wife, Frances, in Charlotte, where he continues to represent the Charlotte Motor Speedway even after retirement. Despite his seventy-plus years, Tim is one of those special people who is perpetually young, with a laughing face and a penchant for humor. He ran and played with a fast crowd. It is only because of Frances, he says, that he has survived when so many of his running mates have passed on.

TIM FLOCK: "My daddy died when I was very young, so young I don't remember him. He drove a taxicab, one of the first cars in Fort Payne, Alabama. He had a mole on his head, and he wore a leather taxicab hat, and kept pulling it over the mole to hide it, and it became irritated, and it turned into cancer, and it finally took his whole face. Really, he died a terrible death.

"When Daddy died in 1928, my mother's brother, a man by the name of Peachtree Williams, asked my brother Carl to move from Fort Payne to Atlanta to work for him. Peachtree, who was known all over Georgia and Florida, was a big kingpin like Capone. He owned everything, making money and buying apartments, becoming filthy rich. He had become a multimillionaire in the bootleg business making moonshine liquor, and he put Carl in business, and when I was five, Carl got to making enough money to move us other eight to Atlanta with him including Mama and all my sisters, and we all growed up in Atlanta.

"When my brothers Bob and Fonty got old enough to where they could drive cars, Carl got them to help him in the moonshine business. You could buy liquor legal, but this was during the Depression and people didn't have enough money to buy government liquor, which was taxed heavily. The liquor coming out of these mountains had no tax attached, and that's why the government jumped all over it. And that's when the government came in and started raiding stills in the mountains, blowing them up with dynamite. A lot of revenuers got shot trying to stop these old farmers making a living in liquor. The farmers would shoot to kill. A farmer might have nine or ten kids, and trying to feed them he was making this liquor, and the guys who were hauling the liquor would come up to his still and load the cars and take the load down to Atlanta and sell it. You could buy a gallon of real good double-twisted liquor for six or seven dollars a gallon, and it was real good liquor. The farmers in the mountains made peach brandy and apple brandy, and people would rather have the bootleg liquor, 'cause they could buy so much of it for not very much money.

"Hauling moonshine was dangerous work, but danger ran in my whole family. In 1939 my brother Carl won the speedboat championship at the Chicago World's Fair, where you got on your knees and ran them little flat boats with the big motor behind you. Reo, my sister, used to jump out of airplanes. There wasn't no silk back then. You had to cut the rip cord with a knife, which she carried on her side. Parachuting was really dangerous, but she made thirty-nine jumps at fairs—got fifty bucks a jump—and she would walk on the wings and hang on to the wheels while the plane was up in the air. She was the first daredevil in the family. She ran away from home, met some guys who owned the airplanes, and they talked her into walking the wings, hanging on to the damn axle. Those airplanes were made of fabric. You wouldn't think some of them could even fly.

"I was growing up through that era, going to school, but I happened to see the liquor brought in from the mountains, saw where they dropped it off at filling stations or old garages, where they'd have a drop-off place, pull in, bring maybe a hundred gallons, and in fifteen minutes all the liquor would be out of the car, and some guy would pick it up who would sell it later. It was a big business.

"I never did haul any liquor, thank goodness. My brothers wanted me to stay in school, which I did. I graduated high school while Bob and Fonty were hauling for Carl, and they made quite a bit of money.

"There were between twenty and thirty bootleggers running two or three loads a day out of Dahlonega, Georgia, up in the north Georgia mountains, to Atlanta. They made around forty dollars a trip, and this was during the Depression when there wasn't any money, and that's why most of these guys got started hauling liquor in the first place, to make a living. There was Bob and Fonty, Roy Hall, and Lloyd Seay, to name a few, and one day they got to arguing about who had the fastest moonshining car. Finally, they found a place right outside Atlanta, down on Highway 54, a great big field, and they started racing these bootleg cars on Sunday and betting against each other, and then people started coming—no admission to watch these bootleg cars trying to outrun each other—but the bootleggers would pass the old helmets around the fence and the spectators'd put quarters in them, half dollars, and the drivers'd collect quite a bit of money on Sunday afternoons. That was the very start of stock car racing.

"Bill France later on found out there was three or four hundred people showing up, and he built some half-mile tracks, and Bob and Fonty would enter Bill's races. Bob and Fonty were friends with a gentleman by the name of Raymond Parks, who built some of the best cars for them and for Red Byron and Lloyd Seay, and on weekends I was out of school and I would go with Bob and Fonty and help them in the pits, change tires, but they weren't going to let me drive, because they had promised Mama I would finish school first.

"Finally one day at North Wilkesboro a man named Bruce Thompson—Speedy Thompson's dad, from Monroe, North Carolina, asked me, 'Are you Tim Flock?' I said, 'Yeah.' He said, 'I have an extra car, but I don't have a driver. Would you like to drive it?' I looked around for Bob and Fonty and saw they were out on the track, and I jumped into that car, and I started running that day, and before the year was up I was outrunning Bob and Fonty both. I was just a natural-born good driver—not bragging mind you—and I won a lot of races.

"I participated in the very first NASCAR race [on June 19, 1949], here in Charlotte off by the Holiday Inn on Little Rock Road. Highway I-85 goes right through where that was, a three-quarter track, dirt, a race run by Bill France, who rented the track from the people who owned it.

"I didn't have a car to drive in that first race. Bob and Fonty had cars. We were at the track, and Bob said to me, 'Tim, if you look over against that fence, there's a brand-new Oldsmobile 88.' And at that time you couldn't find none of them. He said, 'There's a guy sitting in that car watching. Why don't you go over and ask him if you could run that car in the race.' This was on Tuesday. I said, 'He'll think I'm crazy.' Bob said, 'Come on. I'll go with you.' We walked over to the car, and here was this nice-looking couple sitting and watching what was going on in their brand-new 88, their personal car that had 750 miles on it. Their names were Buddy and Betty Elliott, from Hildebran, North Carolina. Buddy had a hosiery mill in Hickory.

"Bob walked up to them and said, 'My name is Bob Flock. I'm qualifying for the race next week with my other brother Fonty, and this is my other brother Tim. He doesn't have a car to drive in the race Sunday. Would you let him drive your car?'

"Betty leaned over and said to her husband, 'Are you crazy?'

"I whispered to Bob, 'See there.'

"But Buddy kept talking to Betty and me, and he said, 'Tim, I'm going to take Betty home, and I'll let you know something tomorrow.' And would you believe the next day he came back with three guys, and we got the car ready in three days and put it in that race!

"These were brand-new cars. You couldn't do much to them. Had to put a safety belt in. The cars had no roll bars. They had full-across seats, didn't have bucket seats, so when you went through the turns, you'd be pulled over almost onto the passenger side holding on to the steering wheel.

"No one knew what to expect. The way Bill France set it up, these had to be brand-new cars, and nobody had ever heard of this before. Twenty-two thousand people showed. The state troopers liked to have a fit because they couldn't get all the people in the race. That was the start of Grand National racing right here in Charlotte. Bill France charged five or six bucks a head. Back then, that was a lot of money. Bill France figured out we had something good going.

"My brother Bob was on the pole, I was on the outside pole driving the Elliotts' Oldsmobile 88, and Fonty was third or fourth. I finished fifth in that race. Bob led the first lap, and I took the lead, but I kept breaking wheels. You know the lugs that would hold the wheels on? We'd go into them turns, and the track would dig up, and the lugs would go all the way through the wheels, and the wheels would come off and hit the fence, sometimes go over the fence into the grandstand.

"I remember those wheels breaking real good. I remember how the track dug up and the dust. They used calcium chloride to hold the dust down, an oil-based product that is really greasy, but the track was really dusty anyway, and it had a lot of holes in it. I remember Lee Petty, Richard's daddy, from Randleman, he was driving the family Buick, and he flipped that thing going through the first and second turn and liked to have killed himself. And he really got in trouble with his old lady when he got home! Lee turned that Buick end over end, sideways, really had a bad one.

"The winner was Glenn Dunnaway, from Gastonia, North Carolina. Glenn Dunnaway was actually flagged the winner. And after the race was over, he got disqualified because he had helper springs like the bootleggers in Georgia and North Carolina used to build up their cars, and you couldn't do that. They had put rules out saying what you could do and couldn't do, and Glenn probably didn't look at the rules. It was supposed to be Strictly Stock cars, so they disqualified Glenn and he couldn't do a thing about it. They gave the race to Jim Roper, in a Lincoln.

"The second race was held on the Daytona Beach and road course.

It was four and three tenths miles around, half of it on Highway A1A, which is still there today where all the motels are built. The backstretches, we called it, for two miles.

"Bill France took bulldozers to the shell rock on the beach and made a turn toward the beach, and we ran down by the water two miles till you got to the north turn and headed back to the asphalt again. Some drivers ran on the edge of the water to cool their brakes, which you needed because the turns were sharp and if you weren't careful you could go off the end of the backstretch. But you also had to be careful not to get trapped in the water when the tide came in.

"I had a strategy that helped me win six Daytona races. I won in all three divisions, modified, convertible, and I won two Grand National races. My strategy was to watch that water, where it came in and went back out, 'cause that sand was harder and I could get a lot better bite on it. I can remember in one modified race, 124 cars started. The back wheels would start jumping and vibrating, and that sand would get dug up, and I'd just move over to where the water had run out on the sand, and it was a lot smoother. That was one of my secrets. Can you imagine starting 124 cars in a race? They did it because the track was so large, but that asphalt backstretch was real narrow, and we were running way over a hundred miles an hour back then. A1A was just wide enough for two cars, and if you ran up on a car that was having problems, you just prayed he didn't move over one foot, or someone would have gotten killed.

"I won that race. I was driving a Joe Wolf car out of Pennsylvania, a Chevrolet coupe with an Oldsmobile engine with fuel injection, had the big cams in it. It could fly. Joe had moved the engine back, and my head was back against the back window, and as the car vibrated, my helmet kept hitting the back window, but that car was so fast we lapped the field.

"We raced the next year in that race car, had it won, when a hose broke. Joe didn't change the hoses and one of them rotted from the year before. We were way out front when we blowed up.

"The biggest problem I had racing on the Daytona beach course was the seagulls. There must have been four hundred million seagulls down and around where the race course was, and every one of them thought we were driving a Porta-John. Ptu, ptu, splat. During the week of sitting in the pits, they'd fly over you and ptu. You'd get a rag out. They thought we were a Porta-John.

"The first lap we knew we were going to have trouble, 'cause there were millions of them birds the whole length of the course, so we put three layers of plastic over our windshields, and we had a tab we could pull. I remember in '55 I was driving a Chrysler 300 and I must have killed three hundred seagulls that first lap, and when they hit the plastic covering the windshield, boom, boom, boom, boom, the blood would ooze and the feathers would stick to it, and you wouldn't be able to see a thing 'cause the windshield would be covered with feathers. You'd pull off the first sheet of plastic, and you'd have a clear view down the backstretch, but there would always be a few stragglers, and they'd hit, and you'd pull off the second piece of plastic, and you'd have a clear window. Another reason we used the plastic, when you'd be running along the water, cars in front of you would spray water and sand onto your windshield. After everybody saw us use it, they started using it too.

"I finished second to Red Byron in that first Daytona beach race. Red was a real fine guy. He had been a fighter pilot in the air corps during the war who had gotten one of his legs shot off. They put a false leg on him; he had one leg shorter than the other, and he had to put a block on the accelerator so he could reach. Or maybe it was on the clutch—I don't know which leg it was.

"Red was only around the first couple of years, which is why nobody knew much about him. Today they just know the name: Red Byron. He was the first NASCAR champion. I got to know Red real good. He was a fine old guy, short, redheaded, had that bad leg.

"We ran eight races that first year in '49. Red won two of them, the second one and a race at Martinsville, Bob two, Lee Petty won one, Jim Roper the first one, [Jack White won in Hamburg, New York] and the race at Langhorne, Pennsylvania, was won by Curtis Turner. I ran an Oldsmobile that day, and we blowed it up. The sportswriters like to talk about the Lady in Black at Darlington, but the Langhorne Speedway was the hardest track to win on. Every driver back then would rather win at Langhorne than Daytona Beach. It was a complete circle, one mile, black oil would get in your radiator, but if you could win at Langhorne, you were a hell of a race driver, cause you run flat out and never did lift nowhere. That was *the* track back then. And everybody you talk to will tell you that.

"Curtis to me was the greatest driver who ever ran in NASCAR. He was the kind of driver who would run the car as hard as it would run every lap until it won or it blowed. He won a lot of races, but he never won a championship because he'd blow the cars up. He was that type of guy.

"Curtis had no problem taking you out of the race if he wanted to get past you. At one of the half-mile tracks Curtis and Bobby Myers got into it, and after the race Bobby was so mad that he picked up a wrench and went looking for Curtis. Thirty minutes after the race Curtis was sitting on his car in the infield, and Bobby came running up with this wrench, and Curtis had a .38 aimed at him. Curtis said, 'Bobby, what are you going to do with that wrench?' Bobby said, 'I'm just trying to find a place to lay it down.'

"Curtis liked to drink a lot, party a lot. He had a house over on Freedom Drive here in Charlotte, it had four or five bedrooms in it, and he'd start a party, and a hundred people would come over, and he'd have a hundred cases of government liquor, with chasers and ice, and girls would be up on tables dancing naked, and the party would go on for six or seven days. Oh God, I went to those parties. They'd last for a week. He'd have the roads blocked, and he'd hire police to keep order.

"Curtis made a lot of money selling timber. He might make two hundred thousand dollars, and it would last him just about thirty days partying. He'd make all that money and throw it away. Then he'd get in his plane, fly people over, and sell another tract. Curtis went through his money like it was water.

"Curtis was a party man. He drank CC [Canadian Club]. One time Curtis was flying his Apache airplane, a twin engine, along with the guy who started the A&P stores. Curtis wanted a drink, and so he landed the plane on a highway somewhere down in South Carolina, and pulled up in front of an ABC liquor store. They got out, bought some CC, got back in the Apache, and taxied on the highway, and when they landed in Charlotte, the FAA was looking for him and took his license. That was the type of guy Curtis was, partied a lot, had a lot of fun, led a full life.

"I can remember one night Curtis was coming home in a brand-new Lincoln, and some guy was following him with his brights on, and Curtis kept blinking his lights, asking him to turn them off, and the guy wouldn't do it. Finally, they came to a red light. They both stopped. Curtis pulled up about thirty feet, put the Lincoln in reverse, and he came straight back and knocked the guy's radiator plumb over his engine. The guy had enough sense to write down Curtis's tag number, and he sued him, and they took away his driver's license for a couple of months. And so now he didn't have a license to drive either a plane or a car!

"But Curtis was so entertaining. Wait till you hear this one: he was with a redheaded baby doll in a motel in Monroe, and he was taking her home down Route 74 coming back at two in the morning when a state trooper pulled him over in that Lincoln. The trooper got out of the car, got his license, gave him a ticket, and it made Curtis madder'n hell. Now Curtis was brilliant, had a sharp mind on him. All state troopers wear a badge with their name on it. Curtis remembered that trooper's name.

"The trooper drove off, and Curtis headed for the first filling station. He found a phone book and looked up the trooper's number, and at two in the morning Curtis had his redheaded baby doll call the trooper's house. The trooper's wife answered, and the redhead got on the phone and said to her, 'I want to tell you something. I've been waiting on Bill at this damn bar, and he hasn't showed up yet!' And she hung up.

"Can you imagine what happened when that trooper got home? That's the way Curtis paid him back. A true story. Curtis was always a foot ahead of everybody.

"I saw him get in a race car one time wearing a brand-new one-hundred-dollar silk suit and a tie. He was drunk all night long, and he showed up at the track just before the race with his silk suit and tie and jumped into the car. Curtis was really, really interesting.

"I lost the Daytona beach race in 1951 because my pit crew was drunk. We had it won. We had a three-mile lead on that four-mile track, but that big Lincoln of mine was burning more gas than we thought. With only a few laps left, the engine started cutting off, and I had to pull into the pits. We didn't have radios, so I didn't have a way of telling my crew what I needed, and when I came into the pits, it was unreal. We didn't have any extra gas in our tanks, and the pit crew was drinking. I mean, they all were drinking, celebrating our victory, and when I pulled in there they didn't know what the hell was happening. There was a lot of drinking going on back then. I mean, *a lot* of drinking. My pit crew just knew we had this race won. We were three miles ahead on a four-mile track.

"The guys started running back and forth up pit road trying to get gas, and as I watched Marshall Teague coming down the backstretch, finally someone loaned us enough gas to finish, but by then, Teague caught up, and I finished second. We had the race sewed up. I know we should have won it. We finished second, won about $750, which was good money back then. There just wasn't any money back then, not like it is now. But we sure had fun. And then in 1952, we started having even more fun, because that year Joe Weatherly, who had run modifieds and who won the AAA motorcycle championship before he came to NASCAR, joined our circuit, and him and Curtis Turner were two of the biggest buddies in NASCAR history. Joe had an Apache, Curtis had an Apache, twin-engine airplanes. Joe drank so much that the call letters of his airplane was Whiskey and the number.

"One time Curtis and Joe rented a car at Daytona from Hertz, the U-drive-it company, and they were partying, drinking, drunk, and at two in the morning they came back to the motel. Instead of parking the car, somehow they drove it into the deep end of the motel swimming pool. That car went all the way to the bottom. The next morning they had to get a derrick to get it out. Of course, that cost them some money. They laughed about it. It made all the papers in Daytona.

"They liked to show off. Both of them were show-offs. At Darlington one year all of us were at a motel drinking, cutting up, and we saw this black man who was plowing with a mule, and we said, 'Let's go get his mule.' We gave him a hundred-dollar bill to borrow the mule. We unhooked that mule, and it took twenty-five of us to push it up the steps onto the second floor of this big motel. The motel is still there in Darlington. Here was this mule walking back and forth along the second-floor balcony, and all the guests who checked in with their bags were greeted by the damn mule. It took the fire department to come out. They put a sling under his belly and lifted him off. Crazy stuff. We were all drunk. These are true stories. You can't make up anything like that.

"It was partying and drinking, a wild bunch. Every one of us. Wild, drinking, cutting up, partying, women. At one time these two guys, Curtis and Joe, were keeping track of the women they had actually put under the sheets. They figured out that Curtis was around 178 women he had gone to bed with, and Joe was around 156. This was back in the early days of modified racing when there were a lot of women at every racetrack, and there were always thirty or forty of them at every track. These little ole gals would be in the pits, and they'd find out where you were staying at in the motel. Most of us had our cars parked in front of our rooms, and they'd come knocking on your door at two in the morning: 'Tiiiiimmmmmmmmyyyyy.' Of course, I wouldn't let them in! [This statement was followed by a wink at his wife, Frances, and ten minutes of laughter.] But there was a lot of them that come to try to find you. Just about every driver. And there wasn't nothing known as AIDS to stop you.

"Beauty queens also were at the tracks, and Curtis and Joe, and other guys, would go after them. Curtis and Joe would take them up in their airplanes. They called it 'Joining the Mile-High club.' They'd try to get into their britches. A lot of these beauty queens were young beauty contest winners who had never been with nobody, and that damn Joe Weatherly, true story, he'd get in the back of the Apache and start playing around with the girl and tell her how much he loved her. He'd actually open the damn door and say, 'I'm going to jump out if you don't git your britches off.' Him and Curtis, they scored a hundred times with tricks they pulled on girls.

"I'd have been dead twenty-five years ago if it hadn't been for Frances Flock. She watches everything I do, stays with me. You'll never see me unless you see her. But she's taken care of me all my life, and that's why I'm still here. We have been married fifty-two years now, fifty-three coming up this November twenty-sixth. She gave me five babies, and all of them are doing really good, no dope, which I'm proud of. And I love her more now than I did when I married her. 'Cause we were wild.

"In 1952 I won the Grand National driving championship points over Herb Thomas the last race of the year at West Palm Beach, Florida. I was leading, and Herb was second, and all I had to do was go around the track and get the flag at the start and that gave me enough points where even if Herb won the race, which he did, he couldn't outdo me.

"I was driving a Hudson Hornet, and the problem with the car was that if you broke an axle, the tire would get hung up in the wheel well, and the axle would lift the car up. Well, several drivers were killed in Hudsons: Frank Luftoe at Lakewood in Atlanta was one of them. He was throwed out of the car and killed. The axle would break, and it would lift the car up and throw it end over end. And on the sixty-eighth lap, that's what happened to me. I was going down into the first turn, and without warning, I was rolling end over end, and there I was, sitting upside down in the car, the last race of the season, the points leader.

"I won a beautiful '52 Hudson Hornet for winning the points championship that year. The car was given to me on the beach at Daytona, and I had to go to the races, and I told Frances not to drive it. She was taking driving lessons. She didn't have a driver's license. She had my mother and the kids in the backseat, and she decided she was going to ride up and down the beach in that Hudson, and she did. She was coming off the beach at Daytona when she missed one of the ramps and turned the car over on its side. She just wrinkled up the whole side. I told her, 'Don't worry about it, Frances. We'll put a number on it, and you can race the car.'

"There was no money back then. For fifteen years if you won the race, you got a $1,000 purse. And you as the driver only got forty percent of that, or $400. I never did own one of my cars, so there was no money around. We ran for chicken feed for years.

"As a result, most of the drivers had something else they did. I sold cars for a while, had a car lot in Atlanta. I had a filling station. Bob had a transmission shop. Joe Weatherly at one time had a motorcycle shop. Many of them hauled liquor. Good money.

"I probably would have won the championship again in '53, but over the July Fourth weekend a car ran over my head before the race in Spartanburg and damn near killed me.

"Herb Thomas and I had raced two days before in Ontario, Canada, and we had to tow the cars all day and all night long to get to the race. We finally got there in the afternoon, and we pulled into the infield. We both were towing Hudsons, and we got out of the cars and just kind of laid down beside the cars to take a nap. The race wasn't scheduled until eight, and it was a chance for us to get some sleep.

"Herb and I laid down next to each other, real close to our cars. Meanwhile, a man hired by Champion spark plugs was putting decals all inside the fence and on poles, and he backed his pickup truck, backed his truck, until he backed it about a hundred and fifty feet onto my dang head. I woke up when I heard the muffler, and before I could move the left rear tire made a track across my head—you can't holler with a car sitting on your chest—and when the car stopped, the tire was up on my head.

"When the driver looked down and saw me, he was so scared he fell out of the car. Herb tried to pull the truck off me, and his hand started bleeding. Some troopers who were there to direct traffic heard Herb hollering from the fence, and about six of them finally lifted the car up and lifted me out from under it. I went to Mary Black Hospital and stayed there a few days. I sued Champion. I was the '52 champion, and it knocked me out of several races trying to win the '53 championship. We collected, but not a big amount of money. Back then you collected what you could. That poor boy who ran over me, I saw him last year [1996], and it still worries him about backing over my head. It was a freak accident. Might have cost me the championship. I had had a good start in '53.

"Then in '54 I won the Daytona beach race. I was running an Oldsmobile out of Kentucky, a real great car. It was the first time a car had a two-way radio in it. We had a pole in the pit with an antenna on it. It puzzled everybody in NASCAR. The officials said, 'This car has so much stuff on it.' Bill France Sr. was after me before the race even started.

"We won the race, and after it was over, France disqualified the car, saying there was something wrong with the carburetor, which there wasn't. There wasn't a thing wrong with that car. We begged them to take the carburetor off, put it on another car and run it down the beach. Bill France said no. They wanted the second-place car to win that race, and by God, that second-place car won the race. They gave the race to Lee Petty, in a Chrysler.

"It was a deal that made me so mad, I went over to Bill France's home where he had an office on Peninsula Avenue in Daytona, and after they called me and said they were going to disqualify me, I slammed the door of his Florida room so hard the glass went flying back into the living room. And I quit racing. This was after the second race of the year in 1954.

"I went home to Atlanta and talked to the Pure Oil company, real good people, and they built me a brand-new filling station. I tried to build it up for seven, eight months. And I liked to starve to death."

4

CURTIS AND LIL' JOE

ANOTHER TOUGH VETERAN SUR-vivor of the early days of stock car racing is Ralph Moody, who was a great sprint car and modified driver-mechanic in the days before NASCAR's emergence as the nation's top racing circuit. Moody won four Grand National races in 1956, and the next year he and John Holman took over and ran the racing program for Ford. Between 1957 and 1973, his race team bred an entire generation of champions.

The first drivers for Holman-Moody that inaugural year of '57 were Bill Amick, Curtis Turner, and Joe Weatherly. Amick was not a problem for Moody, a straitlaced, temperate, family man. Turner and Weatherly, according to Moody, more than made up for him. The two notorious racing rascals, who both died early, courted danger of one kind or another in every aspect of their lives: their modes of transportation, love lives, and jobs all involved close calls and needless risks. For them, that's what life was all about.

RALPH MOODY: "I was intrigued with racing when I was about eight or nine. I had a neighbor by the name of Kingsbury who was a racer. He drove an old boat-tailed thing, great big wheels. Every time I got a chance, I went to help him. Once in a while I'd go to a racetrack. My father told me, 'You ain't never going to be no racer. You stay away from race cars.' But what did he think I was going to do? I had always been around it.

"When I was sixteen I was racing, not near Littleton, Massachusetts, where my father might have found out about it, but in other parts of the country. One night I was scheduled to race in Littleton, and a friend, Nat Whitney, and I pulled in there with a midget racer, and my father come out and said, 'What the hell is that?' I said, 'It's a race car.' He said, 'That little thing ain't a race car.' I told Nat, 'Don't tell him I drive it. Tell him you drive it. 'Cause he'll raise hell.'

"We got down to the track and got in the pits, and I told Nat, 'You make like you're going to get in it. Take the helmet when they push it out there.' My father was bullshitting with people in the pits. They pushed the car out onto the track, and I grabbed the helmet, got in the car, and they pushed me off. My father looked out there and saw that race car, and he looked at Nat standing in the pits, and here he went, raising hell so bad the police had to put him out of the pits! My father told Nat, 'When he gets home, I'll take care of this. I'll bust it up.'

"My uncle said to him, 'You can't go beating on an eighteen-year-old.' My father said, 'The hell I can't.'

"We stopped at a diner on the way home, and on the way to the washroom, I told my uncle, 'As soon as you go in to wash your hands, we ain't gonna be here.' And we left. We went back to my girlfriend [now wife] Mitsy's home, which was in Taunton, seventy-five miles away.

"The next time I saw my father, he was some kind of hog-tied. But when he found out I was racing different places and winning, you ought to hear him, a whole different tune. 'That's my boy.'

"This was in the thirties, before the war, and back then you could make more money driving midgets than you could anywhere else. There were tracks built throughout New England and New York. We could run five, six races a week. We'd run all year.

"I first learned to build race cars with midgets. I always looked for something that didn't fall off or didn't break. Back then, you couldn't buy anything to build a midget. There was no place to go buy parts. You had to make it. You'd buy an old Ford four-cylinder engine, a

Model A gear box. The first midgets had Model T Ford axles on them. They had small spindle pins which would break, so we built something better. I made all my hubs and spindles, machined down the Model A Ford hubs and spindles, put a tube in between them and made a rear end, because the Model T rear ends would fall apart.

"The first midget I drove had four-wheel hydraulic brakes that I built. I used parts from a Studebaker Champion. After I put those sons-a-bitches on, boy, you had to watch out when you were running with someone behind you. You'd put the brakes on, and the guy behind you would run all over your ass because he couldn't stop. Braddie Winters and I began building and selling those brakes for other cars. We rather they had them than not, because that way the other drivers wouldn't run over me. We sold a lot of those brakes.

"Then I got into aluminum chassis, with the help of a guy from New York name of Bennett. I had an open-tube rear end, real light-weight. I won a lot of races.

"We had a racing association. One year we paid a guy a hundred thousand dollars to run the association. We did this because the pro-moters would cheat the hell out of you. You'd win a fifty-lap race on a third-of-a-mile-high bank, running 130 miles an hour, and they'd pay you $500.

"Our association met and we demanded 40 percent of the gate, and to make sure we got it, we said the tracks had to put turnstiles and ticket counters in, or else we weren't going to race. The first race after the meeting, there were no turnstiles, nothing, and everybody went home. The next race, which was at Lonsdale, Rhode Island, there were turnstiles and the crowd was counted at 31,000. It was the first 100-lapper they held there, and my share of the purse was $8,888. That was the difference between turnstiles and no turnstiles. That was a hell of a pile of money back then.

"I can remember sprint car races controlled by a guy named Hatfield. He was a thief. He must have owned thirty goddamn sprint cars. They'd go to fairs across the country, and he'd hip [fix] the races. If you came in with your own car, he'd tell you, 'You run like the rest of them. You get what the rest of them get.' He'd say, 'Boys, don't run over one another and tear them cars up.' Damn, you'd go out and race and put on a show, change positions, and everyone got two or three hundred dollars. Hatfield made a goddamn fortune, and the drivers made a nice living. He was making a ton of money putting people in the grandstands.

"But the midgets kind of petered out because there was too much of it. It was every night of the week. Also the young kids were running what they called jalopies, running the same time the midgets ran. That ruined it. A lot of tracks went out of business. The owners of Lonsdale became involved in a bogus ticket-selling scandal, they were put in jail, and the track became a shopping center.

"After the war everyone was hopped up to do something, and they put in high-bank tracks to run midgets, but a lot of people got hurt, and the midgets never did become as popular as they had been before the war. In the late forties modified racing was the hot ticket. By then I was living in Hollywood, Florida, working as the service manager at Holman Lincoln-Mercury. We had a circuit in Florida where we ran on ten tracks. Fireball Roberts was one of my competitors. He didn't like me too much, especially when I raced against him. 'Cause I beat him most of the time, and he'd have a fit about that. He was a good racer though. He ran cars owned by Fish Carburetor, and they were hard to beat, had good running engines, but the chassis weren't done right, they were too stiff. I'd have an old flathead with stock-looking wheels that no one else wanted to run, but it was lightweight, soft-sprung, the right kind of setup, and we'd go out and beat all the hot shoes. We built a nice four-bedroom house in Hollywood, paid for it and furnished it on my earnings driving a modified race car. It took me two and a half winters to pay for it.

"And it was after the war that I first started racing throughout North Carolina, Virginia, Delaware, and New Jersey. I couldn't believe the junk the southern guys were trying to run. Those southern guys were at a great disadvantage. If they had raced outside their area, they'd have learned more than they did. The only guys they had to race against were the local guys. I had raced all over the country, and I had the advantage of having built all my own race cars starting in my midget days.

"When I first came down to Carolina, all through this area I ran a little black Sportsman car with a big X on it, a '37 Ford coupe with an early flathead engine. Mr. X, they called it. The car had one carburetor with stock ignition. Wire ran up to the ignition in a tube wrapped with masking tape. The tires had white walls! The reason no one else ran Sportsman was that no one could figure out how to make it work right. If you tried to run with a stock ignition, it would skip and sputter all the time. But I knew how to fix it. Everybody else had three or four carburetors. They thought they had the greatest thing.

"I would stop at tracks I hadn't won at before, places where there was good money. I was making my way south, and as I passed through Georgetown, Delaware, I saw a lot of cars going to a racetrack. It was a modified race, a hundred lapper. When I got to the track, I ran into Joe Weatherly and Buddy Shuman. I knew them from racing up North. Shuman asked me what I was doing there. I said, 'I was going south and I saw the race cars, and I figured I'd race.' He said, 'It's a modified race.' I said, 'Yeah, I've been to some of your modified races.' Their cars had big wheels, big floater hubs. All the other drivers were looking at my little car. 'Is that modified?' they asked. I lied to them and told them it was. Joe Weatherly knew different. He said, 'Don't lie to them. Tell them what it is. It's a goddamn Sportsman.' When they saw my little car, they couldn't believe I would dare race them in it.

"I was the last one to qualify, and I set a new track record! Boy, the shit hit the fan right then. They looked at it and looked at it, and when the race started, they decided to start three abreast, with me on the pole, and Weatherly next to me, and Shuman outside. They were driving hogs, cars much heavier than mine, with big ole tires, and I knew I would have to do something different to grab the lead, because I didn't have enough jump off the line.

"We came around to take the green flag. I was smoking a cigarette, and they were looking at me, and we're coming off the corner, and I'm holding the cigarette, and they're looking, and I'm pretending I'm looking at them, and while they were watching I dropped the cigarette, and as they were watching the cigarette, I stood on the gas, and goddamn, I was gone. I blew them all away, won the race, and boy did everyone protest.

"I parked the car in the front stretch, walked away, and when I came back, who crawled out from underneath my car but Buddy Shuman with a drink in one hand and a bottle in the other. Nobody said anything about drivers drinking back then. It was the reason Buddy died.

Drank and set his bed on fire with a cigarette after falling asleep. Buddy was a character. He was looking under the hood to see what made the son of a bitch go!

After he was done looking he came over and shook hands. He said, 'Goddamn, I don't know how you do it with that old bunch of junk.' He was that kind of guy. He wasn't mad when you beat him.

"Joe Wolf, who won big back then, had four cars in the race and he was cussing, raising hell. This was when I first began racing around here, and I was a damn Yankee boy, and if I gave the good ol' boys a rough time on the track, they hated that, and here a little Sportsman had outrun those modifieds. They wanted to disqualify me so badly. They checked my fuel. They checked my engine. I showed them the car had a twenty-one-stud flathead engine and explained to them that there was no way to make it big and race, and boy, that blew their minds. What they didn't understand was that you could run a real early crankshaft with a short stroke. You make the bore big and turn the shit out of it. When you punch it, it jumps. That was my secret that no one else could figure out. But boy, did they hate it when I came around.

"I went to Wilmington, Delaware, with the car for a modified race. I figured that if I didn't qualify good, nobody would pay any attention to me, and I'd get in the damn race. In practice I didn't run hard. It was a hundred-lap race, and I started way back. After about forty laps, I was gone.

"The race ended, and Joe Wolf again was a competitor, and he was hot. You had to go up a flight of steps along the side of a building to get paid. He had all the money laid out for all the positions. The promoter said, 'I'm not paying you. The guy who finished second gets your money.' I turned the table upside down. They wouldn't pay me. I don't know why, except that I had come into someone's hometown and blown them away with a car that wasn't supposed to. We got the hell out of there because I started a half riot. You didn't know who was fighting who.

The promoter called me and said, 'We don't want you back at Wilmington. You're causing too much trouble.' I said, 'Well, you son of a bitch, you wouldn't pay me.'

"I decided to fix him. I went to a junkyard and found a rusty shit-box, put my engine and equipment in it and took it back to that track.

It looked like hell, didn't have a number on it or anything. I had a friend of mine, old Bob Sauls, enter it for me.

"When I arrived at the track, the promoter wanted to know what I was doing there. I said, 'I came looking for a ride.' He said, 'Okay, go ahead.' I went to him and said, 'See that car over there. How about if I drive that one?' So the promoter asked Bob if I could drive it, and of course he said I could. The promoter gave me permission. I told him, 'I'm going to take some tape and put X on it like my old car. Is that all right?' 'Yeah.' So I did, and when the race started, I blew them away, just like I did the first time! And before the race was over, the fans knew exactly what had happened, what I had done. They were jumping up and down, cheering, hollering.

"After I took the checkered flag, the people came out of the stands out onto the racetrack, just raising hell. I climbed those stairs, and once again, they wouldn't pay me. I went back down, and the fans wanted to know whether I had gotten paid. I said, 'No, they wouldn't pay me.' The fans were so mad they burned the damn grandstand down.

"When NASCAR started, I wouldn't run all NASCAR. I ran all over the country, wherever I wanted, in Maine, up North, the Midwest, Texas, everywhere. For a while Bill France had me banned at all the NASCAR tracks, because he wanted me running all NASCAR. France was tough. He wanted me to stay in NASCAR, not run anyplace else.

"In 1955 I was living in Hollywood, Florida, and I drove up to Daytona with the notion of interesting the Pontiac people into letting me drive in the Daytona beach race. First though, I stopped by at the Fish Carburetor shop. Robert Fish had built this carburetor, a fantastic carburetor, simple as hell—the military tried it, really it was fantastic, but he never could peddle it to anybody. I knew the Fish people from my midget days, and I walked in there. The Ford people were working out of the Fish Carburetor shop, and I ran into Fireball Roberts, who was surprised to see me. 'What are you doing here?' I told him I was going over to where the Pontiac people were to talk to them about a ride. Fireball said, 'Hey, don't go over there. I think you can have a ride here.' I wanted to know why, and it turned out that Speedy Thompson was supposed to drive one of the cars, but he quit. Fireball brought me over to see Pete DePaolo, who was in charge of the Ford team. DePaolo was an old-timer who had won the

Indianapolis 500 a while back. DePaolo said to me, 'Since I've been down here a lot of people told me about you. Do you want to drive that other car?' I said, 'Hell, yeah. I won't even go see Pontiac.' I had been fooling around with Fords anyway. So we talked awhile, and Pete said, 'You got it.'

"They just did finish the car as race day approached. I drove the car down the back roads to the beach, went through inspection, I was running late, and when I got to the race, I was on the ass end of the field. They fired the gun, and everyone took off. We got running, got up toward the front, and it was raining, bad raining, and that's when old man Petty got lost in the ocean. He came back crossways, and to avoid him, I couldn't do anything but try to go the other way, and I got into deep sand, dug into the sand, and rolled the car about three times. Boy, I was mad. The car landed on its wheels, and I jabbed it in gear, ran it back and forth and got it out of there.

"Well, when the car turned over, it knocked the windshield out. I came into the pits, and they told me, 'You're the last Ford running.' The rest of them had gone out or wrecked.

"It was raining, and I didn't have a windshield, and I fired around the course a few more laps, and I came in, and back then, they washed the windshield with a bucket of water. I pulled in, and the guy with the bucket in the rain didn't notice the windshield was out, because I got a bucket of water right in the kisser! The force of the water knocked my goggles off. What a mess that was.

"We finished the race, and boy, that was a big deal.

"The beach race was a really fun thing. Trouble was, most of the drivers had run short tracks, and they didn't realize how fast they were running. You'd go down that backstretch on the pavement at over a hundred miles an hour, and they'd get sideways because the road would get sand on it, and when they ran toward the corner, they'd go over the hill. Hell, cars would spin and hit that inside bank, which was as high as the roof of this house—when they hit that corner it was thirty feet over that mound—and when that race was over, there were forty cars one on top of the other in a pile. A guy would go over the hill and crash, and he'd scramble the hell out of there, because he knew it wouldn't be long before someone else was coming. It looked like a junkyard.

"I can remember I was chasing Fireball one year, and he ran down that corner, and it turned around on him, and all I could see was him disappear. I remember Banjo Matthews, all them guys, would go over that hill and down the other side.

"But that's how I started my association with Ford, which was dumping some money into racing, engines, flatheads, overheads, parts, unbeknownst to everyone, though Chevrolet was doing the same thing. I ran out of Daytona a couple of times, and then myself and a guy named Red Vogt moved to Charlotte on the other side of town, to run the team for Pete DePaolo, who was a nice guy but pig-headed because he had won Indy way back. Red was a fantastic guy, a hell of a nice person and about as knowledgeable about engines as you could find. Early on he drove, but building engines for race cars is really where he shined.

"So Red was doing the engine work, but we didn't have any machinery to do the body work. We had to haul it somewhere to do it, and nobody knew what to do with it like we wanted, so we were doing a half-assed job really, until I said to Red, 'I've seen what you do. Leave me with the chassis work. You worry about the engines.'

"The first race after our arrangement was the Peach Bowl in Atlanta. I told Red, 'We'll go there, because it's a short track, tough to handle, and we'll see how we do.' We had Curtis Turner and Joe Weatherly driving for us, and we arrived there late. The field was closed, but I told the promoter, 'We have Turner and Weatherly,' and boy, they wanted them to run. So we got them in the field, and we put the race tires on right at the track and started them in the back of the pack. 'Cause everyone else had qualified and was ready to run.

"They went to the front and were gone! That convinced Vogt I knew what I was doing with race cars.

"So Red was working on the engines and I was the chassis man, and we became so successful that before long there was no way we could do the things we had to do and also run the business. Ford decided we needed someone to be the PR man, the gopher, the person to deal with the Ford people. DePaolo knew this guy John Holman, who had worked with Bill Stroppe in California on the Mexico road race. Holman drove the parts truck. He arranged for parts and made arrangements for shows. Ford knew him too from the road race, and we all agreed to bring him in. John was a guy who claimed to know a lot about racing, but he didn't really.

"Well John and Red didn't get along, and Red quit, and so we became Holman and Moody, and it wasn't long before we *were* Ford, and it wasn't long before we were running six cars. I hired Turner, Weatherly, and Fireball to run along with me in Grand National, which now is Winston Cup, and Marvin Panch and Bill Amick to drive short tracks.

"I had always raced with these guys, and I picked them because I knew who was tough to run with and who wasn't. The problem was, you had to make some of these guys—like Turner and Weatherly—behave. But they put on a hell of a show.

"Amick came from West Tulsa, and John knew him and said he was pretty damn good, and he was. Panch had been running on the West Coast, and he quit there and ran for us, and Panch was a guy who stayed out of trouble, would bring the car home in one piece. If he had been more aggressive, he would have won more races. Everybody liked Fireball. I raced against Fireball a lot of places, and he was a good race driver. Fireball had a lot of sense about what the hell was going on. He didn't deliberately try to wreck anybody. He wouldn't try to shut you off behind a car and get you in trouble or move you into the wall or do things like that. You needed those kind of guys who had sense enough to say, 'Hey, this is a business.' You had to satisfy the people who were putting the money up. You had to have drivers who had the sense to say, 'Jeez, I must have blown a valve,' when the engine blowed up. Like the time Smokey Yunick's engine blew up, and he told everyone, 'The starter fell off.' That's part of the game.

"Weatherly and Turner, if it was broke, they didn't give a damn anyway. They were having a good time. They never complained about anything. And so they never got in trouble with Ford, only with me. Turner and Weatherly had started out as rum runners—Turner was one of the biggest rum runners in the state of Virginia—that was a way of life, and they got along together great, and on the racetrack they liked to beat and bang on each other, loved to put on a show. Turner would bounce off other cars, knock them out of the way, to get to the front. He didn't care. One night Curtis and I were down the other side of Gastonia, a small track, and he had this doctor or lawyer with him, and the guy bet him five hundred dollars he couldn't lead the first lap. Curtis started about sixth. Well, the green flag went down, and he just drove through the middle of them, knocked them out of the way. Well, he led the first lap, but that was all he led, because he tore the car all to hell getting up to there. The other guy paid him off though. He was that way.

"One time at Hickory he was fined fifty dollars for rough driving. I said, 'Dammit, Curtis, I told you.' I would raise hell with him about doing these things. He'd knock his own teammate, Joe Weatherly, out of place, just bang on him. The crowd would go wild, thought that was great.

"At Darlington one year Curtis was leading, and Joe passed him, and Turner just knocked the hell out of him, trying to get back in front. Remember, both these guys were driving for me. I was so pissed off, I said to Curtis, 'If you do that again, we won't pit you.' And he went back out, and he did it again, and when Curtis came in, we just set down. We wouldn't pit him. Curtis was so mad he bounced that car off a cement wall, just knocked the hell out of it.

"He had a new Cadillac, and the next morning he drove it to our shop. We had roll-up garage doors, and he drove his car right through the doors, backed out, and took off. That's how mad he was that I wouldn't pit him.

"Another time, and this was also at Darlington, during the Southern 500, Lee Petty put Curtis into the wall, and Joe Weatherly was so mad, he rammed his car into Petty and put him out of the race. Petty and them two never did get along.

"The Pettys lived out in the country, and they grew up that way. They only talked to people they knew, and if they didn't know them, they shut their mouth. They didn't talk about people, didn't say anything good or bad or nothing else. It was nobody's business.

"But I got along great with them. Lee was always a hell of a nice guy. When he was around racing, we talked a lot. If I was outrunning him, he never got pissed off or ugly about it. 'Great, you won the race.' It didn't make any difference where he finished. He was that type of person. He never begrudged someone else something.

"I ran a lot with Lee. Lee was a good racer, heady, kept thinking, 'Stay out of trouble. Make money.' He didn't take wild chances like some of them did, but he wasn't conservative either. He raced hard. He was hard to beat. He had good race cars. But he didn't want to tear them up. He wanted to bring it home and make money every race he went to. And he did that. That's why Lee won championships. And

he'd run every race they had on the circuit, where we didn't go to a lot
of them. To us they weren't worth going to. You'd go to some of those
places and run a hundred miles at some hole-in-the-wall and win six
hundred dollars. It wasn't worth going to. You tear the cars up. But
Lee'd go to those places with a good car, qualify and run up front or
win and make money, and he'd win championships. And years later
Richard did the same thing. He'd run every race. We didn't.

"Our families always got along good. They'd be at races with their
kids, and our kids and my wife would take all the kids and go somewhere. Socially they were always nice people. Once in a while we had
a scrape with Petty about something to do with racing, but that was
gone when it stopped. And he was that way too. He didn't hold a
grudge against people. They'd have to do something pretty wrong for
him to hold a grudge, and then he'd try to get back at you.

"One night we were running some place up in Virginia, and Curtis
Turner and Petty got into it. Turner won the race, and I guess Petty
was still running at the end. Aw, they used to get into it bad. And it
was senseless. If the guy is going to do stuff like that, wait till you find
him in the right place, and then you get rid of him so he can't run anymore. You just don't go crashing. But Turner and Weatherly didn't do
that. They just ran into a guy. And this evening the guy Turner drove
into was Lee Petty. And boy, Lee was seething.

"There was an old wooden rail fence, and Turner was setting up on
that fence drinking booze out of a bottle, and Petty came over and
said, 'I want to talk to you.' He was slapping himself in the leg with a
rolled-up newspaper. He walked up to Turner, and went *whack*,
slapped him beside the head. The son of a bitch had a torque wrench
in it, and Lee knocked Turner right over the goddamn fence. Hee hee
hee hee hee. Petty shouldn't have done that, because Turner would get
him every time.

"So you knew that evening when Petty put Curtis out of the race
that his buddy, Weatherly, was going to go get him if he could catch
him, and that's just what he did, just knocked the hell out of him, put
him in the wall. Joe drove up behind Petty, and coming off the corner
got his nose up in him and turned him right into the wall. And you
usually can get away with that. If you're gonna do it, as soon as you get
him into the wall, you get on the brakes and try to miss him, and if

you don't, so what? You've got him. That's the way they worked. They were nuts.

"Turner was the sort of guy who could make a ton of money and lose a lot of money. He was a millionaire two or three times. He owned I don't know how many theaters in Virginia. He was in the lumber business. He'd fly in his airplane and fly over timberland and show buyers where it was, and then they'd look at it on the ground and buy it from him.

"One night we went to Winston-Salem to race, and from there he was going to Michigan, where he had bought a whole bunch of timber from the Ford Motor Company, a zillion acres of timber. He had a brown envelope, a folder about six inches thick, and he said to me, 'I better not leave this here. Will you take care of this for me?' I asked him, 'What is it?' He said, 'Documents, money and stuff.' I told him I'd take care of it.

"I was at the racetrack, and I didn't know what the hell to do with the folder, so I put it in my T-shirt in back so I could always feel it.

"After the race we got into the airplane, and Curtis said, 'Goddamn, do you have that envelope?' I said, 'Yeah, I can feel it in my back.' He said, 'You know what's in it?' I told him I didn't. He said, 'Five million dollars in checks and cash.' That's what I was carrying around all night at the racetrack!

"Turner was the sort of guy, we had to make sure we collected the purse and gave him his share, because if he got the money, he would spend it all partying. Turner had a place on the other side of town, a Party Pad, he called it. He'd get these go-go dancers from downtown and have some of the biggest, wildest parties you ever saw.

"The night before we had to fly to Rockingham, he called me up and said, 'Moody, you got to come and get me. I can't get to the airport.' He was at his Party Pad house. I knew he had his airplane. I couldn't figure out what was going on. I said, 'Your airplane doesn't run?' He said, 'I can't get to it.' I asked, 'Why?' He said, 'I got some trouble over here.' I said, 'I'll come and get you.' He said, 'Don't come to the house.' I said, 'Where?' and he described a little side street. I thought, Boy, Curtis *is* in trouble.

"Come to find out he had some guy's wife for a secretary, and she had been with him there for about three days, and that guy finally figured out what was going on. When Curtis tried to go out the back door, the guy had shot at him with a rifle, plugging a bunch of holes in the damn door and the windows.

"So Curtis didn't dare come out of there. I parked where he told me, and Curtis came running out the front door. He ran down the road like a rabbit. I grabbed him, we went to the airport, got my airplane, and we went to Rockingham, and he won the race. And he had been up all night over there partying. Jeez.

"Curtis was always calling me up. One night he kept calling me, and he didn't sound like he had been drinking. He said, 'I got car troubles. You got to come and help me.' So I got over there to his Party Pad, and he had a big brick patio, all lit up, and after I parked in the back, I walked up, and this girl came out, had a big, long dress on, and when she got close, she pulled up the front of her dress, and she said, 'Ain't I pretty?' And she wasn't wearing a thing under that dress! I thought, Oh shit, how do I get out of here! I looked inside, and these girls were dancing, and half of them were naked. I said to Curtis, 'You bastard, you called me over here for this?' Boy, he made me mad. I was a happily married man. I turned around and left. Jeez.

"I never went to those things so I didn't fit in a lot of places. It just wasn't my way of life. I had my own family so in a lot of ways I was an outcast. I didn't quite fit in, but that didn't bother me. I did my job, and that's why I stayed there so long.

"You ever see anyone dance naked? Curtis said to me, 'Think of all the fun you can have.' I said, 'I have enough fun.' Curtis was something. Jeez."

5

MORE CURTIS AND LIL' JOE

MAX MUHLMANN IS ONE OF THE most successful sports marketers in America. When entrepreneur George Shinn wanted to attract a basketball team to Charlotte and when Jerry Richardson wanted an NFL franchise for the city, the man they turned to as the brains behind their PR effort was Max Muhlmann.

But before Muhlmann was a sports mover and shaker, he was a talented columnist for the *Charlotte News*. A sportswriting prodigy, in 1957 the *News* hired Muhlmann away from his hometown Greenville paper when he was only twenty-one to write about stock car racing and college sports. Quickly Muhlmann discovered what wonderful characters inhabited the world of Grand National stock car racing. The two characters who most attracted him were the two wildest: Mssrs. Turner and Weatherly.

MAX MUHLMANN: "I was born on November 19, 1936, in Parkersburg, West Virginia, but I moved to Greenville, South Carolina, when I was four or five. My dad was in the Army Corps of Engineers and he moved there to work at Donaldson Air Force Base, which was just outside of Greenville.

"When I grew up I liked baseball and basketball particularly, and track. I wanted to be Bob Feller. I was a pitcher, and I kicked my leg up high like he did. I didn't care about cars.

41

"When I was in junior high school I was elected to be the home-room reporter. I wrote a column about our homeroom, and it had my name on it. I kind of liked it. And when I got to Greenville High School, that whetted my appetite. The school had a very good journalism class and a weekly paper that perennially won the best high school newspaper in the state. Journalism and writing generally appealed to me, and sportswriting seemed to be something I really enjoyed. And somewhere between the ninth and tenth grades, I got a job taking scores at night on the *Greenville News*, the morning newspaper. I'd be in the office, and they'd call in. There was something called Textile Basketball, twenty to thirty mills that had teams that were almost like semipro teams, and they'd call in to report the score of the Dunning Mills B-boys and A-girls, and some poor sap had to take that, and I was that sap. I was just a little kid, but I got to be around the real reporters.

"By the time I got to the tenth grade, the *Greenville News* decided I could cover high school sports, including my own high school, which was an interesting concept. I'd write about Greenville High and Parker, our rival, and once in a while about something else. And of course I felt I knew more about journalism than Mrs. Becton, the journalism teacher, did, so she and I had a rocky relationship during the three years. She was a little tyrannical in her concept of teaching, and I would suggest that having some real experience might be helpful too.

"In the eleventh grade I became the sports editor of the high school paper. I wanted to be the editor, but the teacher had her chosen person, a gal who was a better student than I was. When her name was announced all the students said, 'You're so much better a writer. We know it's because Mrs. Becton doesn't like you.' Of course I gave Mrs. Becton several reasons not to like me. I did some awful things, like pasting the erasers to the blackboard. I probably got what I deserved.

"By the summer after my junior year I had started working full-time on the *Greenville Piedmont*, the afternoon paper, and my senior year I worked there a lot of days after school. The afternoon paper seemed to have a schedule that suited my personal life better.

"I got to cover one particularly dramatic game, in which our high school's star, all-state, a potential All-American quarterback, broke his leg the week before we were to play Parker, our archrival across town. I wrote a story for the *News* about how the guy got hurt, how the team fell behind and his teammates rallied in a dramatic and cheerful halftime bonding, and they came back with blazing eyes and blew away Parker.

"The sports editor entered it in the state AP writing contest. I didn't think anything of it, and about three months later, the editor said, 'Would you like to come down to Charleston to the awards dinner? You can see what it's like.'

"Fritz Hollings, now Senator Hollings, was the governor of South Carolina, and he was presenting the awards. They began announcing the prizes for sportswriting. Third prize went to the Charleston paper, and second prize went to the *Greenville News,* and they announced, 'First prize goes to Max Muhlmann of the *Greenville Piedmont.'*

"I just about fell out of my chair. I was eighteen years old, still a student in high school. I had one sports coat and no suit. They had voted my story best among all the regular sportswriters! I was just speechless. I couldn't think of anything to say.

"That was in 1955, and that got a lot of people's attention, and that fall I began going to Furman University in Greenville, paying for it by continuing to work at the paper before and after class. Sandy Grady, a sports columnist for the *Charlotte News,* was the only reporter in the South I knew who wrote a regular column about stock car racing. I read him because the sports editor of my paper wanted me to write something about stock car racing. He said, 'We have a track here called Greenville-Pickens and once in a while they run one of these Grand National races,' as they were called then. I fought him. I said, 'I'd rather cover a dog show than stock cars. I can't even start my car.' I didn't know about cars, and I didn't want to know anything about cars. My view of it was having to deal with guys who either drove cars or drove wreckers. I had a very wrong slant, though it was much more true then. I was the classic stick-and-ball fan. I wanted to be Bob Feller. I didn't want to be Fonty Flock. But he made me go.

"I went to Spartanburg, which was only thirty miles away, where they were having a Grand National race. And the first time I covered it, I immediately fell in love with the people, because they were so easy to interview. A lot of times it was hard for me to interview college athletes, never mind coaches, who clearly didn't like the idea of wasting their time with an eighteen-year-old kid. If they had something to say, they wanted the main columnist or the sports editor to hear it.

"The first racer I interviewed was Tim Flock. He was the defending champion. He was sleeping under his car, catching a nap before the race. I said, 'Mr. Flock?' He jumped up right away. Oh gosh, I saw that he was napping, and I thought to myself, 'If this were Bill Murray'—the head football coach at Duke—'that would be it for me.' Tim said, 'Oh no, that's all right.' He treated me as if I were Red Barber instead of Max Muhlmann from Greenville, whoever he was.

"He talked to me, we laughed and joked, and he introduced me to his wife, Frances, and we just became really big buddies. I still didn't know anything about cars, but I knew he was a good guy. He talked about what he was trying to do, about how great the car was, and he was just so easy.

"So I saw that I really did like these people, and I started writing a column called 'Exhaust Smoke.' Sandy Grady's column in the *Charlotte News* had been 'Pit Stops.' And early in '57 Sandy left the *Charlotte News* for the *Philadelphia Daily News*. When Sandy went, the sports editor of the *News* called me up and offered me a job. His name was Bob Quincy, a well-respected writer who died a few years ago. He said, 'We need somebody to write stock car racing and cover high school sports.' I don't think he knew how young I was.

"I thought the *Charlotte News* had the best sports writers in the South. Furman Bisher had just left the paper. Charles Kuralt was writing for the *News*. And sure enough, I came up here in April of '57. I dropped out of college and never did finish. I thought I'd finish at North Carolina, State, or Duke, but I discovered they were 130 miles away.

"The first assignment up here was to interview Buck Baker, another eloquent racer. Buck had one of the best knacks for a quote that I've ever seen. His son Buddy is an extension, but not as good as his dad was. His dad was one of the best ever. I interviewed him when they were running fuel injection Chevies and supercharged Fords, and NASCAR was talking about taking the fuel injectors and superchargers away. Buck had a Chevy. I asked him what he thought about it. He said, 'That would be like running mules in the Kentucky Derby.' The words just flowed out of him. 'And I'll tell you what, that Bill France is going to lose out.' He just kept pouring out all this good stuff.

"It was a pretty good story, and they played it pretty good on the first sports page. So while I was interested in furthering my career by covering college sports, I could see that racing was going to pay dividends, so I kept doing it, took up Sandy's column and just kept writing about the bullrings of the South, which is what Sandy used to call the dirt tracks. The people who went to the Charlotte Fairgrounds were good folks, low-income people who worked on cars or used machinery, farmers and a lot of rural people, people who worked with their hands. They knew that the red dirt would be on them, wore clothes they could go home in and throw away. They understood Fords and Chevys and had their favorites with a wrestling-fan intensity for who they liked and didn't like. Junior Johnson and Curtis Turner were great favorites around that time when I was coming into it.

"Fighting was not as much as part of the sport as in hockey, but it was in that direction. You were prepared to race, win, wreck or fight or all of the above. If you were a competitor, chances were good you could get involved in any of those things, including the fighting. Even guys like Ned Jarrett, who is a calm individual, had a couple of moments when he had to get physical.

"Curtis was a lightning rod, 'cause he had such a passion for winning, and he had so much skill that if he ran second or third or fourth and was on the same lap as the leader, that was an oddity, because his view was he *had* to win or someone was going to pay the price. And like Dale Earnhardt, there were people who liked him for that and just as many who didn't.

"When he came, the competitors said, 'Oh heck, Turner's here. Maybe I'm running for second now if I'm hot tonight. How am I going to handle Turner? Can I afford to wreck this car to keep him from passing me?' because you knew he was going to be uninhibited. The question was on everyone's mind: How am I going to handle Curtis Turner?

"Curtis was intimidating because he would go out there and spin them out and knock them into the fence or through the fence, and of course, they would give it to him sometimes too. At the point I came on the scene in '57 it was difficult to figure out whose grudge came first. I remember seeing a race where Lee Petty clearly wrecked him. And that was some sort of payback for something Curtis had done previously to Lee. The next time Curtis could get at him, he wrecked Lee. This kind of thing would go on and on.

"Some people would take it more than others. But there *was* fighting, and it was based on a carryover from what happened on the track. These dirt tracks were much different from the superspeedways, where the speeds weren't that high and the safety features weren't nearly as good, so maybe the danger was evened out. Guys drove in shirts and pants. There was more danger from fire. But it was very difficult to pass on dirt, unless you made contact. And maintaining control while scraping beside someone else was something Curtis was expert at. He had a sense of balance that was just phenomenal. Curtis could keep the car under control even when nothing was pointing straight except the wheels. He could get through there somehow. It would be impossible to think of a way to keep Curtis from coming through unless you just blocked him or turned him around.

"There were very, very good drivers like Fireball Roberts and Buck Baker, but Curtis had a talent that was obvious even to someone like me who had never driven a car on a racetrack and not very well on the street.

"One afternoon I went to the Charlotte Fairgrounds to cover the race. Curtis was the pace driver in a Grand National race. He was driving a '56 Ford convertible, and he said, 'Pop, get in the backseat and you can see real good.' He called everyone 'Pop.' He started driving, and he said, 'Pop, I'm going to make a lap. Want to make a lap?' I said, 'Hell no, I don't want to make a lap. Let's get out of here.' Curtis said, 'Aw no, we're going to make a lap.'

"Curtis had had a couple shots of Canadian Club, as was his form, and as we were driving around the track, I looked back, and Speedy Thompson in a Chrysler 300 and Buck Baker in a Chevrolet were in the front row, and they dropped the green flag, and Curtis was supposed to pull into the pits, and he wouldn't get off the track! He went into the first turn sideways, and I was in the backseat doing what I could to find a place to hold on. They didn't have seat belts then. I had my fingernails up underneath the seat cushions holding on. I said, 'God almighty, Curtis, get this thing out of here.' And I could see the race cars coming up to us. He could get through the turn as well as they could, but they were yelling and giving us the equivalent of the finger. I screamed, 'They're going to hit us. They're going to hit us.' Curtis said, 'Nah, they won't hit us, and if they do hit us, I'll hit them back!' I said, 'I don't have anything to hold on to. You have a steering wheel.'

"We were yelling back and forth as he made about two laps. It scared the *crap* out of me. I was afraid I was going to bounce out of the car and get run over.

"Another time Curtis was driving his Cadillac. The Charlotte Motor Speedway on U.S. 29 was his original idea, and he had just started building it. Bruton Smith came later. It was a sea of red mud, they were grading it off, and they started building the berm for the back of the grandstand, and he was very proud.

"Curtis had on a silk suit, and we were out driving along on a hot summer day, and Curtis said, 'Let's go out and see it. You want to go over there and ride around in the mud?' I said, 'No, not in this Cadillac.' He said, 'We can do it. It doesn't make any difference.' And all of a sudden he whipped the car, jumped a ditch, and landed in this sea of mud, *whoooooosh*. He turned the windshield wipers on, and the mud started oozing through the air conditioning vents. He was sliding around, driving as fast as he could on this big front yard of the speedway. I can't imagine what that must have looked like. Curtis was an impetuous, impulsive, fun-loving guy. In both of these cases he was having fun—much more fun than I was having! But it certainly made an indelible impression. So you can imagine what Curtis was like when he had his game face on and was driving for money and why he would be a little intimidating to be around. Guys like Fireball Roberts were more under control, more thoughtful, a little smarter in the way they approached it, but Curtis didn't have to be very smart because he was so good. And he wasn't very smart—he lost a lot of races by abusing his equipment. Ralph Moody would stress to guys like Freddie Lorenzen, whom he was teaching, 'To finish first, you first have to finish.' This was one of Ralph's big slogans, but this *never* would have occurred to Curtis. To him, what was important was to be first and stay first until something took it away from you.

"Curtis and Joe Weatherly had a place in Daytona Beach called the Party Pad that they would rent annually when they were down for the February races. At the time the newspaper wouldn't pay travel expenses—the idea of paying somebody's expenses to go cover something was unheard of—so if I went to an out-of-town race, I had to pay my own expenses. So Curtis would take me a lot of times in his plane or whatever, and when I got down there I didn't have a place to stay, and he'd say, 'Stay with us. We have an extra bedroom here.' I was single, and it was a great life for a single guy, as you can imagine. I was a writer watching Greek heroes running around doing Jack Kerouac-like things.

"Joe Weatherly would run around drinking out of a great big glass lamp that he had at the Party Pad. It held at least two quarts of whatever you wanted to pour in it. It had a solid bottom, a big glass thing like a vase, but it was the inside of a lamp. And Joe, who was a short guy, had an even shorter girlfriend whom he called 'Short Track.' She would go 'round with him. She didn't like to share Joe with anyone, so before she arrived, Joe sometimes would get a little frisky, and he and Curtis would keep score of their conquests on a chalkboard in their bedroom where they would put hash marks. Curtis and Joe, who were both from Virginia, called it 'chopping kindling.' Joe would say, 'We're going to go chop a little kindling with this little honey bunny here.' Honey buns and chopping kindling, it was crazy.

"They would go across the street to Robinson's bar, and their idea of prerace training was to have steaks and drink Canadian Club and tell stories late into the night, and go to the Party Pad and party for a couple more hours and take their selected young lady to the scoring room.

"Their lives tended to revolve around the races they went to. Joe used to fly by using an Esso map. He wasn't too far along in this piloting deal. He would fly low enough to see what the highway number was. 'Oops, turn right on 29 East.'

"Of course, when Joe flew with Curtis, Joe was very wary. One time I was flying with them. Curtis was at the controls, I was sitting next to him, and Joe was looking out the window in the back. Curtis said to me, 'Watch me scare the shit out of him.' Curtis cut off one of the engines. It was a two-engine plane. Joe was looking out the window and saw that the engine had feathered, and he said, 'God almighty, the engine is out.' Curtis said, 'God almighty, sure is.' And then he kerned the other one off. Curtis said, 'Joe, I can't get either one of them on.' Joe got all excited, and after we started going down a bit, Curtis finally turned them back on. Curtis thought that was the most fun. He said to me, 'What do you think of that?' It didn't occur to him that I wasn't an uninvolved passenger. I was more on Joe's side than his!

"God, I can't tell you how many rental-car adventures they had. One time I was with Curtis when we went to Columbia. He said,

'Come on, I got you a room.' He picked up a honey bun at the track, and he got drunk, and on the way back to the motel, the girl thought it would be a good idea if he drove the car into the swimming pool, and I believe he made it.

"Then he couldn't remember what room he was staying in. He said he knew he had left the door open. So at two-thirty in the morning as he walked with this girl he started kicking in all the doors as he went along the motel corridor, *blap, blap, blap*. If the door didn't open, he knew it wasn't his room. Finally, he kicked one and it opened up, and it turned out there was somebody else's suitcase in it, so he threw the suitcase out and took the room anyway!

"I always seemed to be the third party he was confiding in. Another time late at night he was scaring a young lady by slaloming the telephone poles along the road. Fortunately there was nobody on the sidewalk at the time. We were in Columbia, and he was driving down a boulevard, and he'd go over the sidewalk on one side of a pole and down the street and go outside, inside, outside, inside at about 90 miles an hour, and then you'd feel the *kaboom* when he went back over the sidewalk onto the street. Hubcaps would go flying in every direction.

"I've been with Curtis and Joe on several occasions when they would start banging into each other in their rental cars. They got to where the Hertz people wouldn't rent them cars. They had an all-points bulletin: If you see these men, do not rent them anything. Do not talk to them. Do not give them anything, not even a map! What they did was awful, but it was awfully funny. It was incredible that they got away with what they got away with.

"Only one time when I was with Curtis did we get stopped by a policeman. We were going somewhere in separate cars, and Curtis passed a great big drink of Canadian Club out the window of his car to me in mine. There was a police officer behind us. I yelled, 'Officer behind us.' The cop turned on his lights and pulled us both over.

"Curtis said, 'Me and this honey bun are going out to this club. I was just offering my buddy here a little pop.' Curtis said, 'You want a pop?' And I was sure the cop was going to throw him in jail. Curtis said, 'I got a race tomorrow. You want to go to a race? Come on. You can be in my pits.'

"And he talked his way out of it. Curtis was something."

MAURICE PETTY

6

THE PERFECTIONIST

WHEN NASCAR BEGAN IN 1949, one of the featured drivers was Lee Petty, winner of fifty races and driving champion in 1954, 1958, and 1959. Following in Lee's footsteps came son Richard, who won 200 races and won driving championships in 1964, 1967, 1971, 1972, 1974, 1975, and 1979. Through most of Lee's career and then throughout most of Richard's, the younger son, Maurice, went along. For several years beginning in 1960 Maurice took a shot at driving, and he was good enough to finish in the top ten in nine of his twenty-six starts, but after Lee Petty was seriously injured at Daytona in 1961, Lee decided that Maurice crashed too often and that Richard would be the son to get behind the wheel of the Petty Enterprises car. It was also decided by Lee that Maurice would be the chief mechanic. Maurice, the dutiful son, accepted his job stoically.

Lee Petty, though still with us, has been such a recluse that I thought it right to include a chapter on a man I call The Invisible Champion. Lee refuses almost all requests for interviews. He says he wants his sons to have all the credit. When you visit the Richard Petty Museum, sometimes you can see Lee Petty standing way out on his property, a lone figure hitting golf balls. He is an intriguing character, perhaps the first true professional racer. I sought out son

Maurice to talk about what it was like growing up under Papa Lee's strong leadership.

In the long barns adjacent to the chockablock Richard Petty Museum in Level Cross, North Carolina, Maurice Petty and his sons work on the Petty Enterprises truck engines. A small wooden and glass trophy case inside the door to this race shop is filled with honors won by Lee and Maurice, important figures in the history of stock car racing but men who for years spurned the media spotlight.

Lee's Hall of Fame induction program lies on a shelf. There are also two large bronze sculptures of a mechanic working on an engine block. Maurice won those in 1964 and 1967 when the Grand National Master Mechanic award was bestowed upon him. Maurice Petty, who maintains the lowest profile of the Pettys, is the winningest engine builder in the history of NASCAR, engine builder of twelve winning Daytona cars, including seven 500s and the chief mechanic for cars that won 198 races.

At age fifty-seven, Maurice Petty remains shy and diffident. It could not have been easy for him to have lived under Lee's heavy thumb or in Richard's long shadow for so many years, and yet he shows no bitterness. Like dad Lee, Maurice Petty is a pragmatist. You do what makes sense. You do what makes you the most money. Over the years car number 43 won a lot of races. Maurice Petty was one of the big reasons why.

MAURICE PETTY: "I was born on March 27, 1939, in Level Cross, right in that house that sits next to the museum, me and Richard both. Our daddy, Lee, was a fanatic about Richard and me working and not lollygagging around. If he didn't have something for Richard and myself, and this was even before we were in racing, if we'd come home from school or in the summertime, Daddy'd make sure there was something to be done, even if it was nothing but cutting weeds or picking up rocks and putting them in the driveway. So we worked.

"He started racing in '49, so I was ten and Richard was twelve. When he first started, we were too young to know anything about it, but there were parts to be cleaned, floors to be swept, the car to be washed, just odds and ends jobs, and from that we progressed to changing rear ends, packing wheel bearings, changing brakes, and then on to building motors. We took it a step at a time.

"When we would come home from school, it would be like a farmer who had kids. They would go to the fields, while we would go to the little shop Daddy had, and we'd do these chores. And there was no *wanting* to do it. We *had* to do it.

"When we went to high school, Richard and I went out for football, basketball, and baseball. Daddy gave us that opportunity, and he was behind us a hundred percent. I played football and basketball. I didn't play much baseball for Randleman. But it wasn't a question of 'if' we were going into racing, it was a question of 'when' we were going to do it.

"Richard and myself didn't want to go to college. We wanted to race. But Lee had gone to King's Business College in Greensboro when he was young, and he insisted we go, and so we both consented to take a business course. In that course you had a handwriting class along with numbers and typing, and at the time they taught that pretty scroll, old-timey writing, and Richard latched on to that, and that's where he learned his autograph from. Me, I ain't much on writing. But that's how all that come about.

"When we started going to the races with Daddy, what I recall most about him was that he didn't take no shit off of nobody. When it came time to lean on somebody, he might lean on him a little bit. And they'd lean on him. To a certain degree he was hot-tempered, not only in racing but in everyday life. He was a perfectionist. He wanted things done his way, and he always wanted it done right. If you done something wrong the first time, you done it wrong, but if you done it wrong the second time, it was your ass. Daddy didn't stand for it to be done wrong twice.

"Two of the more memorable characters Daddy drove against were Curtis Turner and Joe Weatherly. Curtis was a flat-out driver. He would run it until the wheels run off it. We drove a lot of dirt tracks back then, and they had big old holes, and you would think he would finesse his way around them, but no, Curtis would hit the same hole in the same spot lap after lap after lap after lap until something fell off the durn race car. If it didn't, he run good. Weatherly was a nice, easygoing guy, a clown who was always joking, having a good time. He drove hard, but he didn't drive nothing like Curtis, he drove with a lit-tle more finesse, and they both liked to party big-time. I never did attend their parties. They were grown-ups, and Richard and I were young boys. I've heard some wild tales though.

"The difference between Curtis, Joe Weatherly, and the Flock boys, and my daddy was that they all drove *for* people. Lee owned his own deal. It was his livelihood. I mean, if he didn't finish good, we didn't eat good. If he finished good, we made car payments. That makes a hell of a lot of difference how you approach racing. Lee approached it to finish. They approached it to win, but Lee was fortunate enough that he still won a bunch.

"One of my earliest memories was going to the Daytona beach race in 1954. We drove down there in a '53 Dodge. We went over to the Chrysler-Plymouth dealer and bought a '54 New Yorker, and we took the racing items off the Dodge and put them on the Chrysler, and when the race was over, Richard drove the car home on the road, and I rode with him. I was fifteen at the time, and driving the car home is a much stronger memory than Tim Flock getting disqualified and Daddy getting the win.

"The next year I can remember Carl Kiekhaefer coming into rac-ing. He came in with a lot of money, and when he came in, he came in first-class. He brought Chryslers to the track, and whichever one run the best, that's the one he would run. He was also a perfectionist, but he had the money to back it up. In '56 he came in a with a lot of race cars. He hired the Flocks and Speedy Thompson and Herb Thomas to drive for him, and he created a definite problem for the Pettys, because as long as them cars were there, man, they were up front. You just hoped you could run with them long enough for them to have problems. And naturally, on several occasions, Lee just out-smarted them.

"In '57, Lee ran a second car beside himself, when he gave Bobby Myers a chance to drive for him. Bobby was there just a short period of time. He was a terror on the short tracks, the modified or Late Model circuit. Bobby was going to be a top-notch driver, but unfortu-nately he had a bad accident at Darlington, and he lost his life. It sort of happened right in front of us, 'cause Lee and his crowd was pitting on the front stretch, and Richard and myself and some of the boys were pitting on the backstretch with Bobby. Fonty Flock spun out, and they all came up through there, and Bobby hit him. It was a bad scene, and it affected everybody, cause it took forever for the rescue people to get there, and I can remember them running up to that car, shaking their heads, and going over to check on the other drivers.

"And the other thing about that race, Darlington was a one-groove track, and towards the last part Curtis Turner and Lee got together, and Curtis hit the wall, and then Joe Weatherly came back and got back at Lee, but in all fairness, if they could watch the films, the films I have seen of it, they all tried to say that Lee hit Curtis, but the way I seen it, Curtis went and lost it, hit Lee and then went and hit the fence. But everybody has his own opinion. Whatever side you're on, that's the way it's going to come out.

"Back then, the racers took it to heart. One of the better deals was at Greensboro, a half-mile dirt track when Lee and Tiny Lund got into it. After the race Lee and Tiny were wrastling around, and my mother hit Tiny with her pocketbook. That was quite a show. Tiny was a big, strong ox of a guy, and he was young. She was popping Tiny with her pocketbook. Tiny must have been on top of Lee at the time.

"Richard began driving in '58, and I drove some in '60, '61, '62, and '63, but then after Lee got hurt at Daytona in '61, I scaled back a little bit. At that time Richard was making money, finishing races and bringing money in, where I guess I would tear up the car more than it was worth. I remember a race we ran at Greenville-Pickens. It was the early sixties, and we didn't have much money. Richard was running, and his tires wore out, and they changed them, and he went on to win the race, and then my tires were worn out, and I put on the tires they just took off Richard's car. But I was a real racer.

"In '64 it became that I would build the motors and look after the car, and Richard would do the driving, because that just seemed to make more sense than anything going. I liked driving, but at the time Richard was coming into his prime, he was doing good, and it just made more sense to put a hundred percent effort behind him, instead of making fifty percent to him and fifty to me. And at that time, when they made that decision, I'm sure it hurt. But you know, my driving just didn't make sense.

"In '59 I saw the new Daytona track for the first time, and my reaction was like everyone else's: I thought, There ain't no way they're going to be able to race on this racetrack. It was too big. It was ungodly big. It was something none of us had ever seen or dreamed of seeing. It was a whole new ballgame.

"The drivers didn't know what to expect, and I'm sure they were concerned, though I don't know if scared isn't the right word. At the end Lee and Johnny Beauchamp finished neck and neck. Beauchamp [pronounced Bow-champ] came out of the Midwest. He ran a few races in a Thunderbird. He was a good racer who happened just to be there. As they raced to the flag, we were jumping up and down, hollering for Lee. And when it was over, Lee said, 'I won the race. I *know* I won it.' But it was so close from where we were standing looking across the racetrack, it was impossible to tell. It was Lee, Beauchamp, and Joe Weatherly in a lapped car, and hell, there were three of them, and here they come, and you see it, but did you *see* it?

"We didn't go home. We stayed right there. We'd go over to the NASCAR offices, and somebody would say one thing, somebody else something else, and we'd wait and go back, and they called around and asked that if anyone had a snapshot of the finish, would they bring it and let them examine it to see what went on. They finally wound up with a good snapshot that proved that Lee won. But he knew he won it all along. He said, 'I know I won it, because I was there.' And then we packed up and went home.

"And later that year at the Lakewood Speedway in Atlanta, Lee came in first, and Richard came in second, and we were jumping up and down because we knew it was a good payday. You didn't look at the winning and the trophies then as much as you were always thinking, 'Man, there's first-place money and second-place money. That's a big payday.' Trophies didn't mean all that much. You can't eat them trophies.

"In '59 Lee won the driving championship for the third time, and the second year in a row. Richard was driving that year, but there was no rivalry between Lee and Richard. The deal with Richard was that he was learning how to drive. Hopefully, Lee would win a race and Richard would get a good finish out of it. A couple times Lee treated Richard the same way he treated everyone else. We were in Ontario, in Canada, running a little old short track, and Lee and Cotton Owens were running for the lead, and they caught up to Richard to lap him, and Lee just knocked the crap out of Richard, knocked him into the fence to get him out of the way so he could go on and win the race.

"By 1960 Richard was doing well, finishing second in the points to Rex White that year. Rex came out of Maryland. He was a super short-track driver, but he wasn't well liked by the competitors. He was just a—Yankee.

"All along I expected Richard to run good. He was my brother, and I always had confidence in him that he could do it. I never thought no other way. That was the way it was in the Petty family. Our attitude was, 'We're going to do it, and we're going to do it better,' and if you don't have that attitude, you don't need to be in racing. Even the times in the back of your mind you didn't think you had as good equipment or proper tools to get the job done, you still went with the attitude you were going to win the race—under any circumstances.

"Richard won his first race at the Charlotte Fairgrounds, which was a dirty old racetrack. Lee almost spun out Rex White, and Richard was able to win. It didn't make no difference to Lee whether he won or Richard. Later that year, Lee won his fiftieth race, though we weren't counting them. How many races you won didn't matter. You go do it, because that's what I'm supposed to do. So we went to racing because that's what we were supposed to do.

"In '60, the Charlotte Motor Speedway ran its first World 600, and Lee was disqualified after spinning in the pits, and Richard was disqualified and so was Junior Johnson. Nobody knows quite why. There was never no rules. You spun out on the straightaway, and hell, it was dirt between there and pit road, so instead of going all the way around, when you spun out you drove right on into your pits. And there had never been no kind of ruling or anything said about how come you came into the pits, that you had to make another lap to come into pit road, but for some unknown reason, NASCAR pulled another trick out of their hat, and that's what they went with. It cost us two paydays. Bobby Johns run third in our other car. We would have been third, fourth, and fifth.

"That was not a good time around here. That was NASCAR's decision, and they stuck with it. There was no appealing. Why it was done that way, to this day nobody knows.

"In '61, in the first qualifying race at Daytona, Richard hurdled the guardrail. He went out of the racetrack in the number four turn. He got airborne and cleared the guardrail and went off and set down. And then in the second race, Lee and Beauchamp were running, and Banjo Matthews or somebody had a wreck, and Lee checked up and Beauchamp didn't, just kept coming, and it was 'Kady bar the door' as the two cars flew together outside the track. It was a bad accident. Everybody ran across the track, and by the time I got there, Lee's car was out there all twisted and battered and smoking. They took Lee to the hospital, and it was nip and tuck. We didn't know if he was going to make it. It was the scariest moment I ever had.

"I stayed in Daytona in the hospital with Lee and my mother for about a week, and Richard got all the things together and came back home to get ready for the next race. My dad came back, ran several races, but he just decided it wasn't the thing to do. It wasn't that he was scared. The wreck took so much out of him physically. It just drained him, and he never did get his strength back. He couldn't do it anymore."

7

CARL KIEKHAEFER

AFTER WINNING THE DAYTONA BEACH and road course race of 1954 and then having the victory snatched away by NASCAR, Tim Flock quit in a huff and went home to Atlanta to run a gas station. In 1955 he returned to Daytona, as a spectator. By accident, he came across a car owned by a man named Carl Kiekhaefer. Flock had never heard of the man, but circumstance brought them together. The chance meeting would change the course of racing history. Kiekhaefer, a tyrant, but a man who passionately hated to lose, passed away in 1983.

TIM FLOCK: "I had quit racing the second race of '54, and while racing was going on without me, my buddies would come by. I wanted to go back but I told them I had to run my gas station, that I didn't want to go to Daytona. It was February of '55, and the new season was coming, and they finally talked me into coming. I didn't take a helmet with me or anything. I went to watch, and I was standing on the beach with my buddies, drinking beer, when a Chrysler 300 drove by. I said to them, 'Damn, if I had that car, I'd win the race.' The Lord done this, had to. Standing about three feet from me was Tiny Haygood. He said, 'Wait a minute, son. I know who owns that white Chrysler you were talking about. What is your name?' I said, 'Tim Flock.'

59

'You won the race last year, didn't you?' 'I sure did, and I got disqualified.' He said, 'The man who owns that car is worth about forty million dollars. His name of Carl Kiekhaefer. Would you like to meet
him?' I said, 'Man, yeah.'

"I left my buddies to go with Tiny, who was taking me over to
where the car was going to be down the beach later on. Kiekhaefer had
rented a brand-new filling station, and when I arrived about two
hours later, I saw eight to ten guys in white uniforms working on the
car. Tiny pointed to a little, bitty short man with a cigar in his mouth.
He said, 'That's Mr. Kiekhaefer in the back. He's real busy, but wait
around, Tim, and we'll talk a little.'

"Finally Mr. Kiekhaefer walked back to where me and Tiny were,
and Tiny said, 'Mr. Kiekhaefer, this is Tim Flock. You don't have a
driver for your car, and he won the race here last year.' He said,
'What's your name?' 'Tim Flock.' He said, 'You don't have a car for
this year, and you won last year?' I said, 'I sure did.' He said, 'Sit down
in that car.' I sat in the car, and you talk about a race car. I looked up
at the steering wheel, and I said, 'My God.' In a real hoarse voice Mr.
Kiekhaefer said, 'What's the matter, Flock?' I said, 'This car has an
automatic transmission. No car in the history of NASCAR has ever
won at Daytona with an automatic transmission.' Because you go
uphill on the backstretch, and you need to have a second gear to get
you out of the sand. He said, 'Don't worry about it. You want to drive
the damn car?' I said, 'Yes sir. I sure do.'

"I qualified at 139 miles an hour. Of course, the car was wound up
and I didn't have to shift. At the start of the race me and Fireball
Roberts were up front going through the first turn of the first lap. He
was driving a beautiful Buick built by Red Vogt, a known engine man
who had built a lot of bootleggers' cars in Atlanta, and I was right
behind him. Fireball pulled me two hundred yards up the backstretch,
caught second gear running wide open, pulling ahead, and I had to
knock my car into drive trying to get ahold, and I almost would catch
him at the end of the backstretch, and that's the way we ran all day
long. I could not get by him, and I finished second.

"And then Bill France disqualified the car Fireball was driving. He
was disqualified for shortening his push rods a sixteenth of an inch,
the same thing he had disqualified me for the year before. A story-

book finish, really. I hated to see Fireball get disqualified. I knew how he felt. But we got the win.

"We ran that car the next four races, and by the fifth race Kiekhaefer bought me a straight stick built by Chrysler to put in the 300, and after that, nobody could touch us. That was it. We had a big hemi engine, a great car, and that year we went on to win eighteen Grand National races, a record which stood for twelve years, until Richard Petty broke it. I'm proud of this. Petty is the only driver who has ever won more than me in one year. And after we won eighteen, NASCAR was always inspecting every inch of our cars. They never could find anything wrong with the Chrysler 300 I drove.

"Kiekhaefer had so much money. He had the first haulers. We showed up with beautiful trucks with the 300s in the back of them. He had Mercury Outboard motors advertised on them. That was what he was doing, advertising his Mercury engines. He had 2,700 Mercury Outboard dealers throughout the United States. That Mercury motor was a damn good fishing motor. He had the money, and he had Chrysler, and in '55 that man more or less moved into NASCAR and took over.

"This man wanted to win no matter what. Kiekhaefer was an engineer, and he built great engines. He had dynometers, which no one knew about, in his plant in Wisconsin. He would run cars wide open on the dynometer until it blowed. Two or three trips I traveled up there and watched until the pistons and rods went through the ceiling. He'd take the engine apart and see what made it blow. That's why the car was so successful. We won eighteen races in '55.

"That Chrysler was so heavy, the Fords would get up behind me and try to spin me, and I'd just shake them off. They were so mad at me for winning eighteen, everybody was after me to try to block me or spin me, and if you let them get by with it, they'd keep it up. You had to put them in the rail and get away from them. I'd spin them out so they wouldn't hassle me no more the next week.

"I won the driving championship in '55 at Darlington. Seemed like I always had trouble at Darlington. I finished second one time, third one time, but I never could win that race, and I wanted to win there so bad in '55, but that Chrysler was so heavy. We should have won it. We led it, led it, and it kept blowing tires. One of the mechanics hadn't tightened the bolts on the exhaust pipe, and it came loose and was throwing flames right into the gear box and steering, and it got to where I couldn't even turn the wheel. I had to back off, and I don't know how I even finished third, because I could barely turn it. I must have run the last fifteen or twenty laps with the car like that. When we got to the pits after the race the car had completely locked. They couldn't even park the car. They had to pick it up. So Kiekhaefer wasn't too mad. That sewed up the championship. But Kiekhaefer was very disappointed we didn't win the race.

"After we won that first race at Daytona, Kiekhaefer said, 'Tim, I want you to know one thing: every nickel you ever win in one of my cars you can have. The whole hundred percent.' Which had never been heard of before in the history of NASCAR. I won eighteen that year, and he gave me every nickel.

"But he made up for it in the wintertime. I had five kids living with me in Atlanta, and he would call me up from Wisconsin and want to know where I was, and he would fly me to Wisconsin. He had two full-time pilots, and I'd fly out there for two days to play cards. I would stay in his home with him. One time it had snowed and was icy, very cold. I was laying in bed going to sleep, and he came in and covered me up, like a mother would.

"Another time I got there and was there two days, when he called and said, 'Look, I don't need you on this trip. You can go back and be with your family.' And I hadn't even seen him. He wanted to control my life, and he did for the little over a year I drove for him. He had to know where I was at, what I was doing. And with him, there was no drinking, not even beer. I developed an ulcer that year. I had come out of the army with an ulcerated stomach, and that year I was down to 130 pounds and I was throwing up blood. But I was winning races, making more money than I made in my life, $40,000, which was unheard of. It was *big* money. We bought a beautiful home in Atlanta, a new car, had everything we wanted.

"And then in 1956 Kiekhaefer went and hired Junior Johnson, Herb Thomas, Speedy Thompson, Wendell Scott, the black driver out of Virginia, Fonty and Bob. In '56 we showed up with six beautiful Chryslers and Dodges. Kiekhaefer was controlling NASCAR, and it kept them in an uproar.

"I said to him, 'I don't know why you're doing this, Carl. We just got through winning eighteen races, won the championship. How many people are you going to hire?' That question pissed him off at me.

"We went back to Daytona in '56, and I won it again. I outran all of his other cars, almost lapped them, and Buck Baker and everyone else. We won that race, but he just got worse and worse.

"At Daytona he rented a sixty-unit motel and put all his drivers at one end and the wives and girlfriends at the other. We couldn't have sex the night before the race. This was his rule. We were like boxers. And he would watch all night long, and if you didn't play by his rules, you were fired the next morning.

"At six in the morning he'd blow a whistle, and everybody had to meet him out front. The week before the beach race he rented an abandoned airport which the military had used in Daytona. We ran those Chryslers from six in the morning until dark, changing rear ends, experimenting to find what worked best. We even had a fifth wheel that we pulled behind the car to measure distance from one corner to another, and he had everything calculated to the decimal point. We had those cars to where the rpms would be peaking on the beach, and then going down the beach it peaked going into the north turn. And that's why those cars won so many races. And we did it on half-mile tracks, three-quarter mile tracks, mile tracks. Everything was perfect on those cars when we went into a race.

"I won the Wilkesboro race. I returned to Charlotte. I was staying at the Barringer Hotel. Mr. Kiekhaefer called and said, 'Tim, you did a great job. Come up to my room. I have a steak waiting for you.' I went up there and opened the door. He had candles burning, trying to be real nice. He said, 'Come on in, Tim.' I stood in the door. I said, 'No, Mr. Kiekhaefer, I'm not going to come in. That was the last race I'm ever going to run for you.' He said, 'Come on in and sit down, Tim. Eat this steak.'

I said, 'Mr. Kiekhaefer, you've been great. I've enjoyed the whole thing,' and I walked out, and I didn't see him again for eight years when they put him in the Hall of Fame at Darlington. He was still so angry with me that when someone tried to take a picture of me and Junior and him, he tried to grab the camera and destroy the film. He had felt I was like a son to him, that I had betrayed him somehow. I won twenty-three races for that man, but he wasn't satisfied. He wanted to win *every* race.

"And after I quit one of his big wheel millionaire friends who worked for him called me up. He had made me some of those Italian uniforms with the zipper going sideways made of beautiful silk. His friend said, 'Tim, if you send the eight driver's uniforms back to us, we're going to send you your twenty-three trophies.' I had given him all the trophies because he had given me all the money. And I wanted those trophies. I sent the uniforms the next day, and to this day I never did get the trophies. It was one of them crooked deals.

"The next year Herb Thomas, who drove for Kiekhaefer, was going to be the driving champion, but for some reason Kiekhaefer wanted Buck Baker to be the champion. Kiekhaefer rented the track in Shelby to add an extra race. Speedy Thompson went out in a Kiekhaefer car and took poor Herb into the guardrail, and several cars hit him, and they put a plate in Herb's head, which ended his racing for the season. And Buck won the championship. People started throwing bottles at Kiekhaefer's trucks, throwing stuff after they seen what happened at Shelby. He could not take that kind of bad publicity with the millions he spent for his company on advertising. He had the public mad at him. And it was not long after that when the man pulled out of NASCAR.

"I got some revenge against Kiekhaefer in '57 at a road race in Elkhart Lake, Wisconsin, in his backyard. Kiekhaefer had six cars in that race, and all his six thousand employees were there to see his six cars win the race. He had six cars in it, with Buck Baker, Frank Mundy, Junior, Herb, the whole bunch. It's four or five miles over mountains, a lot of turns, right outside Chicago, a road course, and I was so good on road courses. I was pissed off at him, had been since he built all these other cars. I was driving for Bill Stroppe, who built me this Mercury, and I ran off and left them. I won $3,000, which was a good purse in that day. And that killed Kiekhaefer, what with all his employees there. NASCAR held a race there only that one time. Never had it again.

"But I believe that because of Kiekhaefer, the Ford and Chevy teams came back to NASCAR in '57. He was winning all the races, and they couldn't stand it anymore. Carl Kiekhaefer—the man is in the Hall of Fame and he should be—because he did so much to build NASCAR racing. He put the fans in the grandstands. He sure did."

8

THE DEATH OF THE MYERS BROTHERS

BEFORE THERE WAS THE DEATH OF the Allison brothers—Clifford and Davey—there were the Myers brothers, Bobby and Billy, talented modified and Sportsman racers who had just begun their Grand National careers when they died prematurely. Bobby was only thirty when he died, Billy thirty-four.

On September 2, 1957, the day of the Southern 500 at Darlington, Bobby Myers thought he had a good chance to win the race. Driving a Petty Enterprises Olds, he sat on the front row between Cotton Owens, the pole winner, and Curtis Turner. "I can win this one," he told Bob Colvin, track president and friend.

But on the twenty-eighth lap, Myers was driving at top speed when he ran his white Oldsmobile into a stationary Fonty Flock, who had spun out and sat against the outside wall hoping against hope that the oncoming cars could avoid him. Myers apparently never saw Flock's Pontiac until it was too late. According to Tim Flock, Fonty said he could see Bobby Myers's eyes grow large when he realized, too late, that Flock's car blocked his path.

When the cars collided, Myers's car flipped end over end as pieces of metal flew everywhere and the engine was ripped out of the chassis. When rescue workers reached him, Bobby Myers was dead. Fonty Flock was lucky to survive, but was never to race again.

About six months later, on April 12, 1958, Bobby's brother, Billy, who finished sixth in the points in 1956, was driving in a race at Bowman-Gray Stadium in Winston-Salem when he pulled off the track, stopped his car, and died after suffering a heart attack.

Danny "Chocolate" Myers, who today is a member of Richard Childress's crack race team, was nine years old when his daddy, Bobby Myers, died at Darlington. His memories of his dad burn brightly within and haunt him still.

DANNY "CHOCOLATE" MYERS: "I was born on October 17, 1948, in Winston-Salem, the home of Bowman-Gray Stadium and the R. J. Reynolds Tobacco Company. I'm the son of Bobby Myers and the nephew of Bill Myers. I can remember things about him. I can remember him and his friends working on the old cars in the garage behind the house. We'd play out there. I can remember Dad cutting metal with a torch and stepping on something hot. I remember Rex White and Tiny Lund coming by the house. They were just starting out. Rex was from Baltimore, and Tiny from out in Iowa, and because my dad and uncle were racers, they'd come over and sleep in the garage. I can remember going to the races and hearing people cheer for my dad—it wasn't like it is today. The guys had fans, people who followed them, but there was no TV.

"Most of my memories of my dad comes from things people have told me about him or from looking through old pictures, seeing pictures, like the ones I have of my dad and my uncle with Ralph Earnhardt, Dale's dad. They were good friends.

"My dad and my uncle were rivals of Curtis Turner and Glen Wood over at Bowman-Gray Stadium. Bill France Jr. hung out with them. His wife is from Winston-Salem. They have roots here too. He told me this story: He said that Daddy and Curtis got into some kind of deal on the track, and they were beating each other around a little bit. The race was over, and Daddy pulled in and went after Curtis. He picked up a tire tool. Curtis had stepped up on the back of his truck, and Daddy started after him. When Curtis stepped down, he had a pistol. Curtis said, 'Bobby, where are you going with that tire tool?' Daddy said, 'I was just looking for a place to lay it down.'

"I didn't see that, but I do remember what happened after that. A couple miles from Bowman-Gray Stadium is a place called Charles'

Speed Shop. Belonged to a guy named Arnold Charles. He was a cam grinder and engine builder, a real good friend of my daddy and my uncle. Anyway, on Monday or Tuesday anybody who was in racing would be at Arnold's, and they'd be sitting around talking. This day I went with my daddy. Daddy brought a blank gun with him, and he walked in, and he stuck it in Curtis's back. And they were playing this time. They fought on Saturday night, but on Monday they were buddies. And then they fought the next Saturday night. I remember Curtis being scared, but they were just playing.

"Banjo Matthews told me a story. Back then everybody towed the car with a tow bar. They didn't have trailers. He said, 'You would always be telling your daddy, "Daddy, the car is gone." And you told him so many times that this one time you told him, "Daddy, the car is gone," and he didn't believe you.' Banjo said, 'Your dad went about two miles down the road before he realized the car had come unhooked, run off the side of the road somewhere, and was gone.'

"Mama tells the story of going somewhere to race, and the car that we used to pull the race car was not as good as the race car, and we were going up a mountain, and Daddy said, 'Lorraine, slide over here to the steering wheel,' and Daddy would have to crank up the race car to help push the family car up the mountain. It was tough times, but good times for them. They were two kids in love, and he was doing what he wanted. It's hard to complain when you have a deal like that.

"I was at the NASCAR awards banquet last year and Herb Fishel, the main guy at Chevrolet, got up in front of the audience, a full house, and he surprised me when he said, 'We grew up in the South. Growing up in the South we didn't have professional sports. We didn't have anything but stock car racing. We looked to stock car racing for our heroes. And Bobby Myers was my hero.' Last week I went to the lumberyard to get a piece of wood, and a guy said to me, 'Your dad was the greatest dirt track driver I ever knew in my life.' He's been gone almost forty years, and it makes me feel good that people still remember him.

"Most of the guys didn't have anything. They worked all day, and at night they worked on those cars, and then they towed them to the racetrack and raced four nights a week, maybe to Fayetteville on Friday night, Bowman-Gray Stadium Saturday night, and Victory Stadium in Virginia on Sunday. They raced all over the Southeast throughout the year. I remember going to Bowman-Gray Stadium on New Year's Day, going to race on Easter Monday. And when it got too cold in the Carolinas, he'd race in places like Jacksonville. He and my uncle were just getting into Grand National racing.

"My dad was an electrician by trade. Years later I was talking to the guy he worked for. He said, 'Your dad worked for me. I'd fire him every Wednesday or Thursday, because he'd want time off to go racing, and every morning I'd be over your house drinking coffee trying to get him to come back to work for me.' Dad was good at what he did, but was also a racer, and he could not do it and also work a regular job.

"One of the best things I remember: We were kids, and we were used to Dad winning. Sometimes we'd stay at Grandmother's house when Dad went to the races, and when they'd come pick us up the next morning, I'd say, 'Hey, Daddy, Daddy, where's the trophy? Did you get a trophy?' And I'll never forget my dad saying, 'Son, you can't eat those trophies.' So that was telling me he wasn't doing this to put trophies on the mantel. He was doing it to feed the family.

"I was nine years old when he was killed at Darlington. I can remember it like it was yesterday. I have a younger brother Richard, and they call him Pancho. We were kids, so we didn't know much about the danger involved in racing. We were used to Dad turning the car over or running through a wall and bringing us back a picture and saying, 'When I went through that wall, a two-by-four come right by my head.'

"Mom and Dad had gone to Darlington and we were staying at my grandmother Myers's house. We were playing, not sitting in front of the radio, but still listening to the race. My dad was driving for Lee Petty. He was running at the front of the race. Fonty Flock spun out in front of him, and Dad hit him square on. They had a horrendous crash.

"I remember Grandmother started crying. 'What's wrong?' I asked. And then we heard that Dad had been in a wreck, and I can remember saying, 'He probably just broke a couple ribs or something.' As kids, we didn't know. And then family started coming over.

"We went over to Uncle Billy's house, and more people came over, and then later on in the day they called us out and told us Dad had been killed. And as kids, we still didn't realize the impact. We cried a little, but we probably didn't know the impact, what it would mean.

"I can remember going to the funeral home, and they said the only person who had more flowers at that funeral home, which was *the* funeral home in Winston-Salem, was when Mr. Reynolds died. The funeral home was covered with flowers. They had flowers in the design of a checkered flag, flowers in the shape of a steering wheel, all sorts of flower designs pertaining to racing. My mother saved clippings of it all, and she would sit for hours looking at them.

"Dad's death really affected Uncle Bill. They were very different but very close as brothers. They say my dad was a happy-go-lucky, fun-loving guy and my uncle Bill was the opposite. But they said, 'Never, ever try to break up a fight between Bobby and Billy Myers, cause if you get in the middle of it, then they'll both get you.' Uncle Bill was driving at Darlington that day, and he saw the wreck and knew what had happened. Bill stopped and got out of his car. He couldn't go on. Tiny Lund got in Bill's car and finished the race for him. After Dad died, Bill would come in from a race and say, 'I saw Bobby out there with me today.'

"Bill was a workaholic. He had a factory ride for Mercury in Grand National, and he was also running the local shows. Less than a year after Dad was killed, Billy was leading a race at Bowman-Gray Stadium, and he just pulled off the track, pulled into the infield, laid his head on the steering wheel, and died. He had a heart attack or a cerebral hemorrhage, they don't know which.

"And that was really bad. When Dad died, Mom told me, 'Daddy got killed and we know that, and that's done, but we've got Bill. If we need anything, we've got Bill.' Less than a year after Dad died, Bill died, and from that time on it was really rough. When my dad died, he didn't have any insurance, didn't have anything. I can remember someone bringing a bucket of change into the house. NASCAR gave us whatever they could collect in a five-gallon bucket. So the day after my dad got killed, we moved in with my grandmother and lived there. My mother got by with what little Social Security she had. She had a part-time job as a school crossing guard, and that way she could be at home with us. The other day my mother told me, 'You boys didn't have a daddy, and I made a promise to myself that I was going to be a momma and a daddy to you.' She said, 'I stayed home until the day after you graduated from high school.' I mean, I'm always talking about my dad, but my mother deserves so much praise. I really never

gave her all the credit she deserves. She did it all. It was tough growing up. We didn't have a lot, but we made do with what we had.

"Billy left his children a lot better off than my dad. Bill was better
off financially. He had had a factory ride, plus he was a workaholic
and had built his garage business, and he had some insurance. Billy
had two sons, Randy and Gary. They had a brick house on the other
side of town and a car, and we had a frame house over on this side of
town and we dreamed about a car. I'm not complaining. I'm just saying there was a difference.

"After I was older and knew my dad wasn't coming back I would
dream of being a race car driver. That's all I wanted to do. And I wanted to win the Southern 500 and get even for my dad losing his life
there. I had those childhood dreams, and I did drive a race car a little
bit, played around with it, went to Bowman-Gray Stadium and a few
other places, but I didn't really have the desire, the will to do it.
Evidently, I didn't want it bad enough. One time I didn't have a way
to get my car to Bowman-Gray Stadium, and I just fired it up and
drove it over there the back way. If you did that today, you'd be in a
world of trouble.

"I ended up working on cars. I'm a member of Richard Childress's
team, have been for a long time. I've worked there since the last year
Ricky Rudd was there in '83. We've been winning races ever since.
Even today, people say to me, 'Aw man, what happened to your father
was so terrible, how can you want to have anything to do with racing?'
This is the way I explain it to people: There are people dying every
day, and they have no choice. It was unfortunate Dad got killed, but
Dad was doing exactly what he wanted to do, and loving it, when he
died. We don't have that choice.

"Dale Earnhardt once told me a story: the fastest he had ever been
in a race car was down at Concord, and this was when his dad was still
driving. Dale had an old car, and he was racing with his dad, which
would be a dream for me. I often thought about being able to do that.
Coming down the straightaway, his dad running behind him, pushing
him, and he said that was the fastest he had ever been in a corner in
his life. He thought he had been going fast, until his dad got behind
him and pushed him.

"Bobby Allison is a great friend of mine and my wife's, and we were
sitting around talking with Bobby and Davey at Dover one day, and I

said, 'You know, you guys running one and two at Daytona, I dreamed of that all my life to do that with my dad.' To be able to do that, that is so unbelievable.

"Every year we go to Darlington, my wife and I drive around the track, and I still have tears that come to my eyes.

"The most emotional race I've ever won was when Dale won the Southern 500 for the first time. Even though I wasn't driving, I was on the team that won the race, and just knowing I had a small part in this was enough. I felt it was pretty much my payback. A few of other guys knew a little bit about my background, but most of them didn't, and nobody knew what it meant to me. This was a personal deal. I can remember walking into victory circle there, looking up and saying 'Hey, I did it, Dad. This is for you. We won this race. Dad, this is for you.'"

9

THE "CONVERTED YANKEE"

TOM PISTONE, A SHORT MAN WITH the heart of a lion, hails from Chicago, the Windy City. After beginning his career racing on a track built inside the hulking Soldier Field under race promoter Andy Granatelli, he became five-time Chicago champion and won championships at Rockford, Illinois, and at the Milwaukee Speedway. When he first arrived in the South to race in 1955 he found the going rough, because he was a stranger, Italian, and worst of all, a Yankee.

With both financial and psychological help from the late Bill France, whose generosity and autocratic nature both were legendary, Pistone began racing on a regular basis in 1959, when he won two convertible races. In 1961 General Motors sponsored three cars under the table through the efforts of France and Chevy dealer Jim Rathmann. Separate corporations were formed for Tom Pistone, Ned Jarrett, and Johnny Allen. After three races, France pulled the plug on Pistone and Allen while Jarrett ended up with the sponsorship. Pistone came close to winning races in 1966 and 1967, but without factory support he found Grand National racing to be too expensive to compete.

In the early sixties he thought he had his financial problems settled when Andy Granatelli, who worked for STP, a gasoline and oil additive, shook hands with Pistone on a deal that would have given Pistone the STP sponsorship. The deal could have made Pistone one of the front-runners. But Granatelli gave the STP backing instead to Fred Lorenzen, and in 1972 he awarded it to Richard Petty, who has had it ever since. While Petty went on to fame and fortune, Pistone has experienced only bitterness and hardship.

TOM PISTONE: "I was born in 1928, and I grew up in Chicago. As a boy I heard about car racing at Soldier Field, a football stadium. Andy Granatelli, who came from California, was running hot rods and roadsters, and in 1949, the year NASCAR started in the South, Andy decided to run stock cars in Chicago.

"I was a fruit and vegetable peddler, because my dad was a fruit and vegetable man. I didn't know anything about cars at all. What happened was that Vince and Sonny Gondolfo saw this race car, and they wanted to buy one too.

"In them days you went to a junkyard and bought a car. And the way it came from the junkyard, that was the way you raced it when you went to the track. You didn't fix the engine or nothing. You just bought the car and went out and raced. So my friends and I went out and bought a 1942 Ford and started to race there. My first year at Soldier Field I flipped that car twenty-two times. I set a record for flipping the car, though I never got hurt.

"It took me two years to win the championship. I had gotten into Andy Granatelli's clique at Soldier Field. See, Andy used to stage a show. He had six guys on the payroll making the same money, and he'd tell you who was going to win that night. He had four or five guys on the payroll called 'booger artists,' and it was their job to crash you on purpose. 'Cause Andy Granatelli was more or less a circus person. He knew what people wanted to see: accidents. And he staged the races. He would have two guys on the pole, two in the middle, and two at the end, and when the green flag would drop, all those guys would stop dead, and all the cars would crash on top of each other. 'Cause the other drivers didn't expect those cars to stop.

"Andy staged all the wrecks. So it took me two years to get in the clique with Andy, and then I started to win races, 'cause I knew what the heck was going on.

"I didn't hear about NASCAR until 1954, and in 1955 Soldier

Field turned NASCAR. The southern boys came up and raced us at Soldier Field, and that was the first time I met Fonty Flock, Tim Flock, Herb Thomas, Jim Reed, Cotton Owens, all the southern boys. I had won the championship in '54, and Andy Granatelli said, 'Tom, if you win the championship again next year, we're going to promote you to run NASCAR down South.' And at the end of '55, I moved and ran down South.

"My problem when I got there was that I didn't learn my history when I was going to school. I hated history. I didn't know nothing about history, and when I came down South, I never realized how bad it was between the southern people and the Yankees. I just couldn't believe it. I had never even heard the expression 'Yankee,' and I couldn't understand what these people meant when they were saying, 'Hey Yankee, go on home.'

"It was bad, I mean really bad. Darlington was the worst. If you went to Darlington and you were a Yankee, you were history. Especially if you went down into the infield. When Jim Reed, who was from Peekskill, New York, won at Darlington in '59, the papers didn't write, 'Jim Reed wins Southern 500,' they wrote, 'Yankee wins Southern 500.' It was personal. It was bad.

"Soon after I first arrived down South I drove into a gas station in Winston-Salem called the Golden Esso Station. It was owned by Alvin Hawkins, and when I pulled in who was there but Bill France. It was a miracle he was there.

"Bill France Sr. came outside—I didn't know who he was—and he said, 'Son, what are you going to do with this race car?' I said, 'I came down South to race at Martinsville.' He started laughing. He said, 'That race was run last week.' And for some reason he took a liking to me. He said I could work out of his shop, and I moved into it. It was just a miracle. Alvin and Joe Hawkins took me under their wing. They said, 'Tom, about this Yankee thing, paint on your hood, 'A converted Yankee,' and put a lightbulb on it and the words 'I see the light.' After that I started calling myself 'A Southern Wop.'

"I entered my first Grand National race in '55. I raced at North Wilkesboro, and got twenty-eight laps before my Chevy overheated. Then in '56 I ran a convertible and a couple of hard-top races, and in '57 I was picked up by General Motors. I designed the first NASCAR lightweight chassis with aluminum roll bars and screw jacks, a completely adjustable car. All that time I was driving back and forth to Chicago every weekend. I left my family in Chicago until 1965. Between taking care of my cars and equipment and my kids, I didn't have much time for enjoyment.

"In them days you body-slammed each other. There were no rules. If you wanted to get around a guy, you body-slammed him. You had to, or you pushed him out of the way. The tougher you were, the better driver you were. Like I used to tell all those guys at the drivers' meetings, 'I'm five foot four, but we're all the same size in that race car.' I said, 'After the race it's a different story. In Chicago, I used to be twenty strong. Down here I have no friends. I can't fight you guys.' But nobody bothered me. I just went head-to-head with them. That's the way I was. But I never had any problems. The southern boys never gave me any problems at all.

"The toughest of them all was Junior Johnson, but Junior was the only one I really took to. You could go into Junior's truck and take anything you wanted. Junior gave you anything. He was one of the real good old southern boys. There was nothing he wouldn't do, absolutely nothing. He'd give you the world if you asked for it. You could use his shop, use anything he's got. Junior and I were very, very close. There was nothing I couldn't take that he had. And I would do anything for him, even though there wasn't anything I could do for him. I was the taker. I had nothing. See, Junior was sponsored by Ford and Chevy, got a lot of stuff for nothing, but he still shared it with you. I think Junior Johnson was about the best there is. I don't think there was anybody better than him.

"But the thing about Junior, during a race when you really stuffed him into a wall, you'd get him mad, and he'd want to fight you. He'd rather cut your throat than anything. Oh, Junior was bad, very tough. Curtis Turner would laugh at you. When you beat Curtis, you beat the best. Joe Weatherly was a laughable guy. I remember one time Larry Frank and Joe got into a tangle, and after the race Larry was chasing him, and Joe was running on top of the roofs of the cars in the parking lot, jumping from car to car, and Larry couldn't catch him. And the next day Joe walked up to Larry and said, 'What's the matter, Pop? Couldn't you catch me?' And Joe got Larry laughing. That's the way Joe was. In those days the cars had keys in the ignitions, and before a race Joe would steal all the keys, and he'd be the only one with a key. We'd go to start the race, and we couldn't.

"Joe knew all the secrets. One race Joe stole all the gas caps. He stole them all, and we couldn't start the race. Joe was good people.

"Joe and Curtis were party boys. I went to their parties, but I couldn't stay. I had to race the next day. And I was not too good of a drinker.

"I used to fly with Joe and Curtis. They were the craziest. They'd open the door and try to flip you out of the plane. They'd play tag up in the air. They were the best pilots in the world. They'd go up and play tag, turn the plane upside down, try to push you out over the swamps. You'd try to sleep, and all of a sudden you'd be flying straight up, and then you'd fly straight down, and there was no way you could sleep. If they were awake, you were awake. Them days it was good people, very good people.

"We never thought about the danger in any of this. In those days, we never thought about nothing. Danger was nothing to us in them days, absolutely nothing. Never even knew what the word was. There was nothing we wouldn't do. We were crazy, absolutely crazy. We used to fly out when you couldn't see. We'd take off in ground soup. That's the way we were. We didn't care. In our day we were very wild.

"Tiny Lund was another one. We used to hang our helmets upside down attached to the roll bars, and Tiny would sneak over and pour water into the helmets. Or he would pull me over to a gate and hand-cuff me there so I couldn't start the race.

"They used to call Tiny and I 'Mutt and Jeff.' We used to take our Winston Cup cars and run Sportsman shows, by installing a new tail-light into a two-year-old car. We used to go to Macon, Georgia, Jeffco, all over the place. Tiny was a very hard driver and hard to beat. We raced a lot, joked a lot.

"Whenever we went out, I would take Tiny with me and Larry Frank, two of the toughest guys there is, and we used to go into these bars, and I would instigate fights. 'Cause I knew Tiny and Larry were with me. I would stand on top of the bar and tell the people off and instigate fights. Tiny and Larry would do the fighting, and I would wait for them outside laughing. They *loved* to fight. Yep, loved to fight, and they were the best racers ever there was.

"People don't know much about Larry. He's a full-blooded Indian. He's still around. He owns one of the biggest body shops in Greenville, South Carolina.

"Tiny got killed at Talladega. The night before, I saw Tiny at the Hickory Speedway. I was his crew chief on his Cougar, and he owed me money and we had argued. It was over money. Stupid. Absolutely stupid. But we made up our differences that night, before he was killed.

"When I was picked up by General Motors in '57, I thought I had it made. By '57 GM was in it real heavy, and then all of a sudden in the middle of the year they quit. They pulled right out. American Motors was complaining about GM having a business monopoly, and so they all pulled out. Also at that time, I was leading a race at Martinsville, and it started to drizzle, and I slowed down, and Billy Myers came down the straightaway and drove right over the hood of my car and went over a concrete wall in turn number one. There were some spectators standing at the point the car went off the track—they weren't supposed to be standing there, but Myers's car hit them, and a young boy had a bad head laceration. It bothered me quite a bit, because I thought the kid got killed, and I didn't find out until four or five months later that the kid was all right, and that's when I returned to NASCAR. I got eight kids of my own, and just the idea that that kid got hurt bothered me. I didn't come back to racing until '58.

"Then in '59 Bill France opened the Daytona International Speedway and everything changed. The track was very fast, but the speed was no problem at all. The speed was nothing, absolutely nothing. In fact, I often felt my car was going too darn slow. In the second round of qualifying for that first Daytona 500, I had the fastest time.

"During one of the preliminary races before the Daytona 500, Curtis Turner got behind me and Lee Petty and started pushing us. On the racetrack, Curtis would play with you, push you, tap you, body-slam you. He was a joker, a party guy, but one of the greatest drivers who ever lived. During this Daytona preliminary race, Curtis came from the back and drove right between me and Lee Petty, and about ten or fifteen of us spun out, because he hit the draft so hard when he went between us that we didn't know what hit us. We didn't know anything about the effects of drafting.

"Curtis and I were driving T-birds. Holman-Moody built about twenty of them, all built the same. They charged $5,500 with tires and wheels. The car cost $5,500, ready to race. We worked on our own chassis. I ran a smaller tire, about four inches wide, and I put more air pressure in my tires so it could go down the racetrack on the ball of the tire. That's why I had the fastest T-bird down there. The problem was that the tires couldn't handle the speeds and kept coming apart. If we had just slowed down ten miles an hour all of us would have finished. We were just all too stupid. Except Lee Petty. He slowed down, his tires kept together, and that's how he ended up winning the '59 race. Lee was a smart driver. He wasn't a fast driver, but he knew how to pace himself. Curtis, Junior Johnson, Fireball Roberts, me, all we knew was pedal to the metal, no common sense, and when the car blew up, it blew up. We had no sense of anything but, 'Go to the front.' And we were all having tire problems. In fact, at the end of the race there were no more tires available. We kept using them up. And we were stupid. We never slowed down. And all you had to do was slow down. But when you see a guy go by you, how do you slow down? If you're a racer, you try to catch him, like a greyhound chasing a rabbit.

"Lee Petty was smarter than that, and that's what it takes when you run a 500-mile race. Lee had patience. I'm not saying he wasn't a good driver. A good driver has to have patience.

"I hooked up with Curtis in the Daytona 500. We started at the rear, and him and I went right to the front. He discovered that by your pushing him, you both went faster. Curtis Turner caught on right away. In that initial race at the Speedway, I finished eighth and earned something less than two thousand dollars.

"I ran in the Firecracker 250 in '59. Ralph Moody and John Holman were pitting me. They were my crew chiefs, along with Herb Nab. They said, 'We're going to make one pit stop. That's the only way we're going to beat Fireball.' And we almost did it.

"I ran one lap too many, because I couldn't see the pit board, so I ran out of gas on the 126th mile. Lee Petty, whose car had broken, came out of the pits and pushed me in. But we had the race won. I just didn't see the pit board, a two-by-two blackboard. We had Fireball beat. I ran out of gas. Finished seventh.

"That year, '59, I was running as well as anyone. I really thought I was going to be one of the stars of the circuit. In '59, I had a sponsor, Rupert Safety Belts, out of Chicago. And in 1960 Tiny Lund and I flew to Indianapolis and went to see Andy Granatelli about STP sponsoring me and Tiny Lund. Bill France told me there was no way they could put STP on a race car because of Union Oil, so France came up with the idea of STP being sold as an oil treatment, and I told this to Andy, and Andy said, 'Okay, Tom, we're going to sponsor you and Tiny Lund,' and the next thing I knew Andy awarded the STP sponsorship to Freddie Lorenzen. See, I was Freddie Lorenzen's idol. Every place I went, he went. He wanted to grow up to be like me. I sold him his first NASCAR car. He came down South with it from Chicago in 1956. Then all of a sudden he was stealing my sponsors. He stole STP, and then Richard Petty got it. Well, that's the way life is. I said quite a bit to Andy Granatelli. It's too bad I wasn't the Godfather at the time. What he did was a hundred percent wrong. Because I got Bill France to get STP in there, and once I did that, Andy turned against me. And when I saw him at Daytona the next year, I spit right in his face. That's how bad I felt toward him. No, he done me wrong. Look where Petty is today. And he got nobody else to thank but me. I was the one who brought STP into NASCAR.

"In 1960 I went to Daytona, and during practice the engine started missing. A lot of cars had this problem. The engine went *bloop, bloop, bloop,* and nobody could figure out what the problem was. We were flying back and forth to Detroit trying to find the cause of the miss.

"Mario Rossi and Crawford Clemens tried putting in a real high gear to get rid of the miss, and a guy named Bradley Dennis figured the problem was in the distributor. He said, 'Take the dual points out and put a single point in.' He figured out that the wiring was too heavy in the car, that the resistance in the wiring was making the car bloop.

"In them days we rewired the whole car. And my car was actually the fastest car on the track. We came from the rear and went right to the front. I came in the pit, and like a dummy I pulled in and backed up—in those days if you backed up it cost you a lap penalty. So they took the lap away from me.

"I went back out and we made up the lap, and I was trying to pass Junior on the outside, and Bob Welborn tapped me, and I went backwards into a race car owned by a guy named Dixon. It's a good thing that car was there, because I would have gone right through the pit area. I woke up in the hospital the next day. I had a concussion, a broken collarbone, and internal injuries.

"When Bill France visited me in the hospital, I told him there was a hump in the fourth turn where I crashed, that it was a bad deal the way it was situated, that at a certain speed when you hit that hump, the car would go completely sideways. I had been telling people about that hump, but nobody would listen to me. They all thought I was dreaming. But I was a hundred percent right. The next year they cut out that hump.

"In three months, at Darlington, I was back driving. You can't wait to get back in that race car. When you're a racer, you don't care about nothing; you got no pain. Racing is like a disease. When you're in that race car, everything goes away. All your pain goes away.

"In '60 I had the fastest Chevrolet. Everywhere we went, we were fast. But we had a lot of engine problems that year. I was just too stupid. I drove the car too fast. I didn't have any common sense, and I'm still the same. I'd still drive it flat out.

"I drove in the first World 600 at Charlotte in '60. That day the asphalt tore up, became a dirt track. We had to put big screens on the windshield and on the grill. I'd hit the same hole, the same hole, the same hole, and finally the lower control arm broke on my car. That was another race where we were all too stupid, drove too fast.

"I had a porta-power inside the car, a hydraulic jack, and as I kept losing the wedge in the car and couldn't understand why, I kept jacking, kept jacking, and finally the right A-frame broke.

"After the race, they put new asphalt on the track, and nobody wanted to test it because it was so rough. Goodyear said that if I tested and something happened to my car, they would buy it and give me a new one. They never had any contracts like that before. I needed the money, so I went testing. Curtis Turner and Bruton Smith, the Charlotte track owners, stood in the corner, and going into number one my tire just broke in half. I hit the wall and demolished that Chevrolet. Goodyear bought Fireball Roberts's '59 Pontiac for me.

"In '61, Curtis Turner tried to organize the drivers, but that was nothing. I didn't pay any attention to that stuff. I was Bill France's boy. I didn't pay any attention to it. Whatever Bill France wanted me to do, that's what I did. I was strictly for NASCAR.

"By 1961, after the STP deal fell through, I didn't have a sponsor.

Bill France stepped in to help me. Bill France took care of me and my kids ever since I moved South until he left us. [Bill France died on June 7, 1992.] In 1961 Bill found us a sponsor, Lynn Holloway, who owned Grace Steamship Lines. The idea was that they were going to form a three-man team.

"Marvin Panch and I were sitting in the Queen City Motel in Charlotte trying to figure out what drivers to get to drive the other two teams. We hired Ned Jarrett and Johnny Allen. We had 'Go-go-go Corporation,' 'Win-win-win Corporation,' and Dash-Dash-Dash Corporation.' Ned had his own garage, and Johnny had his, and I had my shop behind the Speedway in Daytona.

"I finished tenth in the Daytona 500, Ned seventh, Johnny eighth. I was driving that Pontiac, and I was behind Johnny Beauchamp and Lee Petty when they got together and went over the wall. The biggest mistake I made was stopping and going over to see what happened. I saw Lee Petty inside that car upside down all crumpled up, and when I got back to my race car, I couldn't even buckle my seat belt, that's how nervous I was. I just couldn't believe two guys could go over the wall like that.

"And that's when Bill France came into the pits, and he said to me, 'Get in that car and drive it.' 'Cause then I got my nerve back, and I drove flat out again. But I learned one thing: never stop for an accident.

"At Atlanta I finished eighth, and then I lost my ride. What I didn't realize was that France was looking to see who could run the cheapest operation between me, Ned Jarrett, and Johnny Allen. Jarrett won, because he had a two-car garage, a dirt floor, and no rent. He ran the operation cheap because he was getting parts from Chevrolet for nothing. I had a Pontiac, and I wasn't getting nothing for nothing. So Bill France let Johnny and me go, and Ned took over the operation, and that's when Ned won the points championship in 1961. Ralph Earnhardt got my Pontiac.

"See, Bill France got mad at me, at my shop in Daytona because I painted the floors, had curtains and peg-boards on the walls. Bill knew what it was to be broke. He was never a high roller. He was always very, very economical. He said to me, 'You're spending my money. You're wasting my money.' And I could see he was right. In those days who needed a fancy garage? But I was always like that. Ned Jarrett had a two-car garage, a dirt floor, and here I had a beautiful, I mean gorgeous, place down at Daytona. So he got mad at me, and he let me go.

"I entered four races that year, finished in the top ten in three of them, but with no factory support, I didn't have the money to continue to be competitive, so I quit. A lot of us who owned our own cars did. Junior Johnson, me, we all quit, because we didn't believe in stroking. We had no more money, and we all just pulled out of it. A lot of guys who stayed stroked, and they made money stroking, but a bunch of us, we just quit.

"I should have known better. I was not schooled properly. I never took advantage of promoters. When they liked you, they helped you, but I never took advantage. Like the time Richard Howard at the Charlotte Motor Speedway held a Tom Pistone Day, and there wasn't anything I couldn't get. He would have given me a brand-new car, anything, but I didn't take advantage. David Pearson and a bunch of guys gave me gifts. Bill France gave me a lifetime membership to NASCAR, which I still have.

"So I didn't have the sponsors. I could have been on top if Ralph Moody and John Holman wanted me to. But I wasn't one of the Good Old Boys. I wasn't. Nope.

"Times were very tough for me. I had eight kids to feed. It was very tough. By '63, I was in a hospital in Chicago. I had ulcers, and they busted open, and the doctors had to take out 70 percent of my stomach. I was in the hospital when Tiny Lund won the Daytona 500 in '63.

"In '65, my wife said she had enough, because I was gone so much, and so she sold the house and the two garages up North, and she came down South. I picked her up and drove her straight to Richmond, Virginia, and she gave me the money, and in six months I blew it all on racing. And I'd do it again.

"I raced through '68, and that's when I quit for good. I had no more money. I went broke. Bill France cosigned a note on the Concord Bank and got me started in the parts and chassis business. We started building cars and selling parts, going to all the races. Bill France didn't have enough cars entering his races, so he would sponsor a car, and I would build it, and he'd put certain drivers like Jim Hurtubise in the car.

"Over the years I've started a lot of drivers in racing, brought a lot of people from up North. Rusty Wallace worked for me, Fred Lorenzen, Jimmy Spencer, Randy LaJoie, a lot of guys. Ernie Irvan worked here, and he drove one of our dirt cars. I worked with Harry Gant for five or six years. I built all his Sportsman cars.

"We financed BSR for two years. We put Butch Stevens in business where he is today. [Dick] Hutch[erson] was in the chassis business, and all of a sudden he went into the parts business. Dog eat dog. We always were the cheapest on parts, but I was in the parts business at the wrong time. I gave parts on credit to all the guys who went broke. I have over a million and a half on the books that I can't collect. Today you can collect your money, because the sponsors will make you good. But in our days, a lot of guys went broke, and some of the big companies took you for money. You just can't believe what these guys would do to you.

"And when Bill France left us, that took a big part out of me. Because Bill France was more or less my whole life in NASCAR.

"Today I build Legends cars for the races at Charlotte. If my grandsons weren't in it, I wouldn't be involved with it. In my mind I still belong in Winston Cup. I've been Winston Cup all my life, and that's my desire, to go back and be a successful car owner or crew chief. Even though I'm sixty-seven years old, I want to win the NASCAR championship before I leave.

"I'm a very bitter person. I hold grudges too much. That's my problem. It hurts to see people do people like they do. It just hurts.

"In '87 I was working with Western Auto, and I explained to them that they had fourteen hundred stores, and if each store would give me twenty-five or fifty dollars, in return I would put souvenirs and T-shirts and hats in these stores, and they'd get their money back guaranteed. And it worked. In fact, it made them money. And it was my idea. But I just didn't know the right people at the time, and I was left out in the cold again. I didn't have the right people behind me. But that doesn't bother me as much as all the people I helped, and they all forgot. Every single one of them."

10

FRED LORENZEN

RALPH MOODY AND JOHN HOLMAN, who from 1957 to 1973 ran the Ford factory team, could make or break careers by hiring a driver for their team. One of the drivers from up North who Ralph Moody liked was a youngster by the name of Freddie Lorenzen. He hired the newcomer to drive for him, and the talented Chicagoan won twenty-six races for Holman-Moody between the years 1961 and 1967, when he quit suddenly. Lorenzen returned in 1970 and raced for three more years, but no longer was he the Golden Boy he once had been.

I included Fred Lorenzen in this book because he was a driver who rose to stardom like a shooting star only to come to earth quickly and flame out. Fred, a nervous sort who suffered from ulcers, quit the game on top and disappeared into the normality of selling insurance in his hometown of Chicago.

When I wrote to Fred a couple of years ago, I got the distinct impression from his return letter that he felt he had made a huge mistake by retiring before his time. As a result, I felt an overriding sadness from this man once famous for his million-dollar smile. Sometimes in life we make wrong decisions. As a result, Fred Lorenzen today has been largely forgotten.

Ralph Moody, who gave Lorenzen his start, remembers the Golden Boy.

RALPH MOODY: "I was helping Fred Lorenzen in USAC before he began driving the NASCAR circuit. We had cars running USAC in 1959 and that's when we saw him run. He was all over the racetrack, and the car wouldn't run, but he was driving the hell out of it. I was standing with a guy from USAC. He said, 'Shit, he don't know where he's going.' I said, 'Man, if he had something to drive, he'd be a race driver.'

"So I told the Ford people I had a young, good-looking, ambitious guy, but Fred decided he was going to run his own car. He came down to Charlotte with a Chevrolet and got upside down and quit and went home. In '61 we put together a Ford, and Fred decided to come down, but he wanted the car to be his. He went to Atlanta, and the rear end came apart, and he was so broke I told Ford, 'Why don't we hire him?' Joe Weatherly was leaving Holman-Moody to go to Bud Moore. Holman didn't know about it, and before he found out Ford okayed it, and I told Lorenzen to come down, that he was going to be our race driver, and he came as fast as he could get on an airplane. He didn't believe it.

"John [Holman] didn't like Freddie. Freddie was a carpenter, and John tried to get Freddie to go down to his house and do some work on it, said if he didn't he'd fire him. I told Freddie, 'He ain't gonna fire you. You do what you want to do.' So he told Holman to go to hell. So John never liked Freddie.

"After we run him a few times, boy, let me tell you. His first race was at Atlanta, and he was leading the race when a tire blew. Then we went to Martinsville, and he was leading when it began to rain, and then we went to Darlington. I schooled Freddie for a week on how to beat Curtis Turner. Turner was a guy, if you went outside, he'd shut you off, get you into the wall. I told Freddie, 'Be dumb, keep trying to pass him right at the end of the race on the outside, on the outside, on the outside. He ain't gonna let you. And then the last thing, right at the end, go down inside him and move his ass out of there and then go on.' He did that on the white-flag lap and won the race. And after Freddie crossed the finish line, Turner drove down the backstretch and drove right into Lorenzen two or three times. Boy, Curtis was hot. And that place went up for grabs, because Freddie was a Golden Boy then.

"In '63 Freddie was the best driver. He won six races. There was one race at Martinsville where Freddie and Junior Johnson banged each other around for ten or eleven laps. They were a couple of hardheads. Junior was one especially who resented a young snipe outdoing him. The problem was that Freddie could outrun them if they raced fair and clean. And the reason he could, we had a setup that worked, and he could drive it, and Junior was doing his own, and that year Ford told him to let Holman-Moody set up his car, and when he found out what Ford wanted, Junior wouldn't come to the races. He sent his brother Fred, who was a boozer. After three or four races, Junior showed up, and he wasn't mad at me anymore. I told him what was happening. I said, 'I hate to do this, but this is what Ford says.' So we got Junior's car working. He said, 'I was mad about it, but I ain't mad at you.' Junior showed me something. It was what Ford wanted if Junior was going to stay running a Ford.

"Junior had a yellow rooster-tailed car, and every time he ran it, he busted a tire and hit a wall. Junior was the type of guy who wanted the car the way he wanted it. He wanted the chassis parts hooked on his way. I said, 'Junior, that won't work.' He said, 'I want one like that.' So I asked Bud, 'If he wants a car like that, should I make it?' He said, 'Yeah, whatever he wants.' We put it together and took it to Daytona, and he didn't even make the field. Junior had to go home and get one of his old cars.

"We had a meeting in the infield offices the next day. The Ford people were there, and Junior and me, and I figured I was in trouble for building something that didn't work, 'cause Junior was going to say it was my fault. They came in, and they asked, 'What happened to the car?' Junior said, 'I took it home.' 'How come?' 'It wasn't worth a damn.' 'Why? How come Moody built it for you like that?' And Junior said, 'It was exactly the way I wanted it. It ain't worth a shit. I took it home.' They asked him, 'Was it built the way you wanted it?' Junior said, 'Yeah.' 'And it won't work?' 'Not worth a shit.' And they turned around and walked out. And here I thought I was going to take the blame for it. A lot of people wouldn't have done what he did.

"But getting back to Freddie, Freddie and Junior were racing at Martinsville, and Freddie was trying to pass him, and Junior was shutting him off, trying to push him into the wall or shove him into the infield, and both cars had slowed down to where neither of them were going anywhere. Junior was using up the racetrack. Freddie didn't want to tear up the car, because he figured he'd win the race. But when

Junior kept blocking him, Freddie hit him with his bumper to say, 'Jeez, get the hell out of the way.' But Junior just shut him off. He wasn't going to let him go.

"Freddie finally pushed him into the corner, got him high, and went past him. And they knew Junior would wait for him, and the official told Junior that if he did, he was out of the race. So Junior didn't touch him anymore.

"But the older drivers resented Freddie. Freddie was new. Just like the way the veterans treat Jeff Gordon today. They don't like him because he blows them away. Of course, Junior got his revenge in the National 400. And he wasn't the only one. The day of Fireball Roberts's funeral, in July of '64, Johnny Rutherford and A. J. Foyt decided they were going to put it on him, screw him up good, but they ended up getting the worst end of it. I don't know who did what, but Rutherford went right over Lorenzen, over his left side top fender and the middle of the hood and hit the wall, and A. J. went down through the infield, a hell of a wreck, and Lorenzen stayed in pretty good shape.

"Like I said, these guys didn't like some new hot dog coming along. The worst part of it was that I was helping these other guys run these other Fords, and they were beating on him. But if that happened on a racetrack, you couldn't stop it."

11

ROUGH-TOUGH CHARACTERS

PAUL "LITTLE BUD" MOORE WANT-
ed to be a dirt track, oval track driver ever
since he was a kid watching the pros race at
Darlington. He and his high school friends
would drive their family cars to the newly developed subdivisions of hometown Charleston,
South Carolina, and race in a circle on the
deserted vacant lots. Upon graduating high
school, Moore knew he needed to find someone
who could help him get better equipment to race,
and he went to one of the best, the late Ralph
Earnhardt of Kannapolis, NC, the father of Dale
and one of the finest half-mile dirt track racers in
the history of the sport.

With Ralph Earnhardt's help, Paul Moore
won the Georgia state racing title. In 1964
Moore began driving in NASCAR Grand
National races, and in '65 he won the pole at
Greenville-Pickens, a track Moore says attracted
"the meanest people I have ever seen in my life."
In addition to his association with Ralph
Earnhardt, Moore was close friends with three
legendary drivers who no longer are with us:
LeeRoy Yarbrough, Tiny Lund, and Bobby Isaac.
LeeRoy, Tiny and Bobby were stars of the short
track, dirt track days and all were successful on
the superspeedways as well. They were rough-
hewn characters, and Little Bud, who raced and
fought against them and at the same time clearly

was very fond of them, remembers the rough, tough, but oh-so-very-good old days.

PAUL "LITTLE BUD" MOORE: "I came from Charleston, South Carolina, which is completely different from any other part of the South except New Orleans. There are a lot of different denominations, colors, creeds, a port city, very different, but very southern-oriented. Charleston has had some racetracks, but mainstream Charleston didn't care anything about racing. They were sailboat people, golfers, which today racing people are part of that, but at the time racing was looked down on. But I can remember going to Darlington—everybody in South Carolina went to Darlington. My dad had an old plumbing truck with scaffolding, and he took all the kids, and we'd get on top, and it was the greatest thrill twice a year to go and see people like Tim Flock, Buck Baker, Cotton Owens, and Curtis Turner, who I thought was just the greatest. I could not believe what he could do with a race car. And growing up, I always thought about running Darlington, and the only thing I wanted to be was an excellent dirt track racer.

"And early on I can remember looking at these drivers and thinking, God, how tough can you get? These people were the toughest breed of people I have seen in my entire life. And so I became fascinated by it. It occupied my thoughts all the time. In high school I did a little drag racing—I have high regard for Don Prudhomme and Kenny Bernstein and the people who do it—but I knew I was going to be an oval track racer. When everyone else's kids were running dragsters, we were finding subdivisions that hadn't been paved yet, and at night we would hold our own oval track races, and we were very serious about it. We really had a good time until we had to finally quit doing it. The feel of the car sideways at ninety miles an hour with the wheel cut back to the right was something—like when Curtis Turner would turn his car sideways at the flag stand. Turner sometimes didn't make a faster time that way, but I think he just enjoyed doing it. Richard Petty's philosophy was the straighter you can go around dirt, the faster you run, and who can argue with that? He won a lot of races. But if you watch some of the old films of Curtis Turner on the beach course at Daytona, sometimes he misses the turn completely, goes by it completely sideways. I gotta tell you, that's what influenced me, and I knew someday I would do it, and I was the only kid in high school who graduated owning a stock car. I had an oval track race car in the twelfth grade of high school. This was 1958. And by the time I was in high school, on Thursday nights I began watching the races at Columbia, South Carolina, which to this day still holds the record for more champions—seems like everybody, the Pettys, Cale Yarborough, the Bakers, Bobby Isaacs, the Earnhardts, have come from Columbia Speedway.

"When I first started going to these races in Columbia, David Pearson really fascinated me, the way he built his cars and took care of them. When people today look at those old cars, they have no understanding of what these folks did to them. The early race cars were very precise cars, very good pieces of machinery. They were built to the best of these guys' knowledge. They were craftsmen. They didn't get on the phone and call someone up and say, 'I want a left side chassis, a wheel base so and so, this type of A-frame.' They went out into their shop and made this stuff to make the car work. Consider the magnesium hubs they cast and put on or the stroker motors, the injectors, the different fuels they ran and nitro in some outlaw classes. If I had to pick a favorite at that time, I guess it would be Ralph Earnhardt, Dale's father. Right off, I watched him as to what he done, and to this day I still look up to him.

"I got an early start, and right away after competing in a couple of outlaw-type races, I saw that racing was entering a new era. We were getting away from the old coupes and moving into the Late Model division, '57 Chevrolets and Fords. They were called Sportsman cars, and I saw that Ralph Earnhardt had progressed to where you couldn't hardly outrun his cars. I saw that I needed the equipment that Earnhardt had to win races, so I took a guy from North Carolina with me as a sponsor, and Ralph Earnhardt supplied me with one of his engines, and that's how I got to know him.

"Ralph built his own car, and he built a car for Bobby Isaac, and for a while they ran as a team. And then later there were three cars all painted the same, Isaac was 8, Earnhardt was 6, and I was 9, and I ran my car down in the Georgia circuit and won the state championship with it. Isaac and Earnhardt ran up through the Carolinas most of the time.

"Isaac didn't have any education whatsoever. He came out of the mills, just like David Pearson and a lot of other people. Stock car racing to them was a way to get away from that. It was a gift, something they could do. Isaac was an extremely good racer. And if his crew didn't want any more of racing after three days and nights, he would show up at a racetrack Sunday morning all by himself in an old station wagon pulling the car by hisself. We all did that at times. I went a long time eating potato soup without the potatoes, just the onions and the juice. A long, long time. In this business, you don't get something for nothing. You dig, and you dig hard. That's why the Earnhardts are like they are, why everyone in racing is like that.

"Ralph Earnhardt taught me a lot about racing. He supplied my engines, and he would get pissed at me when I would come back and pieces of my car would have dirt on them. He'd sit down and drill me how that didn't need to be there. He'd say, 'The last time I put it together, the gasket was on it, and it was clean. And that's the way I want to see it when you bring it back.'

"At times he parked me when I really needed the money. He spurned me a couple of times when I had to charge the pit pass to get into the racetrack. I had just enough gas in the race car to finish the race and not enough in the tow car to get home. But that was all part of the process. He made me mean. He taught you how to convince a lot of the other competitors that you were tough enough to be left alone. He had ways, when you went to the track, you already had a lot of people whipped before the race even started.

"It came from the way you warmed up the car. People looked at you like, 'Damn, this guy is getting the job done.' He taught me a lot of stuff. He taught me that when you're willing to do things the others aren't willing to do, when you're willing to hurt yourself, the other drivers have to weigh that, and they'd leave me alone. He knew I could drive a race car, knew I loved running those racetracks, and he helped me a lot. Of course, Ralph was older and a lot smarter than I was. If we ran five races against each other, and I won three and wrecked in two from being overaggressive, you have to remember that he finished second in the three I won, and he won the two that I wrecked in, so when you weigh it out, all I had was one victory more than him and two tore-up cars. He had two victories and three seconds, and was still driving the same car. That's how smart he was as a driver.

"Ralph taught me about tire stagger. He knew that during the race you may not get any faster, but other people slow down. Early on, Ralph taught me that. He'd say, 'When you start the race off, it doesn't matter if you have to hang your ass out the window something terrible, but hang it out there. You may be driving over your head. But they don't know that.' He said, 'If you set your car up in a way that you know it's going to get better, then the longer the race runs, the easier the rest of the race is going to be. Just think in your head what that will do psychologically.' And sure enough, I would run races, and I would drive so hard early on to try to keep the lead with all these other drivers all over you and doing what they were doing, but the first time you saw the front end of the car behind you drop back one inch off the corners, you knew your day had come. From there on out, the race was going to get easier. And that was the best feeling that ever was. And if you've ever watched Dale Earnhardt run a race car, sometimes at the start of the race his car is terrible and you've counted him out, but his crew works on that car the whole race, and he gets dialed in, and he will be there at the end of the race.

"Ralph's cars were so much safer than most cars being built back then. Ralph put bars in the doors of his cars, and one night I drove at the speedway in Savannah, cleared the air and hit the only big pine tree anywhere close to the track midway up. I hit right in the door, hit so hard the steering wheel was centered to the gearshift coming through the floor when it finally stopped. It bent the car completely around me, and those bars saved me. I did not wake up until five-thirty the next day in the hospital.

"I'd drive from Charleston up to Ralph's house to work on the car, because I knew absolutely nothing about engines. I didn't even know how to change a spark plug, but I went back to Georgia with that engine, and I blew everybody away. And the good part about it, we were just kids. We went to the racetrack with a tow car, no trailer. We had one little green toolbox and a bumper jack, and we would jack this car up to change the two front tires, and the pit crew would run because half the time the bumper jack would fall. But when the race would start, we would blow everyone away. And you have to remember the other drivers were big, burly, bad-ass people. I can remember one night the police came to the Oglethorpe Speedway in Savannah, Georgia, and took the drivers of the first six cars to jail. And I was a little guy, didn't weigh more than 135 pounds, and there were times I had to climb on top of the concession stand to get away from the free-for-alls after a race. These people were mean.

"I have been to a lot of places, but the meanest people I have ever seen in my life were from Greenville, South Carolina, a racetrack called Greenville-Pickens. They were so mean, you could not back up against the pit fence, because the women would cut you with a knife. When I say that, people don't want to believe me, but the women were as mean as the men. These people were bad asses. At that time my car owner was from Greenville, and I didn't understand why the people hated me so bad until later, when I learned that he used to sit in the stands and give the rest of the field odds, and he would bet a hundred dollars to each person that I would win. We only went to Greenville for special events, the big events, and I can't remember but one time when we didn't win the race in a big event.

"One time the Highway Patrol had to escort me and my wife, who is a very petite, beautiful, conservative lady, from there, with one patrol car in front and one in back. They took me to the city limits to make sure we'd be safe. That's how mean those people were.

"I can remember Bobby Isaac winning a race and having to get on top of the car and stay there. Bobby taught me something a long, long time ago. He said, "When you get in that damn car, you're just as big as anybody." And I raced three and four nights a week with the likes of Tiny Lund, who was probably as tough an individual as I ever met in my life. You didn't get into a whole lot of physical stuff with Tiny Lund.

"One time down at Daytona I was driving Bondy Long's truck, and Tiny was riding shotgun. He was in his driver's uniform. We had left the racetrack, and he didn't have time to change. We stopped on South Atlantic, and a car tried to pull in front of us from the side road right where Max's bar was, a pretty popular place back then. And this pretty good-size guy made a remark to Tiny, and Tiny said something back to him, and this guy got out of his car with something in his hand. Tiny asked me, 'Is anything in the back of this truck?' I thought to myself, My God, I can't imagine what this is going to turn into.

"The guy almost got to our truck when Tiny leaned over in his seat and kicked the door open, knocking him down. Tiny rolled out of the truck, reached in the back and found a tire iron. About this time the guy realized just how big Tiny was. Tiny was a *big* person, and fast and quick too. He was in good shape.

"This guy started running. All traffic was stopped. Everyone was looking. Tiny started running after him. I started easing along in the truck. They were letting me ride down the middle of the road. I knew this thing was going to get ugly, that this guy was in trouble.

"The guy fell and tripped. Tiny let him get up, and the guy started to run again. I knew that was a big mistake. He ran and tripped again, and this time Tiny just beat the shit out of him, hurt him. I was hollering for Tiny to get off him. Really, he could have killed him. He got in the truck and we drove off. I'll bet that was the last time that guy smarted off at anybody in traffic. I thought, Man, did I come out lucky.

"Because I had done something to Tiny in a race not long before that, and Tiny was such a brute. On the track he did something to me, and I gritted my teeth. I had a policy that if him or LeeRoy Yarbrough ever messed with me, and I let them get away with it one time, I was just going to quit racing. I had made this deal with myself. 'Cause every time someone started to fool with me, I would always picture in my mind me and my wife and daughter sitting at the table, and the tablecloth gets jerked off the table with everything on it. That's how I thought of them, taking food out of my mouth. So when Tiny did something to me that time, I chased him for the next thirty-five laps of the race and caught him with about a lap to go, and I just put it to him and won the race.

"I seen him storming down through the pits coming at me, and I just wondered what was going to be next. When he got there, he just kicked me square in the ass. So I got off pretty lucky. He didn't want to hit me. He never would box me. LeeRoy was not the same. He would. But Tiny didn't. After Tiny beat up that guy, I thought to myself, Tiny could have killed me.

"It is so funny. I can just go on and on and on. One time I was going down the road to Augusta, Georgia, towing an old race car, and I ran up on this old Buick. Tiny had borrowed this old four-door Buick that a doctor friend had owned, and they were going down the highway, and Tiny was in the backseat asleep, and he had his leg hung out the window, and his leg was so big it looked like a telephone pole. This guy who worked with him, his name was Cantelope, a character who had been with Tiny a long time, was driving the Buick, and it was running hot. They had a broomstick tied up under the hood and wired down so more air could get to the radiator. And behind it they had an old '57 Chevrolet race car that Tiny had been running as a Grand National car—he had been running it so long it was now a Sportsman car. And if you don't think they didn't look like a band of gypsies!

"I drove a Sportsman car for Bondy Long, and he and I used to go to races we weren't running in just to watch Tiny and his bunch in the pits. Tiny was such a good, aggressive racer. Didn't come no tougher than him.

"I probably knew LeeRoy better than anybody in that he came along out of Jacksonville, along with his brother, Eldon, who raced for a long time, and I came out of Charleston, so we were two people who came into North Carolina together. Except for Fireball Roberts, we were the first guys from that part of the country to be really competitive. LeeRoy was an extremely good race driver. He won a lot of races. He won seven races with Junior in 1969.

"Like most of the people who came into racing, he was poor, low-class who had to pull himself up from that. And he was violent. He would fistfight in two seconds. A very strange fellow. A questionable kind of person. LeeRoy didn't get along with a lot of people. You would get into things with him. But he also had a sense of fairness about him.

"One time he got into me in a race car, and later in the race I drove the bars in his doors clean in on him, I hit him so hard. His owner made a protest, got awfully big on it, but LeeRoy said, 'Forget it. I had that one coming.'

"Another night LeeRoy was flying to a race in Augusta, and his car owner was there with the car, and LeeRoy was late. They didn't have anyone to warm up the car, and even though I was his toughest competitor, they came and asked me to do it, and I turned the car over! LeeRoy was pissed at me for a while.

"We were forever getting into things. One night we were in a barroom brawl in Savannah, and this big old country boy had him out in the middle of a pond during a downpour, and was about to get the best of him, and while they were fighting the country boy's old lady was running to their car to get a gun. She reached into the glove compartment, and just as she did, I slammed it on her hands to keep her from getting the gun and shooting LeeRoy, and finally the tide turned. LeeRoy was a very physical person, wiry, and he could get the job done, and finally LeeRoy got the best of him, and then he jumped all over me for not jumping in the middle of this pond and helping him with the guy.

"I told him, 'You son of a bitch, that woman was fixing to shoot you.' And I had the hardest time convincing him of that. He was still mad because I didn't jump in there and help him with this big old country boy. This gal was going to shoot him, man!

"LeeRoy ended up in an institution. He had a dislike for a certain breed of people [blacks], and he had problems in that institution he was in. If the truth be known, that's probably what cost him his life, and I have reasons for believing that.

"But Tiny and LeeRoy were two of the worst enemies I ever met, and I always found myself right in the middle of them. Tiny was married to Wanda, who was once LeeRoy Yarbrough's girlfriend, and somewhat because of that, they were always getting into it.

"LeeRoy, Tiny Lund, and myself raced four nights a week. There were nights they were on the pole and me behind them, and one would have a better spot on the track to follow, and when they hung the green, they would run over each other in the parade lap fighting for that spot. And you'd have to stop the race and get the cars apart during the parade lap, because they had already hooked up!

"We were in Darlington one time, and the promoter in Savannah, Georgia, had given us a deal to come to Savannah on Friday night to race. Since we were all running at Darlington, they sent an airplane for us. In those days it was an old fabric-covered plane, a four-seater. I'm telling you, I gave a lot of thought to getting in that airplane with them two characters. I honestly had a lot of concern for the two of them getting in a fistfight in that plane and kicking the fabric off the side of the plane and going down. Truly, that was my number one concern. But it was one of the very few times I can remember that we got in a plane, flew to Savannah, ran one, two, and three and returned without an incident. I don't know how we did that. Nobody fistfought. Nobody wrecked each other, and nobody got mad. Nothing happened in the plane going down or back, and I'll tell you, I was *real* glad! Because Tiny was extremely strong and extremely tough, and LeeRoy was extremely mean, and I was just an awful little guy.

"They were two characters, and I guess I get rated with them sometimes by people just for having been there every time they ran, and I did have the misfortune of getting into it sometimes too. Sometimes I would come out on top, and sometimes I didn't.

When I did, I considered myself extremely lucky. The people in that era were very tough, and I'm not taking anything away from today's drivers, because I think they are all the same breed or they wouldn't be there to start with. They are just limited to throwing bottles of water now, where you used to come across with a tire iron. It's just the nature of the business. It has to be that way. And I'm glad. It's much nicer now that you can go to the infield and put your campers up and take your kids with you and not have to worry about them walking around the infield. Cause back when I ran, nobody could do that! You had to make sure you had as much arsenal as they had to even get through it.

"I look back at those guys who I ran with four nights a week, the pioneers of the sport, LeeRoy [died in mental hospital], Tiny Lund [died in Talladega crash], Bobby Isaac [suffered fatal heart attack], Ralph Earnhardt [fatal heart attack], a guy name Ned Setzer [died of respiratory problems], they're all gone. One thing that bothers me about the sport is that people who have come on board recently have a tendency to think if your name wasn't connected to Winston Cup in a big way then it's not worth mentioning. This year we've nominated Ralph Earnhardt for the Motor Sports Hall of Fame of Alabama, and we're hoping he'll get in.

"I just feel fortunate I'm still here and have those memories, and I hope one of these days I'll see them again."

12

BUCK'S BOY

LIKE RICHARD AND MAURICE Petty, Elzie Wylie "Buddy" Baker grew up under the aegis of a tough, demanding racing champion. In Buddy's case it was his father, Buck, who won driving championships in 1956 and 1957. Buddy Baker was eight when he attended the very first NASCAR race in June of 1949, and he was there when his dad won championships for Carl Kiekhaefer. When Buddy himself began racing in '59, one of his competitors was Tim Flock, who was part of one of three generations of top racers against whom Buddy competed in a stellar career that lasted until 1988.

Buddy learned from racing against the best— Curtis Turner, Joe Weatherly, Ralph Earnhardt, Tiny Lund, LeeRoy Yarbrough—and his hero was the late Fireball Roberts, a master racer on the superspeedways who died after a flaming crash at Charlotte in 1964. According to Buddy, Roberts was "one of the interesting people," as you shall see.

And throughout Buddy Baker's life stood the towering figure of Buck Baker, who today runs his driving school in Rockingham. Buddy, who today is a TV commentator for TNN and CBS, is glib and charming. But on that racetrack he was tough and fearless. He is, after all, Buck's boy.

BUDDY BAKER: "I was born in Florence, South Carolina, in 1941 on January twenty-fifth.

My dad, Buck Baker, started winning races in 1949, so I was brought up not only in a racing family but in a winning environment. I can remember the pioneers, the people who started in the sport. I vaguely remember the first NASCAR Grand National race, what we now call Winston Cup, ever run. It was at Charlotte. I was eight.

"Up to that point my dad had always run in the modified division, which was older model cars. All of a sudden, here are the latest cars on the road during a time when the economy wasn't all that great. It was something to see someone out there in a brand-new car with the headlights taped across. They used leather belts to hold the doors shut, and there was just one seat belt, the one that goes around your lap, and no roll cages in the cars. Of course, the tops of the cars were a lot stouter then. They had a lot more metal to them. The cars had stock wheels, no racing tires at all. You got the best tire you thought they produced, put it on, and raced.

"All I remember about that very first race was that just about everyone fell out. [Only eleven of the thirty-three cars finished. Buck Baker, driving a Kaiser, finished eleventh and won fifty dollars.] The attrition rate back in those days was astronomical.

"When I was a boy, my heroes were all in racing. Most of the other kids had football or baseball heroes. But for me, there was Lee Petty, and Tim Flock, and Fireball Roberts was one of the better drivers back then. As far as I was concerned, Fireball was the thunder and lightning, the first major speedway standout.

"Of course my father was my all-time special person. He won Darlington three times, which was the one superspeedway when I could first recall, around '53.

"In '56, my dad drove for a man named Carl Kiekhaefer. He was a perfectionist. He was the first Hendrick-type car owner of the era. He hired the best drivers, the best mechanics, the best cars. He had a group of people who took the racing tires out and drove them a hundred miles to make sure they didn't have any flaws. He tested the motors on dynos. If he'd take three cars to the racetrack, many times they'd finish first, second, and third.

"Kiekhaefer was quite a guy. He had so many employees. A guy was making a delivery to the back door of his shop. In the middle of unloading racing parts, he got tired and sat down on the dock up against the building to rest a little. Well, this wasn't rest time to

Kiekhaefer, who walked out and asked the guy how much he made a week. The guy told him, and Kiekhaefer said, 'Go in and get your check from Rose because you're done here.' Kiekhaefer fired him, and the guy didn't even work for him!

"And the same token, my father and Kiekhaefer were as close as could be. My father was pretty dominant at the time, and this guy only wanted people who were going to lead every lap and try to win the race. I know that Tim Flock and Kiekhaefer didn't get along, but Tim's philosophy was to protect the car and make the move near the end, where my dad went out and just drove the wheels off it. Within a year's time my father was the number one driver for Kiekhaefer, and then he won the championship for him. [Buck Baker won fourteen races for Kiekhaefer in 1956 and was the racing champion in 1956 and 1957.] Certain things remain true in racing: When you start winning championships and the most races, you automatically get along with the boss most of the time.

"Kiekhaefer was only in racing two years. At the end of '56 he added a race in Shelby. In it, my dad and Herb Thomas, who he was racing for the championship, got together, and Herb was badly hurt. If you go to any half-mile dirt track, that happens all the time. I don't think that's why Kiekhaefer got out. The thing with Carl was that he got out of it what he wanted as far as letting the Southeast and the racing world understand that not only was he the number one outboard motor builder, he was the number one racer, and once you've accomplished what that man did in that short period of time, you really don't have any more to prove.

"I started racing in '59. I even ran a race against Tim Flock. I drove against three generations of racers. When I decided I wanted to be a racer, that was pretty spooky. If you've ever spoken to my dad, he can be pretty hard-line when it comes to things—they have to make a lot of sense. When I decided I wanted to drive, I said to myself, Okay, but I want to make sure I have the blessing of my father.

"I was working for him at the time at the race shop. I walked up to him two or three times during the day. I said, 'Dad, I need to talk to you. Oh never mind.' And I walked away. It took me three passes by him to say, 'I really would like to see if I can do this. I don't know how we're going to go about it, but I would like to drive.'

"His response almost floored me. He said, 'See that old car in the corner over there.' I said, 'Yeah.' He said, 'There are all the parts. Get you some people and put it together, and you can run this weekend.' Whoa.

"So we put the car together and I went to Columbia, South Carolina, with a bunch of friends. I had one guy who really knew what he was doing with the car, and the rest of them were just high school friends. We were out on the racetrack, and I was running dead last. I was running against Curtis Turner, Fireball Roberts, Lee Petty, anybody who could really go at that time. And those guys didn't wait on anybody. When they made a decision, if you didn't get out of their way, they knocked you out of the way.

"My father was leading the race, and I got a little bit wide, and he rapped me, and I was knocked almost into the infield. My own dad! So the first car that ever put a fender on me was my own father!

"So I was running dead last, and I was blaming the car. I said to myself, What a piece of junk. I was thinking it was the car. It was my first race, and I didn't realize it takes a lot of ability to run up front against this quality of people I was running against. This was not a Saturday night special. These were the best drivers in the world.

"About halfway through the race, my father's car expired. I had already lost a lap, been run over by the top ten. He motioned me in, and I got out. He got in the same car, unlapped himself, and brought it all the way back to third place. That pretty well wrote the book: Sonny Boy, you have a long way to go.

"I would ask him what it felt like to turn the car over, and he would never answer that. He said, 'I'm going to tell you that when it happens to you, it's a feeling you'll never forget, but it's something you don't walk around talking about.' After I was driving about a year, I accomplished this end-over-end off the top of a half-mile dirt track. I came stumbling through the house, and my dad said, 'What's it feel like, boy?' I went, 'Waaaaaaaaaaaaaa.'

"But let me tell you about my father. He would not let you sit around and feel sorry for yourself. It's like when a driver would get into me, and I'd say, 'So and so is really giving me a hard time out there.' He'd say, 'Have you made up your mind whether you want to be a driver or not?' I said, 'Yeah.' He said, 'Then you have to make up your mind whether you're going to let him push you around or not.'

Within a week he expected to see that guy going somewhere sideways. And I'd do it. There never was a question about that. That era was a little different than modern-day. Conversation was short. The fight sometimes lasted a long time. Back in those days you could have an enemy for a full year.

"I'd rather not say the name of the first person I tangled with like that. At that time I could go from zero to completely teed off in about a second and a half. He was a guy we all liked a whole bunch, and I got mad and stuck him into the outside wall pretty hard. Unfortunately, I sent him completely out of the racetrack on the back straightaway. The fortunate part was that nobody else was over there, so he didn't get hurt, but it gave me a pretty sound wake-up as far as how to act behind the wheel. I saw it was a lot easier to touch him just a little bit and then after the race go see about it rather than put some-one in that much danger. I guess that's why they call you a profes-sional. As you grow you get a little wiser.

"Once I started racing, I was watching the world's greatest and learning a little bit from every one. I was acquiring driving styles that later on would develop into winning.

"Curtis Turner gave me a good lesson at Hillsboro one time. I was a cub driver who didn't understand that I didn't have the talent that he had in my first year of driving. I walked over and asked him where he was backing off getting in the corner on the mile dirt at Hillsboro. He showed me the point. But when I got there, I might as well have taken a gun and shot the right rear tire. He could get through the cor-ner at that spot, but I couldn't. I went through the damn gate so fast nobody missed me for a lap or two!

"I had the luxury of watching the way the best on each racetrack drove it. I was not under any pressure. Nobody said I had to be an instant success. Nobody said, 'We expect you to win in the first two years of your racing career.' I would watch practice, watch a certain driver who was extremely good at Martinsville or a guy who was great at Daytona, or good at Darlington like my father, who was the best there. I must have learned pretty well from him because he won at Darlington three times, and I won twice. Darlington was home. I was born fifteen miles from the speedway there. At that time, when I first started out, if you won Darlington, you were pretty much there.

"One time he was teaching me, and I was running in his tire tracks, and he blew a motor and I ran into the wall, and we wrecked both cars!

"I watched those guys, and I listened. And there was another driver who came a little farther along, Dale Earnhardt, who did the same thing. He'll tell you that he watched Bobby Allison and Cale and myself and some other guys. You say to yourself, Okay, this is the way I want to run this particular racetrack. This guy really gets around this place well, and I'd watch how he set up for the corner, how he pretty much drove the whole racetrack. At Darlington I also watched David Pearson. It was like he wasn't running half as fast as the other guys, but he'd go out and set a track record, 'cause he had a knack for getting around that place. Every track is that way.

"In '60 and '61 I only drove part-time. There are times in your career when you're not doing really well. At that time I was a father to my oldest son, and quite frankly, I had to make a living. I worked at Martin Guy Motors, which was a Chrysler dealership. I worked with Felix Sabates there. He and I were salesmen. In '62, I was getting closer, and I made $5,000 in winnings, and the nice part, I made another $5,000 selling cars, but I could live on that. I hadn't acquired the living style that some of the winning drivers had acquired. It's like the guy who said to me, 'When you won Daytona, you didn't win but $105,000.' I said, 'Yeah, but back then that would buy something that wasn't a down payment.'

"When I first started out, I ran a lot of local dirt tracks, the eighty-over division, which was the coupes with flathead Fords. I ran at Columbia Thursday nights, raced at three or four other tracks. When I ran Grand National, that was a bonus. I was making money at these other races. That was one part of my racing career I would not change for anything, being able to go into a guy's backyard and race with a totally different group of drivers. When you jump into one division and stay there your whole career, I think you miss a lot.

"I ran against Dale Earnhardt's dad, Ralph, and against David Pearson, Tiny Lund, and LeeRoy Yarbrough. To win there, if you beat that group it was like winning Daytona. I'll put it this way: If you could stay up with that group, you could go home pretty happy with yourself. Those guys were tough to handle.

"Ralph was the sort of driver, if there were two or three laps to go, you didn't want to look in your rearview mirror and see Ralph's car. Talk about a guy who knew how to win races! He'd never wreck you, but he'd get under you and touch you just enough to get you off-line. He didn't even touch you hard enough to get you mad. He just taught you a good lesson. It was like getting the last three hairs in line. He had that ability. When you start running halfway decent with Ralph Earnhardt and some of the others, Billy Scott, who was from down around Blacksburg, South Carolina, or Dink Widenhouse, another one who was quite a driver. Dink drove for the preacher, Marion Cox. This guy would never drive on Sunday. At one minute after midnight, he would stop on the way home, park his car and get a hotel. He wouldn't even pull his race car on Sunday. Dink was another guy like Ralph Earnhardt, as good as I've ever run against. He was a guy like Red Farmer, who ran local tracks in Alabama. Bobby Allison told me one time, 'If Red Farmer had come our way instead of staying in Birmingham and running the modifieds and dirt tracks, he'd a made everyone's win records look like nothing.

"There are people who run on these local levels, great talents, but they have absolutely no concern to move up. They are happy right where they are. Ninety-three percent of the people around the country would never know who you're talking about, but boy, could they put a dusting on you!

"In addition to these guys, there was LeeRoy Yarbrough and Cale and I, and I can put myself in that category because we ran wide open, half turned over all the time. Someone said to me, 'How many times did you win the Daytona 500?' I said, 'Twice, but I won the Daytona 475 eleven times!' I ran wide open. Had the cars at that time been as dependable as they are now, my God! But unfortunately, NASCAR can claim that I was one of the first 500-mile dynos!

"Early in my career I got to race against Joe Weatherly and Curtis Turner. Weatherly was kind of happy-go-lucky, fun to be around, but very serious when he got into a race car. He was tough on the racetrack, and he and Curtis had classic battles. They'd run for the same race team and beat each other half to death. They were both very talented. They'd get out and cut up and carry on, and the minute they dropped the green flag, they'd run right into each other! It was fun to be around those guys. It was a time I wouldn't change for anything.

"The good part was that Curtis was at his best before I began run-

ning, 'cause we'd have been like gasoline and a match. I've often
thought about that. Boy, that would have been a fight. Joe was tough
and all, but he wasn't like Turner. They called Turner 'Leadfoot.' He
had one style. When they dropped the green flag, it was wide open,
and if the car lasted, he won. That's why he didn't win any more races
than he did, because many times he paid the price for running so hard.
Certainly, as far as drivers go, I'd put him in the top ten of all time as
far as being able to control a race car and just sheer fan delight.
Certain people do a lot for the racing world that isn't measured by
wins. Curtis was the epitome of wide open.

"I rode with Curtis one time in his airplane coming from Daytona.
Nobody else in the airplane knew a damn thing about flying. He set
an alarm clock, put the airplane on automatic pilot, slid the seat back
and went to sleep. All the way back I was sitting there white-knuckled.
Just about fifteen minutes from Charlotte, the alarm clock went off;
he reared up, and landed it. I went, 'You're a nut.' Curtis said, 'Not
with you in the airplane. If anything happened, I knew you'd be right
up!' I said, 'Thank you, pal.'

"Oh yeah. Nothing could have gone wrong because I was sitting
right there. He knew I'd have said, 'Hey, hey, wake up.' He flew an airplane just like he drove a race car. Just got in it, cranked it up, and
went. Curtis made me love the ground.

"I also knew Fireball Roberts. It's tough to talk about him, because
he was my superspeedway hero. Every chance I got, I would sit down
next to him like a bug in a corner and listen to him talk about what
he was doing, how he approached the corners at Daytona. He was the
first superspeedway technician we ever had. Fireball was the one
everyone used to gauge how well they were running. If they were
within two or three miles an hour of him, they felt they were really in
business.

"Fireball had a little thing he always did the first of the year. I was
young and kind of confused about the major speedways. I would take
one of the my new cars out, and I'd be going down the back straightaway looking over the gauges and making sure everything was just so,
and Fireball would come down and take a dive at you and usually miss
you by two or three inches and just scare you half to death. It sounded like a bomb went off when he'd pass you like that. He scared me so

bad, I stood up in my seat. I came in, and he was laughing. He did that just for the fun.

"A few years later, after I was running better and better, he had a new car down there, and he was going down the back straightaway, and I liked to turn him over. I went by, *Whooooom*. I came in, and he looked over and shook his finger at me. Fireball was something else.

"I was there when he crashed and burned at Charlotte in '64. I did not see the wreck, thank goodness. I had already fallen out of the race. After he was injured, I spent quite a bit of time with his brother, Tommy Roberts. Fireball was in such bad shape that it was pretty tough to go in and see him. I can tell you, Fireball was one of the interesting people.

"In '64 I was driving for my father. That was the first year I really had a pretty good race car, and in '65 my dad had a really bad accident at Daytona. My father has never really liked Daytona; he never liked Talladega. Seemed the places I loved the best, he disliked the most, except for Darlington.

"In '65 at Atlanta, I had a pretty good run, finished fifth. That was the first time I ever ran with the leaders. That was the first power steering race car I remember in Winston Cup. Dad had put power steering on this Oldsmobile. I wondered, Why? Because in '65 I could lift that car. But I was getting a lot better. Just racing as much as I did, I was beginning to understand a lot more about what was going on.

"My father tried the best he possibly could to have top-notch cars, but my father would have won a lot more races had he raced for someone like Ray Fox, but he always loved to have his own race team. And he did quite well with it. But if you look at his championship years, he was driving for someone else.

"Back then it was tougher to be a car owner, because you couldn't go and buy a front end piece you needed to make the car go straight. You had to build one. To own a race team back then, you had to have people in the garage who could do everything. You had to have a lot of general mechanics, not specialists.

"I finished second to A. J. Foyt in the Firecracker 400 at Daytona in '65. I had all kinds of trouble that day. I had an alternator belt that had to be replaced, and I got behind. But quite frankly, all day long the car was as fast as anything out there. That car, when we built it, people laughed. It was a Fury 3. The windshield on the car looked like a milk truck, just stood straight up. You didn't have to worry about getting trapped in there. We had a hemi engine, and it was a super-good driving car, and quite frankly, by that time I had gotten to where I could go pretty well. People were starting to say, 'If you really get in a good race car, you're ready.'

"And by this time I was starting to outrun my father. In '65 I actually finished ahead of him, but there were times before that I had run better than him and didn't finish. By that time I was starting to get better and understand a lot more, and I was on my way up. I never thought about doing better than my father. I always respected my father, always have, always will. It was just like the changing of the guard. Richard Petty went through the same thing with Lee. I never went, 'I beat my father.' I never did that. Never. I never had any joy of finishing ahead of him, even later on when I had better cars and was running up front. My father lasted a long, long time.

"Then in '66 I drove for Joan Petre. Bless his heart, his budget was about two hundred dollars for the year. I mean, he did a remarkable job for what he had to work with. I hate to tell this, but one time I needed a wheel at a half-mile dirt track in Monroe, and Goodyear said, 'Which one of these broken wheels do you want on the right front?'

"At this point, I had almost decided that maybe this wasn't the thing I was going to do. I couldn't win, and quite frankly, I felt I had been in the sport long enough to get the opportunity to drive a good race car. There is nothing more frustrating than being in a position that you know you've spent the time it takes to be as good as most of the racers, but you're not able to get the quality race car it takes to win. And I was really juggling the idea of getting out of it.

"I would ask myself, Am I doing the right thing? I'm getting better, but golly. Some of the guys I went to school with were doing really well in business. Then I'd say, Yeah, but they aren't doing what they want to do. And that stands for a whole bunch. I never went into a racetrack that I wanted to leave. Some people go to work Monday morning and say, 'I don't want to do this this week. How many months until my vacation?' All my life to this day I have never done anything I didn't enjoy.

"On the other hand, I knew if I quit racing, I'd have plenty to do.

Bill France's most far-reaching, brilliant idea was that the cars that ran in all NASCAR events would be late-model cars. "He was a master politician with a great sense of timing," says Bob Latford. (DAYTONA INTERNATIONAL SPEEDWAY)

The first thing people who know Slick Owens will tell you about him is that he once jumped out of an airplane without a parachute and lived. (COURTESY OF SLICK OWENS)

Cotton Owens could thread a needle with a race car. (DAYTONA RACING ARCHIVES)

Bob, Tim, and Fonty Flock (from left) were among NASCAR's early daredevil heroes. Their sister, Reo, used to wingwalk and perform in airshows. (DAYTONA INTERNATIONAL SPEEDWAY)

Tim Flock and his fabulous Hudson Hornet in 1952. (COURTESY OF TIM FLOCK)

In 1955, Tim Flock won eighteen races in this Chrysler owned by the legendary Carl Kiekhiefer. (COURTESY OF TIM FLOCK)

Drivers Buck Baker (left) and Tim Flock (right) discuss spark plugs and valve lifters with one of the local beauty queens. (DAYTONA RACING ARCHIVES)

Bud Moore (left) and Buck Baker (right). Bud has entered more winning cars than any other owner except Lee and Richard Petty. Buck won back-to-back championships in 1956 and 1957. (DAYTONA INTERNATIONAL SPEEDWAY)

Red Vogt was as knowledgeable about engines as anyone you could ever find. (COURTESY OF SLICK OWENS)

Curtis Turner had to win or someone was going to pay the price. (DAYTONA INTERNATIONAL SPEEDWAY)

Joe Weatherly won back-to-back racing championships in 1962 and 1963 while driving for Bud Moore. (DAYTONA INTERNATIONAL SPEEDWAY)

LeeRoy Yarbrough and
Miss Dixie 1966.
(DAYTONA INTERNATIONAL
SPEEDWAY)

Tiny Lund "was probably
as tough an individual
as I ever met in my life,"
says Paul "Little Bud"
Moore. (COURTESY OF
WANDA LUND EARLY)

Bob and Lorraine Myers. In the words of their son, Danny "Chocolate" Myers, "It was tough times, but it was good times for them." (DAYTONA RACING ARCHIVES)

Bobby and Billy Myers, young brothers, died six months apart in 1956.
(DAYTONA RACING ARCHIVES)

Ralph Moody. His dad didn't want him to race — until he found out Ralph was winning. (COURTESY OF RALPH MOODY)

Curtis Turner and Miss Pure Oil. Curtis was a party animal. (DAYTONA RACING ARCHIVES)

The Holman–Moody racing team in the basement of Ralph Moody's home. Top row, from left: Marvin Panch, Curtis Turner, Dick Hutchinson, Junior Johnson, and Cale Yarbrough. Bottom row: Fred Lorenzen, Ned Jarrett, and A.J. Foyt. (COURTESY OF RALPH MOODY)

The Holman–Moody pit crew in action. (COURTESY OF RALPH MOODY)

Glenn Roberts, who had the great nickname "Fireball," was a "thoughtful, intellectual guy," says close friend Max Muhlman. (DAYTONA INTERNATIONAL SPEEDWAY)

Tiny Lund (left) and Curtis Turner (right). "Tiny had a few run-ins with Curtis," says Wanda Lund Early, "but Tiny liked Curtis. Curtis could throw a hell of a party." (DAYTONA RACING ARCHIVES)

Holman–Moody's finest. At their peak, Holman–Moody were an indomitable force in racing. From left: Dick Hutchinson, A.J. Foyt, Fred Lorenzen, Carl Yarbrough, Ned Jarrett, Curtis Turner, Junior Johnson, Ralph Moody, and John Holman. (COURTESY OF RALPH MOODY)

Ned Jarrett (left) and Marvin Panch (right) were great drivers who were also gentlemen. Jarrett once pulled Fireball Roberts from a flaming crash. (DAYTONA INTERNATIONAL SPEEDWAY)

The death of Fireball Roberts was the most shocking loss that racing had ever faced and affected the entire sport. (COURTESY OF RALPH MOODY)

Tiny Lund with his wife, Wanda. When they met, Wanda says, "He turned me over his knee and set my heinie-end on fire like a two-year-old kid. Then we were an item after that." (Courtesy of Wanda Lund Early)

From left: Tiny Lund, Wanda Lund, Paul "Little Bud" Moore, and Buddy Baker jamming during the '60s. (Courtesy of Wanda Lund Early)

Everyone loved Tiny Lund, pictured here with his wife and young admirers
after yet another victory. (COURTESY OF WANDA LUND EARLY)

Tiny, Wanda, and son Chris Lund. Wanda remembers, "We used to tease Tiny about the song, 'Old Dogs, Young Children, and Watermelon Wine.' That about summed up his philosophy of life." (COURTESY OF WANDA LUND EARLY)

Curtis and Bunny Turner. She was 19 when she first met "Pops" Turner. She was a trainee at a bank in Charlotte. He walked up and asked her to cash a check for $27,000. "I didn't blink an eye. I opened the drawer and cashed the check." (COURTESY OF BUNNY TURNER HALL)

You hear people complain they can't get work. I've always felt if you work hard enough, there will be no shortage of jobs. I had worked hard to get myself in a position for a good race car, and it was just a question whether a good race car would ever come my way."

MARVIN PANCH

13

ESCAPE FROM A FIERY DEATH

IN HIS GRAND NATIONAL CAREER racer Marvin Panch won seventeen races, including the Daytona 500 in 1961 while driving for mechanical wizard Smokey Yunick. In 1957 Panch finished second in the points championship to Buck Baker, an amazing accomplishment, considering that he hadn't made a concerted effort to try to win it. During his most competitive years driving for the Wood Brothers, Marvin Panch was a top contender. If he didn't win a race, he would most often finish in the top ten, an indication that Marvin Panch was indeed a very talented race car driver.

But as all drivers know, danger lurks around every turn, and after an excellent qualifying run for the Daytona 500 in 1963, a few days later Panch was injured badly in a flaming crash of a Maserati he was testing for car owner Briggs Cunningham. If several bystanders, including Tiny Lund, hadn't picked up the burning car and freed him from the flaming wreckage, Marvin Panch would not have survived. Confined to a hospital bed, Panch turned his ride over to Lund, who in storybook fashion won the Daytona 500 for the Wood Brothers. It is one of the great heroic stories of racing, and I was looking forward to hearing from Marvin Panch exactly what happened that fateful day.

Marvin and Betty Panch live down a dirt road

111

on ten treed acres several miles down I-95 south of the mammoth Daytona International Speedway. There are horse farms next door and across the street. Adjacent to their home sits a large travel trailer, and next to it stands a motorcycle and sidecar on which the couple that morning had ridden to Deltona, a small town twenty miles away, for breakfast.

When I entered their home, Betty Panch asked me what I did for a living. "I write books," I said, and then I told her about my first book on stock car racing, *American Zoom,* describing some of the race personalities I had interviewed including Richard Petty, Ralph Moody, and Smokey Yunick.

"That's the book where Smokey said that Marvin was a bad driver, isn't it?" she asked acidly. I couldn't remember what Smokey had said, but I meekly concluded that it was a possibility.

"You shouldn't have written that," she said.

"But Smokey said it. I didn't say it," I said defensively. "He's entitled to his opinion, isn't he?"

Betty Panch acted like a mama bear protecting a loved one. "You shouldn't have put that in the book," she snapped. "In fact, I told everyone I know not to buy that book."

While Betty Panch raged, Marvin Panch sat quietly in an armchair. When she finished, Marvin said to me, "I didn't mind. That's just Smokey. You have to know where it's coming from."

In a career that went from 1951 through 1966, Marvin Panch, who was devoted to his wife and two children, drew little attention to himself away from the racetrack. Like Geoff Bodine, Ricky Rudd, and Terry Labonte today, Panch was never a favorite of the media, an outstanding driver who let his driving do the talking for him.

Marvin Panch and I talked for the better part of the afternoon about his life in racing, his successes, and the difficulty he had raising money during the hard times before the age of sponsors, when the auto factories dropped out of racing.

Every once in a while from the back of the room, Betty Panch, whom Marvin met in California in the early fifties ("I was opening brake shops in California, and her folks had a supermarket next door. I'd go over there and buy lunch meat, and she took advantage of me," he joked.) would speak up to correct a minor error or to indicate her disapproval of someone who had hurt Marvin in some way. One time

I mentioned Curtis Turner and Joe Weatherly and their party life. I asked whether he ever joined them.

"I did my own thing at night," said Marvin Panch, indicating that, like Ralph Moody, the antics of Turner and Weatherly offended his sensibilities and values. But Betty saw the deeper result of his shying away from more colorful activity.

"Marvin was a family man," she said, "which is why they never wrote about him." She added, "Our children were the first ones to go to Victory Lane."

Said Marvin, "We were more family. We didn't run around at night. So they had no reason to write about us."

When I mentioned Marvin's crash and how Tiny Lund had been given his ride and then went on to win the Daytona 500, Betty Panch bristled. "Tiny Lund never visited Marvin, didn't even call him," she said. Though Tiny is gone, she has never forgiven him for it.

"Did Tiny ever visit you in the hospital?" I asked Marvin.

"He never did come," said Betty Panch.

"Race drivers are a little weird," Marvin said, defending Lund. "They don't like going to hospitals."

"He should have called," said Betty acidly.

"I'm that way," Marvin said softly.

"Yeah, but you would have called, Marvin. You gave him the ride."

"The Wood Brothers actually gave him the ride, honey."

When the factories pulled out of racing in the late sixties, owning a race car became a financial impossibility for many car owners and drivers, including Marvin Panch. In an era before the coming of the corporate sponsors, racing had become too expensive an enterprise for just about everyone. When Ford pulled out of racing in 1966, Panch took a ride driving a Plymouth for Petty Enterprises, and when Ford returned to racing at the end of the year, rather than continue his constant struggle for rides and sponsorship, the forty-year-old Panch accepted a job with a brake-line company. Marvin Panch had tempted and bested fate before, and this time he decided it was time to get out.

MARVIN PANCH: "I was born in Wisconsin on May 28, 1926. I lost my dad when I was three years old. I lived with uncles and aunts, and when I was around seventeen I drove out to Oakland, California, with a friend of mine who was in the Merchant Marines.

"When he joined up, I bought his car, and after he came home on leave, we drove the car out there. When he took off again, I went to work in a shipyard and also started managing brake shops for a company called Four-Wheel Brake Service, and while I was doing that, I started racing.

"After I got out to Oakland, I liked to go to the racetrack at Oakland Stadium, where they held roadster races, '32 Fords. This one fellow who drove by the name of Lloyd Ragon had a six-cylinder Ford he was running against the V-8s, and he was real smooth, and he'd either win them or run second or third. They announced a stock car race coming up at the Oakland Wall in a couple weeks, and after watching Lloyd race, I thought to myself, I'll run my car and maybe Lloyd will drive it.

"I went down to the pits and asked him, and he said he would do it, and he did real good. He was very consistent, and when they started a group out there called The Hardtops, your '39 and '40 Ford coupes, I built one of those for him, and we went out and the first night we raced it, we won the race, but he got spun out at the finish line, came across the line backwards, and he didn't like that too well. He said, 'These guys aren't racers. They're just running all over you.' And the next Saturday he didn't show up. So I started driving myself. And when they announced a stock car race at the Bay Meadows horse track, I had a '50 Mercury, and I decided, I'll run my own stock car. And that's how I got started. Most of the tracks were quarter-mile dirt. We ran Bay Meadows horse track, Balboa Stadium in San Diego. The Oakland Wall was asphalt. That was a high-banked paved track with a lip, and in order to get around there real good you had to go up and smack the wall a few times to get the car curved in the right direction. Matter of fact, I still hold the track record there, because after I set it they tore the track down.

"I started winning races in a Mercury, and I began driving for Dick Meyer in a '53 Dodge Red Ram V-8, and between him and me, we won practically all the races on the West Coast. Chrysler helped us out by giving us sheet metal and parts, obsolete stuff from the manufacturing plant in Oakland. We'd go and pick out what we wanted. That was about all the help we had.

"I always had good cars. I was very competitive. I was doing real well in that Mercury, and John Holman, who was working for Bill

Stroppe, they were working together in a Mercury deal, and Stroppe asked me, 'Why don't you come and drive for us?' I knew they were big, but hey, I was doing good with the car I had. When you're young, you're stupid. I turned him down.

"In '53 I raced against the southerners for the first time at the Oakland Speedway when they came west in the spring. I finished second to Dick Rathmann, who had a Hudson Hornet. When they came back that fall I had an extra car, and Chrysler asked if I'd let Lee Petty drive one of my cars.

"Then in '54 I was drafted into the military. I took my basic at Fort Ord, transferred to Fort McArther in San Pedro, and got discharged on a hardship before I got shipped overseas. I was in not quite a year. After that, I came back to North Carolina and drove in a race for Lee's brother, Julie. He had a Chevrolet, and I drove that at Darlington. Julian was Lee's younger brother. He was shorter than Lee, a nice guy.

"I liked Darlington, which was the same as it is now. I was used to the Oakland Wall, which was more treacherous than Darlington. You had to race against the racetrack. If you did that and passed whoever you could whenever you could, you had no problems. I never won a race there, but I finished second many times. There was nothing different racing against the southerners than it was out West. They knew more than we did, had cars that were a little quicker, so when I came South to race, I had no problems. If someone shoved me around, I shoved them back, and that was the end of it. I got along real well with everyone. I had no problems back here at all. But you have to remember, I came here with good equipment. I was always in the front-running pack.

"In September of '55 I came in fourth at Langhorne, which was oil-dirt and was rough. It was sort of a circle and if you looked down at your gauges while going down the backstretch you were liable to run into the wall. What made Langhorne difficult, you had to put a lot of shaker screens in the front to keep that oil-dirt out, because otherwise it would pack in your radiator and you'd have heating problems.

"I drove for Beryl Jackson in his old Oldsmobile, and after the Langhorne race I pulled in the pits and the front end fell right down over the tires, shook all apart. Tom Harbison, who was an Oldsmobile dealer there, came to the pits and he said, 'Would you like to stay back here and run for me?'

"Ford had come with that 312 engine. I said, 'It looks like the Ford is going to be the race car for a while.' He said, 'If you stay back here with me, I'll get you a Ford.' And we built a Ford right there in the Harbison Oldsmobile garage in Langhorne. We towed out of there, and I raced for Tom.

"One day Tim Flock came over to see me. Tim was driving for Carl Kiekhaefer, who was a very good race owner, a very smart individual. Mercury Outboards were on top then. That was his main business, and he was some businessman. Tim said, 'Carl wants to talk to you. Why don't you come over and talk to him?' I thought, I have a good ride, and I didn't even bother to go over. I still kick myself for that. That's one of the biggest mistakes I ever made. Because he had Chrysler 300s, and those Dodges were real quick cars. Kiekhaefer was really the first to come with first-class race equipment. And he didn't leave anything to chance. We ran a lot of hundred-mile dirt races, and you were just borderline whether you could finish without having to refuel. Kiekhaefer showed up with his gas wrapped in dry ice, to shrink the gas, to get more fuel inside the tank. He'd top off the tank right before the race started, so he could make the hundred miles without stopping. Yup. He was good. He really was.

"Tim Flock was a nice guy. When I came back to run Darlington, Tim came over. I was running good, and he said, 'So you don't end up in downtown Darlington, cut a hole in the floorboard, make a trap-door, and keep checking your tire.' I never will forget that, because I did what he told me, and after that race I had a face full of tire. But he did help me keep from blowing the tires.

"And though I didn't go with Kiekhaefer, I'm not fussing. It turned out okay because after I was running Fords with Tom Harbison, Pete DePaolo came along and asked me if I wanted to run for him, and working for him led me to drive for Holman-Moody.

"Meanwhile, in October of '55, I finished second to Speedy Thompson at the Memphis-Arkansas Speedway in Tom Harbison's Ford. My wife and I went to Detroit, got the car, and brought it to Little Rock, where we built it. Speedy was driving a factory car. At the time I was making $100 a week and a percentage. That year I made about $4,300. It was not a good living, but it was a living. I could make more doing that than working.

"In February of '56 I entered the Daytona beach race in a Dodge.

When I got on the throttle my distributor rotor broke. I came around into the pits, helped by a shove from the guy behind me. We didn't have an extra rotor so my mechanic, Gus David, pulled up the hood of one of the Chrysler station wagon emergency cars, ripped the rotor out, put it in my car and got me going.

"When I pulled out of the pits, everyone had already come around and were fixing to lap me, and when I took off everyone in the north turn thought I was leading the race. And that day I didn't have any trouble seeing because I was ahead of them, almost a lap down, but ahead of them. The cars in front would sandblast the cars behind, making it very hard to see. I can remember a driver by the name of Johnny Beauchamp marked the end of the beach straightaway by a family sitting on the bank. When he saw them, he'd throw it sideways and get ready to go into the north turn. What happened, the family got up and moved down aways, and the next time Johnny came through there, he threw it sideways and went right off the end of the course! That's how bad it was to see.

"I didn't race again that year until July 4 at Raleigh, and in Montgomery at the end of the month I won my first NASCAR race. Montgomery had a big track. I sat on the pole, won the race, and earned $950 in purses. All the hundred milers paid a thousand to win, and we ran them all when we had the equipment to do it. Once you're a goofy race driver, you race regardless, whether it makes financial sense or not. That's what it amounts to.

"At the time Pete DePaolo asked me to drive for him, Bill Amick and myself were the short track drivers for Ford. Ralph Moody and Fireball were the large track drivers, and Curtis and Joe were the convertible guys. Like at Darlington, we'd all run.

"That year Ford came in with a Thunderbird to run in sports car racing at New Smyrna, near Daytona. Pete put me in one with the smaller engine. He put Curtis Turner in the one with the big engine. All my job was was to outrun the Corvettes. That was the only thing I had to do. Not only did I do that, but I ended up running second overall. The man who beat me was Carol Shelby in a Ferrari.

"In '57, driving for Pete, I won six NASCAR races. I won the first two races of the season at Willow Springs out in California, and at the Concord Speedway, a dirt track. I remember that race. I was driving a Ford, and so was Curtis Turner. Curtis was a showman on dirt. He liked to cross it up at the start/finish line and go all the way through the corner crossed up. I had no trouble with Curtis. At Concord I was on the pole, and he was on the outside pole. We came down the backstretch side by side, and I knew he was in trouble so I shut him off, and he went out, and I ran off, ran away with the race. Curtis tried hard. I could see him in the mirror all crossed up trying his doggonedest to catch up to me. He finally crashed.

"I liked Curtis, liked Joe Weatherly too. They were good guys, but I never ran around with them at night. I was serious about my racing. And I was faithful to my wife, Betty. My family was very important to me.

"In '57 I finished second in the points to Buck Baker, though I never went after the championship. Never even thought of it. Winning the championship didn't pay a whole lot in those days so I didn't concentrate on it, never even thought about it.

"I really liked ole' Buck. He was a hard charger. I always got along good with Buck, though I've been told he has a temper. One night after a race a fan came to his shop, and I understand he jumped through a window and went after the fan. He didn't take anything from anybody, which I don't blame him for.

"In '57 I started forty-two races, and I finished in the top ten in twenty-seven of them, the top five in twenty-two. I was there to win the race, but I wouldn't go over my head to do it. I always believed this: why race forty or fifty guys at the beginning of the race when if you sat back and were patient, at the end of the race you only had to race three or four. Makes sense, doesn't it? I stayed out of trouble, and towards the last I'd do what I had to do.

"After the Martinsville race in '57, the car companies got out of racing. When Ford pulled out, they gave us a handful of parts and a race car and said, 'You're on your own.' After a while we also got our one-ton trucks we towed with. That was after the Chevy drivers got theirs, and Ford decided to give us ours. But then I was on my own. I was back to driving my own cars. We had to hunt our own sponsors. Times became tough. There was no TV money, and the purses stayed the same. Fireball Roberts made the most money that year, $32,000. I made $4,100. In '58 I was only able to afford to enter eleven races.

"In '59 the Daytona International Speedway opened. I liked it, and I picked up the deal on drafting real quick. Matter of fact, Fireball and

I drafted together an awful lot. We learned it in '59, and applied it in '60. We were the first ones to hook up and go on.

"In that first Daytona 500 Bill France gave an extra thousand dollars to anyone who would cut the tops off the cars. I took the money. I never will forget when they started the preliminary race I was glad I was wearing my shoulder harnesses and all the goodies, because the vaccuum wanted to suck you right out of the car. And after I cut the top off, we snapped on a tonneau cover, and as soon as we started running, the doggone thing came loose and beat the daylights out of me. I had to drive with one hand and hold the canvas cover with the other. It was disastrous. I had to hold on to it the whole race. If I had pulled into the pits, I wouldn't have finished second.

"I started the 500 in the second row. They started the convertibles on the outside and the hardtops on the inside. Cutting the top off turned out to be was one of the biggest mistakes I made, because the hardtops lapped us about every ten laps it seemed. The vaccuum and bucking the wind was so bad in the convertible that you couldn't run with the hardtops. So the thousand dollars didn't pay off very well because between the two, the hardtops and convertibles, it wasn't any race at all. I finished seventeenth that day. The first fifteen finishers were hardtops, and only one convertible finished in front of me. It was the only time they ran it that way. NASCAR doesn't brag about it.

"Nineteen-fifty-nine was a difficult year, a bad year. We were in trouble because all the factories were out, and just a few drivers had sponsors. Junior Johnson had Holly Farms. Lee Petty had Oldsmobile and Plymouth. Fireball had Pontiac. That was about it. We were drivers. What did we know about finding sponsors? And we weren't smart enough to have agents like they have today, people who do nothing but hunt sponsors. In our case we'd go to a town, go to a car dealership, and if they gave us a couple hundred dollars, we were in hog heaven, and we'd put the name on the side of the car. One of my sponsors was a Vanceboro, North Carolina, car dealer, John Whitford. Later I drove with the name of a Ford dealer, Tom Vernon, on my car. Another one was Billy Ridgeway.

"In '60 I only drove in eleven races, and then in 1961 I got a ride driving part-time for Smokey Yunick. Fireball drove a '61 Pontiac, and I drove a '60 Pontiac, his old car. It didn't bother me to drive the older car, because I was looking for a ride. I needed a ride—bad.

"We went to Daytona, and I finished second in the preliminary race. In that race Lee Petty and Johnny Beauchamp went off the track by the tunnel and took a nasty. Lee ran little after that.

"Before the 500, Smokey told me to stay a half a lap behind Fireball, so in case Fireball got involved in an accident, we both wouldn't get taken out at the same time. With less than fifteen laps left in the race Fireball had that half-lap lead, and I was running second, and then he blew an engine. The story at that time was that when he came in, the starter was hanging on the cable, fell off, hit the track, bounced up, and poked a hole in the oil pan. That was the story they had because they didn't want people to think the Pontiac engine blew up.

"When that happened Smokey gave me the okay to go, and I won the race, breaking the previous record by an average of almost fifteen miles an hour.

"It was great, because I was broke. That really helped me. I had a 40 percent deal to drive for Smokey, and after I won the race Smokey said, 'I'll tell you what. Anybody who's good enough to win the race is worth 50 percent to me.' He's the only guy I ever drove for who upped the ante. I liked Smokey. He was real fair. I won $21,000, and at that time, man, my share was great. We used the money to buy the land and the house that we still live in today in Daytona.

"The car I drove for Smokey at Daytona was his second car, and I finished fourth in it at the Firecracker 500, and that car was only available one more time, and that was at Charlotte in May and October, when we wrecked in both races.

"Sixty-one was the year Curtis tried to organize the drivers. I don't remember Curtis's approach, but I was out here at home cutting grass in the front yard when Bill France came by. He wanted to know if I was going to sign up with Curtis. I said, 'No, I hadn't planned to.' NASCAR was good to me. I wasn't going to fuss about it. So that was the end of it. Bill was a nice guy. He always treated me great.

"In '62 I was driving for Bob Osiecki in a Dodge, and the car wasn't that great, and we fell out of the Daytona 500. Speedy Thompson was driving for the Wood Brothers, and Speedy was complaining about a vibration in the car. He came in, and they changed tires, did everything, and Speedy went back out and came back in again still complaining about the vibration. I was standing there, so when Speedy's car came into the pits, Glen Wood said, 'Jump in that car.' And I did. I didn't feel any vibration, but they probably corrected whatever the problem was during that pit stop. Matter of fact, that was a good ride. That car was tough, and that's when I left Osiecki and started driving for the Wood Brothers.

"We should have won the Southern 500 at Darlington in '62. I figured we did win it. To start with they gave it to Junior Johnson, and then they changed the ruling and gave it to Larry Frank. The Wood Brothers said I had a lap on Larry, although Larry finished across the line ahead of me. I was coming up to lap him. Larry is a real fine guy, and Larry needed it, and I'm glad he got credit for it. Of course, I would have liked to have it too, but I didn't. The scorers didn't want to run the score sheets again. I don't blame the scorers. They just didn't feel like it eight hours after the race.

"Glen was the car owner and did the dealing, and Leonard was the man who made the cars run. I'll tell you about the Wood Brothers: they are about as honest folks as you're going to find anywhere. The custom was that after races NASCAR would have us stand in line, and the drivers would get paid their share, and then you'd give the rest to the car owner. After a particular race we did that. I got back home, and a week later I got a check through the mail for fifty dollars with Glen Wood's signature on it and no explanation.

"At the next race I said, 'Glen, what in the world was that check for fifty dollars for?' He kind of laughed. He said, 'An old boy gave me a hundred dollars to put his sticker on the rear quarter panel by the rear glass there. I figured you were entitled to half of it.' That's how straight they are.

"When I got home, I called Mary Bruner of NASCAR. I said, 'I'm not standing in line after a race anymore. As long as I'm driving for the Wood Brothers, send the check to Bernice,' Glen's wife. So I never stood in line again after that.

"Another time I was at Charlotte. I went to practice, and the car in front of me was running low on the racetrack, and I saw a bunch of lead BBs running out of that car and running down the track. The crew chief evidently used those to meet the weight spec, and when we got ready to play racer, he tripped the switch and ejected the balls to lighten their car.

"When I came in I told Leonard Wood about it. I said, 'We should do something like that.' He said, 'I'll tell you what. You drive the car. We'll take care of it.' He was a straight arrow.

"Leonard was pretty bashful, and when you drove for them, your night out was going out in their pickup truck, stopping at the drugstore and having a sandwich. Those boys were straight. I never will forget winning a race at North Wilkesboro. [Beauty queen] Linda Vaughn was giving out the trophies. I said, 'Linda, I have a cold. How about giving the trophy to Glen?' She smacked him on the cheek, and afterward Leonard said to Glen, 'You acted like a darn fool up there.' That's how straight they were.

"In '63 we went to Daytona, and I had the Wood Brothers car qualified for the 500. Briggs Cunningham, who ran Maseratis at LeMans and all over, wanted to experiment with a Grand National engine for a Maserati. They were looking for a dummy to try it out, and I was eager, so I got in it. I took it easy at first, and it didn't feel just right. They had those old Indy tires on it, half-tread, half-slick, hard as a rock. I came in and took on fuel. Leonard Wood came over, and since I was driving for him, I told him what I was doing, and he made some changes on it, and it felt pretty good.

"At the time Bill France was offering $10,000 for the first driver to go over 180 miles an hour, and I figured, I can knock this off, and I got almost to the third turn, and that sucker airborned, didn't have spoilers, and it came down on its side and rolled over on its top and upside down slid all the way over to the tunnel.

"It was a bird cage. The doors closed in the top, so I couldn't get out even though I kicked and frammed. The firemen came with the fire truck. Through that tiny windshield around the carburetor I could see fire. I said, 'Right there at the engine. Get it.' And I don't know if the firemen froze or if the equipment malfunctioned, but it didn't work. And before you knew it, the fire was going pretty good. I was kicking and framming and trying to get out, and I couldn't. No way. There wasn't a hole big enough to crawl through.

"Around that time Tiny Lund, Bill Wimble, Ernie Gahan, Jerry Rabon, and an engineer from Firestone, Steve Petrasek, were coming through the tunnel, and when they saw the crash they came and jumped over the fence. They came and tried to lift the car, and as they did I kicked the door out, and I got halfway out when the gas tank blew. Naturally they had to drop the car. And as this was happening everything bad I did in my life flashed before me like I was watching a TV screen, and I thought, What's going to happen to Betty? How is she going to get on?' All in a matter of split seconds, but it seemed like an hour.

"Steve Petrasek said, 'Come on. He's still kicking,' and they ran right into the flames and lifted the car, burning their hands and arms. Matter of fact, Steve went temporarily blind after that. Tiny Lund grabbed me by the leg and jerked me out. If it wasn't for those guys, you wouldn't be talking to me now. I'm just lucky to be here. And the happiest day of my life was when I was rolling on the ground away from that fire.

"When I was in the hospital Glen and Len came up to visit me. Tiny didn't have a ride, and they decided it would be a good idea to put Tiny in the car in my place. I thought it was a good idea, too, because I was obligated to him too.

"I went out to the racetrack for a little while. They taped me all up and took me in an ambulance. They wanted me to talk to Tiny about how to run the race. And that's when Tiny won the Daytona 500 in my car.

"After my crash, everybody told me, 'You're going to think about it.' The first time I practiced at Daytona, I saw the burned spot, and I said to myself, 'That's where it happened,' and that was the end of it. After the accident, I probably drove a little smarter, didn't get into anything that didn't handle good. No more testing foreign cars. But it didn't affect my driving. In fact, I had my best year after that.

"I returned in June and finished sixth in the World 600 at Charlotte, was third at Atlanta, third in the Firecracker 400 behind Fireball and Freddie Lorenzen, fourth at Bristol, and was second to Fireball in the Southern 500. At Martinsville in September I finished second to Freddie, and then I won the race at North Wilkesboro with Freddie coming in second. That was a fairy-tale–type thing. I got more publicity out of that than in all the years I was driving. I then had two more top-five finishes. In the twelve races I ran in '63, I finished in the top five nine times.

"We went to Riverside in January of '64. Dan Gurney and I were driving for the Wood Brothers. Dan didn't get around all that great at Daytona, but he was supergood on those road courses. Midway through the race, Joe Weatherly had a crash. I didn't see it happen, but evidently he lost his brakes coming down the esses, and there was a sharp right at the bottom, and what it looked like, knowing he was in trouble, he cut across the corner, and when he did, the car leaped and hit the wall on the driver's side. When I came around and saw it, his car was smashed on the left side, but I had no idea that Joe was even hurt. The car didn't look that bad. But his head evidently hit the wall. That was before they put in window nets.

"Nothing was said to me except 'Joe is hurt bad.' Later I learned that Joe had died. Then in late May we raced at Charlotte. Early in the race, there was a crash. Fireball's car caught fire. I was ahead of Fireball, and right away they threw the cloth and slowed everybody way down, and by the time I came back around the flames were out. Fireball was my teammate, and I went to visit him in the hospital. I don't know too much of what he had. When you're burned, they doctor you up so much. Don't get me wrong. You have pain. Fire is bad stuff. Real bad stuff. It isn't like breaking an arm or a leg. They grow back. It's hard to grow back after a fire. Sure is. I wasn't with him long, because he couldn't have visitors. It was one of those deals where I just slipped in. Fireball said to me, 'I don't know how you made it through it.'

"In addition to Joe and Fireball being gone, in '65 Richard Petty and David Pearson also were gone because Chrysler pulled out of racing. Ned Jarrett won the driving championship that year. He had Du Pont money behind him. His car was owned by Bondy Long, who was related. That year I won four races, including Atlanta twice. At Atlanta, your neck has a tendency to work on your arm and muscles. In the April race I was leading the race, and someone in the pits told me to move on a little more because Freddie Lorenzen hadn't made a stop yet, and he was coming. So I was running pretty hard going down the backstretch, passing people, and a real fine gentleman by the name of J. T. Putney was driving a Chevrolet, which evidently was one of Bill France's cars—that was when they had more Fords than Chevrolets—and J. T. tried to get out of my way. If he had stayed where he was, he would have been all right, but he crossed down in front of me, and my arm was kind of paralyzed, and I couldn't quite miss him. J. T. was a nice guy. I wouldn't hit him on purpose for anything in the world. I just tapped him, and when I did he went flipping end over end. He didn't get hurt, thank goodness, but it wiped out Bill France's car.

"From the tower you could hear Bill France's voice: 'Get him out of that car.' I had a two-lap lead, and when I made my regular pit stop, they put A. J. Foyt in the car to finish the race. I didn't complain. I felt, what the heck, why fight city hall? When Daddy upstairs said, 'Get him out of there,' the Wood Brothers didn't want to fight him. I still got credit for the win.

"In June at Atlanta, I was way behind. I called in and said I was running hot. There were a lot of cautions, and I was able to make it all up. Late in the race they said, 'Run it into the ground.' I said, 'Okay,' and we did. We ran all day and it never puked. Evidently the gauge was eager.

"And then in 1966 I was hired by Ford to go to LeMans to drive a GT-40. We went to Riverside and practiced with the car. Ford told us, 'If Bill France calls and wants to know why you're not running, tell them you don't have a car to run.' So Bill Sr. called and asked, 'Are you going to run Charlotte?' I said, 'No.' He said, 'Why not?' I said, 'I don't have a car.' He said, 'What if I get you a car?' I said, 'It has to be as good as the one I have.' He said, 'How about a Petty Plymouth?'

"Well, I couldn't say no. I called Ford to find out what my standing would be with Ford if I left them. They said, 'Go ahead. As long as they've come up with equipment good enough to race, go ahead.' So they canceled me out of the GT-40 program and I drove for Petty.

"Well, what I didn't know was that the car the Pettys gave me was a dirt car. The springs and everything were set up for dirt, and that was one of the roughest rides in the world. And the car was so dirty that after the race it looked like I had just come off a dirt track.

"I ended up winning the race. A few laps from the finish Richard was down in the pits. He wanted to finish the race, so he ran the last forty or so laps. It was my seventeenth Grand National win and my last. Ford wasn't figuring I was going to win the race, and I guess that disturbed Ford a little bit. So when Ford came back, I just finished out the season with Petty, and that was the end of it.

"I was forty years old, and I saw so many guys at forty start going downhill, and I thought, I'm winning races up here, and there's no need to go down into the grave. I was offered a job for Greyrock, brake-lining people, to do test work. I did the high-speed brake testing for them at the Daytona Speedway.

"While I was still driving, I went to Daytona to do some of their police car testing. Bill Taus, one of their engineers, rode with me. He said, 'When are you going to retire from racing?' I said, 'I don't know anything else.' He said, 'You know anything about trucks?' I said, 'No.' He made the sound of a hydraulic brake. He said, 'You want a job as an engineer?' So I took the job as a field service engineer for Greyrock in their truck division.

"I called a press conference and told them I was leaving, and that was it. I worked at Grayrock for thirty years. A couple of years ago I retired from there."

14

CRASH AND BURN

THE EARLY 1960S WAS A TRAGIC period for motor sports. The crash and subsequent fire in Marvin Panch's Maserati at Daytona in 1963 was one of three serious accidents involving the Italian sports car and only a precursor to the horror that would follow. The next year came one fatality after another.

Joe Weatherly was killed in a crash at Riverside early in 1964, and then at Indianapolis drivers Eddie Sachs and Dave McDonald were killed in a fiery wreck on the first lap.

Another huge loss was yet to come. In May 1964 at the Charlotte Motor Speedway, Fireball Roberts, the most popular driver in America at the time, crashed and burned early in the World 600. He would linger in great pain in the hospital for two months before dying from complications from his burns and injuries.

During this period Bob Latford was working in PR for the Charlotte Motor Speedway. He remembers the tragic period and what he had to do to help racing restore its reputation and the confidence of its fans.

BOB LATFORD: "I was working at Daytona for the speedway in '63 when Marvin Panch was burned in a crash of the Maserati he was testing. Tiny Lund pulled the door ajar just enough to get ahold of Marvin's ankles and pull him out.

127

They took him to Halifax Memorial Hospital. I went over to the hospital that night. Marvin and I were friends. When Marvin won the '61 Daytona 500, that was one of the first times when numbers became important. I noticed his speed, 149.601 miles an hour, and I started going back and looking, and I found that was the fastest single lap that had been turned at Indianapolis the year before in a race won by Jim Hurtubise, and here Marvin had averaged that for the whole 500 miles, which firmly established stock car racing as the fastest form of motorsports at the time.

"Marvin crashed in a birdcage Maserati when he got burned. Three of the worst wrecks we had at Daytona in the early years were all birdcage Maseratis. Augie Pabst got hurt in one, and John Martin, a movie theater owner out of Columbus, Georgia, had a bad wreck and was involved in a bad fire, and he was badly burned. They weren't designed for that kind of impact.

"After Marvin crashed and was hospitalized, Glen Wood put Tiny in the car since Tiny didn't have a ride. And of course, Tiny won the race. They never changed a Firestone tire on the car, ran the whole 500 on it, ran out of fuel on the last lap, a storybook finish, the biggest win of Tiny's career. But while Marvin was recuperating, I would go over and talk to him and found he was reticent about public speaking.

"I said, 'You're a race driver. People want to know what it's like out there. Everybody sees you do it, and you make it seem so easy.' And I started giving him a public speaking course out of my old college freshman English textbook, and we became friends, and while he was recuperating we kept two of their dogs, and their children, Marlette and Richie, who were seven and five, stayed with us about a week. One of the dogs, a poodle, was going to have pups, and Marvin and Betty wanted the kids to see the birth.

"We all knew the potential for injury and death existed, but we hadn't had any for quite a while. Joe Weatherly was killed at Riverside early in '64, and that was also the year Eddie Sachs and David McDonald were killed on the first lap of Indy in a big fire.

"When I first started working at Daytona, Fireball Roberts used to come by all the time. Edward Glenn Roberts Jr. grew up in the Daytona area. He moved there from Tavares, which is in central Florida. He went to the University of Florida, but got knocked out by the math courses. He wanted to be an engineer, and he ended up being a resource person for engineers because he knew so much about cars. Back then all the guys worked on their own cars, so they knew what made them work. The successful ones, like Fireball, looked for ways of improving that performance.

"He was a big guy, athletic-looking, and he could speak well, which made him an excellent representative. When he became really successful with the advent of the superspeedways, he became a spokesman for the sport. Fireball Roberts was the first superstar. He and I rode over to Orlando to do TV shows together. Like a lot of the early ones, he wasn't boastful. He just went out and did what he was hired to do, which was to drive race cars. And he did it very effectively.

"Fireball was a smart driver. He was one of the first who drove with his head as much as with his foot. A lot of the early pioneers were just flat-out drivers. Curtis Turner was like that, and Marshall Teague was the same way. Lee Petty was one of the first smart drivers. He realized where the money was and how to take care of the equipment. Fireball was that way.

"In the early years of the Daytona 500, first place paid $25,000, but the track would sell laps at $25 to $100 to augment that. If you led lap forty-seven and it was a sponsored lap, you got the $25. It was part of the promotion and a way of raising additional money. Doris Roberts, Fireball's wife, was one of the ones who went out and sold them along with Betty Falk. And Fireball always had a list of which laps were sponsored taped to his dash, and you could almost tell which ones were sponsored, because he'd suddenly hit the accelerator and go blowing by somebody, lead that lap, and then he'd back off and let someone else lead for a while.

"In May of '64 I was at Charlotte promoting the July race in Daytona. Joe Epton and I brought the pace car up and did a lap before the race. Fireball was burned on the seventh lap of the World 600. We heard about it as we were driving all the way back to Daytona. We were very concerned. We had just started using flame retardants, putting chemicals on driving suits, or T-shirts, or whatever the driver wore. They dipped them in a mixture of chemicals and hung them on a fence in the garage area to dry. Glenn was allergic to the chemicals and didn't like it. Like all drivers, he thought accidents and injuries were going to happen to someone else. He was injured May 24 and died July 2, and I was hired in August by the Charlotte Motor

Speedway when the original PR director, Earl Kelly, left. The track was in Chapter Ten, in financial reorganization. Curtis Turner and Bruton Smith were gone. They owed a lot of people for services, products, and construction, and someone figured out that the old railroad bankruptcy laws could be applied to the track. The precedent was that the only thing you could do with a railroad was run trains up and down. The only thing you can do with a racetrack is run races around it. So the same bankruptcy law was applied, Chapter 10. The creditors brought the suit. People like A. C. Goings, Richard Howard, Fred Wilson and others who bought stock because they were fans or because they knew Curtis or Bruton, in order to protect their investment, formed a stockholders' committee to try to raise money to stave off bankruptcy, and this is when the courts got involved; they had to remove management, Curtis and Bruton, and they reorganized to hold off the creditors, and it was this stockholders' committee that hired me on a trial basis.

"When I got there I saw that the track had a picture on the brochure of the accident, the smoke, and the fire, and immediately I had the brochure redone and took the picture out. But it was a tragedy for the sport, almost a setback, because one of our major stars, if not *the* major star, had died. Richard Petty had not yet emerged as a superstar.

"It was a time when NASCAR was having a lot of trouble. Despite boycotts by the factories, we had to find ways to gradually regain the confidence of the business public as well as the fans in the Charlotte Motor Speedway. Richard Howard was a very innovative manager of the track, and we were quite innovative. If Chrysler boycotted, he got Chevrolets. He got Chevrolets when Ford boycotted. Both Chrysler and Ford were both saying that the competition wouldn't be good because they were not in it, and a lot of the tracks were buying that line of thinking and presented their shows as less than what was available. We would never buy that, and we did a lot of things to try to maintain interest. Richard Howard bought Curtis Turner, Marvin Panch and Ned Jarrett out of their contracts and put them in cars. And Marvin Panch won the 600 that year.

"I didn't realize it until years later and started studying public relations, but I found out that we were doing exactly what we were supposed to be doing: trying to do something for all of our publics, whether it was increased purses or shower rooms for the competitors, a bigger return on investment for the stockholders, better seating or shade for the public, and we did something for the employees as well.

"And we were getting some of the best crowds on the circuit. When [Charlotte track owners] Curtis [Turner] and Bruton [Smith] left, the stock was worth about sixteen cents a share. Bruton was broke when he left the Concord area. He was a used car salesman. He went to Illinois, got involved in the automobile industry, and came back a millionaire. Quietly he began buying up all the stock. At that point it was worth three or four dollars a share, because of the continuous growth in the sport and the good management at the track. Before long, he had bought controlling interest in the track, and he owns it to this day along with a half dozen other tracks."

15

DEATH WHOLESALE

RALPH MOODY WAS AT THE RACE-way in Riverside, California, the day Joe Weatherly died. Looking back, it is Moody's opinion that Weatherly's car should not have been allowed back on the track in the condition it was in when he had his fatal crash. But Joe Weatherly, like most drivers, believed himself to be immortal. That something could go so wrong never occured to him. Getting back out there and racing was all that mattered.

Moody was in his plane en route to Charlotte at the time of Fireball Roberts's crash. After landing, he went directly to the hospital to find the charred body of the great racer. Moody, a blunt man, told Roberts's wife not to expect him to survive.

Again, Moody is convinced that Roberts's death had been unnecessary. Moody had made a strong lining around the gas tanks of his cars, only to have NASCAR make him take them out because they hadn't been approved. After the crash, NASCAR permitted him to install his safer fuel cell, a boon to racing, but too late to save Fireball Roberts.

Moody was witness too to the deaths of racers Jimmy Pardue and Billy Wade, killed during dangerous tire testing. Moody had wanted to install a submarine strap into his cars to protect his drivers from the effect of a lap belt squeezing too hard against a driver's intestines, and again NASCAR said no. But when Wade was killed in a crash in which he could have been saved with such a device, again, NASCAR quickly approved Moody's new safety measure.

In defense of NASCAR, Bill France Sr. had been a racer. Like the drivers, he thought added precautions to be unnecessary. Before Fireball Roberts's crash, drivers just did not die in flames. France didn't forsee the need, as with Wade. It took an automotive genius like Ralph Moody to prove him wrong.

RALPH MOODY: "Joe Weatherly was killed at Riverside in January of 1964, and that was kind of stupid. They broke the transmission, and they came into the pits, and they changed the clutch and transmission. He was setting there in the pits and they changed all that crap, which was red-hot, hard-to-handle, and they sent him back out there. He was God knows how many laps down. I understand from some officials up in the corner with their radios that when Joe tried to downshift, he couldn't get it in gear, that he never got the gear in and he went and slammed the wall. The wall was on the left side about head high, and they didn't have any nets in the window, and he hit the wall with his head and died. But Joe never should have been out there. He was so many laps down, he was there for nothing. I was surprised at [car owner] Bud Moore. Bud ordinarily wouldn't use up his tires for no reason. I don't know why it ever happened. He wasn't going to get any points, he was so far behind. What was the point? It was just one of those things that happen, but you wonder why.

"Fireball was killed at the World 600 at Charlotte that same year. I wasn't at the track, because at Daytona I had been sick, having a hell of a time with my back. I had broken it in a couple of places during my racing career, and it was all closed up and pinching a nerve, and when the nerve shuts you off, you can't do nothing. And at Daytona I had to wear a brace, and I didn't fly home until the day of the World 600.

"I was flying home, and we were to this side of Columbia, South Carolina, and I had the radio on, when I heard that Fireball had crashed. 'Goddamn.' And they were saying, 'He isn't getting out. He isn't getting out.' And they described how the car was on fire and Ned Jarrett was pulling him out. I said to myself, Man, he's going to burn up in fire. They finally got him out.

"I went straight to the hospital to see him. Fireball's legs looked like charred logs. Charred. No way he could survive. No way. And he was sedated so I guess he wasn't hurting that much. The nurse came in, and Fireball was lying there singing western songs. She said, 'If you keep that up, you're going to hurt yourself.' Fireball said, 'If I'd be worried about that, I wouldn't have been racing.' He kept on singing.

"Fireball's wife went to see him once and didn't want to go back. When she did, she told him she didn't want to look at him. She told him, 'You keep covered up.' The fire had burned his hands, his arms. I didn't know how the hell he was still alive.

"She said to me, 'Is he healing up in any way?' I was blunt. I told her, 'He ain't ever going to heal up. Make up your mind to that. He's just hurt too bad. Make up your mind that he ain't gonna be here.'

"She had a fit. I said, 'Doris, I'm not going to sit here and lie to you, to say something is going to happen when I know better.' The doctors knew he'd never make it.

"Later I found out that on the morning of the Charlotte race, his crew had changed his setup on the chassis from what he always ran. He didn't have but a few laps in the goddamn car, and he got out of shape coming out of two, and Junior hit him in the ass, was going to knock him out of the way coming down the backstretch, and Ford and myself had already hollered about the configuration of the backstretch wall, and how dangerous it was with the gates open with the end of the cement wall exposed to the cars, and when Fireball spun, his car turned around and he slammed into that cement wall backwards at a very high speed.

"And at that time cars didn't have fuel cells in them. I had taken Weatherly and Turner's cars in the previous Darlington race and built a strong box around the gas tank, and NASCAR made us take them sons a bitches home and take them out for the Charlotte race. And if it had been in Fireball's car, it might have saved him—it had a hell of a chance of saving him, because it was real strong. NASCAR wanted to put on shows, but they didn't have someone knowledgeable enough who was sitting there thinking about making something better.

"But after his crash, we went to Canada and had some fiberglass fuel cells made—they were oval and held twenty-two gallons, and we put that tin box around it, and that was approved, but too late to save Fireball.

"But to start with, if his crew had left his setup alone, he wouldn't have gotten out of shape in the first place, Junior wouldn't have hit him, and he wouldn't have backed into the goddamn wall.

"A hell of a lot of people came to the funeral. It was held in Florida. They buried him out back of the Daytona racetrack, just the other side of the airport in a nice cemetery. The place was full of people. It was just a shame cause he was talking about quitting and going into something else a year before the crash. He had a partner and he was going to get into some kind of business. Cause Fireball had made a good deal of money racing. He was working on 50 percent. That was pretty good money back then.

"It wasn't long after their deaths that Jimmy Pardue and Billy Wade were killed while tire testing. Jimmy Pardue drove Car 54. Remember the TV show, 'Car 54, Where Are You?' He was a nice guy too. He was tire testing, running a Chrysler car, and I showed him how to get around Charlotte, rode him around, showed him what to do, and he went over into the corner and a tire blew, and when it blew, he locked it down, and he went straight into the wall, right through the fence, and out of there. He landed on a wire chainlink fence. A post hit him side the head and went through his helmet.

"I went to the hospital with him holding his mouth open to keep his tongue from choking him. He bit my fingers on the ride to Concord. When we got there, I figured he'd never make it. His head was busted and bleeding. I could see his pulse going.

"Billy Wade got killed on the Daytona Beach track tire testing. Unbeknownst to somebody, they were testing tires with inner liners. They had started doing it, and then they quit. What they were doing, on the backstretch they had a stake, and you ran the tire over it and blew the tire. Darel Dieringer ran the test and hit the wall two or three times, and he decided the tire company was doing something wrong. And what they were doing, the inner liner was only an inch and a quarter from the tire, and when the tire hit the stake, both the tube and the inner liner both would be cut, so they quit that for a while.

"So they got Billy Wade down there, and they were testing tires. At the time I was campaigning to put a submarine strap in the driver's seat of all the cars, but nobody wanted them. They thought it would squeeze their balls. But I had experienced getting in wrecks, and afterward I couldn't swallow, couldn't eat, spit up blood, 'cause what would happen, the belt would come up and push your guts up through your mouth. So to prevent that, I wanted to put that submarine belt in the car. And what finally convinced them to do it was the death of Billy Wade.

"He was running this tire test, and he blew a tire and hit the wall head-on. I went down to get him. He was a little guy, and he had slipped through the lap belt, and his guts were hanging out of his mouth. Boy, when Bud Moore walked up on that, it liked to ruin him. But after that, they started putting in those submarine belts.

"After so many people died or got hurt, Fred Lorenzen quit. He didn't want to get married while he was still driving. He had enough money, and he was working the stock market. He was getting so he was solvent as hell, so he decided to get the hell out before he got hurt."

16

THE DEATH OF
FIREBALL ROBERTS

M AX MUHLMANN COVERED STOCK
car racing for the *Charlotte News* from 1957
until 1964, when his close friend, Fireball
Roberts, was killed in that fiery crash at
Charlotte. At the time, Muhlmann was working
with Roberts on his autobiography. They were
close, and when Roberts died, Muhlmann was
devastated, so much so that he left the worlds of
sportswriting and stock car racing, never to
return.

MAX MUHLMANN: "The only races I personally miss today from the old days are the Daytona
beach races. You should have seen the cars slide
out of turns toward the beach and kiss the water,
and the hundreds of yards of broadsliding they'd
do as they prepared to exit the beach and go back
up the road course. It was just spectacular. It was
hard to get a position to watch it, but if you
could, it was fabulous.

"Bill France was a master politician with a
great sense of timing. In the late fifties a lot of
the drivers thought France was too much of a
dictator. In fact, I wrote a column in the *Charlotte
News* in '59. Fulgencio Batista had just fled Cuba
and had actually taken up temporary residency in
Daytona Beach, and I wrote this column that
started out, 'Now there are two dictators in
Daytona Beach, Fulgencio Batista and Bill

France,' and I went on to say that it wasn't necessarily in the best interests of the drivers and fans, but that this was the way he wanted it. I don't remember the issues, but France got so mad he flew his airplane up to Charlotte and visited my editor and tried to get me fired. I was a close friend of Fireball Roberts, and I sent the clipping to Fireball, and he just loved it. He thought that was wonderful. He told me, 'Boy, you have it just perfect. That's exactly right. You have him covered.'

"Needless to say, I was not number one on Bill France's list for a while. Having said that, my company today does a lot of work with the NFL and the NBA, and you see how much they depend on public money to build their stadiums. Public money never built a single racetrack, much less Bill France's superspeedway of 1959, when it opened. At the time France built the Daytona track, I thought it was a mistake, but I didn't know much about the business side of racing, how hard it was to manage the crowds at the beach races, how limited the number of tickets you could sell. Looking back, building that track turned out to be the right thing to do.

"I didn't realize what a feat it was to pay for, to get it done politically and financially, but it was just an unbelievable facility. Darlington was the only speedway. Darlington didn't look anything like this. Daytona was two and a half miles compared to one and a half, and Darlington still looked smaller than its real length because it had one little tin-roof grandstand. Daytona was a stunner.

"My first reaction when I saw it was, 'It looks dangerous.' I thought people were going to get killed left and right. When Lee Petty flew off the track in '61, he flew out of the track, absolutely out. I said, 'Well, he's dead. That's all there is to it.' And Lee did hurt himself badly.

"Daytona was awesome in terms of the fearful fascination that it created. You almost hated yourself for going because you wanted to see what was going to happen to these drivers, the men you cared for and lived with. I think a lot of them were nervous about it too. It didn't bother guys like Curtis or Junior, but there were a lot of them who didn't know what to expect, and neither did the fans or the media.

"Over the years France became more and more of a benevolent dictator. Now I see what he did and what he had to put up with and how difficult it must have been. Some of the things he did by themselves maybe he shouldn't have done, but on balance, on which hopefully most of us are judged, clearly the man was a genius.

"Curtis Turner didn't have as much success with his racetrack in Charlotte. He opened Charlotte Motor Speedway in '61. For some reason Bruton Smith wanted in on the deal, and Bruton said he would start a track on the other side of town, and it made Curtis mad. Curtis felt competitive about Bruton. But Curtis was enough of a business-man and a politician to say, Maybe I can take in an old rival, if not an enemy, and maybe help myself. That was his attitude.

"And after he took Bruton in, Bruton became more and more involved. Bruton promoted a lot of the local races. He had to break up fights. He was always a tough guy, had been a paratrooper, and I imag-ine Bruton could have whipped any of these guys. When the con-struction workers threatened to strike over not getting paid, either Curtis or Bruton went out with a shotgun and threatened them to keep them working. Bruton certainly worked his way into a very important role, especially since Curtis was flying all over the country. Bruton was the more dedicated guy to the project. Curtis wanted it to happen very badly, but he had to fly off to make a timber deal or to race. Though it didn't start that way, they finally became pretty com-patible.

"In January of '64 Joe Weatherly died in a crash at Riverside, California. It was a real shock. He was the first big-name racer I can think of who got killed, although others did die. And it was the first time any of us realized that even the best guys could get killed that way they did in Formula 1 or Indy. You just didn't think they could die at this. Everybody wanted to know how it happened. Joe's head went out the window and hit the wall when the car crashed in turn six. It led to restraining nets in the windows.

"And around this time I was working with Fireball Roberts on a book. When he would race in the Charlotte area, he would come and stay in my apartment with me. Fireball was a thoughtful, intellectual guy. He had that great nickname. He had been a baseball pitcher in college and apparently a pretty good one. He was the first racer who worked out with weights regularly. He was very thoughtful, and I enjoyed talking to him. Fireball thought through the politics of rac-ing. The number 22 black-and-gold Pontiacs Smokey Yunick turned out was one of the great images I had of those days and to anyone who saw them running out front ahead of everyone. It was a comedown to think of Fireball in the purple 22 Ford, but for him to go with a Ford product at the time was smart because that was one of the best rides. Ford had more money than anybody, and it was coincidental that he was in a Ford when he was killed at Charlotte in May of '64.

"He was concerned about getting good cars. He wanted to lead. He and Smokey Yunick had that great union, because they were both from Daytona Beach. Fireball got along with Smokey as well as anyone gets along with Smokey. Smokey had the clear feeling of, 'I'm the coach. I'm in charge.' Where a lot of chief mechanics worshiped the driver and did everything he wanted, Smokey's job was to turn out this ass-kicking machine and find a driver who was up to it, who would listen to him and do what he wanted. Smokey would make a few changes, but nothing like what the driver would want. But Smokey worked with Fireball better than any other driver who drove for Smokey, for sure.

"Fireball and I spent close to two seasons trying to develop his autobiography. My ability to spend money was pretty restricted, and whenever he'd come up to Charlotte, we'd get the tape recorder out again. He was interested in doing it, but there were aspects of his personal life that may have held him back. When he died I dropped the project. I didn't want to embarrass anybody.

"That day in Charlotte I was in the radio booth doing color commentary with Fonty Flock and a guy named Sammy Bland. We were on the front stretch side, and the crash happened on the backstretch. I could see cars spinning, and then a huge, *huge* plume of black smoke, clearly a gasoline fire.

"I always looked for Fireball's car first, 'cause we were actively writing the book and were close. I did a quick look, and immediately I couldn't see it. And I knew about where he was. I said, 'Ooooh boy, I'm afraid it's him.' And about that time Fonty leaned over and whispered, 'It's Fireball.'

"Both of us had that same eerie feeling. People have sent me photos of the crash. The car was upside down, and Ned Jarrett was pulling him out of the car, and you could see he looked charred.

"There was a long vigil at the hospital. They wouldn't let me in. Immediate family only. I thought about trying to find a nurse to help me get in, but I was getting reports that he was okay. His infection was what they worried about most. I ran into one of the kids who put him into the warm bath, and he told me he was washing off the gangrene, and Fireball said, 'Look at me. I'm the Jolly Green Giant.' I'd hear stories like that, and then he got this fever and went downhill, and then he died.

"Ralph Moody flew me down to the funeral in Daytona Beach, and I got emotional during the flight down. Ralph was very calming. You know how he can be, he and his wife Mitzy. I would visit the gravesite in Daytona. I wrote a lot about his death and funeral.

"I was very touched by his death. It was a big loss. It was the most shocking loss that racing had had up to that time. Losing Fireball Roberts would be like losing Dale Earnhardt now. Not that one life isn't as important as the next. It was a bad death, an ugly one, and a lot of changes came from it.

"About that time I had an offer from Carol Shelby and Ford in Los Angeles to be on his staff as the director of public relations for the Cobra sports car. I don't think I would have been interested if Fireball hadn't been killed. But after he died, I wanted to get away from stock car racing. I was just sick about it. It took away all the excitement and enthusiasm I had for it. I was just devastated and wanted to get away. But I had to have a job, and it was almost providential that this offer came at this time. We didn't know anyone west of Gastonia at the time. And after my wife surprised me by saying she would go way out West, I accepted and went to work for the Ford Motor Company. Later, when I got into sports marketing, my first big client was a hockey league. I spent three years trying to get an NBA franchise for Charlotte and six years working on an NFL franchise. Coming from a writing background, I never thought of getting into the business of sports, but the experience with Ford helped me tremendously. They taught me business. So I got my education after all."

17

NED AND JUNIOR

THE DEATHS OF THE COLORFUL Joe Weatherly and the beloved Fireball Roberts in 1964 cast a pall over the sport. So did the pullout of the Ford Motor Company from racing. As a result of the two deaths, some racers were reminded that they were not immortal after all. Freddie Lorenzen left racing, and so did two legendary racers, Ned Jarrett and Junior Johnson, who had both earned fifty Grand National victories.

Ned, a close friend of Fireball Roberts, had helped pull the driver from his burning car. Roberts had pleaded with Jarrett, "Help me, Ned. I'm burning up."

Johnson, who had won everything there was to win but a championship, quit because he had run out of challenges. After Jarrett quit, he went into broadcasting, where his popularity has grown. Johnson became a very successful car owner. Among those who drove for him were LeeRoy Yarbrough, Bobby Allison, and Neil Bonnett, three star-crossed drivers. Bob Latford, who once worked for Johnson, recalls them all.

BOB LATFORD: "Junior Johnson never won a championship as a driver, but he ran hard, won fifty races, the same as Ned Jarrett. Ned and Junior quit at the same time. The fall race at Rockingham in '66 was the last race for both of

145

them. They both finished in the top five in that race. Fred Lorenzen won it, Ned finished third, and Junior fifth.

"When they retired both were very young. Ned was thirty-four and Junior thirty-five when they quit driving. They quit in part because Ford got out of it, and partially because Joe and Fireball were killed, and Nelson Stacy got hurt at Atlanta and retired.

"Junior said he started thinking about quitting when he won Charlotte the second time, 'cause he said it didn't mean that much to him. He had done it before. And by '65, Junior had won Darlington, Atlanta, Daytona, Charlotte, Martinsville, Wilkesboro. He was repeating something he had already done. The challenge wasn't there. He felt the challenge was in building and preparing cars, so he got out of his car and started getting it ready for other drivers. Also, it was a chance to quit while he was on top. It's the difference between Babe Ruth and Lou Gehrig. Some drivers keep going way past when they should, and the fans forget when they did win and their careers are damaged. Others, like Junior and Ned, quit on top and maintain their reputation.

"Consider that Ned had two championships and fifty wins, and Junior had fifty wins, and neither of them won a half a million dollars in their entire driving careers! Since he quit driving, Junior has won another six championships and another 120 plus races, and at the time he quit in '95, he won more money than any owner in the history of auto racing. And again, it quit being fun. It became bottom-line, an activity he no longer enjoyed. Ned kept his hand in racing by broadcasting and has become even better known now than when he was a driver.

"In 1984 I went to work for Budweiser, and we were sponsoring Junior's cars. The first three years he had one of the first two-car operations with Darrell Waltrip and Neil Bonnett. Neil was a very nice man, just like Benny Parsons. He remembered names and was an excellent storyteller, was good at explaining things, and when he was driving for Junior, all I needed to do was make one phone call, and I'd have enough quotes to do three press releases.

"When I went to work for Junior, I discovered that he is much deeper than the surface that most people see, which is a guy who ran liquor and ran hard and well and who built cars. Junior's interested in different things. He's a strong believer in the almanac as a guide for planting his garden. He's curious about nature. He had an apple tree next to his house onto which he spliced five different types of apples.

Just out of curiosity. They had different blossoms at different times producing different kinds of apples. He believes in plowing his garden with a mule, not a tractor, though he has access to the finest machinery. He took good care of his hunting dogs. He has as many trophies for coon dogs as he does for racing.

"Junior was a philosopher. When I first joined him, he had a large stack of résumés of people wanting to go to work for him. I asked him, 'What characteristic do you look for most in somebody you're going to hire?' I figured he would want someone with an understanding of metalurgy or physics or mathematics.

"He answered very straightforwardly, 'What I look for is honesty. You give a man a try. Everyone makes a mistake. If he makes a mistake, you advise him how to correct it. If they deny the fact they made that mistake or if they don't learn, they're gone.' To Junior repeating a mistake is a serious error. To be successful in this sport, you have to be running at the finish.

"Junior started with Darel Dieringer driving, and in '68 he hired LeeRoy Yarbrough to drive for him. LeeRoy was an outstanding short track driver out of Jacksonville, Florida. He had run in Savannah, Valdosta, and Jacksonville, and had been very successful in the Firecracker 400 in July, won it a couple of times in a Mercury and a Ford. He had several lesser rides, and then he joined Junior in '68, and in '69 he had a phenomenal year with Ford, winning what would have been the Winston Million. He won Daytona, Charlotte, and Darlington—there was no Talladega that year. Unfortunately for LeeRoy, the prize didn't come in until 1985.

"LeeRoy was another one without a great deal of formal education but he could drive a race car. He knew how to make it go, and how to talk to Herb Nab, Turkey Minton and the crew. Ted Lowe, who had been with the team, had died of leukemia just before LeeRoy won the Daytona 500 in '69. I was in the pace car, and I drove LeeRoy around for a victory lap, and as we went down into the first turn he said, 'It's a shame Ted didn't live long enough to see this.' It was the first time Junior's car won Daytona since Junior himself won it in 1960. After LeeRoy and Junior parted in '70, he went and tried some Indy racing, and he got burned badly in a crash at Indianapolis, and he got hooked on the painkillers and then alcohol, and eventually it ended his career.

"When it first became obvious, LeeRoy'd show up in pretty bad shape and always have an excuse why he couldn't last in a car or why he couldn't make it go fast enough, when he had been one of the best. Frank Wiley, the bureau chief of Chrysler, said that LeeRoy in a Ford was one of the best at getting in and out of the pits during a stop.

"LeeRoy was spaced out on whatever he was taking, and his drinking became real bad, and he basically lost everything. His wife Gloria and his kids moved out. He was broke.

"LeeRoy was convinced he had money someplace, that he had an airplane somewhere that someone was keeping from him. He had had one once, but it had all been dissipated. After he tried to kill his mother, he ended up in a psychiatric unit. Junior and Ralph Seagraves went to visit him. They tried to find out if mental evaluation or chemotherapy or anything could resurrect him, because he had been such a racing talent. He was one of our own, and we wanted to do everything we could to take care of him. We had a charity softball game in Charlotte to raise money for that purpose. Unfortunately it was a pathetic situation.

"LeeRoy was one of those talents who enjoyed a short span of high success. Some people can't handle failure, and others can't handle success, and he was one of those.

"He died in a mental hospital, which was a real tragedy. He just quit living. It may have been like prisoners in Korea. Futility sets in, and you give up the desire to live.

"Bobby Allison led the last eight races of '71 while driving for Holman-Moody, and in 1972 he hooked up with Junior. Bobby led every race in '72 that year until the finale, thirty-eight consecutive events. Bobby had made up his mind he was leaving. He wanted part of the Coke sponsorship, and Junior felt that since he had the majority of the cost—salaries, engines, cars, tires—that the sponsorship money should go to the owner. Bobby had won his last two races at Charlotte and Rockingham. Junior called him in before the season-ending race in Texas, and they began screaming over the distribution of the money. Bobby left a good ride.

"Bobby was the only driver who drove for every factory there was, Plymouth and Dodge, Ford and Mercury, Chevy, Buick, Oldsmobile, American Motors Matador, and he won in all of them! And he won for a variety of owners.

"What has happened to Bobby is also a tragedy, beginning with a

freak accident at Pocono in 1988. [After the crash, Bobby Allison suffered brain damage. For a while he found it difficult to form sen-
tences.] Neil Bonnett and Bobby both got hurt the same year. Neil
had a concussion, which led to amnesia. Neil told me that he and
Bobby got together later that year, and he said, 'Bobby was trying to
think of what he was saying, and I was trying to remember what he
said.' Neil said, 'It made for some great conversations.'

"Eventually Neil came back, because it was what he loved. He had
had some bad crashes, but no one ever spun out not trying hard
enough. That's what I tell young drivers when they go out and loop
one. It was the thing Neil loved to do. He knew the risk, the potential for injury. It's a shame he crashed and was killed. But he was doing
what he loved most."

18

THE RELUCTANT CHAMPION

DAVID PEARSON HAS BEEN A country boy all his life. Like so many racing personalities who came from rural South Carolina, Pearson, who came from Spartanburg, left school as soon as he legally was able to work at what he loved most: building and racing cars. Pearson would have been content to race on the small tracks within several hours of his home, but his talent was so obvious that his admirers raised money by passing the hat for him to buy a car and go racing on NASCAR's Grand National circuit.

From his first superspeedway appearance, David Pearson felt at home. He never considered the danger. From the start, he felt he could compete with any driver. When Weatherly and Fireball Roberts were killed in 1964, he choked back the tears like everyone else. Pearson, in fact, was the last one to speak to Fireball before his crash.

In 1964 Pearson won eight races and finished third in the points. He was on his way. By the time he retired, David Pearson was a three-time racing champion and the winner of 105 races, second on the all-time list behind Richard Petty, with whom he battled for the checkered flag throughout his long career.

DAVID PEARSON: "I always lie about my age now, but I was really born on December 22, 1934.

151

I grew up in a little mill village, what they call Whitney, right out of Spartanburg. I still own the house that I lived in back then.

"My father worked in the cotton mill, the Whitney Cotton Mill, and my mother did too. It was a yarn mill, and they made cloth. Growing up, we didn't feel like we was poor. We always had something to eat. Naw, we didn't feel poor because everybody around us was poor. And we had more or less what we wanted. We didn't know no better, I guess. We didn't have anybody who was rich live next to us, and we just made do with whatever we had.

"I didn't go to high school. I passed to the tenth grade, and I quit, and the reason I quit, if you want to know the truth, was that I was wanting a car.

"I quit school one day and I started working in the cotton mill the next day. I worked the second shift, had to work at night. I took the cloth off the looms. I'd be in there working, and I'd look out the windows and saw all my buddies working at the little service station/hot dog joint we always hung around at, and I just couldn't stand it, seeing all of them out there. So I didn't last very long at the cotton mill. I had to quit and find something else.

"My older brother Bill—his name is James, but we call him Bill—ran a body shop. A lot of times after school he would make me help him, and I ended up painting cars. I didn't want to do that either. So I growed up doing that, working with him around the body shop. And when I quit the cotton mill, I went back to working with my brother.

"I was driving when I was ten years old. My brother always had some kind of car. Or I drove my dad's car. While they would go to work, I'd slip in the car and run it a little bit. In fact, our neighbor told my dad I was doing that, but he said, 'I know better than that because I have the keys in my pocket. Don't be telling things like that.' Dad told me, 'I know she's not telling me the truth.'

"At the time I agreed with him, but what he didn't know was I could push open the side vent with my hand, reach my arm in there and unlock the car, and I'd straight-wire it. I'd ride it around and always park it back in the same place.

"One time my brother had this little ole' stripdown. I was getting in it and driving it around. He thought I was doing it, 'cause the gas would get going, so one time he put a stick on the back housing of the rear end, and when I moved it, the stick fell off. When he came back, the back wheel was sitting on the stick. So he caught me. And he would get mad when he caught me.

"Every once in a while he'd let me drive it around the block. This one time I was spinning the wheels and he could hear me up on the next street, and he took off across the people's yard looking for me, and I seen him coming, and I stopped real quick and got out and ran.

"I always wanted to drive a race car, ever since I first seen one over here at the Spartanburg Fairgrounds. I climbed a tree to watch the race. Cotton Owens, Joe Eubanks, Banjo Matthews, and Fireball Roberts were running dirt tracks back then, and I always said when I got old enough, that's what I wanted to do. I wanted to do that for a living, because I had always been crazy about cars.

"Spartanburg at this time was a hub of stock car racing. Quite a few of the top racers had shops here: Rex White, Tom Pistone, Tiny Lund, Buck Baker, Bud Moore, Jack Smith. Before I started racing, I would go around to their shops. I'd go visit Rex. He was a real good short track driver, real tough. Rex came here with Crawford Clemens and Louis Clemens, his mechanics, and G. C. Spencer—they was all from Kentucky. They ran real strong. I'd go to his shop and Bud Moore's shop and look and try to find out something, just wishing I could be driving too. It was a thrill to me just to get to look at those places.

"When I was probably fifteen I was working with my brother in the body shop, and I decided I wanted to build me a car. My first car was a '35 Ford, an old car. I didn't know what to do to it. We chopped the fenders off of it. I knew to cut the flywheel down. I always heard that. And I shaved the heads down. I wasn't a mechanic, but I did all the work myself. I took the motor out, and I had it on the floor under the house. I took the heads off, did what I knew to do, had it shaved and put it back. Just whatever you would hear that would help you, that's what we'd do. We was me and my friends, who didn't know any more than I did. We were a bunch of boys getting together and doing that.

"The first time I ran was down at Woodruff on a little ole' quarter-mile track. I enjoyed it. It was a lot of fun. The first race I probably wasn't running fast enough to slide the car, to tell the truth. I ran real good. I know I finished third. Of course, a lot of the others was just like me too, learners.

"I kept on running, and I started going to different places around Spartanburg. I run Columbia on Thursday night, and Greenville-

Pickens on Saturday, and sometimes I'd go to Asheville on Sunday. I ran as many races as I could.

"I started running NASCAR at Greenville-Pickens, and in fact I won the championship at Greenville-Pickens in 1959. I won thirty out of forty-two races altogether. At that time I was making about a hundred and fifty dollars a week and driving a race car, and that's what I was wanting to do. That's more than I was making in the cotton mill. Of course, there were tough times too when I'd wreck or need a part. I'd have to wait until I worked a while at the body shop to pay for it. I'd work a week or two until I got enough money to buy it, and I'd go racing again. It wasn't all peaches and cream. It was hard going but I was happy running the little dirt tracks. Of course, I was winning a lot of races, but I was happy just because it was racing. I'd be working on my old car under a tree or the house back when I was running the short tracks, and they'd talk about running at Darlington and rubbing the guardrail, running 130 miles an hour, and I'd think, Them people are crazy. Man, I wouldn't do that.

"At the time I was working at a service station downtown, Rogers' Esso. A friend of mine, the late Ralph Sawyer, who was a policeman, got the idea of raising money for me to go racing Grand National. I really didn't want to go Grand National, 'cause I was happy doing what I was doing, but Ralph and Rogers got to talking. Ralph said, 'I think we ought to start a fan club and raise the money to buy a car from Jack Smith.' I said, 'No, I can't do that.' They said, 'Why not?' They had gotten fans to buy Cotton Owens his Thunderbird. I said, 'No, I can't do that.' They said, 'Oh, yeah, we're going to do it,' and at that time we had a mobile radio advertising the service station. Old crazy Ralph got on the radio, and he said, 'We're going to start a fan club for David Pearson, and we're going to raise some money and go to Daytona in February.' Ralph rode a motorcycle on the police force, and wherever he'd ride, he'd collect money. When he brought that money to me, I was forced to buy that car. I'd have given the money back, but I didn't know who to return it to. 'Cause he was getting nickels, quarters, anything, whatever it took. But I couldn't give it back, because I didn't know who to give it to so I had to go ahead and buy the car. It wasn't near enough, so I had to borrow the rest of it from my dad. So I bought that '59 Chevrolet and went to Daytona in 1960.

"So if it hadn't been for Ralph, I probably never would have gotten into Grand National racing, if you want to know the truth. Like I say, I was happy running the short tracks and making money. But the way it turned out, it turned out all right.

"Running in my first Daytona 500 was a lot different from running a quarter-miler on dirt. I was used to throwing my arm out the window and waving to the guys behind me when there was a wreck, and I never will forget, there was a wreck in the 500, and I did that, and the wind blowed my arm back against the quarter panel, and I felt like I broke my arm! That was the first and last time I did that.

"Daytona was big, but it didn't bother me. Uh-uh. From the first, I always said that I could do it if anybody else could. I always said, 'The car doesn't know who's driving it. It doesn't know whether it's me or Fireball Roberts or Cotton Owens.' So I just always said, 'If that guy could do it, I could do it.' I was just determined that I was going to do it.

"I never did think about danger. Never did. It never did enter my mind about that part of it. If you get to thinking about something like that, that it's dangerous, you're not going to run as good as you can, you ain't gonna have a hundred percent in it. If you're scared, afraid something is going to happen to you, before you know it someone is going to outrun you.

"So when they dropped the flag at that first 500, I just took off and run. I finished, but I had trouble. The distributor went bad. Lost quite a few laps changing the distributor. I bought the car from Bud Moore here in Spartanburg. We put another distributor in. He just listened to it and set the timing. He didn't put the timing light on it. I got it cranked up and ran some more, finished way back. I lost quite a few laps changing that distributor.

"I ran in the very first World 600 in Charlotte. At that time they had 125-mile qualifying races, and Junior Johnson drove my car in the 125-miler and finished third, so I started third in the 600 with that car, and as soon as they throwed the green flag, I cut across the grass, a dog leg, and took the lead during the first lap. Fireball retook it before the start/finish line.

"There were a lot of cars, and the track tore up. Pieces of asphalt busted gas tanks and radiators. We had sprain wire up on the hood to keep the asphalt from coming in and busting the windshield, just like on the dirt tracks. We put it on before the race, because we knew the track was tearing up. It was so rough the frame of my car broke right over the rear axle-housing and the whole back end was hanging down. Still, I managed to finish tenth.

"In '61 I bought a '59 Chevrolet from Jack Smith, which Bud Moore maintained in his shop. I was working on it, getting it ready to run at Charlotte, when Bud Moore, Joe Littlejohn, and Cotton Owens went to see Ray Fox about letting me drive for him. Ray didn't have a driver for his car, so they talked to him, told him he ought to give me a chance at it.

"When I got the phone call, Ray wanted to know if I wanted to run his car. I knew it was a factory car, that his car was always fast and run good, that he won races, and it just tickled me to death. I throwed everything down right then, and said, 'Yeah, I'm ready to go.'

"I went to Charlotte and the first time I practiced in that Pontiac car. Ray asked me, 'How does it feel?' I said, 'It felt good to me.' He said, 'Is it tight or is it loose?' I said, 'I can't tell you. To be honest with you, I ain't ever run this fast before in my life.'

"And I led about four hundred miles of the 600. With two laps to go a tire went flat. There were a lot of tires blowed that day. I blowed a bunch of them. At the time I was seven laps ahead, which I didn't know then. See, we didn't have radios. All Ray and them was doing was giving me the times by holding up a board. I blew the rear tire going down the backstretch, so when I come off the fourth turn, I saw them waving the white flag, so I just went ahead. I thought, I haven't but one lap to go. I'll still finish pretty good. In fact, Fireball passed me two or three times while I was making the two laps with the flat tire, and I thought maybe he had won, but when I came off four and saw the guy waving the checkered flag for me, I thought, I'm still leading this race, and when I went under that was the biggest thrill I ever had in my life right there, just knowing that this little ole' boy from Whitney Mill village had come to Charlotte and won the World 600.

"And when the press came, I didn't know what to say. I remember them asking me about the pit crew, and I said, 'I don't even know their names.' All I knew was Ray Fox.

"We went to the Firecracker 250 in Daytona. Fireball was leading the race and had problems. He got I don't know how many laps down, and when he came back out, he was flying, and I drafted with him, stayed with him, which helped me win the race. I passed Freddie

Lorenzen with just a few laps to go.

"And in September I beat Junior to win the Atlanta race. I didn't really know him. I just knowed his name. Because see, I never did go to the big tracks.

"To that time nobody had won Charlotte, Daytona, and Atlanta in one year. Like I said, whoever I was running with, Junior or Fireball or anybody, I always felt if they could do it, I could do it.

"In '62 I drove a race or two for Julie Petty, Lee's brother, and then I left Ray Fox and went to drive for Cotton Owens because Ray didn't run but a few races, just the big ones. But Cotton, he made a deal with Chrysler to run all of them, and he was right here at home in Spartanburg, so he asked me, and I figured I'd run more races, so I got with him.

"The problem was that Chrysler was just getting into racing. I was driving a Dodge Coronet, and here was a car that had never been in racing, and we had a lot of engine problems, and of course, we were just learning. So it was a learning process not only for us but for Chrysler, 'cause we had to figure out what made it work, and the first couple of years was real bad. We didn't finish very many races.

"Joe Weatherly won the driving championship in '62 and '63. I'd see Joe every once in a while at Bud Moore's. I didn't spend much time with him. I do know he was really superstitious. Course, people say I am too. I tell them, 'I'm not superstitious. I just don't want to take no chances.' Yeah, the neighbors across the street have a dadgam old black cat, and a lot of times at night I come in one way and the cat runs across the front of me, and I have to stop, back up and go around the block the other way and come back in again. So it doesn't cost me but a little bit of time. Who knows? There might be something to it. I say, I just don't want to take no chances.

"Joe was killed at Riverside in '64. I'm sure everybody missed him, but I didn't know Joe that well. Still, it hurts. It hurts any time a driver gets hurt or killed. You don't want to see it. But when you're driving and there's a wreck, your first reaction is, 'I'm glad he went out. That's one more car I don't have to worry about.' Of course, if he is hurt, you feel bad afterward.

"Not too long after that Fireball was killed at Charlotte. I was in the race. In fact, I might have been the last one to talk to him, cause I was talking to him right before we got in our cars to start the race.

I started in the back, and the last thing he said to me was, 'Cuz, be careful. This is a long day. You have plenty of time.'

"I was the next car behind Fireball when it happened. But I got through. Me and Fireball got pretty close. We got to where we hung out together a little bit. He enjoyed getting out and partying a little bit, talking to people. He wasn't the type to sit by hisself. I really enjoyed him. He was kind of my hero.

"Fireball run hard. He led a lot of races, sat on poles. He ran for Smokey Yunick, and Smokey was always experimenting, always seemed to have like fifty horsepower more than anybody else. His cars didn't last as good as some of the other cars, but when he was running, Fireball would fly.

"After Fireball crashed, I didn't go visit him in the hospital. I didn't want to see him that way. When he died, that hurt everybody, 'cause he was real popular, number one in my book.

"In '64 I won eight races and finished third in the points to Richard [Petty] and Ned Jarrett. We finally had that Dodge going, but then in '65 Chrysler boycotted because NASCAR wouldn't run the hemi. Chrysler put Richard and me into drag racing. My job more or less was to follow Fred Lorenzen and the Fords around. Fred and I would have match races. The idea was for the Dodge to beat the Fords, which we did, because we had so much more horsepower than they did. We could beat them pretty easy.

"I also ran some USAC races with Ray Nichels. I ran good. I blowed up a lot too.

"I'd look at the NASCAR results in the paper Monday morning, and I'd say to myself, 'Gee, I wish I was there,' because there wasn't nobody there running you had to worry about. Every week I'd look in the paper and I'd say to myself, I could have won that.

"In '66, NASCAR let us run the hemis, and that year I won fifteen races and the driving championship. Then in April of '67 me and Cotton split up after ten races. We were fixing to run at Columbia. We had the car loaded, and the truck was outside the shop. Cotton was inside. The crew were there, and we said, 'We'll go get some ice.' So we left to get ice to fill up our coolers, Cotton came out, and when he saw we were gone, he thought, Them boys have run off and left me here with the truck to take it to the track by myself. He got mad. He said to himself, I ain't gonna go by myself, and he pulled the truck back inside the building.

"When we came back from getting ice, we looked and saw that the truck was gone, and we said, 'Cotton has already gone,' so we took off. And when we got to Columbia Speedway, Cotton wasn't there. The car wasn't there or nothing else. We said, 'Now where is he at?' And by the time we reached him at his home, it was too late. We were a hundred miles away.

"The next morning Cotton was raising sand when the boys came in, and he fired a couple of them. Still to this day, it wasn't their fault. It was his fault. Those boys wouldn't run off like that. So I walked in, and I said, 'Cotton, this ain't right. What are you going to do, fire everybody?' He said, 'Yeah, and if you don't like it, you can leave too.' So I left. That's the way it happened. It was his fault. Like I say, we just went and got ice. He oughta knowed we wouldn't have run off and left him.

"I didn't do nothing for a while until the ride come open at Holman-Moody. And then I went with them."

19

THE DEMISE OF DIRT

WHILE RACERS LIKE DAVID PEARson thrived from the start on the big asphalt tracks, there were other racers accustomed to short track, rock 'em-sock 'em, out-of-control mayhem dirt track racing who found their world changing much too quickly. Those in the sport long enough experienced not only the passing of some great racers, but also the demise of its dirt track origins. As the popularity of NASCAR grew, it made sense financially to remove the small tracks from the schedule, consign them to the less prestigious Sportsman circuit, and replace them with superspeedway dates. Darlington had proved so successful, followed by Daytona, which quickly became the premier racing event in America, close behind the Indianapolis 500, until finally it surpassed even that, followed by the opening of big tracks in Atlanta and Charlotte in 1961.

But with the huge crowds and bigger purses and the pricier ticket prices came a big-dollar cost of running a car on the track and maintaining it. Drivers like Little Bud Moore, Tiny Lund, Bobby Isaac, and many others no longer could afford to run in the big time. As Little Bud Moore experienced firsthand, they were forced to choose between running Grand National/ Winston Cup superspeedways on asphalt fulltime or continuing what they did best, driving

161

the smaller dirt ovals. As you will see, the danger inherent in racing never fazed Little Bud, but when the going got too tough financially, he chose to get out entirely, moments before the racing boom.

"LITTLE BUD" MOORE: "In the early sixties I teamed with a guy named Ronnie Hopkins out of Greenville, a very successful car builder. We had a very successful three years together in which we were pretty much the dominant Sportsman car and during that time I also got my taste of what's now Winston Cup racing because Humpy Wheeler was with Firestone tires, and he'd seen me run a lot down in the Carolinas, and he talked me into moving to Charlotte and becoming involved with Winston Cup cars.

"They don't run dirt any more. It's not feasible. It's a different era. But the dirt races were the greatest show that ever was. Dirt racing made racing what it was. It was so much more fun. You're going sideways at a hundred miles an hour with the wheel turned all the way to the right, with your foot on the throttle. That's no greater feeling. To a race driver, that's the ultimate. When you get cars on the damn rail on a superspeedway, you lose something. Nobody cares whether these cars go around a racetrack in eighteen seconds or thirteen seconds. They care about competition, and when you get everybody on a rail, what have you accomplished?

"I went to Darlington to race my first time on asphalt. I was driving one of the Pettys' older cars. Richard had run a lap or two in the car. It had one problem, he told me. The left front brake was dragging. This was in 1964, the darkest year in racing. We had had some deaths during that year—Joe Weatherly had died earlier at Riverside, and later in the year Fireball Roberts would be killed at Charlotte. Along about that time Jimmy Pardue got killed, and Billy Wade. We were going through a transition from dirt track racing, where I felt very comfortable, so comfortable I could sleep on the hood of my car between the heat race and the feature, to superspeedway racing, where I didn't have a clue. I was just beginning to try to get a foothold in this sport, and God, that was a tough era to come along. The guys in this sport were so tough, and the deaths probably weighed more heavily on me than most people trying to get into the business. I got to tell you, it affected me some. I wasn't getting a lot of encouragement. I'd been married young, and I had a daughter, and I loved my wife and daughter, and racing scared my wife to death. She didn't think very highly of it, even though that's how I made my living for a long time. These people, who had been my heroes, were dying, and it scared me. I got to admit at my age I was not as strong a person as Ned Jarrett was—Ned had pulled Fireball Roberts out of that car.

"I had an idea of what it was going to take to win on the super-speedways, but I didn't feel confidence 'cause racing on asphalt was so different, and because my operation was somewhat slack, the people on the pit crew were just helping out, filling in, and this was affecting me too though it didn't stop me from going racing. I was still pretty young, and Darlington was the first time I had ever been on asphalt. I had this vision that these people were all professionals, unlike some of the characters I had been around. Before the race I told myself, 'When they hang the green, we're not going to have the same type of situation we've had at some of these other events.'

"Oh man, was I wrong! They hung that green. I went down in the first corner with guys like Darel Dieringer, Fireball Roberts, Curtis Turner, Fred Lorenzen, Junior Johnson, all these people I had been looking up to, my heroes, and I could not believe what I was in the middle of, like a hornet's nest. They were to me just the toughest characters in the world.

"As this race progressed, I was doing pretty good, tell you the truth. I just had a problem with this brake grabbing. We never did get it fixed, and every time I'd go into the corner, I'd have to allow for it and cut the wheel back to the right. The first time it happened, something slapped me on the side of the face. I had forgotten to buckle my helmet. This helmet, by the way, had come from a Sears & Roebuck catalogue, and on the box it said, 'Fragile. Do Not Drop.' That always pissed me off. I wondered what would happen to my head. Finally one day Ned Jarrett saw my helmet and gave me one of his.

"But anyway, I finally slowed down under a caution and got my helmet buckled, and as the race kept going, we were in the top twelve cars. I had been a pretty experienced racer when I got there and we were going along pretty good, and there was a wreck on the back straightaway, and the guy in front of me, G. C. Spencer, one of the real hard-nosed old-timers, he popped the brakes, and I did too, and when I did, my car jerked to the left, and I slammed right into the back of Junior Johnson, who had been in the wreck. Junior ran in those paperweight Fords. They were made of paper. It pushed the back bumper of Junior's car, fuel tank and all, clean up to his behind. I hit so hard, the shoulder straps dug into me so bad, it turned all blue, and it knocked my glasses off. My head hit the windshield, and I'm sure the windshield popped off.

"Before the race I had spent the week in the Myrtle Beach hospital because I had a throttle hang up on me and I went end to end down through a swamp. My face hit the roll bar going down, and the car went through this black swampwater, and it just covered me. Big stumps ripped through the top of the car, and I knew I was hurt. When Cale Yarborough and Buddy Baker saw me crawling back through the woods and up to the racetrack, I was so black they thought I had been burned. I had hurt my neck so bad I couldn't move it, and then at Darlington, after I hit Junior, I discovered after that I could move my neck fine!

"I got out of my car, and Junior never said a word to me. We both headed for the hospital. I had been breaking myself up pretty regular, and I thought, God, this has got to stop. It took me a long time to learn there are times when you have to let off a car.

"Junior was always a hero to me. One time he told me, 'Never give the car up. Never.' In other words, no matter what's happening, drive that son of a bitch just like you're going to win the race.

"One night in Myrtle Beach, South Carolina, they were running these big block cars, and I had a little block Chevrolet, and the racetrack was real muddy. I was running about tenth, and I thought to myself, 'This is tough.' I was discouraged. It was a hundred-lap race, and the cars up front were flying. But then the track got a little drier, and what Junior told me kept coming to mind. 'Never give the car up.' I passed a car, and got to seventh, and as the track kept drying, I kept moving up, and with two laps to go, I was in third. I passed the third car, and I put the left front wheel in the infield going by the leader on the last lap, and I won that race. When the race was over, that car was so hot the motor wouldn't even cut off, the way the mud was throwed back into it. I can't remember fans getting off on a race more than that. And I did too. That taught me a lesson, thanks to Junior.

"The next year, 1965, Chrysler was boycotting racing. The promoters wanted a Chrysler product in the race, and so I got hooked up with a guy who owned a Plymouth, and again I ran very well. I sat on a pole and made a lot of seconds, thirds, and fourths. We had led some races, seemed to have them won, but you could not beat the Holman-Moody factory Fords. They had a field of drivers like Junior Johnson, Dick Hutcherson, and Ned Jarrett, to name a few. And one of those guys would get you in the end, even when you thought you had them beat.

"One night in Greenville, I was leading with twenty laps to go when I broke a right front spindle and went flying through the air. Our equipment was running out, and keep in mind, the Ford drivers were very good racers. These people were the best there were. Dick Hutcherson came from Iowa, and before he came south he was a heck of a dirt track racer.

"Ralph Moody was the Moody from Holman-Moody. I'll tell you what kind of guy he was. We were running with a Plymouth. As I said, Chrysler was boycotting that year, and I was the only Plymouth in the race, the only competition the Fords had, and while I was warming up, I flipped the car, and things looked tough. Ralph Moody ordered the back glass taken out of Cale Yarborough's car because he wasn't running for the points, wasn't in the race. Moody's car was in the points lead with Dick Hutcherson and Ned Jarrett, and even though Ralph knew I was their strongest competition, he had the back glass taken out of Cale's car and had his own people fix my car, put in the glass, and taped it all in. Keep in mind his Fords had won every race. Nobody had beat them yet. But he was working just as hard to get me in that race as he would if I would have been a Ford factory car. I came back and set that car on the pole and almost won that race. And Ralph was needling them just as bad as if he had been on the other side.

"I still think of things Ralph has told me. Whenever I walk out to the end of my driveway, I always look down and pick up debris. Everybody's driveway has enough stuff in it to make a tire go flat. He taught me, 'When that car is sitting in the pits of a racetrack, I don't care how many people are working on it, if you're driving it, when you get out of it, look around and pick up stuff, because there will be popped rivets or something that could cost you your behind on that racetrack.' He said, 'Always look,' and to this day I do. I'll be jogging down the street and come to an intersection, and I'll see something and stop and go get it and put it out of the way.

"In 1965 I drove a Sportsman car for the Bondy Long racing operation, which Ned Jarrett drove for and won the Grand National championship. It was Bondy and his schoolmates. Bondy was an heir to the Du Pont fortune. Bondy's mother had married a Du Pont after his father got killed in a plane crash.

"They were all from Camden, South Carolina. Bondy was a car owner for Bobby Isaac, Ned Jarrett, Dick Hutcherson, and LeeRoy Yarbrough, who won the modified race at Daytona. They were racing people. Bondy had a big farm in the middle of Camden called Red Bank Farms. They also had racehorses, and one year they won a leg of the Triple Crown.

"I always thought they were the ultimate in southern living. They lived in this real richy section of Camden where all the streets were rock, and they had a lamp post, and the homes and quarters for the help, and they had beach homes out at Charleston, with big posts on the beds, and ringing the bell for dinnertime. I mean, it was something out of a storybook.

"I can remember when all these ladies, aristocrats, came down to the country—they had a country cabin—and they were characters. They partied too. They were well-known women in the fashion industry, and they were pretty sporty.

"Bondy and his group were very good racers. They were *real* crazy. I just caught the operation right toward the end when they were going out of business. We all fit perfect. I was about as crazy as they were. Here we were, real loose. Ned tried to keep away from us. He was trying to win a National championship. Sometimes we were out of hand!

"I can remember leaving Camden and going to Daytona for the Fourth of July races. Bondy went downtown and bought everyone an instrument to play so that when we got there we could form a band of rock and rollers. Bondy asked me if I could play, and I told him I couldn't play anything. He said, 'Okay, then you be the singer.' He bought me a tambourine and a microphone.

"We left with a whole truckload of band instruments, going to Daytona. I said, 'Bondy, we're gonna get throwed out of the motel the minute we get there.' He said, 'We'll be okay.' We also loaded up a fuel-burning Triumph motorcycle with straight pipes, a drag pipe.

"We started the bike up, started down the beach, and about a half block on the beach the police got us. We got back to the motel, cranked up the band, and thirty seconds later the motel called and said we had to get out. We were forever doing things like that. We were just really nuts.

"This was Bondy's operation, and he was a young guy, and these other guys were his schoolmates who didn't pay much attention to him. But when they came downtown to go racing, brother, they got the job done. They didn't fool around. They may have been crazy, but this was an era when *everyone* was some crazy.

"Look at Junior Johnson's bunch. The moonshine era was supposed to be over, but it went right on. Into the late sixties there was drugs. I can remember running Bondy's car at Darlington, and we had flower-power decals on it, and we were rednecks. Robert Yates's first assignment in Winston Cup racing was to be gasman for our car. We always laugh about this. We were redneck flower children, and we had a band, and we were playing up this whole thing, and we were into it.

"Unlike anybody else in racing, Bondy had Iron Butterfly albums, just in complete contrast to what everyone else was listening to, but everybody loved him. If I walk up to Junior Johnson, the first thing he'll ask me is, 'How's Bondy?'

"We were one big family, something I really miss. I can remember the body man getting loaded, and we couldn't find him for three or four days, and we'd have to go find him, and when he came back, he'd work for a week straight, day and night. I remember one of the truck drivers, a guy who went to school with Bondy, snorting sterno out of those cans. He'd go down the road and call back two or three hours later and ask where he was. How the hell were we supposed to know? It goes on and on. There's so much I can't even get into, but it was so much fun that I wouldn't trade any of it for just having gone through the experience.

"I just wish at this time I would have been more serious about it, would have looked at it from Ned's point of view and learned the business side of it more. Because Ned was extremely good at what he did, and he had a tough row to hoe. He had a tough group to keep under control, and keep in mind, he still won the National championship along with a lot of races while he was doing this. But the flip side was, these people were devoted to him when it came to race time. They prepared his cars. They went to the racetrack. They were very tough racing people. They were just a little bit on the crazy side.

"In 1967 Humpy Wheeler introduced me to the Firestone side of racing, introduced me to a gentleman, A. J. King, who had a Dodge out of Tennessee. King had another gentleman by the name of Jim Ruggles, who went on to develop the Buick V-6, became a very prominent engine builder. The problem was that Jim didn't have the time to build engines for my car. I guess you would say we were pretty successful. In our first superspeedway race, at Atlanta, we finished fifth, the best independent finish. The racetrack was so rough down the back straightaway that you'd have to take your hand and hold up your head, because your neck felt like it was going to break. Richard Petty won that one. We went straight to Rockingham and ran fifth or sixth, and Chrysler noticed and the next year gave us a factory car and a partial sponsorship. At the time I was the youngest factory driver. But there is a huge difference between finishing fifth and winning on the superspeedways. Everything has to jell. You had to punish your equipment more. I looked at my short track program, and we had it under control. Every piece fit the puzzle, and then we'd go race in Winston Cup superspeedways, and even though we ran fifth, every element was *not* in place, and that was the difference between fifth and first, and maybe I was a part of that. And that discouraged me a lot.

"If you want to say that's losing, go ahead. But I can remember a race at Martinsville, where I was fourth, and Bobby Isaac was fifth, and it was so hot and so tough, I had run 480 laps, and I kept looking in the mirror because it felt like I was going slower and slower. The car was sliding around, and right at that point with twenty laps to go, fourth place was not too bad. And I kept waiting on Isaac to gain on me, and just before I took the checkered flag, I saw I was actually gaining on him! I could have slowed down.

"So in some races we ran decent, but we blew a lot of engines, because Jim Ruggles didn't have the time to build ours. The one time Ruggles did build the engine was for the World 600 at Charlotte, and we backed off the truck running the best we ever ran. We missed winning the race by ten seconds. Buddy Baker was leading, and I was second, and the rains came.

"Buddy said to me, 'God, I hate that you didn't win the race.' And that's as close as I ever came to winning on a superspeedway. Keep in mind I didn't run those cars but a year and a half. Today it takes a lot longer to accomplish what we did.

"But back then I was running Grand National against the same people I had been running on the dirt tracks three, four nights a week, Cale Yarborough, Buddy Baker, Bobby Allison, and Donnie Allison, the new era of drivers, and so that made it somewhat easier. I didn't feel out of place. This was a tough set too.

"Race drivers never have been a close breed with each other. We've all had people who were good friends killed. Isaac and Pearson were close, but they were the only ones. I hung around with Buddy Baker a lot. We were close friends. When Buddy won the World 600, and I blew it, he sold me his home and his wife Coleen's Mustang cause he won a new Dodge and didn't need the Mustang any more. Sold it at a hell of a price. I was living down the street from him in a little apartment. He lived up on the hill. He built a new home, and sold me his old one. We were close, and Buddy was not the kind of person to get close to a lot of people. Buddy was a very competitive person. He and Cale were about as tough as they come on superspeedways.

"Buddy was a big, strapping guy. Ray Fox's son used to run track, and Buddy would tell him, 'Go for it.' We'd be at a hotel somewhere, and the boy would start running, and Buddy would just blow by him. I had the opportunity to see Buddy in some fisticuffs, and he didn't have a bit of trouble defending himself. He could take the offensive pretty quick, so I was always very careful what I said to him. He wasn't the type of person to take a lot of kidding. He took things pretty serious.

"Cale was one of the toughest characters I've ever seen. I don't think he had the God-given talent of a Bobby Isaac. But the only thing Isaac and myself could do was drive a race car. Cale could do anything. He could wrassle, play football, play softball. He excelled in all of them. He also was a very good race car driver, and in a very short period of time developed himself into one of the all-time great racers.

"Cale could endure anything, racing with broken steering or kicking the flames under his feet. I've seen his face blistered, his feet blistered. They just don't come tougher than that. Until the day he retired, Cale was as tough as Dale Earnhardt, and that's saying something.

"And Bobby Allison was tough. Bobby and I never got along very well, though we became close years later. I always admired his driving ability. When Bobby and his brother Donnie first came here, they were asphalt racers, and we were all dirt racers. First time they came, they had these late model modified cars, caught us on an asphalt track and blew us all away. The next race was on a half-mile dirt, and they had the same thing done to them that they did to us.

"Bobby was another guy where racing was everything. You got to remember that these people worked day and night, day and night. It's all they did. Dale Earnhardt had enough respect for Bobby that he didn't fool with him. It's them odds. Bobby and the Pettys had one of the classic feuds. Richard told me that one time Bobby knocked his car off the trailer in the pits!

"Richard is a special type person. He is very intelligent, and he's a giving person. What other person would sit and sign autographs like he does? At his picnics I've watched him sign from sunup to sundown two lines going down the highway as far as you could see. But the Pettys are competitive people. They are not Goody Two-shoes. They are racers. That's why his feud with Bobby Allison was so intense. I watched one race where with ten laps to go, Richard put left side tires on the right side of his car in a late pit stop in Columbia, to beat Bobby Allison. On that night he outfoxed him. With ten laps to go Richard knew the left side tires would hold up that long and they were softer, and he threw them on there, and that was the difference.

"I was still breaking bones, which finally I learned to stop doing. At Darlington one year I had a cast on my leg, and it was painted red with Firestone decals all over it. That goes to show that the sponsorship era was coming.

"And unfortunately for me, at that time Firestone was leaving racing. Back in those days there were more drivers than there were cars, and so there were four or five people in line for every deal, and if you got a deal, all you had to do was screw up once or twice, and somebody else got it. The factory philosophy was, 'If the damn front tire fell off two weeks in a row, change the driver.' This was something the driver couldn't control at all. These factories were very, very demanding, and both tire companies were a big part of racing then. I was fortunate to do a lot of testing for Firestone along with David Pearson on short tracks and Buddy Baker on the big speedways.

"The problem Firestone had was that there was a clause in the contract that even though you had a Firestone contract, if you didn't think the tire was safe, you didn't have to run it, and if the Goodyears were a split second quicker and Ford demanded you run on Goodyears, you had to do it. There would be nothing wrong with the Firestone tire, but if Richard Petty was running Goodyears, then the clause allowed you to run Goodyears too.

"Finally, the Firestone CEOs sat around a big table in Akron, Ohio, and they said, 'Why did Cale Yarborough win the race in Daytona on Goodyears when we have him under a Firestone contract? The hell with this. We spent a quarter of a million dollars to go to Daytona to test, and we come up with a good tire, and our guy wins the race, and he's not even on our tire.'

"And so Firestone pulled out of racing. Buddy Baker and I were the last two cars from Firestone.

"And the problem I had was that to be a racer, you had to give up almost everything else in your life. Racing was your whole life. It was *everything*. It consumed all of your time. You ate it, breathed it, slept it, everything. And that was tough for me, because I'm an old rock and roller. I liked music and the beach. I grew up on the beach. When I first started, I used to race cars on the weekend and go to the beach and drink beer on the beach during the week. I'd work all night on the car. It was a commitment you had to make. It was your life, what you had to do. And when the superspeedway era came in, I had to make a choice. I was making more money winning short track races on dirt than showing up at Daytona, running 200 miles an hour and blowing an engine or backing the car into the wall. I had to decide whether I wanted to jeopardize my short track program for the superspeedways. I didn't want to do that, but then Firestone came along, and I signed on with them, made a good living, but when Firestone went away, my desire to race full-time was over. Right at the end of the sixties. I knew I didn't want to do it any more, and I got out.

"People say to me all the time, 'Little Bud, you made a big mistake when you didn't go forward in racing,' and maybe I did, but I felt I had to do it, and I'm not sorry I did."

20

A SMALL BAND OF GYPSIES

IN THE LATE SIXTIES, STOCK CAR racing was still a small clique of devoted drivers, mechanics, and friends. The prize money was still small, and those in it ran because it was in their blood. Bob Latford, who worked PR for the Daytona Speedway, went on a northern circuit when one night he helped a young Bobby Allison repair his engine and win the first of his eighty-five Winston Cup victories. Latford ate and slept with Bobby, Tiny Lund, and Elmo Langley, and the others, and he saw the camaraderie as drivers and mechanics loaned one another parts and equipment as needed.

By the early seventies, sponsors had entered the sport, paying big money to advertise on the cars. With that money came an obligation on the part of drivers to represent the sponsor at meetings and shows. From then on it wasn't enough to be a great driver. You had to be a PR man as well. The days of the scraggly, roughneck race driver were coming to an end.

BOB LATFORD: "We used to leave Daytona after the July race and run a series of races up North out of the Southeast heat. We'd go to Old Bridge, New Jersey; Islip, Long Island; Bridgehampton, Long Island; Oxford, Maine; Fonda, New York; and the Lincoln Speedway in Pennsylvania.

"In July of '66 we had run Bridgehampton. Bobby Allison had an independent little operation, and he blew up his little Chevelle there. The car was owned by J. D. Bracken, number 2, a little white-and-maroon Chevelle that was racing against the factory cars. Bobby had gone to a truck garage and bought a short-block 350 engine, and he needed someplace to work on it and rebuild the engine. Our next stop was Oxford, Maine, the first year we ran there, a little third-of-a-mile track, a beautiful facility seating 13,000 in the middle of scrub oak. I was up at the track there waiting for the tour to arrive when Bobby called and said he needed a garage to work in. I called the local Chevy dealer to see if Bobby and his crew could work there that night when they got in. He said, 'Sure. We don't need the place until we reopen in the morning.' Bobby, his brother Eddie, and the whole crew went over there. Bobby put me to work, and we built an engine that night, and he went out and sat on the pole and won the race, the first of his eighty-five Winston Cup victories. Bobby claims I was his crew chief for that one. It was a thrill.

"The next race was at Fonda, New York, a half-mile track alongside the Erie Canal that didn't have any guardrails. A little parallel road behind the backstretch ran right along the edge of the canal. I was driving the pace car that night, and J. T. Putney in a Chevrolet was leading the race, and as he was coming out of turn two, he left the track and went down that road and came right back up in the middle of the lead pack going into three. J. T. caused what seemed like a nineteen-car pileup.

"They threw the caution, and I pulled out with the pace car. As I started down the backstretch, I could read the '94' on top of Don Biederman's Chevrolet which was parked up against a light pole up in the air, and when I got there, I found the track was totally blocked. There was no room for me to lead the cars that had made it through the wreck, so I turned right at turn three to go around the outside of the track. I turned the headlights of my pace car on, and I saw tombstones. I was in the middle of the graveyard! I had to weave my way through the markers so the race cars didn't crash an oil pan or smash a radiator on a marker. We did that for two laps, until they could make a hole big enough to take the field through while they cleaned up the wreckage. Tiny Lund was one of the drivers put out of the race by the crash. When Putney came over to apologize, Tiny dropped him with one punch. Bobby Allison was in that wreck too. His car was short-ened by two and a half feet on the right side. He had to fix it, and he came back and won Islip the next week. After Islip, we all moved south again.

"We all traveled together. I remember Tiny and Elmo Langley were in a bar in Elkridge, Maryland. They had little teardrop-shaped, glass candles on the table, and the test was whether you could hold your hand over the top of the candle long enough to starve it for oxygen and make the flame go out. We all had burns on the palms of our hands, but we got it done.

"There was more camaraderie back then than we have today. People would lend other people gears or hubs or axles or whatever they need-ed, 'cause we were all in the same family, just a bunch of gypsies going up and down the highway, much more so than today with the high-buck rigs you see going now.

"One time at Watkins Glen, Junior had a bad radiator. At that time in the sixties we didn't have that many spare parts. The factory teams were used to just putting in a new one. This was the third or fourth race of the northern tour, and Junior had used up a couple, and they started looking for Stopleak, something you put in the radiator to seal the hole. The only person who had any was Wendell Scott, who didn't have a new radiator, so he used Stopleak all the time. Wendell was happy to lend it to Junior.

"Another time Dick Hutcherson's car got run into on the way to Watkins Glen. It was on a flatbed being towed when someone ran into it and messed it up, so Dick borrowed one of Junior's cars to run the race. I remember sitting down at the Glen Motor Court overlooking Seneca Falls, New York, and watching Junior's number 26 car being repainted into number 29.

"The teams don't loan each other anything today. They're more aloof. Back then we all ate in the same little greasy diners on the road between Hickory and Richmond, down by the Greenville-Pickens Speedway. We ran a race there, and afterward everyone was in that lit-tle diner getting a sandwich, getting ready to head back to Charlotte. Buddy Baker came in. He hadn't done well that night. He was still driving for his dad. We asked him, 'Buddy, are you going to have something to eat?' He said, 'No, Daddy won't let us eat unless we win.' He said it more in jest than in seriousness.

"We spent a lot of times at two o'clock in the morning driving to the next track. One time Richard Petty got out of the truck he usually drove in, climbed over into the pace car, and rode with me. Other times it would be Bobby or Donnie Allison, Tom Pistone or Buddy Baker. We all traveled together, going from Point A to Point B.

"The most we ever ran in one season was sixty-four races in 1969. A lot of those were one-day events. You came in, practiced, qualified, ran the race, and went on all in one day.

"The last time NASCAR ran a dirt race was in 1970 at the Raleigh Fairgrounds, a little half-mile track made of red Carolina clay. It was a hundred-miler. Richard Petty had to borrow a dirt car from Jabe Thomas, whom he had sold one of his old cars to, and they refurbished it and ran it in the race and won. It was the last time I can remember seeing people smiling. You could actually see their teeth during qualifying. They would come down and throw their car sideways on the first turn, and they'd get on it. At that time most of the guys came from dirt. You had a better feel for the car, because you always ran on the edge, much more so than asphalt, where the tendency is to keep everything in a straight line. But with dirt, dust was always a problem. At that time the pace cars were all convertibles. You had the top down, and the dust would settle during the evening into all the nooks and crannies. Most of the tracks used calcium chloride to keep it from being too dusty, and it would take you two weeks to get it out of the car.

"One time in Maryville, Tennessee, Bobby Isaac was leading in a K&K car. As the flagman, John Brunner, Jr., brought the checkered flag down, the rains opened up. By the time Isaac crossed the finish line, you couldn't even see the cars in turn four it was raining so hard. The top was down on my pace car, and all the dirt turned to mud before I could get the top up.

"Maryville was the track where Buddy Baker got hurt one night. They put him in the back of the ambulance, and as they pulled off, the back door of the ambulance opened up and here came Buddy rolling out on the gurney. He ended up sitting in front with the driver.

"Maryville was so steeply banked that the only way they could water it down was to take a fire truck on the apron and spray it. There were a lot of tracks like that back then. And most of the drivers were independents. The biggest races would have a whole contingent of factory cars, but the little races would only have one or two as the norm, Petty in a Chrysler, David Pearson or Bobby Isaac in a Ford, so there were a lot of races where basically two cars were running for the win, and everyone else was battling for third.

"Bobby was one of those drivers from the old school. He had very little formal education but he knew a lot about driving a race car. When he first started out he won a race at Columbia Speedway, and he went and hid in the infield because he was afraid people would want his autograph, and he didn't know how to sign his name. His wife, Patsy, later taught him how to read and write.

"Bobby Isaac was the kind of guy who couldn't get a ride now because all he could do was drive. He couldn't have gone to a national sales meeting and talked to customers. But he came up on dirt, and he won the driving championship in '71, and he set all kinds of records at Bonneville and Pikes Peak. He could drive a car, and he knew what made them work, and he could tell Harry Hyde what it needed. There were a lot of drivers like that. They could work on them and drive them, but they didn't want any part of the other aspects of it, the PR and the appearances, which now is a necessity in the sport."

21

LIFE WITH RICHARD

I F EVER THERE WAS A RACER WHO could drive a race car *and* represent a big company, that man was Richard Petty, who drove the Petty blue-and-red car for Petty Enterprises. He was handsome and always wore a smile, and he'd sign an autograph for anyone who asked and pose for anyone with a camera. He was the King.

On this family-oriented team, Richard had his younger brother Maurice as his engine builder and second cousin Dale Inman by his side. And Poppa Lee Petty was always there in the background for advice when needed.

Maurice Petty experienced the ups and downs of stock car racing during the stormy sixties. He was with Richard when they went drag racing in 1965 after NASCAR outlawed their car's hemi engine. He watched in horror when Richard ran off the road and killed a spectator drag racing in Georgia. After they were allowed to return, and with Chrysler firmly behind him, the 43 car had the best equipment and won a lot of races. In 1967, Richard Petty won twenty-seven races, including ten in a row during one incredible run. Richard's driver unionization try in 1969 was a failure.

When the Pettys won the STP sponsorship in 1972, it was the deal that set NASCAR's future course. Once Petty had STP's money, other teams had to go out and get their own financial backing, until today the name of the sponsor on the car is as well-known to the fans as the driver and owner. Maurice Petty saw the sport grow from its infancy to what it has become today.

Like David Pearson, Maurice Petty wonders whether he hurt himself by spending so much time under the car and not enough effort promoting himself to the public and the press. It rankles him that though his engines have won more races than any other in racing history, a glib, easy talker like Smokey Yunick becomes the center of attention wherever he goes while Maurice remains in the shadows. But Maurice, who is nothing if not realistic, realizes that like his dad, Lee, he has always been both shy and a workaholic, and that he spent all that time under the hoods of race cars because that was where he was supposed to be. And no, he's not famous like Smokey, but his hard work produced the wins, and so he can live with and be content with that.

MAURICE PETTY: "In '62 Fireball Roberts won the Daytona 500. He probably could have beat everybody by ten miles an hour, but Richard drafted and hung on, and to my knowledge to this day, that was the first time anybody noticed that the draft could be used, because if Fireball's car had run by itself, it would be ten miles an hour faster than anyone. Our theory was that when Fireball pit, we should pit, when he went out, we'd go out and follow Fireball and hope we could hang on to him so you could run second. It was a matter of running second, not winning the race. And that's what happened.

"Fireball was a good driver. He was big-time superstitious about thirteen and green and peanuts. For the longest time the racing world hated green. You didn't wear nothing green to the racetrack. You didn't associate yourself with green. And if someone came around the pits with peanuts, it was, 'Get the hell out of here. Get away from us.'

"In '62 we hired a guy named Jim Paschal to drive for us. He was a local guy from High Point, a lot like Lee, good, smart, and steady. There's racers who are winners and racers that are moneymakers, and Jim was a moneymaker, and he was a prince of a person, easygoing, a smooth racer.

"Richard was starting to win a lot that year. He won three races in a week. You didn't work on the cars the way you do now. You'd just change oil, beat the damn dents out, and make sure everything was fastened down good, and you'd go racing again. You didn't pull hubs and spindles and lugs apart after every race. There was no time. And they were short races, hundred-milers. They were not sophisticated race cars like they are now. Although at the time it was just as hard to win a race as it is now, it's different. You didn't have to put in as much effort and work and time, but still you put in as much time as anybody.

"Two people worked instead of twenty or thirty. A lot of times you worked till you dropped. Back then you fixed a piece that broke and waited for another piece to break. Today after a race every piece is tore off and replaced.

"Freddie Lorenzen began racing that year. It was funny. Before he got to drive with Ford, Lee was in the hospital, and Freddie called here wanting to ride. He was from up there in Chicago. I said to myself, Who the hell is Freddie Lorenzen? It was a chance of a lifetime to get someone like that to drive for you. But we said no. We didn't have the facilities or the extra car to go at it a hundred percent like he wanted to. We never did get together. Freddie was a smart driver, a thinking driver, and he ended up driving for the Ford factory team.

"The '64 season began badly, with the death of Joe Weatherly in January at Riverside. I didn't know him, because he was a lot older than I was. It was a sad time for everyone when he was killed. Weatherly was the type who never met a stranger. You could go and talk to him. Some of the drivers you stayed clear of, because they didn't seem to blend in like the others. Joe blended with everyone.

"We had been getting a little help from Chrysler with cars, sheet metal, and a few parts, but they didn't get serious about racing until '64, when they came in with the hemi engine. When I saw that motor for the first time, I thought to myself, I want to go watch it race. I want to race this thing. Let's see what it's going to do. It was a monster of a motor, compared to what we had always worked with. This was a full-fledged racing engine, a nice piece. Everything built for it was built for racing. Where in the past you had to scrape and make the other pieces work, this was already pretty well laid out there for you.

"And that year Richard won the Daytona 500, his first superspeedway win. In life you have certain things you remember as being great, and that was one of them, because Richard had won a bunch of short track races, but this was the first time he had a car that was competitive on a superspeedway, and therefore he proved he could get the job done.

"At Charlotte for the World 600, Jim Paschal won and Richard came in second, and our two cars earned $34,000. I had been building engines, and after that race I got the nod from Lee that because we had done so well I could buy me an air conditioner to go in my engine shop. It was great, the first air conditioner that was ever in a Petty Enterprises shop!

"But what ruined the day for everyone was the terrible crash and the fire that killed Fireball Roberts. All I can remember about it is the smoke coming on up. It was really a bad scene.

"Hey, to quote Mr. Lee Petty, 'Every hair on your head is counted, and when it's your day, it's your day.' If you're in this game, that's the only way you better be thinking about it. And it wasn't long after that that Jimmy Pardue died tire testing. We tested a lot of tires for Firestone and Goodyear, but tire testing is the same as going to the races: You never think anything is going to happen, and if it does, you always say, 'It'll happen to the other guy.' Just as you do driving up and down the highway in your car. You never think like that. You never let that come into play.

"At that time tire testing money was pretty good. They paid you to go test and paid you x amount of dollars for every lap you ran. The more you ran, the more dollars you made. That was part of making a living. We didn't do it just to help Firestone or Goodyear. It was because it was a good payday. And as a result everybody wanted to go tire testing. If you blowed the motor, the tire company paid for it. If you wrecked the car, they paid for the car. Other than when your driver lost his life, it was an all-win, no-lose situation. It was easier money than racing.

"In '65 NASCAR decided they didn't want us running the hemi. It was the same deal when we were disqualified for cutting across the infield at Charlotte to go into the pits. They are in control. They got the best ball game in town. As far as I'm concerned, they have the *only* ball game in town. If you want to play ball with them, you use their ball.

"But we had contracted with Chrysler for the year, and we had to go where they wanted us to go. That year we ran a Barracuda and went match racing all over the United States. And when we were on our own, we'd try to race every weekend somewhere. It's not that we wanted to go drag racing, it was a matter of knowing that it was just a matter of time before Chrysler went back to NASCAR. It was a matter of when and how.

"They had to appease Chrysler. They had to appease Ford, which couldn't compete with the hemi. It was the same old bullshit that goes on right now, only they do it every week now, where back then it was once a year. But I can't say they are wrong, because they're putting on some good shows. People keep coming. It's the best thing going.

"We might have had another dozen wins if we hadn't set out all of '65. One of the match races in '65 was at the Southern Dragway in Dallas, Georgia. You hate to have this happen, and I'm not passing the blame, but there were so many people there who came to watch Richard drive that they were stacked on top of each other. Here was a little old teeny fence, a wire fence, next to the road.

"Well, the race began, and our car got loose because a part broke on the steering linkage, and the car took off and hit that fence, and the people were stacked so deep they couldn't run and get away from it. They trampled each other, and it was an unfortunate thing. That was really a sad, sad situation for all of us. It was another one of them things. You hate it. You wished it would never have happened. You'd like to recall it back, but you have to go on.

"In '66, Ford withdrew from racing, retaliating for them letting Chrysler back in. That year Bobby Allison started in NASCAR, and when he first came in he was a pain in our side. Bobby was a good racer, and he won races. Here we are rolling along, running pretty good, and here comes somebody into your playground. Bobby was like a thorn in our side.

"There was one race in Islip, New York. We were lapping Bobby about the second time, and he wouldn't pull over, and we got a tire cut down, and he went on to win the race. Like I said, he was like a thorn in your side. But hell, you're going to protect your turf. After the race I guess I sort of got fined for fighting. Got suspended two or three weeks. I went after Bobby. But for some reason, Bobby and myself became good friends. He's one of my better competitor friends. Bobby is good people. It was the damn heat of battle.

"By '66, our real nemesis was David Pearson. Either Richard won or he did. We went round and round on that too. David was just smooth, a hard driver but smooth. If Richard and him were running, you could depend that if one was on the inside, they weren't going to take each other out. They were there to race each other, and whoever came out on top came out on top. Not like some of the other drivers, who would try to run into you, try to drive you out. If you're going to race side by side with somebody, you want to race someone like David.

"Then in '67 we won twenty-seven races. Ten in a row. Even then, the records didn't mean anything because there still was not that much money in racing. Don't get me wrong: if you win races, you win money, but we were not counting. And I don't say what I'm going to say lightly: we were out there doing a job, and the trophies and records didn't mean that much. It wasn't the numbers. It was the fact that you won.

"The self-satisfaction was getting the job done any time you went out to run. It was satisfying being there and being part of it, and as we came through racing in my life, a lot of people bring up things that happened, can remember wins, can recall a lot of things that happened, but I don't ever think of any of those things unless someone else brings it up first. It's like going to the office and sharpening ten pencils in one day. You had to do it, and so you did it.

"There are plenty of people who could have done what I did, and I'll be the first person to admit that. And I could not have accomplished what I accomplished had I not had good people working for me and under me. I hear 'I, I, I' so much, it about makes you sick. There ain't no one person, not Smokey Yunick or Robert Yates, or anybody, who's a one-man operation. It's a team.

"We had Dale Inman working with us. Dale is kin people, a second cousin or something. He helped as far back as when Lee was driving. He was good friends. He lived a short piece from our home. He would go and help out on Sundays, and then he went into the service [in the Korean War], and when he got out, he went to work for Western Electric, and then he went back to going to the races with us on the weekends. We'd been after him to go to work for us, and finally he did, and he's been around ever since.

"We had lots of good people, and I think without bragging it's a deal where you got to be smart enough to surround yourself with good people, to be able to pick the qualities out of the people you keep. Hell, we've had tons of people who worked for us. Some of them couldn't cut it, didn't fit in. They didn't stay around long. But anybody who was willing to give you a good day's work, you can train them to do it the way you want it done.

"I learned from Lee, and they learned from me. I wasn't a teacher or anything. I never put myself in the category that I could teach anybody anything. I could show you how to do it. But if you said to me, 'I want a job. Teach me,' man, that would scare me to damn death. But if you're willing to work, then I will show you. I ain't going to teach you nothing. You gotta learn. For me to get up in front of a crowd and say, 'I'm the teacher. This is the way it's going to be done,' noooo way, Jose.

"And so the year we were winning all those races, Ford was screaming. They wanted to know what we were doing and how we were doing it. Here's how: a good honest day's work and a very good driver. And we knew it was just a matter of time before Ford came up with something to even things out. Like football, basketball, and baseball teams that win championships; the next year they might not be shit. But our curve was good. If it went up, it stayed up. It might come down some, but it was not straight up and straight down. We took a long, good, smooth ride.

"Ford and David Pearson were able to win the driving championship in '68 because they threw a lot of Fords out there, a lot of drivers. They just kept throwing them out there, and we kept beating them. Sooner or later, numbers will get you. That's how they approached it.

"In '69 Richard attempted to form the drivers' association. It all stemmed from Talladega. At that time you couldn't run two or three laps when the tires would be all wore out. And it wasn't they were running too fast. They were running too fast for the tires. And Richard decided he wasn't going to run there.

Bobby Isaac was about the only driver who ran the race. I don't know what went on there, except maybe he needed a payday. But nobody held it against him or against Tiny.

"So Bill France ran a controlled race at Talladega. After so many laps, there was a caution, and everybody had to change tires.

"I had nothing to do with what Richard was doing. He felt he had to do it, but that hurt for a while. We didn't make points with NASCAR in that era. It made it harder on us when we went to the racetrack. The inspectors came down harder on us. We felt the aftershock. But that year Richard still came in second in the points. They didn't take anything away from us, except you knew it was coming down the ladder to the inspectors. They were a little more nitpicky about things.

"In the fall of '69 we were in Texas, and the word got around that Andy Granatelli wanted to meet with us. We went out to eat with him, and then on the way to Riverside in January of '70, we dickered back and forth about getting the STP sponsorship. On the way there Richard and I went through Chicago to the head office, and we went in and met with him. The only controversy that we argued about was that he would give us a $50,000 bonus if we would paint our car all red. Richard held firm he was not going to do that, that he was still going to have blue on it. Which is why you see the blue and red today.

"The way it worked, because of the Pure Oil Company's involvement in NASCAR, we could not display a gas additive sticker on the car, but we could an oil additive, and that's what it's always been to this day. And with the STP money, it was a new day for us. Before that, we never had a sponsor other than the factories. We had never had a big-time outside sponsor on the car. And what it did, it gave us money to hire more people, to do things to prepare the race car better. And we went on to win two hundred races and win seven championships.

"Let me tell you, I'm fifty-six now, and it all seems to have gone by in a flash. And looking back, I should have taken better advantage of the situation as I came through. My deal was that the harder you worked, the farther ahead you got. There were events I was invited to that I didn't go to because I stayed home and worked on the car. I missed out on a lot of things. And I should have done better PR. And yet, if I hadn't worked as I did, would we have done what we done? So it's damned if you do, and damned if you don't. Maybe I could have ended up more like Smokey Yunick. Whenever someone mentions Smokey, everyone falls all over themselves. Smokey was good. I like Smokey. He's a character. I love to be around when he's talking, but I don't see all the wins and championships in his column. Yet don't get me wrong, I'm not kicking, I'm just wondering how it might be if I had played the political game better. Even so, I thank the good Lord every day for what I had.

"I guess I had a certain amount of workaholic about me. I'd work and do my job and go back and eat and go to bed, and go back and do my job, where a lot of people did a lot of nighttime activity after the race. And one more thing, anytime I got a chance to take my wife and kids with me, they went, especially in the summertime. Very seldom did you see me without them. That was one thing I was really big on, and to this day I'm proud of it.

"Right now today, I got my three sons working on Richard's Dodge truck program. We build the motors here. Rich Bickle drives the truck, and my oldest son, Timmy, goes to all the races like what I used to. I was totally out of racing in '85, other than messing with my boys. I got away from it, and then Richard got this deal with Chrysler, and we had had such good luck with the Chrysler products, and I had worked on these type engines that he came and wanted to know if I would oversee that, and I told him, 'Yeah,' if the boys would do the work. So here I am back in it again. I was supposed to be retired. But I enjoy doing it. It's better than being retired."

22

MOMENTS GREAT AND NOT SO GOOD

AFTER RICHARD PETTY DOMINATED in 1967, David Pearson, driving for Holman-Moody, won the racing championship back-to-back in 1968 and 1969. But Pearson's racing luck ran out when Ford quit racing, and Holman-Moody left the racing scene soon after. Pearson, like most of the drivers, now had to struggle for work. He ran in only nineteen of the forty-eight races in 1970 and was the driver for Holman-Moody's last hurrah in 1971.

In 1972 Pearson was hired by the Wood Brothers, for whom he won six races driving a limited schedule. The next year was perhaps Pearson's most outstanding, as he won eleven of the eighteen races he entered, only falling out of the top five four times and earning more than $228,000.

In 1976, Pearson won perhaps the most famous race in the history of NASCAR, the Daytona 500, at the end of which Richard Petty and Pearson crashed right before the finish line. When Pearson was able to recover, and Petty could not, Pearson was flagged the winner. Then, as with Cotton Owens, in 1979 Pearson and the Wood Brothers had a falling-out, and for the remainder of his career, he struggled, battling a bad back until his retirement.

David Pearson's 105 Winston Cup victories rank him second on the all-time list to his nemesis Petty, and his fifty-five superspeedway victories mark his stardom. David Pearson may not have had much to say to the media, but he will always have an exalted spot in the history of NASCAR.

While he was racing, David Pearson fought the battle between profits and privacy. He watched as Richard Petty turned his success, a broad smile, and a ready handshake into a legacy that made him the most popular athlete in the history of American sports. At the time Pearson may have been Petty's equal on the track, but off it the quiet South Carolinian was too private to accommodate reporters and woo fans. Pearson was close to some of the other drivers: He made friends with Bobby Isaac when no one else could, and Tiny Lund and he were very close. But Pearson had dropped out of school at a young age and didn't trust himself verbally sparring with newspaper reporters, and so he shunned them.

While Petty hung on as a driver and was given a rousing multimillion-dollar send-off in 1992, when Pearson's time was up in 1986, no one said a word. David Pearson paid a steep price for his privacy.

It was his way. His hometown of Spartanburg at one time provided half the peach crop of the State of South Carolina, the leader in supplying fresh peaches to the nation. After Pearson earned enough money to buy the homestead on which he lives, he decided he would take advantage of the peach bounty, and he hired migrant workers to harvest the peaches growing on his many trees. But Pearson became upset with all the strange people walking about his property as they picked his fruit, and he decided that his privacy was more important than profits. He sent the workers on their way and cut down all his peach trees.

Pearson still lives in that house amid the sights of rural America. A large barn for storing bales of hay marks the entrance to his street. You can see cows down the road, but his property is being surrounded by evidence of growth as dots of new homes rise around him in the Carolinas of the nineties.

Today amid the new faces in racing we see on TV, David Pearson has become an invisible figure. On some level, he wishes it weren't so, but David Pearson is not the sort of man to look back and second-guess himself. He well knows that he is who he is and so there wasn't very much he could have done about it.

He did it his way, and he can live with that. I spent an afternoon interviewing David Pearson at his home. He was warm, and he seemed to enjoy talking about his life in racing. When we were done, he said, "You know, I really enjoyed that." He smiled quizzically and added, "Maybe I should have done it more."

DAVID PEARSON: "When I joined Holman-Moody in '67, they *were* Ford. They did all the factory work for them. I joined the team in mid-May at Darlington. I'd a won the race if I hadn't blowed a tire. I blew a tire and tore the whole right front fender off, so I had to pit. But I could have won the race.

"Then in '68 once again I was running in all the races. I won sixteen races, and won the racing championship again, and in '69 I won it a third time. In my whole career I only ran for the championship three times, and I won it all three years.

"I enjoyed running all the races. Back then, I would have raced for nothing, if somebody had just let me get into the car. Today drivers get too much money right up front, so they don't care if they run well or not. That's what's wrong with racing today. It ought to be where they kind of earn it. I guess I'm a little bit jealous. These drivers are out there getting half a million dollars, never winning a race. That ain't right. That's like these ballplayers getting millions of dollars to play ball. Ain't nobody worth that, I don't care who they are. If I owned a car today, I wouldn't pay a driver that. He'd have to earn it some way or another. I'd pay him, but it would have to be earned.

"Bobby Isaac finished second to me in the points race that year, and the next year in '70 he won it. He was a heck of a race car driver. He always wanted to win. Didn't matter where he was at or what he was in, he was hard to beat. And that just made me like him that much more. Bobby didn't have too many friends. Nobody could get too close to him. Even back when I was running short tracks when I first started, he would come and run. He'd always get out of the race car and walk over and be by himself, and if somebody'd go up to him, he'd walk away. He was real shy, or felt self-conscious, or something. I don't know, I'd just walk up to him and ask him questions, anything, to make him say something. I just *made* him talk to me. Bobby and I were real close. I feel like perhaps I was his best friend. We played golf together. He used to come to my home, and he'd fly to races with me. One day we flew down to Talladega together. He was driving in the race, and in the middle he pulled his car into the pits and quit. Just quit. He told me on the way back home, 'I just quit.' I said, 'What do you mean?' He said, 'I quit driving.' He was driving for Bud Moore. He said, 'I told them to get somebody else to drive.' That's all he ever said to me about it.

"Of course, Bobby was having trouble with his heart, and he knew it. Nobody else knew it. He said things to me that I didn't really think nothing about like, 'If anything happens to me, my car and my keys are here,' or 'I'm staying at a certain motel.' I didn't realize it, but he meant if he died. I thought he meant if he wrecked. But I didn't know he was having heart problems and wasn't letting anyone know it. Bobby had come around asking Dr. Jerry Punch questions like, 'How does it feel if you're fixing to have a heart attack?' So he knew there was something wrong with him.

"The day he died [August 14, 1977] he was running at Hickory, and when he got out of the car he was hurting. They say he had a heart attack.

"Tiny Lund was another good friend of mine. I really enjoyed Tiny. He was another one who always pulled jokes on you. I never will forget we were racing at Hickory one time, and he was in my way. I was about to lap him, and I kept bumping him, bumping him, and he would not get out of my way.

"Tiny threw that big old arm out the window, and he shook his fist at me. I said to myself, If I don't hit him now, he's going to think I'm scared of him. So the next corner I just went and laid into him, spun him out, and I went on and won the race.

"After the race Tiny came up to me. Somebody had given him a cherry pie, and he was eating a piece of that pie, and he said, 'I want to ask you something. Why did you hit me?' I said, 'You know exactly why I hit you. I don't have to tell you that. When you stuck that arm out the window and shook that fist at me, I said right then that you'd think I was scared of you if I didn't hit you.'

"When I told him that, he put his arm around me and said, 'You know, I ain't mad,' and *wham*, Tiny hit me in the face with that pie! He put it right up to my face, and I had that pie all over my face!

"Tiny laughed, and from then on we were perfect friends. How could you get mad at somebody who did something like that? Everybody around was laughing. Yeah, ole' Tiny was a good one. I enjoyed Tiny. I really did. He died in a crash at Talladega [August 17, 1975]. I was there. There was a big ole' pileup, and Tiny was sitting crossways to the track, and a car came and hit him in the door.

"In '70 I didn't run for the championship because Ford pulled out that year. I figured when Ford pulled out, quit racing, that Holman-Moody had enough equipment and engine parts to run a car two or three years if they wanted to. But when Ford quit, Holman-Moody just quit.

"We were in Ontario, California, that morning. The crew was changing the heads on the engine. A crew member dropped a head on his finger, cut his finger off. When we got back from lunch, they told us, 'Ford just pulled out of racing. Stop the test. Don't run no more.' And so we loaded up and came back home. That cut everything off, cut off my money, and I had to find another ride. I ran a few races for Ray Nichels, and then I went and drove for the Wood Brothers, which is what I wanted even when I was driving for Holman-Moody, if you want to know the truth, because I knowed it'd fly. I had run against that thing and behind it, and I just knew it knew how to run. I always said, 'I'd like to get in that car one time just to show everyone.'

"One time down at Daytona I drove their car just practicing, and that was the best-driving car I ever sat in. I told them, 'If I could get my car driving as good as you-all is driving, I'd win the race.' Of course, that tickled Leonard and them.

"Finally, I got my chance, and in my very first race driving for the Wood Brothers, I won the Rebel 400 at Darlington. That's another thing: People always told me how tough Darlington was. I never did think it was that though. I always said, 'If anyone was going to tame it, I was going to do it.'

"That year either Bobby Allison won, or Richard Petty or me. During this period Richard and I won a lot of races. We ran one and two a bunch of times.

"Richard and I always got along good. I always respected him, and he did me, I'm sure, from what everybody says. As far as I know, we never had a hard word as far as saying something about the other. I can't remember arguing about anything.

"On the track I trusted Richard. I didn't have to worry about him hitting me. He's never done anything to cause a wreck—of course he kind of halfway blamed me for what happened down in the

Firecracker 400 in Daytona in July of 1972. Before the race somebody told me that Richard had said that I was not going to outsmart him in this race like I had done two or three races before.

"In the Firecracker 400 I took the lead, and toward the end I did everything in the world to try to get that boy to pass me, and he would not do it. I backed off, and Richard would not pass me. He was waiting for that last-lap deal. He wanted to be able to blow past me at the end. I told the Wood Brothers that the only thing I knew to do to stop him was to pull to the inside and let him pass. So with about one lap left as I was going through the dogleg, I cut sharp to the left down to the inside, and then I backed off. I got out of his way and made him pass so I could have the last pass at the end. He didn't ever have to back out of the throttle, because I was down there that quick. But he complained that I cut back off the front of him, which I did. After the race he talked about how dangerous was what I done to him. But I was not in his way. There was *no way* I was in his way. The dangerous part was when he tried to keep me from passing him. It made him mad. I understand that.

"With one lap to go I came on through in three and four and tried to pass him, but he ran me all the way down on the apron. I still was able to beat him on the last lap, but it wasn't dangerous or nothing.

"Richard, unlike me, was always good to the media. Richard always liked that fame and stuff. In fact, one time I heard him come up to a guy and ask him if he wanted to interview him. Course, doing things like that paid off in the long run for him. Me, I went and hid from them, didn't like talking to them. See, I was like Bobby Isaac. I didn't have an education, and I was kind of shy myself. If anybody talked to me, they had to come up and talk. I would not put myself in a position to go first. But that's just the way I was. I was afraid I'd say the wrong thing, so I really didn't like to talk to them. I mean, I was friendly when I did talk to them, but they were not friends. If I seen a bunch of them over here talking, I'd go around them. I'd say to myself, I don't want to talk to them. And I know it hurt me in the long run. I know that. Not that I regret it. I've had a good life in racing. I can't complain. Sure can't.

"In '73 I won eleven of the eighteen races I entered. The Woods and I won seven superspeedway wins in '74, three more in '75, and in

'76 I won ten more, including perhaps the most famous race ever run, the Daytona 500, when Richard and I wrecked.

"That day Richard had me beat bad, really bad. I knew the only way I could pass him was to draft by him—if I had enough power to do that. Richard led the race, and I was right behind him going into the final lap. Going down the backstretch, I got me a running start and drafted by him. He had more power than I did, so going into three he just pulled down and started right back by me just like I wasn't there. I knew he had more power and was running better than I was. I also didn't know what he had in his mind but I suspected he was going to try to block me, to try to keep me from coming back by him. My guess was he was going to pull in front of me coming off four.

"Well, coming off four, I was all the way over by the wall. I wasn't but an inch from the wall. In fact I believe I even touched it a little bit, or thought I did. And here he came, trying to get in front of me to block me. But he wasn't all the way by me, and he hit my left front fender with his right rear, and when he did, it just spun him right around and me too. We tangled up and wrecked, but I managed to mash the clutch in and keep the engine running, which he didn't.

"While I was spinning around I was wondering who was going to win the race. There was so much smoke I couldn't tell where Richard was at. The Wood Brothers said I was hollering on the radio, 'Where's Richard? Where's Richard?' 'Cause if he got past the start/finish line, he won the race.

"After I stopped spinning, I backed up, turned, and went on. As I headed for the start/finish line I saw him on the grass and I kind of smiled as I passed him and went on by.

"That race was exciting, no doubt about it. But that year we won often. The combination of me and the Wood Brothers was a really good combination. I just don't believe you can find anybody smarter than Leonard Wood as far as doing fine-tuning. I'd talk to him. I'd say, 'It doesn't have quite enough power. You need to do this,' or I'd say, 'I wish I could have that,' and he would say, 'We could move the timing a half a degree,' and he'd do it, and we'd get better.

"We did things nobody was doing, like staggering the tires. Instead of putting wedges in the car, we'd use different amounts of air pressure in the tires. The Woods would measure the tires and not let anyone see what they were doing. If the car needed tightening up, they'd put a bigger tire on the left rear. If the car was loose, we'd put a bigger tire on the right rear. We'd switch the tires around. Nobody else was doing this. Like I say, the Wood Brothers are smart people. They know racing. All of them.

"Our association ended in '79 with an incident that happened during the Rebel 500 at Darlington. During the race somebody had throwed oil all over my windshield, and I could hardly see. In fact, I done rubbed the wall a time or two. It was coming down close, and when I pitted I wanted my windshield cleaned. I told Leonard, 'Be sure and clean the windshield.' But they were in such a hurry to get me in and out of the pits, they didn't.

"I went out again, and I couldn't hardly see. I *had* to have that windshield cleaned. The sun was getting late to where it was shining. I told them again, 'I *have* to have it cleaned. I can't see.'

"I came in to change tires, and they always tell me whether they're changing two or four so I know whether to stop close to the wall or stay away from the wall. But we were talking so much about cleaning the windshield that they didn't tell me.

"Darrell Waltrip was leading the race at the time, so I had to beat Darrell out of the pits. That was a must. They had to hurry up and do a quick pit stop to beat him out, because Darrell was pitting right there in front of me. And I was watching him.

I came in, and they changed the two right-side tires. Meanwhile, someone was leaning over and cleaning my windshield, and I couldn't see them taking the tires loose on the left side. Back then you could take the tires loose on the left side while someone else was changing the right. Once they came around, all they had to do was jack them up and take them off.

"When they dropped the jack on the right side, that was the signal to go. Only they didn't tell me they were going to change four tires. So when they dropped that jack, I took off to beat Darrell out of the pits.

"Of course, I didn't get very far. I got down to the end of pit road, and the left-side tires fell off.

"I didn't really know what had happened, if you want to know the truth. And I don't have no idea what happened after that. It might have been that I just got out right then. 'Cause we done lost the race anyway. I probably just undid my belts and jumped out and said the heck with it.

"It was just a mistake. But now everybody says that that was the reason we split up. But that's not really the reason. I had been with the Wood Brothers for so long that we had already got to where we'd argue, nag things back and forth at each other. No matter what it was, if one of us had a chance to get something on the other one, we'd nag him. And that was just because we had been together for so long. If we hadn't been picking at each other and the tires hadn't fallen off, I'd have stayed with them.

"I always regretted what happened between me and the Wood Brothers. We had an awfully good relationship, and neither one of us realized it. Both Leonard and me are a little bit hardheaded. That's exactly what it was, so we just decided the best thing was to split up.

"I didn't run much after that. Some owners talked to me about different things, but I was having back trouble all along. I ran here and there, every now and then. I didn't run regular or get me a job full-time though I won a race driving for Hoss Ellington. Two or three times they put me in traction in the hospital. I'd stay there for two or three days and get up and walk like nothing ever happened. And it would be good for a year or two, and all at once it would hit me again.

"In '88 I tried running for the Woods Brothers once again. They wanted me to run, and I was going to drive their car at Charlotte, and I run that day, and the next morning I couldn't hardly get out of bed my back was hurting so bad. I called them and told them I couldn't, that they might as well get somebody else 'cause there was no way I could run 500 miles. My back was killing me. It wouldn't have been fair to the Woods if I got out there and ran a hundred miles or two and came in and put someone else in the car. I said, 'That won't be right, so I'll just quit.' The reporters said, 'If you can't run here, you can't run nowhere else, can you?' I said, 'No, reckon not.' And it dawned on me what they were after. They wanted me to say I was retiring. But I wouldn't say it.

"Later they called me at home. I wasn't going to say it. I was just going to say I wasn't going to run. I wasn't going to say I retired. But they made me, and that was the hardest thing I ever done in my life, to say that I retired. Man, that puts tears in your eyes doing something like that, to have to say that. It's rough, I guarantee you, to say that. After doing it all your life.

"After I retired, I ran a Sportsman car. My son Larry drove it. My boy was running and winning. He won the championship a couple of years. I would get in the car a few times testing, run around the track.

"I now rent my shop to Buckshot Jones. He started racing last year, and my boys are running it. One of them is the crew chief and the other works over there. Buckshot is a young kid out of Georgia. This year was his first year, and he done real good. He won Milwaukee. We talk quite a bit. He's always asking for driving advice. I try to help him all I can. I always give them my advice. They don't take it all the time. I have to rag them a little bit. They listen, but they don't always do what I tell them."

"SUITCASE" JAKE ELDER

23

ONE GREAT CHASSIS MAN

J. C. "JAKE" ELDER BEGAN HIS racing career in 1963 as a welder with Petty Enterprises, and in 1965 he went to work for Holman-Moody. In just one year he proved to be such a genius for setting a car that by 1966 he had become crew chief for driver Dick Hutcherson. While at Holman-Moody, Elder worked and won races with Mario Andretti and a young Bobby Allison, and he helped David Pearson win driving championships in 1968 and 1969.

After he left Holman-Moody, Elder acquired the nickname "Suitcase" Jake because his fiery nature prompted him to jump from team to team. Among the drivers for whom he has served as crew chief are Darrell Waltrip, Dale Earnhardt, Terry Labonte, and Sterling Marlin.

JAKE ELDER: "I was born on November 22, 1936. I grew up in Statesville, North Carolina. Since I was a boy I was a farmer. I farmed for about twelve years. We were raising corn, potatoes, grain mostly for cattle. It was just a bunch of hard work, and I couldn't see it getting nowhere. So around 1960 I decided I would move on and do something else, and I became a welder. I went to work for a company out of Statesville called Kiwanic Technical building metal frames. After working there about four years, one day someone told me that Richard Petty was wanting a welder, so I just thought, I'll ride over and see what he has in mind. So sure 'nough, I went over there, and Richard hired me at $97 a week. That was big money back then.

"My job was to put roll bars in the cars. Back then, you didn't go to Mike Laughlin to build a chassis. You did it all by yourself. We got the sheet metal from Chrysler, and we built the cars from the ground up. The winter of '63 we must have built four or five cars, and that was a lot of cars then.

"What made Richard's cars better was him. It was *him*. 'Cause Richard could take an average car and win with it, where the rest of the guys couldn't. He was just that much better than anyone else at that time. He was as good as David Pearson. That's the way he drove. Richard was good back in them days.

"In '65 Chrysler pulled out of NASCAR because of the hemi. Richard didn't know what to do, and he had to lay off some people. I said, 'Hell, don't worry about me. I'll go to work for somebody else.' Richard went and ran drag cars. I didn't want anything to do with no drag cars. So I quit Richard and went to work for Holman-Moody. I was hired by John Holman and Ralph Moody.

"Sixty-five was the height of Holman-Moody. You wouldn't believe that place. They built everything there. They built fuel cells. They built race cars. They built everything you use on a race car, right there in that shop. They didn't go out and hire nothing to be done. They did it all right there.

"They built the motors, and it was just like an assembly line. If you wanted a motor, you went and picked it out.

"They hired me as a welder. I worked in the assembly shop in the back. We had to do all the suspension work, put the running gear on. Then when we wanted a motor, we'd go up to the big shop and say, 'We want so-and-so engine, number so-and-so,' and give the number of the engine they had built for our car. We'd put the motor in, and we'd go racing.

"I welded for about two years, and one day Ralph came back and said, 'I need a mechanic to go on the road.' And me and J. P. Burkelette took Dick Hutcherson's car, and I worked on his car a couple of years.

"Dick was a dirt track champ in Keokuk, Iowa. He ran IMCA up there. Ford wanted to bring him down from Keokuk and put him in NASCAR. Dick was an expert dirt track driver, and even when he went up against Bobby Isaac and Richard Petty, he ran real good.

"Hutch started off driving dirt, and he had to switch to asphalt. At first he wasn't so good. He had to learn.

"After a couple of years working with Dick, John Holman came up and said, 'I need you to work on Mario Andretti's car and take it to Daytona Beach. I want you to go down there and test it and work on the car during the race.'

"To get Mario ready for the '67 Daytona 500, we had to change five or six motors in about eight days. They weren't running. Mario at that time wasn't so bright about what was going on in NASCAR. John Holman figured he could pull something on Mario, so they did it for a while. Freddie Lorenzen and Dick Hutcherson were running high risers, which deliver a lot of horsepower, and Mario was running a medium riser. They figured that Mario was coming into NASCAR, that he had been used to racing lightweight cars, and they figured to give him an average car and see what he could do.

"In the preliminary races he didn't do too good. Mario came over to me one day, and he said, 'I want to tell you something. I got to looking at Fred's motor and Hutch's motor,' and he said, 'There is something different about them motors, and I can't figure out what it is. How 'bout you telling me what it is?'

"I said, 'I can't really tell you right now, but I'll tell you later.' He said, 'Nah, tell me now.' So I said, 'Mario, you all are running medium risers, and the rest of them is running high risers.' And he jumped about three feet off the damn floor. He said, 'I'm going to straighten out John Holman.' He didn't even stop at Ralph Moody's office. He said to Holman, 'I want to know what's going on?' John said, 'What do you mean?' Mario said, 'I'm running medium risers, and your other teams are running high risers.' Holman made like he hadn't known anything about it. Holman said, 'I'll get with you later.' After Mario left Holman's office he came over to me and said, 'Don't worry. I got it all handled.'

"Mario called Jacques Passano from the Ford Motor Company and told Jacques he needed a different motor. Jack said, 'You call John Holman and tell him to get you what you need to have.'

"They flew the motor from Charlotte to Daytona Beach, and we had to put that motor in Mario's car. At that time we were running 177 miles an hour, and everybody else was running 180. We were putting the new motor in, and we had to install a lot of different oil lines, different filters, a lot of work. We had a special set of headers we put in that car, got rid of the old stock manifold headers, which added more horsepower too.

"Hutch's car was parked right beside us, and while we were putting the motor in, Hutch came over and said, 'I'll bet you don't run 180 miles an hour.' I said, 'Might not. We're running Firestone tires,' which were two miles an hour slower than Goodyear.

"Mario went out, and goddamn, when he went down that backstretch you *knew* that motor had a lot of horsepower. Mario said, 'Don't tell me how fast I ran. I know I ran fast.'

"I said, 'Yeah, you ran fast.' He had run 180. Mario said, 'Let's shake them up. Put the Goodyears on there.' and he ran 181.5. We were the fastest.

"We ran Firestones, which we knew were a little slower, in the 500. Mario said, 'Don't worry about it. I'll make up the difference.' I said, 'Mario, you must know something I don't know. Five hundred miles is a long way.' And sure enough, Mario led 79 laps out of 200 that day, and he won that race. I had been jackman for Richard Petty one year when he won, but this was the first time I was involved as a regular chief mechanic.

"And after Daytona, I went with Mario on the USAC circuit, ran all them road courses, and when their season ended, I returned to Holman-Moody in October. I don't know what the deal was, but Freddie Lorenzen said, 'I want to take Bobby Allison and run.' Freddie had retired in April, and Bobby didn't have a ride. Bobby was a young guy, and he had been building and racing his own cars. Ralph Moody liked Bobby. Fred was like the team manager. He said to me, 'I'll take care of everything that has to be done. You just work on the car, and we'll go from there.' Sure enough, we ran Bobby Allison's car, and we won the last two races of the season at Rockingham and Weaverville. We beat out David Pearson at Rockingham and Richard Petty, who won twenty-seven races that year, at Weaverville. That year it was pretty hard to beat Richard with that hemi, let me tell you. At that time that hemi engine dominated. The rest of the teams were just a little short. We got caught with our britches down, know what I mean? It was, 'What's going on?' So Richard, he won a lot of races before the rest of the teams got caught up. Eventually Ford built a better motor, built better cars, cause they had the money to do what they wanted to do. Once we caught up, Richard lost his advantage.

"At the end of '67 Bobby went off and did his own deal, and I worked with David Pearson for the next few years. You never could figure David out, couldn't tell how hard he was running. I used to call him 'Sandbagger.' A sandbagger is a driver who won't show everything he has. David never would run hard until the time it came either to qualify, run for the pole, or run to win the race. And when that time came, that's when he put the hammer down and come on. You could never figure him out. He would not tell you. That's just the way he operated.

"David Pearson was a good race car driver. In fact, right now I'd put him up against anybody right this day if his back hadn't given out. His back is what put him out of racing. But I could never figure David out. He never got a scratch the whole time he raced. No sir. Never got hurt. Right now he still holds the record for winning on superspeedway tracks.

"We'd get mad at David at times, but he was the type of guy you couldn't stay mad at. He was always joking around. David won the driving championship three times with Holman-Moody. He was a good one.

"In 1970 Ford pulled out of racing, and that's when I quit Holman-Moody. Dick Hutcherson formed his own business and I figured I might as well go work for him. At that time I really didn't know what I wanted to do. Hutch was building race cars, and I worked for him for two years.

"I don't know why I was able to make a difference. I guess I was just a better mechanic than the others. Everyone used to say I was the best chassis man they ever saw. They never could figure out how I did it.

"I didn't keep no records. I kept a race book, but we didn't keep a lot of records like they do now. Hell, today they keep more records than I've ever seen in my life, a damn bookful. I never saw so many records.

"I had a *feel* of what was going to happen as the race went on. I could go outside and look up at the sky and tell you what the weather was going to do, and how we were going to run, and how it was going to affect the setup. Everybody would say to me, 'Are you going to go outside today, Jake? What's the weather going to be, Jake?' I'd go out and look and say, 'We got to do this, and got to do that.' And sure enough, it would work. I could figure it out. Yes sirree."

24

HOLMAN AND MOODY'S DEMISE

CHARLES "SLICK" OWENS WORKS as the parts acquisition man for Cale Yarborough Motorsports, a garage not far from the Charlotte airport and down the street from the dilapidated shell of the former Ford engineering powerhouse Holman-Moody, where Slick once worked during Holman-Moody's golden age. Holman-Moody was Ford, and its cars were driven by many of NASCAR's greats. Slick was on the pit crews of a young David Pearson and Freddie Lorenzen.

Slick handled the job of ordering parts for Holman-Moody's racing machine, and he enjoyed secretly helping out youngsters coming up like Darrell Waltrip and Bobby Allison. While there, he hired a youngster by the name of Cale Yarborough to stock shelves and do odd jobs. Slick and Cale became close friends, and Slick watched Yarborough become one of the greatest racers in the game.

After Holman-Moody's breakup in 1975, Slick went off on his own. In 1988 he returned to work near his old haunt, now employed by his former worker Cale Yarborough. It's been a lot of years since the time when Holman-Moody was the pride of NASCAR's race shops. It just doesn't seem possible that she's now a pile of scrap metal. Where has the time gone?

S L I C K O W E N S : "In '64 I went to work for Bill Stroppe in Atlanta and worked with Parnelli Jones, Rodger Ward and Darel Dieringer. The company was out of California, and I commuted back and forth. Stroppe was teamed up with John Holman and Ralph Moody in the marine end of their business.

"I worked for Holman-Moody from '65 to '70. Ralph Moody knew about cars and Mr. Holman knew about the business. Mr. Holman was a fine man. He and Ralph had some differences. I don't think Mr. Holman gave Ralph the credit for what he was really worth. But I thought a lot of John Holman, a lot of Ralph Moody. It was a deal where there were two people who didn't agree on a lot of things, but they were both good at what they did.

"I was in their parts department and issued the parts to most of the race teams. I also pitted the cars for David Pearson and Fred Lorenzen.

"David and I grew up together. I'm from Spartanburg, and I didn't live far from David. I can remember there was an Esso station not far from my father's house at the fork in the road, and David drove a car for them. David was a heck of a race car driver. He knew where to be. He never has even gotten a skin from a race car, never had a broken nose or a broken finger or anything. He knew who to be careful of. He knew who to follow. He would pick a driver out, and if he was a known wrecker and couldn't get by him in a certain amount of laps, he'd just back off and wait till something happened to him.

"David came up just like Cotton Owens, but Cotton got his eyes messed up, and David never had a problem. David was second in wins to Richard Petty, but David was only running seventeen or eighteen races a year and Richard was running fifty-one. Had David run as many races as Richard, who knows, he might have won 200 races himself.

"David had a lot of savvy about what to do under most any circumstance. As a matter of fact, he wouldn't give his secrets out. And when he was racing for the points—he was champion in 1966, 1968, and 1969—there were races when he was in second, and maybe he could have won, but he didn't want to take the chance of wrecking when he knows he's going to finish in second.

"David was never written about the way Richard was. To David, driving was just like shooting a game of pool. He didn't even talk racing that much, didn't talk about the setup. He'd come in and they'd say, 'How's the car feeling?' David would say, 'Leave it alone.' I'm not saying this in disrespect, but I don't think he knew much about the workings of the car, not as much as people might think. He'd come in and say, 'Don't touch it. It's okay.'

"Leonard Wood used to say that David was the best. Leonard is a Christian person, doesn't curse or smoke, never as long as I've known him, and David said, 'When Leonard was calling you a scoundrel, he was calling you an SOB.' David has a lot of dry humor. He's a lot of fun to be around, really. He's sharp and really witty.

"When I worked for Holman-Moody, they were involved in so much. They had all kinds of cars. It was interesting every single day. They ran NASCAR. They ran USAC. They ran LeMans, making Mark 2s and Mark 4s. I remember John Holman most from that company. He was an innovator. He was always busy trying to go in different directions and to please the Ford people he was working with. He was a much better man than he gets credit for, believe me.

"Ralph didn't like John, and like I said, Ralph is a fine person. In his part of the business, I didn't know anyone better than Ralph. But why Mr. Holman couldn't see that, I don't know.

"It hurt me bad when they separated. I can tell you that. But I have a lot of respect for both of them.

"After Ford got out of racing, business wasn't as good as it had been. The racing part wasn't there. I don't know the whole deal, but I guess Mr. Holman offered him a deal to get out. Ralph didn't care about the boat part of the business. He was a racer, a true racer, and if the company had stayed in racing, it would have stayed like it was. They didn't get along that good, but each one knew what the other one was worth to him.

"When Ford announced they were getting out, it wasn't thought about that much. We wondered what would happen, but Ford had talked about getting out before, and they got out for a few weeks and came back in again. I thought at the time that maybe they were trying to get concessions from NASCAR, and then they'd be back. But it was years and years before they ever got involved again.

"After the factories got out of it and I saw its effect, I said to myself, 'This is the end of racing.'

"But what happened, so long as the factories sponsored teams, you couldn't buck the factories. How were you going to make a camshaft or a crankshaft that would last as long as theirs and get them at the price they could? Crane cams has been around, but they didn't have connecting rods that would last five hundred miles. The factories, in fact, gave the parts to the twelve or so teams they backed, the racers we called 'hot dogs,' and the rest were independent, had no sponsors, no money. But after the factories got out, you had small companies who started making parts for the cars. Moroso was one of the first.

"Holman-Moody went from two hundred employees down to a handful. I left in '74, and then when they hired Bill Kitts and put him in charge, I came back to sell race parts. I had hopes of the company getting back on its feet. Mr. Kitts was a good man. But at the time racing wasn't that good, and he didn't know much about the racing business, and they had a meeting, and Mr. Holman decided to get rid of Mr. Kitts, and that's when I decided to leave for good. It was '76, and Darrell Waltrip and I went into business together and opened a parts place in Franklin, Tennessee.

"When I was working for Holman-Moody, I sold Darrell his first race car. Sold him a Mercury. We rented Darrell engines. As a matter of fact, I was in charge of the parts, and Darrell's father-in-law sent him money through a friend, Ed Sanders. Before Darrell came to NASCAR he was known as The Wild Child, and this Ed Sanders would tell me, 'He's a hell of a race car driver. Talk to John Holman and see if you can't get him a ride.'

"We had Fred Lorenzen and all those other great drivers, and Darrell was unknown. To make a long story short, Darrell came up with the money to buy a car, and I sold it to him on the cheap along with a motor, a 429 semihemi, we called it. Darrell went racing, and I helped him. He is one of the best racers I've ever had contact with. He was young. He and Stevie hadn't been married long. Stevie's father sent the $17,000 to buy the car, although Darrell paid it all back. Darrell bought some gears and other parts and got in debt and owed Mr. Holman some money, and Jake Elder was working for him, and I wasn't supposed to do it, but I'd let him have a gear, and they'd bring it back and borrow another, and bring it back. I kept trying to help them out. Darrell ended up paying everything he owed. He worked hard. It wasn't that easy for Darrell, though everyone thinks he was born with a silver spoon in his mouth. He really wasn't. I know that for a fact.

"When I was with Darrell I sold a lot of parts to Bobby Allison in Hueytown. He ran a car for Coca-Cola. In fact, the last car he drove at Holman-Moody's was backed by Coca-Cola. Bobby is a fine person, and so is his brother Donnie.

"I lived there about six months. I didn't particularly like that part of the country. I missed being home, and I let that go.

"After I left Holman-Moody in '75, I worked some for myself, Slick's Racing Parts, which I still have, a place that was downtown in Charlotte but which is in my basement now. After that, I went to work for Banjo Matthews out of Asheville. I sold parts for him at the racetrack in a truck. Banjo is responsible for a lot of drivers not getting hurt and perhaps not getting killed, because he built a really safe car. He emphasized that.

"Banjo was another one who was sort of a loner, but Banjo was really a good fellow. Banjo was one of those guys who if you were around him, he could say 'Good morning' and really tick you off. He had his ways. A lot of us have. But if you did your job, you didn't have to worry about getting your paycheck the next week.

"I first got involved in selling parts at the track in 1960 with Rex White. I can remember when Richard Petty used to bring bubble goggles to the racetrack and sell them on the side. The same lady who sold the bubble glasses then is still in business. We used pit boards then, and I got the idea to sell chalk, and I also sold the boards, and Rex and I went into business together.

"I'm still in the parts business. I've worked for Cale Yarborough's race team since 1988. I buy the parts and do whatever they need done. Cale used to work for me at Holman-Moody. I had Cale setting up parts, stacking parts, going through gears and that kind of thing when he was a young chap. Cale and I used to run around quite a bit together. As a matter of fact he was on the back of my motorcycle one time when we wrecked.

"We had run downtown to get some whiskey. The store closed at dark when the sun went down. Cale put the two fifths in his bosom and we were on our way back to his home on Anne Smith Road—Mr. Holman's home is still there—a road that curves around a lake, and we were going around those curves when this car came way over to our side. I was right at the ditch, and it hit the pedal, and I was worried about Cale's foot because he was scheduled to drive at Indianapolis. I had to go down that bank, and I tried to get the motorcycle back up but there was a culvert that I didn't see in the dark, and the back of the bike flew up, and Cale went over my back. I heard those bottles going 'clink, clink, clink,' and he hit and went 'Uh.'

"The passengers in the car were young kids, seventeen, eighteen, and they came back to see if we were all right. We weren't hurt. Cale said, 'If this liquor is broke, I'm going to go and lick them.' I said, 'No, don't do that.' He said, 'If it is, I'm going to whip them.' But it wasn't broke, not either bottle.

"We got back on that motorcycle thinking it was all right, but the front wheel was bent so bad we couldn't ride it. We had to walk back to the house. It wasn't very far.

"Cale would have won a lot more races if he had not gone to race at Indianapolis two and a half years. He missed those years, and he was another one who only raced seventeen times a year, and he won eighty-three. Cale was as near to Curtis Turner as you could be. As a matter of fact, I ain't sure he wasn't better, and I'm not saying that because I work for Cale. But he didn't plan no strategy. He just went flat out. I just wonder how many races Cale could have won if he had planned a little strategy and hadn't run so hard. It didn't matter to him if he was a lap ahead, he wouldn't slow down.

"Cale is building a new race shop across town, and I'll go over there for a year or so and then retire. I'm not really looking forward to it. I'll stay busy doing something. I won't quit."

25

HE BROKE THE 200 MPH BARRIER

BUDDY BAKER, THE SON OF BUCK, began his racing career in 1959 and went eight long, excruciatingly painful years before he won his first Grand National race. NASCAR was changing from the small tracks to a preponderance of superspeedways, and it became much harder for a driver to roar onto the scene and start winning races than it used to be, because without a factory-backed ride, it had become too expensive to race. Each year Buddy knew he was improving, but the big guy wasn't offered the opportunity to drive for top race teams, and his frustration grew.

He thought he was going to drive full time for Ray Fox, a Chrysler factory team owner, in 1966, but Chrysler overruled Fox's selection of Baker. His disappointment was great but Fox told him to be patient, and the next year he got the ride and his first win, at Charlotte, breaking Richard Petty's ten-race win streak.

Baker drove for Ray Fox until 1969, when the acerbic Fox hurt his feelings, and he quit in a huff. Baker then drove for Cotton Owens, and under Owens proved he could run up front on the superspeedways. He led many of the races he was in, though many times his car broke before the finish, in part because of his aggressive, pedal-to-the-metal driving style. Like Curtis

Turner before him, his win total wasn't as great as others, but Buddy
Baker was one great driver on the big tracks.

In 1970 in a tire test for Goodyear Buddy Baker drove a lap over
200 miles an hour in Cotton Owens's Dodge. Baker was the first driver in racing history to go over the 200 mark. His record has become
part of the NASCAR legend.

BUDDY BAKER: "I hate to tell this story because it really chokes
me up. The first time Ray Fox spoke to me about driving for him on
a permanent basis was in 1966. I actually went from Charlotte to
Daytona on a bus. I went to the track and put my seat in his car, and
I was just so excited because it was going to be the greatest thing that
ever happened to me, and then about fifteen or twenty minutes later,
I got a call that the ride was not going to be available to me. I went,
'Owwwwww, man.' Quite frankly, some of the people in Chrysler
Corporation decided that was a thing they shouldn't do, put me in one
of their cars. 'Cause I really didn't have any background to sell them.

"It took a full year before Ray and I got together again. He kept
saying, 'You just keep the faith and keep on trying as hard as you are
right now, and eventually things will come around for you.' He didn't
say, 'with me.' And so the next time he talked about my driving for
him, I wasn't so excited. I was going, 'Yeah, right, okay.'

"I was supposed to drive the Charlotte race for him in '67, and as I
drove to the track, I said to myself, All the talk, all the times you've told
everyone that all you needed was a good race car—okay, it's today. Then
I thought, Oh, my God. It gives me cold chills just to think about it.

"The first time I went out in practice in Ray's Dodge, this car was
so good that I thought I had run bad. Everything was all new. It handled so well. It had great power. You didn't have to drive it hard. So I
went out and I felt I ran pretty good, but I wasn't sure how good. I got
to Ray and I said, 'I know the time wasn't that good, but when I really lay down on that thing, I think we'll have a good race car.' Ray said,
'When you lay down on it, the rest of them can go home. We're about
a half a second quicker than anybody here!'

"All those years I had spent in race cars that weren't quite up to
speed, I had developed a driving style of running a little bit better
than the car was capable of. Then when I got the opportunity to drive
a really good race car, it was pretty much over. When they dropped the

green flag at Charlotte, I jumped in front and was gone. I have pictures. We finished seventh. Then in July I led the Firecracker 400
until my suspension broke.

"That was the year Richard Petty ran the hemi engine. In '67
Richard won twenty-seven races. I remember at Daytona my father
and I were having dinner at a local restaurant. We were talking: 'We
could run at 167 miles an hour tops.' Somebody said, 'Ole' Richard
did pretty well today up in the test program for Goodyear.' I said,
'Yeah, how fast?' He said, 'A hundred and eighty!' I went,
'Oooooooooh.' You talk about getting a bone in your throat. Yeah, they
were awesome. Talk about catching everyone with their left hand
down. Buddy, they had it.

"There were times when Petty Enterprises had an advantage. The
cars were well engineered. Richard is an engineer, and a lot of people
don't realize that. When I was driving for them, we had brake systems
on the cars no one else had. 'Cause they worked real hard to put great
brake systems in their cars. I mean, the last half of the race, if Richard
Petty was in the race, he was going to get you, 'cause he could go and
he could stop. That was the year Richard Petty won ten races in a row
in August and September. As a matter of fact, I broke the win streak
he had going by winning the National 500 at Charlotte. It was my
first Grand National victory.

"My most vivid memory of that day is pulling into the winner's circle and seeing my father standing there. Up until then, it was hearsay,
and all of a sudden, to see him standing there as I turned to the winner's circle at Charlotte and realizing, No matter what happens from
this day forward, okay, I'm in there. I've won. To see the enjoyment my
father had from the victory was as much as what I felt for myself.

"My dad and I have had an interesting relationship. You know
what? He's still tough on things, but as I get a little bit older I realize
that everything we discussed in the early part of my career was always
to make me better, not to ever pull me down.

"In '68, I was still running just major races and a few selected short
tracks. I never really ran a full schedule. I did a lot of tire testing for
Goodyear and Firestone. Ray Fox and I must have done a million
miles testing. I was making two, three thousand dollars a week, when
somebody who won a hundred-mile race was making a thousand. It
didn't take me long to figure that out! And the other thing, when you

do a lot of testing, you have a leg up when you go out there to race. Today people die for a test program, and I was getting paid to do it.

"In May of '68 I won the World 600. That car was so good, when you backed down, you got a better entry into the corner, and I would have a faster time around the track. I had a good lead, and it seemed the slower I tried to make the car run, the smoother it would come off the corner, and the faster it would run down the straightaway. It must have worked, because I won four times at Charlotte. I mean, I learned a lot that day. Every time I ever got into a race car, I always learned a little something.

"In '69, I didn't win, but I led a lot of races. As far as sheer horsepower, we had their behinds a lot of times. I guess if I had been a little easier on the car, we'd have won a lot more races, but everybody has a style that they race, and it was alien to me to sit out there and ride around. Ray and I were down in Daytona not long ago, and we went over some of the races we ran together, and he said, 'Did you ever think about how many races you would have won if the car had lasted the whole way?'

"I left Ray after the Atlanta race at the end of March in '69. Ray has always been one of my real favorites, but he had a real fiery temper. And I did too. I was nicknamed 'The Gentle Giant.' My wife said, 'Where in the hell did they get that?'

And it was over the silliest thing in the world. We were discussing a race I had won, and he made a comment that, 'Anybody could win in my car.' And I looked up at him and said, 'Do you really mean that?' And he said, 'Yep.' And I said, 'Well, by golly, you can go get anybody.'

"At Chrysler they called me 'Number one charger,' and I was pretty proud, and Ray was proud of what he did, and it was a shame, because we had good race cars. You know, I love the man as much today as the day I drove for him. I wish that hadn't happened. But the comment he made, it ruffled the wrong feathers. And then it was done. Once you have that first real heated deal, it's over. We had a couple of phone conversations where they tried to put us back together, and it escalated to the point where it couldn't be rectified.

"When I went back to the shop, they were hanging body parts. They asked me how I wanted to hang the quarter panel. I told them, 'I don't give a damn if you hook it to the roof.' Then I said to myself, They haven't done anything, and I apologized.

"But we were finished, and Chrysler placed me with Cotton

Owens. Frank Wiley was the head of PR for Dodge, and he decided who went where, and when they realized that I was gone from the ranks as far as Ray and I, they sent me to interview with Cotton in Spartanburg. Right away I liked the car, liked the people.

"The closest I came to winning in '69 was the Firecracker 400 at Daytona in July. It was the only time they allowed you to run the exhaust directly out the back of the car.

"I had the fastest car. LeeRoy Yarbrough, who was driving for Junior Johnson, was running his exhaust pipe out the back of his car. His crew chief, Herb Nab, had put it there.

"I ran LeeRoy down from seventeen seconds back, and I had him set up pretty good, because back then without the restrictor plate, if you were in second spot, you pretty much had the race won on the last lap, so after I caught up to him, I didn't try to pass. I set there, and I was thinking, I'm going to make my move at the end of the straight-away, and I began to smell something. I looked down at the water temperature, and I went, 'My God, it's on the peg. I've cooked this thing.' The hot exhaust coming from LeeRoy's car straight back into my radiator had made me overheat.

I was lucky to finish second. I had to fall back and cool it back down enough to finish the race.

"The next race we showed up with the same exhaust system, and two or three people got behind me, and I cooked them down within about three laps. So they outlawed them and wouldn't let you run them any more.

"In '69, two things happened. Talladega opened, and Richard Petty started the PDA, the Professional Drivers Association. The PDA start-ed with good intentions. I was on the board of directors at the begin-ning. It was set up to be like the PTA. Today the drivers make enough money that they don't have to worry, but back then we were trying to set up retirement funds. At the same time, when Talladega opened, like any new concept, there are problems, and the biggest was that we didn't have time to develop a 200-mile-an-hour tire. We would go out in three or four laps and absolutely skin the tire down to the core. And it was not a problem they could fix. We could not run the cars to their capability on the tires we had to race on. And that's not saying anything against the tire company. I do know we had a real problem.

"It was explained to us that we could back off, run slower. In review, maybe that's what we should have done. But I think if you get a bunch of young bootheads like us out on the track, I'm going to tell you, if Cale passes me, I'm going to pass him back, and pretty soon both of us would have been in the wall. Sure we could have backed off, and we could have run 168 miles an hour until the final three laps and then run 200 and finished it that way, but that wasn't going to happen, and as a result most of the drivers boycotted the race, feeling it was going to be too dangerous. Bobby Isaac was the one driver who raced. One thing about Bobby: he never told anybody he was not going to race. So you have to respect him. He was not a member of the PDA. I had given my word I would not compete, so I didn't. The people I feel kind of indignant about are the—nah, never mind. I don't want to get into that. I'll just pass by that. Anyway, the boycott was the best thing in the world to happen to Talladega, because everybody in the world read about Talladega, and the next race we had there we ran at 200 miles an hour and put on one of the best races ever. But the boycott also pretty much told me from that day forward that drivers have to look out for themselves, and when they have an event, if I have a car there I shall be in it.

"From then on whenever anyone talked about, 'We need to get another drivers' group together,' I say, 'You all go and do whatever you please. Have a good time and enjoy yourself. 'Cause I'm doing pretty well in this race car. That's the way I make my living, not sitting out.'

"And in March of 1970 I went back to Talladega, and during a tire test for Goodyear I ran 200 miles an hour. It was a big deal, because no one had done it before. We had gone down to do some testing with the wing car, and my warm-up lap was right around 200. They said, 'Whoa, we have history here.' So they got Joe Epton with NASCAR with the official clock, set it up, got it ready. They could have told me I was going 215, and I wouldn't have known the difference. I went out and set the world record, and like I say, at the time it was prestigious because it had never been done before. Now it's part of history. I didn't realize exactly how big a deal it was. From that day forward it went with me on my résumé. Any time they introduce you, it's part of what they say. Yeah, I've had records that have been broken, but some records you get to keep for your lifetime. That is one, and I was the first driver to win a five-hundred-mile race under three hours. Those kind of things you can't put a price on."

26

CURTIS TURNER'S LOSING GAMBIT

C URTIS TURNER, WHO PEERS SAID was the best of the early racers, was a debonair man who loved women, drink, fun, and the way money could provide all of the above. Turner, like Bill France, was a visionary who foresaw the growth of his great sport, and in the early sixties he laid plans for a state-of-the-art superspeedway to be built on the wide expanse of empty fields of Harrisburg, North Carolina, just north of Charlotte.

Turner saw that the superspeedways were going to be NASCAR's future, and in that he was very right. But for his brainchild to succeed, he would need things to go smoothly.

In his life Curtis Turner had been rich and he had been broke. He was a high-stakes gambler who figured the odds, but when the contractors digging the Charlotte Motor Speedway oval struck hard granite, his dice came up craps. The cost overruns were enormous, and Turner didn't have enough money to keep his head above water. In 1960, he decided the only way he could survive financially and not lose his speedway was to cut a deal with the Teamsters Union, led by mobster Jimmy Hoffa.

In exchange for a loan of $800,000 from Hoffa, Turner would organize the NASCAR drivers into a union. Part of the deal, which Turner kept quiet, was that Turner would also get NASCAR to allow pari-mutuel betting on the races.

What Turner and Hoffa hadn't reckoned with, however, was the ferocity of the resistance to a union put up by NASCAR boss Bill France Sr., who banned Turner for life—and, using a pistol to emphasize his seriousness during a meeting with the drivers, threatened to shut down all the tracks if they even considered joining a union. Quickly all union talk union ended, and Turner was out his $800,000, ultimately causing him to lose his stake in the Charlotte Motor Speedway.

Tim Flock, the only driver to remain loyal to Turner and who also was banned for life by France, recalls those fateful events.

TIM FLOCK: "Bruton Smith had already been a promoter when Curtis announced he was going to build a mile-and-a-half track here in Charlotte. Me and my brothers Bob and Fonty had run for Bruton on these half-mile tracks. Bruton told Curtis, 'If you're going to build a mile-and-a-half track on Highway 29, then I'm going to build a mile-and-a-half track on South Boulevard.' They tell me he scared old Curtis so bad that he said, 'You come in with me as a partner, and we'll build Charlotte,' and that's what they done.

"When they started digging, they hit real granite. It cost Curtis hundreds of thousands of dollars trying to blast that infield out. It was solid granite under the whole racetrack. They had to drill down and put dynamite sticks in and blow it up. It cost him so much money with dynamite and crews. It was very expensive getting the granite out of there, but they finally finished it.

"As they were building the track at Charlotte, we would fly down over the backstretch lower than the grandstands. The workmen were up on this big hill, and Curtis would fly so low and pull up so late, the workmen would jump and roll down.

"Everybody said Curtis could land a twin-engine Apache on top of a big barn, that he was that good a pilot. In fact, he was a dangerous pilot. He never did check his plane. He'd get in the plane, didn't warm it up, crank it up, and take off. Unreal.

"I must have flown with him a hundred times. One time we flew from Charlotte to Darlington to qualify, and I wish I hadn't done that. He said, 'We're going to fly down instead of drive.' I said, 'There ain't no airport at Darlington. Just for single engines.' He said, 'I can land an Apache on that little strip behind the track.' I shouldn't have gotten in the plane.

"We got down there, and here was this little ole' bitty strip. We flew over the track, buzzed the pits, and they came over and picked us up. We came in, and he landed the plane, and he had to spin it to keep it from hitting a barbed wire fence at the end of the runway.

"I worried all day. We qualified the cars. Now I had to get back in that plane. There was no way that plane was going to get airborne in such a short space. The guys pulled the tail of the plane against the barbed wire fence. The brakes were on top of the Apache, and Curtis mashed both of them down, and he ran both engines wide open. The plane was setting there vibrating, and he released the brakes, and we started rolling, and I could see telephone poles and trees coming at us at fifty miles an hour. Sixty. Seventy. There was no way he was going to pick it up and get over those telephone lines, so he flew under them. I heard the undercarriage of the plane hitting the tops of the bushes and trees, and I said to myself, I will never get in this plane again. And I never did. This was how dangerous he was.

"Here's the real story: Before the first race at Charlotte, Bill France made Curtis and Bruton come up with a hundred thousand dollars for the purse before he would allow the race to be run. Turner jumped into his twin-engine Apache and flew to a bank—he was from Virginia and had a great friend who owned a bank—and he talked that guy into writing him a cashier's check for $100,000, made out to NASCAR. And they made enough money to pay the guy back. But that was some chance that banker took.

"I was in that first Charlotte race. Curtis bought me an old car from Holman-Moody because he thought I'd draw some of my fans. At that first race the track was dug all up. The asphalt hadn't cured, and they started the race a week late, but the track started digging up, and there were asphalt chunks, big chunks. They knew it would come up, so they let us put big bars on the windshields, and chicken wire, and let us put big ole' truck flags behind the wheels. Jack Smith had a six-lap lead in a Pontiac, and a chunk of asphalt busted his gas tank. They put rags in it trying to keep the car together. He had a six-lap lead in the first 600, and he couldn't make it in. They black-flagged him because he was leaking gas onto the track.

"I ran two hundred something laps and blowed an engine. I had smoke coming off that thing.

"Curtis was overextended, and he turned to the Teamsters Union. He was going to organize the drivers, and the Teamsters were going to give him a lot of money. Curtis invited me and Fireball and Buck Baker to fly to see Jimmy Hoffa. By the time the wheels got off the ground in Charlotte, Curtis said to Buck, who was sitting in front next to him, 'Hand me that satchel back there.' There was a fifth of Canadian Club in it. Fireball handed it to him, and he took a big swallow and then finished the bottle. Buck also liked to drink, and he had brought a fifth for himself, which Fireball and I found and finished.

"We were flying over the mountains on our way to Detroit to see Jimmy Hoffa, and we got into a storm, and the radio went out. Buck got scared. Buck said, 'Hand me that fifth I put in the plane before we left.' Fireball said, 'Buck, what fifth?' Me and Fireball had already drank it! Buck liked to have died.

"We got to Detroit, and it was fogged in, and we didn't have a radio. Curtis had seen this airliner go down through the clouds, and we followed that damn airliner down and landed at that airport out of gas.

"When we got to Detroit, I never did meet Hoffa. I met all of his lawyers. They were going to back Curtis one hundred percent. I never did see no big money. Curtis probably got some. I was working for Curtis on salary at the Speedway.

"Curtis wanted the promoters to pay the drivers 40 percent of the actual purses. 'Cause we weren't making no money. We were only getting a thousand dollars for first place in most races. They were paying around 7 percent of the gross, and probably still are today. They are taking in millions of dollars, but the purses are still too short. If you read the papers, a guy wins a golf tournament and wins $270,000 hitting a golf ball. Rusty Wallace wins Michigan running 180 miles an hour, and wins $78,000. Does that sound right to you? So this is what Curtis had in mind forty-something years ago. He wanted to unionize the drivers and raise our pay. But it's never worked. NASCAR has too much control.

"Initially, a lot of the drivers signed up. We made Fireball some kind of secretary. Buck Baker was vice president, Richard Petty the president. We had everybody tied up, and then Bill France called a meeting of the drivers in Winston-Salem at Bowman-Gray Stadium, and everybody showed up. Me and Curtis went, but they wouldn't let us inside.

"Bill France said, 'I'm going to get a pistol. I'll tell every one of you drivers who are making your living right now, I'm going to close every track I've got if you stay with this union deal.' And we lost every ass that was with us. We lost Buck, Fireball, every dang driver we had. They all went back to NASCAR. They left me and Curtis holding the damn bag. We had to look through the windows to see what was going on at that meeting. The guards wouldn't let us in, because we were the instigators.

"Anyway we lost, so we sued NASCAR. We had Jimmy Hoffa and his six or seven million-dollar lawyers, but we had to sue them in Daytona—we should have sued in North Carolina—and that old judge was on Bill France's payroll. He read comic books all the time in court while our lawyer was trying to explain what we were trying to do, get the 40 percent. That judge was seventy years old. They kept Curtis on the witness stand three and a half hours, kept me up there twenty minutes, and that old man judge wasn't paying attention. Hoffa's lawyers told us we had lost the suit before we even walked into the courthouse. Bill France owned Daytona, and he owned that old man.

"After we lost the lawsuit, I just more of less faded out. NASCAR banned Curtis and me for life. France said, 'You cannot run for NASCAR.' We couldn't do a damn thing about it. After we lost Hoffa, we didn't see them union people no more.

"I sold cars, did a little bit of everything, but Bill France started getting thousands of letters—I heard up to a hundred thousand letters on Curtis and me, asking NASCAR to let us go back, and the press was helping us, and after four years France reinstated us. Curtis went back to racing, and I went to work for the Charlotte Motor Speedway. I didn't go back racing.

"After he came back, Curtis won at Rockingham, which thrilled me to death, 'cause he hadn't been in a car in four years. He went and out-ran all them hot dogs. Shows you the kind of driver he was. Hell of a race driver.

"Because Curtis couldn't make good on his promise to start the union, he didn't get the money he needed from the Teamsters, and the government closed down the track and threw them both out. Bruton went off for about seven years and started seventeen Ford dealerships all over the country, in Florida, Texas, and up in Illinois, and he came back with enough money, started buying stock in the Speedway, and finally he bought every bit of it, took over control.

"As for me, when the Speedway started back up again, Bruton hired me back. I'm still there. I've been there thirty-eight years. But I don't have to go to the office no more, because I'm retired, but they still furnish me with a pace car. They put signs on it, and we go to a lot of different tracks.

"Bruton built a track in Texas, bought Atlanta, Wilkesboro, Bristol. Everyone says Bruton is buying enough tracks where he could start his own NASCAR circuit. I didn't say that, and I doubt that, but that's what everyone else is saying.

"No telling how much money Bruton's got today. He's building a $400 million track down in Texas, and he offered $150 million for the Charlotte Hornets basketball team. I guess the man is worth close to a billion dollars. Unreal."

27

THE DAY THE MUSIC DIED

CURTIS TURNER, THE RACER MORE than any other who embodied all that was fun and crazy about the stock car racing business in the early years, died on October 4, 1970, in a plane crash. His Aero Commander 500 plowed into the side of a mountain near Du Bois, Pennsylvania. When they found the wreckage, a close friend, Clarence King, who was a golf pro, was found strapped in the pilot's seat. Turner was found nearby. It was Turner's habit to sleep in the back while the plane was on automatic pilot. In this case, something went wrong, and Turner obviously didn't get to the controls quickly enough to avert disaster.

When Curtis Turner died, it marked the end of an era. The devil-may-care days of NASCAR were officially over. The days of drivers with portfolios and business managers and briefcases were about to begin. Curtis Turner was the Babe Ruth of stock car racing. He was bigger than life, an idol to all those who knew him, laughed along with him, and loved him.

Three of Turner's closest friends, Tim Flock, Max Muhlmann, and Ralph Moody, recall their flying experiences with the most legendary of all racers.

TIM FLOCK: "I heard about Curtis's death on the news. I had a pilot's license to fly a single-engine plane, and Curtis knew this, and sometimes he'd let me fly his plane while he'd go and lay down. He had a big old Air Commander at the time, had a sofa in it, and he let me take over. He'd say, 'Watch the needles. If you can fly single-engine, you can do this.' He'd go in the back and go to sleep. On the day of his death, Curtis was coming back from a meeting in New York, and he was flying with Clarence King, a known drinker who had had several heart attacks. On the way back from New York to Roanoke, Virginia, they were over Pennsylvania, and I just know Curtis was back there sleeping, and this old man had a heart attack, because a farmer who saw it said the plane spiraled down into the woods. I know that old man was flying the plane and had a heart attack and didn't wake Curtis up, because Curtis would have landed the airplane. And another thing, there was a hole in the top of the fuselage, and his body went through the top of that plane. The deer hunters who found the plane said they found Curtis about a half a block from the plane, while the old man was still strapped in dead—he got all smashed up—but he was still buckled in the flying position. So I think Clarence had a heart attack. That's my theory, but you'll never know. 'Cause if Curtis had been in the cockpit, he'd have been strapped into his safety belt.

"Too bad Curtis couldn't have seen what happened at Charlotte. 'Cause Charlotte was nothing before Bruton Smith started adding all the beautiful stuff they got now. If Curtis had seen that track today, he'd probably have a heart attack. It's unreal what they've done. If Curtis hadn't started it, and Bruton hadn't jumped in there with him, it never would have been built."

MAX MUHLMANN: "I was out West when I heard about Curtis's death. I couldn't believe it, because he was just as skilled in an airplane as he was in a car. I remember calling Bruton Smith, because I figured he'd know about it. He agreed with me that Curtis was too skillful to have had anything mechanical happen to the plane, 'cause Curtis would have figured out some way to do something other than drive it straight into the ground.

"When I flew with Curtis he used to say to me, 'I need to take a nap. I have it on automatic pilot. Sit up here, and if you see anything, call me.' Bruton's theory was that he had that golf pro in that seat, and the guy could have had a heart attack, and when you start down the G forces are too much, and Curtis couldn't get to the controls in time. That was Bruton's theory, and it made as much sense to me as anything."

RALPH MOODY: "Curtis was reckless as hell in that airplane. One night Curtis, Joe Weatherly, and I were at Spartanburg, and he had rented an LTD Ford at the airport. Curtis wasn't racing that night, and during the whole race he was in the pits boozing it up with his lawyer and another friend. In the middle of the race there was a caution, and Curtis and his friends decided to leave. I got in the backseat for the ride to the airport, where my Bonanza was parked two planes from his twin-engine Commander.

"He went down the road driving like a maniac on the side of the road, and Jesus Christ, he hit forty cars on the way to that airport. I told Curtis, 'You son of a bitch, if I ever get you stopped, I'll beat your head in.' Man, he made me mad as hell. He could have hurt other people.

"We got to the airport, and he jumped out of that car, and they all got to the airplane, and by this time they were all feeling pretty good. I said, 'Turner, you leave your airplane here. I'll fly you home.' He said, 'I'll fly myself.' He jumped into that son of a bitch, and fired it up without checking it out, turned on the taxiway, and took off! I had just cranked up my Bonanza, and the tower called and asked me, 'Who just took off left side of you?' I lied. I said, 'I don't know. I saw that thing leave, but I don't know who it was.'

"I took off for Charlotte. Turner had headed south, the wrong way, and he came back to where I could see him. We got to Gastonia, where there's a mountain, and he was flying at less than a thousand feet. I called him, 'Hey Pops, is that you? Where are you?' I said, 'What the hell are you doing flying so low? Don't you know King's Mountain is right in front of you with the light on it?' He said, 'Oh, I see it.' Instead of going up, he flew around it.

"He went in and landed, and I followed him in. He parked on a downhill slope, and his airplane slid down backward into a ditch. He and his friends acted like they hadn't even noticed. They just walked off, leaving the plane in that ditch. Goddamn, I don't know how Curtis lived as long as he did.

"One time my wife saw Curtis riding on a motor scooter. He had lost his pilot's license after he went through a town in South Carolina flying low. He landed in this little town, people were coming out of church, and he like to run over a police car, flew right down Main Street in an Air Commander. He pulled that thing up, and wiped out every traffic light and cut all the phone lines in the town! Then he flew down near the treetops to keep from being seen and he set down somewhere near Charleston. Didn't make any difference. They were waiting for him.

"My wife said to him, 'What are you doing driving that motor scooter?' He said, 'I don't have a driver's license, and by now I don't even have a hunting license.' But he drove his Air Commander anyway. He landed it in a field out behind the Charlotte Motor Speedway. License or no, he kept right on.

"When Curtis first got an airplane, he bought a Tri-Pacer, a little single-engine plane, and he decided to fly to New York. Though he told the authorities he knew how to fly, he had never flown an airplane in his life. He didn't know where he was going. He landed at the wrong airport, and they about put him in jail.

"He flew to Atlanta, where he landed on the road. He came back home to Winston-Salem, ran out of gas and landed in somebody's hay field. Somebody went and got him gas, poured it in, and he finally got back to Winston-Salem. But he turned out to be a hell of a pilot. Careless as hell, though.

"One night a bunch of us were setting in the shop, and I had a shortwave. The weather was bad, snowing and sleet, and I heard Curtis's call number coming on. He'd flown from Texas with that Commander, six people in it. All the airports around Charlotte were closed. He said, 'I'm coming in to land.' They said, 'The airports are closed. You can't land.' He said, 'I'm out of fuel. I have to land.' Oh shit, I thought.

"I got in my car and drove to the airport, where I met Dick Beaty, who was the Charlotte airport's manager at the time. Dick had a Jeep, and I jumped in with him, and up in the sky you could hear the plane circling.

"Dick had the lights turned on, but it was snowing so badly and everything was so frozen you could hardly see them. It was just raising hell out there, and here comes the plane. I could hear it back off a little, and pretty soon I could hear the goddamnedest noise. There was a foot of ice and snow, and when the plane landed, that plane plowed the ice and snow, and pretty soon one engine quit, and then the other. That son of a bitch was out of gas! He was out of gas! Goddamn. The guy was the luckiest bastard in the world.

"One time Curtis flew from Norfolk to Winston-Salem, and then we flew together from Winston-Salem to Detroit to meet with the Ford people. In midflight his Twin Commanche started skipping. Curtis said, 'Oh shit.' I said, 'What's the matter?' He said, 'I only got one set of mags [magnetos] to work. The other ones don't work.' You're supposed to have two sets, in case one set goes bad. The other set had been bad a long time, and he didn't bother to fix it. Goddamn. Boy, we put it down this side of Chicago somewhere. It just about quit running. We had to have it fixed.

"The last time I flew with him we went from Indianapolis to Baltimore. He had a road race up there. We flew in a single-engine Piper with a friend of his, landing at this little airport. The road race ran through the night, and when it was over, we got back in the plane. I said to Curtis, 'Are you sure they filled this thing up with gas?' He said, 'Yeah. They filled it up.'

"We were flying back to Indianapolis, and we got in the Goddamnedest storm you've ever seen. The guy in the back was scared to death. We got closer and closer to Indianapolis, and I said to him, 'Don't you think we ought to switch over to the other tank?' But he wasn't doing it. I said, 'Curtis, change the damn thing right now.' Curtis said, 'Pop, that tank don't have any fuel in it.' I thought, Aw shit. I knew we were not going to make the Indianapolis airport.

"We flew past this little airport, which had a tower that must have been eight hundred feet high. I said to Curtis, 'Do you know where we are?' He didn't. I said, 'I know where we are. Let me fly this thing. You watch for that big tower.'

"I called the airport, and they turned on all the lights, 'cause they knew we were in trouble. Curtis was pretty uptight, and the guy in back was about to die. I saw the lights, turned that plane ninety degrees, went down because I knew there was nothing but houses next to the airport, and I got it down to five hundred feet, backed off, and we hit the ground just like we landed in a lake, just whomped the front nose down because the wheels were dragging in the water, and goddamn, the runway was like a river. We taxied off, and right then, the son of a bitch quit running. We were out of gas. We never would have made it to the main airport, and it wasn't but another ten miles. And that's the last time I flew with him. He took all kinds of stupid chances. He was something else.

"Before he died, Curtis had left his wife and got married again. He owned a lot of property in Detroit which he had bought from Ford—when Ford built cars, it bought the property for the wood to put in the cars. But they didn't need wood any more, and Curtis made a deal with Ford, bought a cartload of property out there, and as part of the deal, he had to build recreational places with roads and lakes, and the lumber had to be taken out in a way designated by the government. So much money went to Ford, and so much to Turner, a percentage deal, and eventually Curtis owned it all, so when he died, all that went to his second wife, Bunny, who wound up with all the property and money. But they hadn't been together that long."

28

"SWEET THANG"

IT WASN'T EASY TO FIND BUNNY Turner, Curtis Turner's widow. I knew only that she lived in a small town nestled somewhere in the Blue Ridge Mountains of southern Virginia. After interviewing H. Clay Earles, the president of the Martinsville Speedway, it occurred to me that perhaps the Virginia track had invited the elusive Mrs. Turner to one of their Legends functions, and after asking around the speedway office, I learned that Mrs. Turner worked for a Ford dealer in Floyd, Virginia, the small town up in the mountains where her late husband, Curtis Turner, had grown up.

From Martinsville, I rode west on Highway 58, until I came to state road 40, where at Woolwine I found secluded state road 8. I then drove the one-lane back roads of woodsy Virginia, climbing a tall mountain around and around and around at a painfully slow pace behind a large struggling tractor trailer hauling felled timber. On the other side of the mountain, miraculously, appeared a sign announcing the town of Floyd. As I entered the town, a blue Ford Mustang passed me and took the 35 mile-an-hour turns at 75. I knew I had arrived.

It wasn't hard to find the Skyline Ford dealership. The town has one traffic light at its lone intersection. As Mrs. Turner, now Hall, would explain to me later, as a young boy Curtis used to enjoy shooting out the light with his .22. I made a right at the light and saw the rows of new Ford cars and vans in the lot of the dealership. Inside, sitting at her desk was the comptroller, Bunny Turner Hall. I told her why I had made the trek from Martinsville to find her. Would she talk to me about Curtis?

In a husky voice that was a dead ringer for Lauren Bacall's in the movie *Key Largo,* Bunny Turner Hall spent the better part of the afternoon talking about Pops, a man she met in 1963 when she was nineteen years old. She talked of her whirlwind courtship, their life together, and his tragic death after only seven years of marriage. More than twenty-five years later, she made me understand more clearly that Curtis "Pops" Turner indeed had been one of a kind.

CAROLINE "BUNNY" VANCE TURNER HALL: "My family was raising baby rabbits at the time they brought me home from the hospital. My brother Danny, who was two, said, 'Oh Mommy, a baby bunny.' And I was Baby Bunny until I was five years old when the 'Baby' was dropped.

"I'm from a small town in North Carolina called Spruce Pine. It was just a really neat place to grow up in, a beautiful little area near the parkway about thirty-five minutes from Blowing Rock. My daddy was a warden. There was a wrong way, a right way, and Virgil Vance's way. That had its advantages and its disadvantages. When the boys got in trouble with their mufflers and fast driving, it helped them with the Highway Patrol. But Daddy was strict, really strict. I was the baby of eight, and the two youngest closest to me were boys, so they were very protective over who I saw, dated, and what I did. When we were kids, it was war. When I was little, my brother Danny tried to smother me. And now we're so close.

"It was a dry county, no liquor and I mean, Spruce Pine was so small there was nothing for the young people to do. It had a drive-in theater, and on Friday and Saturday nights you had drag racing on the highways, and that was the entertainment. Everybody had their cars, and my brothers used to put me at the wheel of theirs and I'd drag race, and they thought it was the greatest thing in the world when a girl would beat the guys.

"I shouldn't be telling this, but guys would haul their cars down from Detroit and go so far as to bet title for title. If you lost the race, you lost the title to the car. That wasn't usually the case. Most of the time they raced as a matter of pride. But one time a guy brought a gold Plymouth Fury down to race. That's when it had that hemi engine. My brother Danny had a '64 Ford, and it flew, and they bet title for title. I watched Danny beat him, but he didn't take his title.

"I was seventeen when I graduated high school. I applied to Appalachian State University, and in the meantime after graduation I went to Charlotte, because I had a sister and a brother living there, and during the summer I worked for a short time as a teller at the Bank of Charlotte on Main Street. I was a trainee, and the rule was, if anyone brought in a check over $25, I was supposed to call up book-keeping and get it approved to make sure the check was good.

"One Saturday Curtis Turner walked up to my window and handed me a check for $27,000 and change. I didn't bat an eye. I didn't bother to call upstairs to see if it was any good. I opened the drawer and cashed the check. And I almost got fired over it. If it hadn't been who it was, I would have been fired.

"Curtis was a lot older than I was, twenty-four years older, and he kept trying to get my telephone number, and I wouldn't give it to him. This was in 1963. The man scared me to death. I had seen him race at Bristol, and he was my favorite among the race car drivers, and I just was in shock, I guess. I was just a little mountain girl who had never been anywhere. I really hadn't been around very much, and I don't know if that was what appealed to him. I don't know. I really don't. But after three months I finally gave him my phone number—it took me that long to get up the nerve to give it to him—I was living with three other girls in an apartment, and on our first date he said he wanted to take me out to dinner, and I thought that that was safe enough.

"He came to the apartment to pick me up, and we headed for the airport. He had a 500V Air Commander, and I was so overwhelmed I should have said no, but I didn't. So we went to the airport, and we got on his private plane. I had never been on a private plane before. I had no idea where we were going, when we were coming back, whether I was going to live, whether he was a serial murderer or not.

"'We're going to race at Atlanta,' he said. A limo picked us up at the Atlanta airport and took us to the racetrack. There had been a big storm, and the race was rained out, and the storm wasn't finished, and

Curtis informed me that we had to spend the night in Atlanta. He checked us into the Peachtree Hotel. It was comical. I was so young and naive. We were getting ready to go up in the elevator, and I said, 'What floor are our rooms on?' He told me. We got to the floor, and he got the key and unlocked the door, and I held my hand out and said, "Where's the key to my room?" He said he only got one room. I said, 'Well, you'll be the only one sleeping in it.' He didn't say a word. He turned around and went back downstairs and got another room—adjoining his. And so we spent the night in Atlanta. I called the girls to tell them I wouldn't be back. I was really nervous. I mean I was all to pieces, and they thought it was the greatest thing in the world.

"We had a beautiful dinner. He couldn't have been more of a gentleman. We flew back the next morning. He took me back home. He brought me to the door and kissed me on the forehead and told me, 'I'm going to marry you.' And that was on our first date.

"The next day at the bank Curtis sent me a rose. The next day he sent me two roses, then three, then four, then five, until it got up to four or five dozen. The bank was filled with roses. And my roommates and everybody at the bank thought it was the most wonderful thing. And I was just terrified. I was scared to death. I really didn't know how to handle it. After two months or so he asked me to marry him, and he gave me a two and a half carat diamond, and I kept it in the box. I didn't even put it on. I said, 'I have to go home.' He said, 'I'll take you.' I said, 'No. I have to go home and see my mama.' 'Cause my daddy had died the year before.

"I went home and spent the week with my mama. She said, 'Let me ask you a question. What are you going to do when he's eighty-something years old, and he's all crippled up and in a wheelchair?' I said, 'Push him.' And she said, 'Then you have my blessings.' And from then on, it was just a whirlwind, a merry-go-round, and as I look back on it now, it doesn't even seem like it really happened 'cause it's been so long ago.

"See, I knew a different side of Curtis Turner. Those who were really close to him—they were few and far between—knew a different Curtis. He wasn't the Curtis Turner the fans knew and expected. There were always stories about him, and I'm not saying they weren't true, that he didn't do that, the partying, the carousing, because he could out-party anyone. He *did* do a lot of crazy things, he and Joe

Weatherly—I didn't know Joe, he was killed before I met Curtis—they would get a U-drive-it and put it in swimming pools, take out mailboxes. They'd play. It did damage, which they'd pay for, but it was really in fun. Nobody's life was at stake. But Curtis was one of a kind.

"Sportswriters loved him. He was always good about giving interviews. The older sportswriters adored him because he was always doing something crazy they could write about. There was always news, and it didn't necessarily have anything to do with racing. And he was so good to the fans. Whenever we were having dinner or had to be somewhere, most drivers don't like to be bothered, but Curtis was a hands-on hero to these people. He would answer fan letters if they were touching or from kids.

"I can't imagine the commercials Curtis would be doing if he were racing today. Because he was a good-looking man, and very well spoken, articulate and charismatic. He never saw an ugly woman. No matter what she looked like, he made her feel like a queen.

"Curtis was a doll. Everybody loved him. Curtis was this kind of person: 'If you want to go with me, great. I'll be happy to have you. I'll even pay your way. If you don't, get out of the way.' It's documented that he won 360-something races, and that's just when they started keeping records. God knows what he won before that. But he'd win, and some cute little teenage girl would walk up and admire his trophy, and he'd say, 'Here, sweet thang, you can have it.' I've got maybe fifty trophies. He gave the rest of them away. They didn't mean a thing to him.

"Curtis was a bloody genius. He didn't make any money racing. He lost money in racing. Where he made his money was in the timber business. He could fly over a hundred thousand acres of timber, and he could tell you how much of it was oak, how many feet of pine. He was awesome. He was brilliant. He was something else. Curtis did a lot of business with Ford, sold a lot of land, bought a lot of land. He didn't require but two hours' sleep. The man could go forever. We'd pack the night before. He'd get up at three in the morning, pick me up like a doll, take me out and lay me in the back of the limo, and I'd sleep until we got there. I'd never even wake up.

"We'd get up in the middle of night. He'd call Don and Carol Reeves, our good friends in Charlotte, and he'd say, 'Pop, we're heading for Daytona Beach. You all want to go?' He'd slam that telephone down and say, 'Sweet thang, grab your overnight bag.' And we'd go and pick them up and go and get the plane. It would be snowing, and we'd leave in winter clothes, and when we'd land in Daytona, and it would be so warm. I can still feel that air when we got off the plane.

"When Curtis started Charlotte Motor Speedway, he had the option on the land to purchase. Bruton Smith was promoting the other little Charlotte Motor Speedway, which is now in Concord, and Bruton had been talking about building a track, talking, talking, and he approached Curtis about going in together. Curtis was very apprehensive. Curtis had started on his own, and he wanted to continue on his own. But from what I understand—because I was not around when this took place—Curtis and Bruton were close friends, and so he went in with Bruton as partners, and then when they hit rock, Curtis got in trouble money-wise, and he got in the whole mess with the union. Curtis needed money, and he turned to the Teamsters. They would loan him money if he would help them organize the drivers. When he tried to organize a union, the only one who stood by him was Tim Flock. They were tight, good friends. You have to understand that Curtis was also a close friend of Bill France, like a brother to him. Bill France was a fine, fine man. He really helped a lot of people, and that's what hurt Bill so bad when Curtis tried to start a union. Curtis and Bill had raced together on the Mexican road course. But Curtis started the union because he wanted greater benefits for the drivers. He had seen them get all busted-up, their kids go hungry. They had nothing. But he did it to help build the Charlotte track too. Bill was so hurt. I think that's why the punishment didn't fit the crime. Curtis had been so close to him. Curtis did what he had to do, and Bill did what he had to do. And Bill France suspended Curtis and Tim both for a lifetime. Curtis and Bill patched it up before Curtis's death. Bill was one of the pallbearers at Curtis's funeral. But Bill took them back in '65, though Tim never did go back to racing.

"I was in a bar with Tim Flock in Atlanta, the night before Richard's [Petty] last race [in November 1992]. We all went out to eat crab legs, and Tim looked over at me, and there was a bunch of racing people there. We had gone into a karaoke bar, and Tim was about half-shot, and he looked over to this guy, and he said, 'Do you know who this little lady sitting here with me is?' The guy looked at him as though he had lost his mind. 'No, who?' Tim said, 'She was married to Curtis Turner. Do you have any idea who Curtis Turner was?' And the guy said no. And it made Tim mad, just broke his heart. He looked at that guy, and he said, 'Let me tell you something, if I could put any two drivers together today to race each other, it would be Dale Earnhardt and Curtis Turner, and Curtis would run right over the top of him, over him, and under him.' Tim was crazy about Curtis and loyal to him.

"The fans pitched a pretty big fit to get Curtis and Tim back into racing. I wonder sometimes what Curtis would have done in those years when he was out, 'cause those were his prime years.

"When France lifted Curtis's suspension in '65, one of his first races back was at Rockingham. He won the race with a broken rib. I thought about Curtis when Dale was driving with broken ribs. It's five hundred miles of hard racing. And back then they didn't have the comfort in the cars that they have now.

"When he came back, he was going to go with Ford, but the ride wasn't there. Fred Lorenzen had it. It just galled Curtis. He couldn't stand Fred. Fred was a new guy coming up sort of like with Earnhardt and Jeff Gordon. Of course, when Curtis got in that Plymouth, Ford couldn't stand it, so they got him a Ford to drive. Ford approached him at the Speedway. Glen Wood and Curtis were real tight. Glen put him in the car, and that's the one he won at Rockingham.

"Curtis was a wild man. Just like Glen Wood said, 'I can't tell you how many races Curtis would have won for us if he had only let us set the car up for him.' Glen said they'd work on the car and talk to Curtis, and he would never get in it before the race, never practice. He'd just get in and race. The cars were never set up for him. He just drove them. And he made them do things nobody could make them do. And when he'd be running out on the track, they'd stick the pit sign out, and he'd turn his radio off, make like it was torn up. He wouldn't look at the pits and he wouldn't hear them. Curtis didn't want anyone telling him what to do. He said he'd feel it when he had to come in, which he never did.

"At the time of his death Curtis had gotten to where he liked to play golf better than he liked to drive. Clarence King, who was a golf pro, was his best buddy. The last six months before his death they had traveled with us extensively. We had been to Las Vegas two or three times, just here, there, and everywhere. Going to Las Vegas with Curtis was wild. He would give me five one-hundred-dollar bills before we left home, and he'd say, 'Sweet thang, if I get down on my hands and knees and beg you for this money, don't give it to me, cause we got to get home on this.' 'Cause he had maxed-out every credit card we had, and he'd call the banks and have them wire money. Usually he won, but when he lost, he lost big. We had a ball.

"Curtis made millions and millions of dollars in his lifetime, and he blew every penny of it. Curtis lived every day like it was his last day. When he wanted something, he bought it. The week before he got killed, he tried out a Learjet. He'd always wanted one, and he was getting ready to buy it. It was a beautiful airplane, just awesome. Curtis loved speed. I guess most drivers do.

"When the union effort failed, Curtis and Bruton went broke, and the Speedway went into receivership. The next thing Bruton did was talk Curtis into resigning from the board as president, and after he lost his board seat, Bruton used his vote to get Curtis all the way out of Charlotte Motor Speedway. I don't know why Bruton wanted him to resign, and I don't know why he did resign. I was so young then. I wish I knew. I just wish . . . I would love to have him back and have some questions answered I didn't ask him, because I didn't know so much of what was going on. Curtis was so protective of me. 'Cause Curtis would teeter right on the fence between some things that were just not perfectly right. As far as out-and-out illegal, I never saw it. I saw him come close, but he didn't do anything *really* illegal. But I would love to ask Curtis some questions, and I can't do that.

"To make a long story short, Curtis always felt that Bruton cost him the track. He felt that Bruton had been his friend, and he turned out not to be a friend. And after they took the track away, Bruton went North, made all these millions, sold used cars, and came back and bought the Speedway for a zillion, gazillion dollars. Go figure.

"Curtis was very bitter about leaving the Speedway. Lord, yes. The whole time I was married to Curtis, Bruton Smith was the only man who Curtis despised.

"At the time of his death Curtis was getting ready to build another Speedway in Monroe, just right across the river from Charlotte. He had met with five different men, and the money was there, everything was all set. They were finalizing everything that weekend about the track. It was going to be a two-and-a-half-mile track, with a jet airstrip, and he had the sponsorship. Sure it was a vendetta against Bruton. I don't blame him.

"Until three years ago, I never laid eyes on Bruton Smith. Bob Myers took me to a party at the Charlotte Motor Speedway. Bruton was cordial but curt. Later Tim Flock had me in a parade at the Speedway. Do you know when that parade was over, our car was marked to leave. No provisions were made for us to sit in the VIP suites. I had never been to a track in this country where I wasn't welcomed with open arms and treated like a queen, except for the track my husband built. There's never been a tower named after him, never been grandstands named after him. There's a quote Walk of Legends, and the first name that should have been there was Curtis Turner's. And in fact, it's not there. I don't know what went on between them, but I do know you can't buy class. And as far as I'm concerned, Bruton Smith doesn't have any. And you can print that.

"Curtis was killed on the fourth of October, 1970, eighteen days before little Curtis was born. Curtis never got to see him. And he's so much like his daddy in so many ways, and in other ways he's entirely different. Little Curtis tried driving for a while. We had a great sponsor. But it was a lot of pressure.

"After Curtis was killed, I married a surgeon about four years later. He had a hard time competing with Curtis's legacy. We got divorced after eight years, and then I was single for twelve years. Tommy, my present husband, used to be my boss at Pulaski Motors, a Ford dealership. He was the sales manager there. Tommy is down-to-earth, just special. Today he works for Shearer Chevrolet, as does Little Curtis. We're all in the car business.

"Everybody has always wanted me to do a book on Curtis, but I don't know if I ever want to do that. I don't know if I want to share what I had with him."

29

BROOKLYN MEETS ROBERT GEE

LOU LAROSA, WHO GREW UP IN the borough of Brooklyn, city of New York, was fascinated by the workings of the automobile ever since he was a little boy. He read books about engines and would go to the junkyard, take a carburetor out of a jalopy and bring the greasy hunk of metal home to study. After he graduated high school, LaRosa worked in a bank by day, at a gas station as a mechanic by night. Two years later he quit the bank and concentrated on the cars.

After a stint in Vietnam, he raced briefly on Long Island. When he learned from an acquaintance that the DiGard race team was looking for help, LaRosa drove south to watch the Southern 500 in Darlington, then continued to Daytona where he walked in cold to the DiGard shop and told owner Jim Gardner that he'd "work for a month for nothing."

It was at DiGard that LaRosa met legendary engine builder Robert Gee, who would become a big influence on a man who would go on to build winning motors for some of NASCAR's legendary race teams.

LOU LAROSA: "I was born on October 8, 1943, in New York City. We lived on Manhattan's East Side while my father was in the service, lived with my grandmother on my mother's side in a brownstone down by Fort Greene in Brooklyn toward the end of the war, and when my father got out in 1945, we moved to Bensonhurst. My father was a rabid Yankee fan, and he also liked boxing. He boxed in the AAUs when he was younger, going under the false name of Joe Rivers, because his parents, who were from Italy, didn't approve of boxing. They thought it was all hoodlums and criminals.

"We grew up really poor, very, very poor. It was hard to make ends meet. My father worked two jobs. He was a correction officer during the day, and he worked nights at the Todd shipyard. We had a medical problem with my young sister, and that's where all the money went. He didn't drink, didn't run around with women, all the bills went to medical, and at the time there were no free giveaways like today. It came out of your pocket.

"We always drove an old car, fifteen years old or older—now they're classic cars, but back then they were junk.

"My father had a friend, Cammy Falcone, who owned a junkyard down by Coney Island. Ever since I was twelve years old, I had an interest in old cars and anything mechanical. I'd buy books and read about engines, and Cammy would let me go down and pick out an engine and take it apart, let me take the parts home. I'd take a carburetor into my bedroom, and I never could get it back together. I'd have extra pieces. I'd have a mess in there.

"Cammy would instruct me, and so did some of the older guys I got to know who were seventeen, eighteen years old and had cars. Back then it was common to put an Oldsmobile engine in a Ford, a Caddy engine in a Chevrolet. These guys were doing that because back then you could not go down to the local speed store and buy parts for your car. The guys who got out of the service were inquisitive, had ingenuity, and they went out and built parts. I ran with them, and I'd do that too, and that's how I learned mechanics.

"When I was fifteen I went to work in Sam's Neptune Service, a gas station on McDonald Avenue in Brooklyn. After I graduated high school in 1961, I went to work for the Chemical Bank from nine to five. They were first putting in a computer system, big mainframe computers, the forerunner of what you have today. They were account reconciliation tabulators, old machine punch cards. After I came home, I worked in the garage and did repairs until midnight.

"After two years I quit my job at the bank and went to work for the gas station full-time as a mechanic. I built my own car to race at Freeport on Long Island. Sam's was my sponsor. I was driver, builder, and owner. I raced in '64 and '65, and then I got drafted into the army in '65.

"I really liked it, for a couple of reasons. Being from Brooklyn, which was concrete and crowded, I really liked the outdoors, loved going to upstate New York with the Boy Scouts. I liked to shoot guns, enjoyed the challenge of making five bullets go through a hole the size of a dime at a hundred yards. That takes skill. So when I got drafted, it really didn't bother me.

"From June '66 to June of 67, I went to Vietnam. It was no big deal. I got shot at, but I didn't get shot. I did what I was told to do. It was scary for everybody, but it was no big deal. The way I grew up, I believe in serving your country. The President is Commander in Chief. If the government tells you to go, it's your duty to go. When you're a soldier, you don't sit there and think, Is this politically correct? If you questioned every order, you'd have chaos. My father went. My grandfather was in the Spanish-American war, World War I, and when he was sixty, he volunteered for World War II. I'm real high on Mom, apple pie, and America. People just don't know what a good country this is until you go and experience a Third World country like Vietnam, see what a dictatorship can do to the people, see how the people live in dirt poverty. These people lived in shacks with dirt floors. They lived like crap. Was it right to go to war? That's not my judgment call.

"What threat was Vietnam? Go back to the politics of the time. The Domino effect. If one country falls, another falls. We made a stand there, right or wrong.

"When I came home I went back and raced. I was average. I never had good equipment, 'cause I was doing it out of my pocket. I ran awhile, got married, crashed, got married again, got out of it, went into drag racing with my cousin, got out, then got back into it in the early seventies, until Freeport changed the rules on me. Freeport is like Bowman-Gray in Winston-Salem, just a football field with a track around it. In the middle of the season they changed the rules that forced you to change tires. They wanted you to go back to the eight-inch tires. But I had two or three thousand dollars tied up in the fatter tires. I couldn't afford to switch. So I sold the car and the equipment, and a guy I knew who worked for a paper in Jersey told me that the DiGard race team, which was down in Daytona Beach, was looking for help.

"So I drove down to Darlington and watched the Southern 500, continued to Daytona, and walked in and told the receptionist at DiGard I was with friends and I would like an application. She said, 'You can fill one out, but we have a stack this tall,' putting her hands about a foot apart. About that time Jim Gardner, the brother of owner Bill Gardner, walked in. He was all pissed off because they had blown up for the umpteeth time, or wrecked, so he was growling and all bent out of shape when I went in and told him what I could do.

"I had a brainstorm. I said, 'I'll tell you what I can do. I'll work for you for nothing for a month, and if you like it, you hire me, and if you don't, that's fine.' He liked that deal. He didn't have to pay me.

"He said, 'Fine,' so I went home and put the house up for sale, came back and went to work for him. At the time DiGard was based in Daytona Beach, which was a bone of contention at DiGard. They'd race and have to go down to Daytona Beach and drive back, so they were always a day behind. When they ran at tracks around here—at the end of the year was Wilkesboro, Rockingham, and Charlotte—they'd run out of Robert Gee's garage.

"At the time Mario Rossi was the team manager and chief engine builder. Mario had come down in the late sixties and worked with Banjo Matthews and had run his own car successfully out of Spartanburg with Bobby Allison. When the factories pulled out in the late sixties, he lost everything, and DiGard hired him to run the shop. When I went to work there, they had me sweeping the floors and tarring the parking lot. Being a Yankee, nobody liked you. It was a closed sport, and you had to prove yourself. I learned that very quickly from Robert Gee.

"When Robert first met me, he asked me what I wanted to do. I said I wanted to build motors. He said, 'You ain't ever going to make it. You have two strikes against you.' I said, 'What's that?' He said, 'One, you're a Yankee, and two, you're one of them Eye-talians.' Robert wasn't being vindictive or hateful. He was just telling it the way it was. Other than Rossi, there were no Italian-Yankee engine builders, and people certainly held it against Mario. They'll tell you other reasons, this or that, but there was always an underlying current of distrust until people got to know you. Here's the reason: When I grew up in Brooklyn, I learned the history of the Civil War from the Northern point of view, how Lincoln freed the slaves. But for the southerners, it wasn't about that. They feel the North actually invaded the South, kind of like if Russia had invaded the United States. Southern culture, southern ways were very different, and they felt the North wrecked havoc on the South. And it really did. Not only Sherman. The civilian population was punished. These people were put in poverty and starvation. And everyone who comes from here has had somebody killed or wounded in the Civil War or suffered deprivations from the war, so the hostility has been passed down from the great-grandfather to the grandfather, who told stories of carpetbaggers and Yankees, and how they raped the South and exploited it. They did. So in a way that bitterness is justified.

"So Robert Gee wasn't being hateful. He was just telling it like it is, like somebody telling Jackie Robinson, 'You ain't gonna play white man's baseball.' So blacks weren't the only ones being discriminated against. I caught it too. What I told myself was, Bite your lip and show people.

"I truly believe the cream rises to the top, that you can't keep a good man down. I have always felt that if you work hard enough and long enough and are determined enough, they can't hold you back. Jews may have been trodden down, but with hard work they come right back up. When you give up, you're finished. People got prejudice, doesn't matter if you're black or white. You ain't gonna change that prejudice by talking to them. You got to show them that 'I'm just like you. I'm not after your daughter or wife, I'm here to work.' Yeah the southerners were clanned, but they were that way because they've been screwed going back to the carpetbaggers. I don't justify the Ku Klux Klan, but there are reasons things happen.

"So Robert Gee wasn't being hateful. He was just telling me the way it was. Robert Gee was a good-hearted guy, who gave a lot away. Robert had a lot to do with making Darrell Waltrip, put Darrell up at his house, let him use his tools. The same with Dale Earnhardt. Robert was Dale's father-in-law. Robert's daughter was his second wife. Robert had a lot to do with making Dale. Robert was a joy to be around.

"The first two, three months I was at DiGard, the cars weren't running, the motors were blowing up. The place was in chaos. There was no organization. Byzantine politics was going on. The question was who was going to screw who. Some people wanted Darrell Waltrip as the driver. Others were loyal to Donnie Allison, who used to drive there. Half the people didn't like Mario and wanted someone else for crew chief. It was total chaos.

"The motors would blow up. Robert Gee used to say, 'Ain't no sense setting the pits up, because it ain't gonna run but a hundred miles and blow up.'

"Mario was always looking to get that extra horsepower. Darrell would say, 'By the time he gets done, the motor is all wore out.' Ironically when I went to work for Darrell many years later if you didn't hunt for that extra two horsepower, you were a son of a bitch. Things change in time.

"Mario would run the engine, and change this or that, and run it again. Mario was on the edge. He would have been a better drag racer than Winston Cupper. People said Mario was stupid, but he was *not* stupid. He was a smart man. He was always looking for that extra edge, lightweight cranks, things people talk about now. They had just switched from the big block engine, the 427s that you could run forever and would never blow up, to a little puny 350 cubic inches. You take 80 cubic inches away and you get a motor nobody has worked on, and shoot, you're down 500 horsepower with no torque. Torque is what makes the wheels turn. And the cars were still heavy, running 4,000 pounds. Now they're down to 3,400. A hundred pounds makes a lot of difference. So everybody was struggling, and they were lost. Cars wouldn't run. Some people knew how to cheat them up and make them run. Everything was in transition. Nevertheless, it was one of the best times in racing for me.

"Back then, I'd work on engines. David Ifft, a funny crazy guy, was the crew chief who worked on the car; Nick Olatta, who now works for John Andretti, did the transmissions—he had come from Penske and was well trained and well versed; and Kenny Trout was the fabricator. At fourteen Kenny had built his own supercharged hot rod. These were people who had talent, who could make a car go. These guys were in their thirties, and then there was old Robert Gee.

"You'd work on the cars, load the car, get on the truck, a sleeper, and drive the truck to the racetrack. When you got there, you'd unload the car, get the car ready, race the car. After the race, we'd load the car and drive it home. Just the five people. Today you have hood-pin specialists, a decal specialist.

"Racing was real small. There were good crowds, but no one thought to make show of getting a sponsor. People were happy to get a sponsor like Joe's Steak House for one race. DiGard was a pioneer. It was one of the first major teams, in that they had an airplane. Bill Gardner had a vision of racing turning out the way it is today. He had tractor trailers. His shop was a showroom. Bill Gardner was always one who tried to impress people. He was a businessman. He knew how business worked. I can remember he had people from Stokely Van Camp, the parent company of Gatorade, to dinner at Gene's Steak House on US 92 going away from the Daytona Speedway. He had all the big wigs there, all the hot shots, and that was something new. Now it's common in racing. They were in their suits and ties, and in his way of impressing people, Bill said, 'We're going to drink this three-hundred-dollar bottle of champagne.'

"Everybody was sitting there. Robert Gee was a little lit, and the waiter, who was French, came over with a little towel over his arm, and he said to Robert, 'Sir, would you like some Chateau LaFitte?' Robert, who always had a cigarette hanging out of his mouth, with a real southern drawl replied, 'Chateau de shit. Bring me a bourbon and Coke.' And them people from Stokely Van Camp just sat back and looked at him in shock!

"Robert Gee was a person I admired. I liked the heck out of Robert. He probably didn't get out of the third grade but he built some of the fastest modified race cars. In that little garage on Route 29 near the Charlotte Speedway he built some of the fastest cars ever to come out of the Carolinas. They ought to make a movie about a boy like that.

"I can remember one time the car was running crappy, and Bill Gardner called a team meeting. He held one every Monday after the race to critique our performance, which also was a first. You came back and everybody knew what they had to do. You didn't need a meeting to tell you. He had this big old oak table about twelve feet long, and the whole team was sitting around it.

"Robert Gee was paid on a contract basis. The Gardners paid him so much to come down and put the bodies on the car and work on them down in Daytona. He'd stay out all night, go to the Macombo Lounge or to Tommy Brown's Band of Renowned, a country and western place, and after partying all night, he'd come in and be sitting there, smoking that cigarette, and he'd smoke it down until it was about an eighth of an inch long and the ash would be three inches long. He had eyes that looked liked like a Chinaman's, big old eyes that were slits, and he'd be watching as they were going through this boring meeting, a Cheech and Chong experience, because Bill Gardner would say, 'What do we need?' Kenny Trout would say, 'We need a band saw.' Bill would say, 'Get a band saw, Jim. Write that down.' 'Okay, Bill.'

"We'd come back for the next meeting. 'What do we need?' 'We need that band saw.' 'Where's the band saw, Jim?' 'It's back-ordered, Bill.' That was bullshit. The Gardners were prone to getting money but not to spending it. They were *never* going to buy it. So the meetings were futile. So one day Robert Gee leaned over, and he had that cigarette dangling, his eyes closed, and Bill said, 'Anything else?' Now remember Bill Gardner doesn't know Robert Gee. Robert was there because Darrell wanted him. Robert said, 'Yup,' just like that. 'Well, what is it, Robert?' asked Bill Gardner. Robert said, 'You need to do something about the goddamn commode.' Bill said, 'What's wrong with the commode?' Robert Gee said, 'You either need to lower the water or give me an inner tube because my balls are sloshing around in there.' And Kenny Trout and I peed in our pants. And Robert Gee never cracked a smile. And Old Bill, boy did he get red!

"They made a movie, *Greased Lightning,* about Wendell Scott, the only black driver in NASCAR. Richard Pryor was playing Wendell Scott, and Richard told Robert Gee, 'You're the funniest white man I ever met in my life.'

"DiGard hired Stump Davis from the Shadow team, which ran a Can Am car. Stump's background was fuel injection, Indy cars, drag racing. He had worked with Danny Ongais. Mario and Stump had a conflict, and Darrell was in the middle pissing and moaning. All Darrell's done for twenty-five years is piss and moan, never take a stand. Like a chameleon he changes colors in a heartbeat, going with whatever's popular and suits him. That's how he got the name 'Jaws.' He was always complaining, bitching. Sometimes it was valid. There are times when you have to say something, but I also believe that you have to take a stand, say what you mean, and mean what you say. Needless to say, he pissed and moaned enough that they fired Stump, fired Mario. He just had to have Robert Yates, who had worked at Holman-Moody, worked for Junior Johnson. So they brought in Robert Yates to be the chief engine builder.

"And I, being a hardheaded Italian, didn't get along with Robert from day one, because my loyalty was to Rossi. It's what happens when a new regime takes over. He's going to put in his people. And so there was no love lost there between Robert Yates and me. The good part was that DiGard brought Ducky Newman from Bud Moore's to work with Robert. Bud wasn't big on paying back then. Bud would pay you by the hour, and Ducky was making next to nothing. I got to be good friends with Ducky. He taught me assembly, machine work, honing, and balancing. Another person who came with Robert Yates was Lee Willyuh, a certified genius. Lee, who came from Junior's, worked with Robert on the first steel main caps, which hold the crankshaft in place. Chevrolet had cast iron ones, and they were prone to break. As Chevy added more power, the whole bottom end would blow out. Robert had come down with the idea at Junior's, and when he came over to us, he handmade these caps, put them on our car, and David Ifft and I drove the car out to Riverside, California, to test it before the first race in January of '74.

"We towed the car on an open trailer behind us. Driving west I said to David, 'Shouldn't we drain the motor?' David was real rough. He said, 'Piss on it. Goddamn, we're going to California. Sunny weather.' He disconnected the radiator hose but didn't take out the drain plugs.

"Around the time we reached Arizona, David looked back and said, 'Stop. The bungee came off and you ran over it.' Bungee is Southern lingo for the tie-down strap. I didn't know what a bungee was. I swear I thought I had run over a Japanese kamikaze pilot.

"I got out, and I tied it, and I said, 'David, there's water coming out from under the race car.' He said, 'That's just goddamn condensation.' I said, 'David, it's running out of the goddamn motor.'

"What had happened, even though the hoses were off, the motor had frozen going through Louisiana, where it was 32 degrees out. Cracked the goddamn block. And I was supposed to be in charge of looking out for Robert's motor.

"David said, 'What are we going to do?' I said, 'David, start that son of a bitch up, and we'll drive it over to the Grand Canyon and jump out.' Because I didn't want to have to face Robert. David said, 'No, no, let's get a bottle and think about this.'

"We drove on to Riverside and got there about eleven at night. We borrowed a lift from Bud Moore's crew, drove to a shopping center, and at twelve at night in the shopping center, if you can picture it, me and David changed the motor by ourselves.

"We took it out to the racetrack the next day. We had never started it. We got it ready, got it through inspection. David said, 'Fire that son of a bitch up.' It started smoking. I thought, Holy shit, we've blown up the second motor too, but it was only oil on the head.

"We ran good, qualified third. But when I got back, and Yates found out about the first motor, he held me responsible for freezing it up. I was on his shit list, and I didn't see eye to eye with him, so I left."

30

TROUBLES ON THE LAST LAP

AFTER LEAVING COTTON OWENS after the 1970 season, in 1971 the thirty-one-year-old Buddy Baker became a force to be reckoned with on the superspeedways. In addition to a win at Darlington that year, he finished second six times and third five times. Perhaps Baker's most remarkable statistic was the high percentage of races that he led. Of the nineteen races he entered in the Petty Enterprises Dodge in 1971, Baker led fifteen of them. If he didn't finish in the top five, it was because his car broke or he crashed. Throughout his career his near wins would gall him. Had he been luckier or driven less all-out, his record would have shown far more than the nineteen wins he garnered.

In 1971 Baker teamed with the King, Richard Petty. He drove in the shadow of the sport's top attraction. Desirous of being top dog again, Baker then moved on to the K&K Insurance team, owned by Nord Krauskopf and led by Harry Hyde. Baker had an outstanding year in 1973, winning two, finishing second four times and third six times. His battles on the big tracks against Richard Petty, David Pearson, Cale Yarborough, and Bobby Allison were fierce and exciting.

In his quest to find a team that would lead him to his personal quest—winning the Daytona 500—in 1974 he switched to the Bud Moore race

team. Baker drove for Big Bud for four seasons, and though he won
five important superspeedway races, he still was unable to win the Big
One in February at Daytona.

BUDDY BAKER: "Cotton Owens was an ex-driver. He had been
with David Pearson before me and had great success with him. I just
walked into an awfully good race team. Cotton was the mildest car
owner I ever had any experience with. He understood the ups and
downs of the sport. Sometimes we had huge leads, and the car would
break something, and he would keep calm. He was like a father figure
to drive for. But when he got mad, you would listen because it meant
something. A lot of people talk, and I don't give a hoot. I just fly back
at them. In Cotton's case, I always felt Cotton gave a hundred percent
to me, and I always gave a hundred percent back. We kept falling out
of the race, having problems, breaking things.

"For example, I lost the April Talladega race in '70 when a tire
ripped apart with thirteen laps to go. I probably ran over something.
Goodyear had fixed the tire problem from the year before, but back
then, before interliners, if you got a puncture, it was like somebody
shot the tire. It was pretty much like going over the Alps in a hot air
balloon and realizing you're out of gas. There's not much you can do
about it, but say, 'Uh-oh.'

"His crew even gave me a trophy one time, 'cause we were having
so much trouble. It said, 'You're our horse even if we never win a race.'
When the crew feels that way, it isn't very long before we're sitting in
the winner's circle.

"I won the Darlington race that September in Cotton's car.

"In '71, Chrysler went from six teams to two. Richard Petty had
both teams, so I had to leave Cotton and run out of Richard's shop.
That was another Chrysler placement. There wasn't big conversation
between Petty Engineering and me. And this was tough for Petty
Engineering and it was hard on me, because one of my friends who
was let go so I could come in was Pete Hamilton. The Pettys loved
Pete. Richie Baerz, who later was my crew chief, was like a brother to
Pete. Any time you go into a place where you're taking the place of
somebody who meant a lot to the group, it's tough. And I liked Pete.
That made it double tough. It wasn't anything I had anything to do

with. But whew, when I walked in there, I could almost feel the cold fingers.

"It took about five races before I could feel it was warming up. Another reason going to the Pettys was hard on me was that with Cotton, I was numero uno. I was *the* guy, and when I went to Richard's team, I am no longer uno. I'm two-oh. In the literal sense I went from uno to two-oh.

"Richard and I always got along great. Richard has always been a friend of mine, and it was never a problem between Richard and me. Like I said, Pete had had pretty good success with the Petty Engineering car, and I was a foe before I walked in the door. Believe me, just because you ran for Chrysler, that didn't make you everybody's buddy.

"We managed to get through the first year and make a pretty good year of it and also acquired a pretty good friendship with Richard. I felt like we really came along. Starting out good was the biggest thing. Everyone was expecting us to do well, and the first race together at Daytona Richard and I ran one and two. Did you see how many times we ran one and two? Richard finished first, and I finished second, never the other way around.

"First of all, there was never any question in my mind who the number one team was. And when you're running one and two, you don't go out there and take the chance of taking out both cars. One time Lee Petty told me just that. He said, 'One thing that our race team does not do. If we got first and second, we don't take each other out.' That was good enough for me. When they explain their position, you pretty much know what to do from there. Richard was the number one team, and it was Petty Engineering, not Baker Engineering. And yet, I was able to win races. In May I won the Rebel 400 at Darlington when Donnie Allison's engine blew. It was a great experience, because Richard's car had had problems, and Richard was in the pits calling the shots. It was a nice family relationship. But after having done what we did the first year, the second year was kind of a disappointment.

"Part of it had to do with the fact that Chrysler had pulled out of racing. That was a shock, for sure. We still had parts enough to race forever, I guess. Richard had not run out of resources by any means.

He had STP, so we were pretty well still there. But that second year is never the same as first on a race team.

"The first race out in '72, I came off the corner running right up front, and Walter Ballard and I got together, and it tore the brand-new race car all to pieces. It just didn't start out well. Even though we had had a great first year, you're only as good as the last race you've run. At the same time Bobby Isaac was not altogether happy with what he was doing, and I was talking with Harry Hyde about going over to the K&K team. My first concern was Bobby. I had already been through one of those deals where a popular driver was replaced. I said to Harry, 'By no means would I consider it unless Bobby Isaac himself has decided he does not want to be there.' When that's what Bobby decided, there was no question then. It was an opportunity to drive for Harry Hyde. I had won the World 600 at Charlotte for the Pettys, but if you look at my history, winning didn't mean that much. It had to do with what I felt was going to be best for my future. The opportunity to be the number one driver again meant a lot to me.

"I went with Harry, and he provided probably as good a race car as I've ever driven. Harry was incredible. He was the best storyteller who ever lived. He would take a little card out of his pocket and show you exactly what you were going to qualify at down to the thousandths. He'd say, 'We're going to win the pole, and we're going to be this much faster than everybody else.' You'd go, 'Whaaat?' You'd think, Wait a minute. Where is his pointed hat? He's a magician.

"The races I won for Harry were as memorable as any I ever won, 'cause just the stories going home were worth the winning. You felt so good about winning with him it was incredible. I've won races for people, huge races, races you would think would make your career, and you'd get back, and they'd go, 'We were supposed to win. What was so big about that?' And you'd go, 'Aw, excuse me. Let me get my little self out of here. I feel like a brick now.'

"Harry just always had a perfect race car. In their time his cars were as good as the Petty group or anybody else. He and Bobby Isaac had had a tremendous amount of success. Harry always said he found five miles an hour when I came over there. We got along great, and part of it was the chemistry. I very much respected him. At one time we were so much faster than everyone else on the major speedways that it was sometimes four and five miles an hour better than the other cars.

"In '72 fans got to watch some fierce competition between me and Cale and Bobby Allison and Richard. Have you ever watched *King of the Hill*? Sometimes you are left standing but you look a little ruffled. That's where we wanted to be. Cale and I had several run-ins like that, and it was because we wanted the same thing out of the sport. Our driving styles were a lot alike on the major speedways, and though Cale and I were the best of friends off the track, sometimes on the racetrack I don't know of anybody I disliked more. The old saying is, 'Good guys finish last.' People don't understand when a guy gets out of the car after a race and goes after another driver. They don't realize these are spirited people, or they wouldn't be able to do what they do. I don't feel hard at somebody getting mad at me. When I first started racing, what you said didn't mean a whole lot. You had to be able to back it up. It helped to be mean to the point of taking up for yourself.

"In '73 I ran for the points for the very first time. I finished sixth that year. I can't tell you how many times I had David or Richard beat, and we'd get in trouble. I mean, that goes for anyone who was in the top five or six of a generation of drivers. Donnie Allison was leading a lot of races he never got credit for. He ran up front and ran well, but you have to go all the way.

"One time I was leading the Daytona 500 and I called in to Harry Hyde and I said, 'Harry, this thing just quit.' He said, 'Buddy Baker, you better be telling a lie.' I said, 'Do you hear anything?' I never heard another reply. I came in, and everyone had gone to the garage. It's a sickening feeling. One time I was in sight of the checkered flag, and the car just quit running. This must have happened to me at least ten times in my career.

"In May of '73 at Talladega I was leading, and then I was involved in a twenty-one-car pileup. Ramo Stott had problems coming off turn two, and this awful chain reaction started. We were running well over 200 miles an hour. And this will tell you something about David Pearson, the luckiest son of a gun who ever lived! If you look in the dictionary next to the word 'lucky,' they ought to have a full-size head shot of David Pearson. David started that race outside the pole. He fouled his plugs out, so when we took off, he couldn't go. He was running so poorly we were almost ready to lap him. When the huge wreck started, it started directly behind him, and from there back everybody was wiped clean.

"The front group came around, and we were not that far from starting to lap traffic, and I ran into what looked like a junkyard. People were sliding, wrecking. Dirt was flying. There was smoke. I saw motors. We rode off into this cloud bank of destroyed race cars, and we crashed. I knocked the motor out of my car. Cale went over the top of me still accelerating. Bobby Allison hit James Hylton and cut the car just about in half. It was just a huge wreck. And here came David Pearson in high gear, running about three miles an hour, *chuga-chuga-chuga-chug*. He was so far behind that the smoke had dissipated. He drove through, hit the gear, went around, and the pace car came out. He went in and changed all the spark plugs, went out and won the race. Now tell me!

"I won my first race for Harry Hyde in Charlotte at the World 600 in '73. That was a unique race. I blew a right rear tire going into turn three, never looped the car, just stayed sideways all the way, slid right to the pit entrance, went right down pit road, changed the tires, came back out and never lost the lead.

"At the Talladega 500 I finished second to Dick Brooks, who had a fast car. That was the race that Bobby Isaac quit in the middle. He said voices told him to get out of the car. That wasn't like him at all. I don't know what the problem was. Maybe he just decided that was it. I know if I heard someone tell me something in a race car, I'd look to see who was in there with me. But when you hear that, it's time to quit. He did the right thing.

"I finished third at Darlington, third at Dover, fourth at North Wilkesboro, fourth at Martinsville. At Charlotte we had a good race car but we were disqualified when Nord Krauskopf wouldn't let NASCAR look at our engine after the race. Back then there was a lot of experimentation going on as far as how to get by with what they had. Nord hated the restrictor plate rules. But everyone was trying to get a competitive edge. It really wasn't cheating. Everybody was experimenting. That was a good dodge, wasn't it? Unfortunately, when we went to race at Daytona in '74, Nord boycotted over the rules, and that left me with an awful good race team and nowhere to go. At that time, I was on top of my game, and I wanted to race. To this day I think the world of Harry Hyde and Nord Krauskopf. Both have departed. It was one of those situations: I'm a race car driver, and I want to race. I was sitting around doing nothing, and they were fixing to do a hill climb at Pike's Peak. I went, 'Boy, is this out of character for me or what?'

"Bud Moore called me and asked if I wanted to drive for him. Bud Moore at that time had as good a race car as anybody. I thought to myself, Pike's Peak or the World 600? Give me a break. I went over and talked to Nord. I explained to him, 'These special events I'd love to stick with you, but I want to go race.' Nord said, 'We can't tell you we're going to be ready to race again in three months, or whether we will ever race again.' I said, 'That pretty much answers my question.'

"This was the only race team in my career that I didn't choose to leave. If was just that they weren't racing anymore. Can you see me at Pike's Peak? Whoa. Put army parachutes on that one.

"Bud was special. He's kind of like Bill France. He's been here since Day One. The first time they threw up a handful of red dirt, Bud ran through it. Of all the people I ever drove for, he was the boss more so than anybody. He was a driving coach. He would talk to you during the race. Not that I always listened. He'd get so mad at me sometimes he'd take the headset off and throw it off into the infield. He'd want me to slow down, and I'd lift, and I'd pick up speed. We won a race at Ontario one time, and he wouldn't even come to the winner's circle. He told me to slow down, and I lifted, and I picked up speed. I had a 28-second lead over David Pearson. Bud said, 'I told you to slow down.' I said, 'Bud, I am slowing down.' He said, 'You're picking up speed, Buddy. Don't tell me.' While we were having this discussion, I picked up another second on David. Bud was getting madder and madder. I had to go to Spartanburg to sit down and talk with him for a long time to make him understand, 'cause he just flat lost it.

"But Bud and I got along great. I was driving for Bud during the Firecracker 400 in '74. I was sitting right behind Richard Petty and David Pearson as they went for the checkered flag. Richard and David had some classic duels near the end of races, and this was one of them. That was a race I should have won. In fact, I had almost a lap lead on the field, and the accelerator cable went back to almost half throttle. It had a stainless steel ball on the accelerator, and it slipped back on the cable, and I was running half throttle.

"David led Richard past the white flag, and then Richard took the lead back. Richard was on the inside and started moving up toward the outside, and David Pearson, in sight of the checkered flag, was not going to lift. David Pearson was headed for the Union 76 station when Joe Frasson hit him in the left front and straightened him out, and he went on to beat Richard and to win the race, and that was incredible. I mean, David was a goner, and Joe Frasson drove into one side and knocked him back straight. When that happened, I was on the brakes pretty good then.

"I mean my car was flying that day. Cale and I tied for third and fourth. I was battling Cale. Cale and I were going at it. We had locked into the two red faces looking in at each other and grinding the sides off the race cars. That was the only dead heat that's ever been declared by NASCAR.

"The next race at Bristol I was leading Cale going into the final lap, and he put me into the grandstand. I may have crowded him, and he may have decided he didn't want to be crowded. Then I tried to get him, and he tried to get me, and we both went up on the wall. He slid a little bit better than I did. I mean, both of us climbed up on the wall and we ended up sliding across the finish line first and second, and his car was a little straighter sliding than mine.

"In '74 Darrell Waltrip was a rookie. Darrell was extremely talented as far as this: What he didn't know about the draft, he would ask. All of a sudden it didn't take him very long to move into the forefront, and he was so damn cocky he made everybody mad right at first.

"I was at a gathering at Daytona one night, and he was on the stage, and he walked up there to do a radio show, and he said, 'I know you don't know me. I'm Darrell Waltrip from Owensboro, Kentucky, and I'm here to take Richard Petty's place.' The people in those stands would have killed for Richard Petty. I went, 'Boooooooo.' And everybody sat there for a second and went, 'Boooooooo.' It didn't take Darrell but a second to turn the racing world against him. They used to say when he drove down Interstate 77, people booed him here in Charlotte! Then Cale named him 'Jaws.' Incredible.

"At the end of '74 Bud lost his sponsor, RC Cola. He asked me what I was going to do. I said, 'I'm going to stay with you.' I ran well every time I ran with Bud. I won three Talladegas for him, won Atlanta with him, and we had a good race team. We picked up different sponsors during the '75 season, Coppertone, Shoney's, United Gunite, the army, but where we killed everybody was when we got with Norris Industries.

"We won Talladega in '75. I was leading David Pearson in the final lap, and he went high, and I made sure he didn't get ahead of me, and I beat him. See, Talladega was unique. The finishing line is about a hundred yards farther down the racetrack than it is at Daytona, so when David made his move, he showed his hand way back. Once he showed me what he was going to try to do, I just made sure I took a better line and didn't leave a whole lot of racetrack for that 21 car to run on. He was smart on that racetrack, but that particular day, I had a better race car.

"Talladega was my potatoes anyhow. That was my smokehouse. I'd go there and have something extremely good or extremely bad happen. I got burned there once. But overall the racetrack was the strongest I ran on as far as my driving style.

"In August of '75 Tiny Lund was killed at Talladega. Tiny was like a big brother. He and I fished together. He pulled practical jokes on me. One night he took the mascot for the Charlotte Motor Speedway—a cheetah—and put it in my bedroom. I went in. It was the middle of the night, and you don't turn on lights. I crawled in bed in the buff. I heard this, *Chhhhhhhh* sound.

"I turned the light on, and here was this cheetah standing six inches from my face. Not in a cage. A real cheetah.

"I can tell you one thing: Don't let anyone tell you that a cheetah is the fastest running animal on earth! 'Cause I was in the hall before that cat knew that damn light was on.

"I made my appearance well known when I came through that door. I didn't even bother to ask who was at fault. I knew it was Tiny.

"Another time we were fishing down in his fishing camp. It was a hundred degrees. I said, 'I'm going swimming.' So I dived in off the back of the boat. All of a sudden, a pain hit me. We had been talking about alligators, and underneath me I could hear a bubbling sound. I said to myself, 'Tiny Lund has me.' He dove off the front of the boat, caught me by my privates, squeezed and started swimming toward the bottom. Of course, I'm going with him.

"I got up in the boat, took a paddle, and I wouldn't let him get in. It took him twenty minutes to get in the boat. I think you have a picture of Tiny Lund.

"Of all the races I won, I can't remember anything jarring me quite as bad as learning Tiny had crashed and died. In the winner's circle after the race I was unaware that he was dead. During the interview someone said, 'Oh, by the way,' just like, 'Oh, by the way, it's sunny outside.' I was talking, saying, 'The car handled great,' and this guy said, 'Oh, by the way, Tiny died today.' I almost fell out of the chair. I just said, 'Guys, you all will just have to excuse me. That's the interview.' That was the hardest thing I ever had to hear. Tiny was a good friend. Racing means a lot, but it's just not that important."

WANDA LUND

31

THEY WERE ALL CRAZY

WANDA LUND MET HER FUTURE husband, Tiny, at a race at Columbia, South Carolina, in 1968, when she was a nineteen-year-old farm girl. He was a six-foot-five, 250-pound stock car racer. She was not impressed. For Tiny, it was love at first sight. It was only after Tiny gave her a good spanking that they began dating.

Theirs was a classic love story that ended in a crash at Talladega in 1975. Tiny had semiretired, and racing that day didn't feel right to him. He raced only because he had given his word. For many years after his death, Wanda, who lives in Charlotte, felt anger and bitterness toward her husband. She refused to go to a racetrack. Only after driver Larry Frank got her to come to the Charlotte Motor Speedway to watch him race in a Legends event did she forgive Tiny, and at the same time, the sport itself.

WANDA LUND EARLY: "I was born December 10, 1948, in Haywood County, North Carolina, and was raised there on a farm. I enjoyed growing up on a farm. We were very poor, but we were very close and very happy. You'll never hear me say I have all these emotional and mental problems because of my childhood. I had a very happy childhood. It was a dairy farm, and I enjoyed helping my dad. I'd get up early in the morning, about three-thirty, four o'clock and go

259

round up the hundred or so milk cows. I enjoyed doing it. I can remember very well the pleasure of the early morning in the summers, the dew still on the grass. I went barefoot my whole life. The only time I wore shoes was when it snowed and I had to. So I enjoyed feeling the dew on my toes, hearing the sounds of the unusual bird, and I'd think, God, I'm on top of the world. I love this feeling.

"I'd roam those mountains, get down on my knees and look at the little flowers, climb the trees. I about drove my mom nuts.

"I was very much a tom boy. I can remember overhearing a conversation between my mom and dad. My mother said, 'She's a young lady now. She's going to have to start wearing dresses and acting like a young lady.' My dad was saying, 'Ev, she's the best help I've ever had. Leave her alone. I need the help. She'll come out of it maybe.'

"I never did get over being a hillbilly farm girl. To this day I have no regrets, and I make no apologies. What you see is what you get. You either can handle it or you can't.

"I went to school at Crabtree-Ironduff. Crabtree and Ironduff were little communities. We're not talking towns, just little farm communities next to each other. There were 250 to 300 students in grades one through twelve.

"When I was nineteen, I moved to Florence, South Carolina, over the summer with my cousin. I went for the excitement. I had never been off the farm. When I moved to Florence, I met this lady, Doris Bowman. She and I were good friends. We were working together at the Howard Johnson.

"The next summer Doris was living in Columbia, South Carolina, and we got an apartment together, and since the same man was managing the Howard Johnson in both Florence and Columbia, we got jobs working at Howard Johnson's in Columbia. Doris's boyfriend was the biggest race nut that's ever been. Every Thursday night we would go to the dirt track in Columbia.

"This was 1968, and one Thursday night everyone was so excited. They said, 'Oh, those big NASCAR boys are going to be in town. We got to go to the race tonight.' So we went. I remember Buck Baker won the race so when Doris's boyfriend introduced me to Tiny, I was not at all excited about meeting Tiny. If I was to meet a real race car driver, I wanted to meet Buck Baker. He had won. So when I was introduced to Tiny, I said, 'Yeah, yeah, yeah, how are you? Fine.' Tiny was sizing me up and down, but I wanted to meet Buck Baker.

"What was weird, Doris and her boyfriend were intent on finding Wanda a guy. And so on Sunday they dragged me along to Rockingham, and I was totally not interested. I was not interested at all. This was before women and children were allowed in the pits.

"At this race at Rockingham I had never seen so many people in my life. I had never been so hot and aggravated in my life. I thought I would die. The heat was just awful so I climbed up on somebody's truck in the infield and I laid there and went sound to sleep.

"I laid there sound asleep, and I woke up because I was so hot. I just sat there watching the cars for a few minutes, and then I had to go to the bathroom so I got down off the truck and started for the rest rooms. Tiny had fallen out of the race, and he was walking by where we were, and I looked at this guy because he was so dirty and his hands had blood running off them. He stopped to talk to Doris and her boyfriend for a second. I was by the truck standing there observing. I said to him, 'Do you drive race cars too?' He said, 'Well, you have a long memory. I just met you Thursday night.' I said, 'What is wrong with your hands?' He said, 'A damn ill-handling race car.'

"Tiny asked me for my phone number, and it was like, 'I don't think so.' He said, 'You might as well cooperate with me today right now, because I am going to marry you.' And I said, 'Honey, my momma would kill me if I dragged someone like you home.' There was no way. I was looking him up and down, and I mean, this guy was *huge*. I was thinking, I'm five foot two, and there ain't no way in your wildest dreams.

"I can tell you that we didn't start dating immediately. He'd call friends of mine wanting to know, 'Where is Wanda? Where is she going to be?' He'd call and ask me for dates, and I'd say, 'No, thank you.' But he was so persistent. He kept right on. I said to myself, I can't get rid of this guy, so I made a date and stood him up. I was terrible, awful, figuring that sooner or later he'd get the message.

"One Sunday Doris and her boyfriend and a bunch of us went to Lake Murray where they were going to teach me how to water-ski. The boyfriend told Tiny.

"I was off the side of the boat with a ski belt on feeling so proud and cocky. I was thinking, This is cool. I'm not drowning. I would just pop back up. Tiny came aboard, and he said, 'You really shouldn't do that without putting a vest on. You don't know how to swim and sometimes those belts will break.' I thought to myself, Oh yeah, right. Who do you think you are?

"I no more thought this than it broke, and Tiny had to jump in and pull me out 'cause I was sinking like a rock. I was choking and sputtering, and he starting shaking me, saying, 'I told you. You wouldn't listen.'

"He turned me over his knee and set my heinie-end on fire like a two-year-old kid. Then we were an item after that.

"He was one of the biggest people I had ever seen in my life. I was not afraid that he would hurt me physically, but I was a little bit scared. I was very young, and he was so overpowering.

"I never met anyone like him. He seemed to have no fear of anything. He seemed to not have any common sense about anything.

"Tiny could not believe anyone couldn't swim. He was an incredible skier and swimmer. Over the years we were dating and married, Tiny thought if he threw me in enough times, I would swim. 'You're gonna swim.' So he'd throw me in and see how long I'd bubble. He'd finally drag me out. 'Well, I guess today is not the day you're gonna swim.'

"Tiny was a big overgrown puppy who liked to play. Tiny could hurt you just loving you, playing with you, hugging you. He was very, very strong. I know a lot of times he'd be playing with the mechanics, and they'd say, 'My God, he about broke my neck.' I called him 'Baby Huey,' you know, the big duck who never had any harmful intentions whatsoever, but every time he turned around, he was tearing up or screwing up something. That was Tiny in a nutshell.

"After we started dating, the first race I went to see was at Daytona. My prior racing experience had been short dirt tracks, and this was very exciting. But once again I was atop a truck in the infield, and after watching him practice and qualify, I laid down on the truck and went to sleep. Later, he was all excited. He asked me, 'What did you think?'

"I said, 'I went to sleep.' He said, 'You went to sleep? For God's sake, why?' I said, 'Well, it took you too long to come around.' He said, 'Hell, I was going 180 miles an hour. It took too long to come around?' Well, Daytona was a big track, and compared to the little short tracks I'd been watching, it did take longer to come around. So I got bored and went to sleep.

"His feelings were so hurt, but in the long run I think it was good for him. He tried so hard to impress me that I didn't realize he was trying hard to impress me. 'Cause I had never been off the farm.

"I should have been excited, and I was, to see all these different people. The first guy I met in racing was an executive with Grayrock Brakelines. Tiny introduced me to this man, and I said, 'Hi, how are you? It's nice to meet you.' He said, 'What's so nice about it?' Well, I had never had anybody speak to me like that in my life. Oh God, he was hateful. I have never met anyone who was such a crab as this man.

"I almost started crying. My lip was trembling. I said, 'Nothing really, and if everybody else I meet in racing acts like you, I'd just as soon go back home to the farm right now.'

"He looked at Tiny and said, 'Is this an act?' Tiny said, 'No Bill, this is genuine. She really is like this.'

"The guy felt so bad that he had hurt my feelings, after that all the times I saw him he went out of his way to be kind and nice, because I guess he thought my country accent was an act.

"Tiny didn't make enough money racing to support himself, so he owned a fish camp, and he went fishing every single day. To Tiny it was still something he loved to do. People would book to come in fishing, and when he wasn't racing, he'd be a guide. He'd take them out on the lake in a boat fishing for bass or rockfish, which was Tiny's specialty. In 1963 Tiny caught the world's record rockfish for freshwater, 55 pounds, and he held that record until 1976. It was a big fish, and it's on display at the Joe Weatherly Museum in Darlington now. And it stayed a state record until 1992. I was doing an autograph session in Charlotte, and somebody asked me about Tiny's fish, and I said, 'I think the waters are so fished out now that I don't think that record will ever be broken,' and I no more said that when some guy came up and handed me a newspaper article. Some guy had broken Tiny's record, and just for a second I felt like somebody had died. Then I heard this voice in my head saying, What the hell. Records are made to be broken. And I just laughed. I said to myself, If this guy had as much fun with his fish as Tiny did his, then I really commend this ole' boy. And then later I met the guy, and he brought the fish for me to see. It was not a whole lot bigger than what Tiny had caught, but it was larger. I had heard that he ran up and down the lake trying to get the fish weighed in. It was weighed several times. This went through my mind: They finally weighed it until it broke 55 pounds. But when I actually saw the fish, I was content, because the fish was bigger, and the ole' boy who caught it was so nice. He said, 'Wanda, if I'da known you were this nice, hell, I'd have eaten the damn fish. I really feel bad about it now that I've met you.'

"I said, 'Now don't, because that's something to be proud of.' His fish was 56 pounds, 7 ounces, a huge fish.

"Tiny's life was racing, fishing, and old dogs. I used to tease him about the song, 'Old Dogs, Young Children and Watermelon Wine.' That about summed up his philosophy in life.

"One of Tiny's closest friends was LeeRoy Yarbrough. I actually knew LeeRoy before I knew Tiny. LeeRoy lived in Columbia and raced at this little dirt track every Thursday night. LeeRoy raced there about every week, and he won a lot of races there. LeeRoy was a big NASCAR driver at the time, but it never dawned on me that the two of them were involved in the same type of racing.

"I have to say this—back then they were all crazy. There wasn't a sane one in the crowd. LeeRoy was a lot of fun. He was a cutup. He was focused, had a quick temper. The least little thing could set him off. LeeRoy wouldn't think if he got mad. He'd take a swing. After Tiny and I started dating two or three times I saw him start fights. Tiny would step in and break it up—or take up for LeeRoy. One time LeeRoy made Tiny mad, and Tiny beat the hell out of LeeRoy. Tiny knocked him plum across the hood of the car, knocked him out of his shoes. I said, 'Tiny, he's your friend.' He said, 'I can straighten him out, but no one else can.' And then he picked LeeRoy up and dusted him off and started petting him, saying, 'You shouldn't have done that.' And LeeRoy said, 'Yeah, I know Tiny. I'm sorry.'

"I thought, God, these guys are nuts. You'd be sitting back and watching this, thinking, These guys really do care about each other. These guys will really help each other out, and they did, loaning each other parts, sharing motel rooms, 'cause they didn't make the money then they make today, but on that track they were bitter enemies. They raced for that win. Off the track, they were the best friends in the world.

"I know one time at a short dirt track Tiny was the only one with a new set of tires. Larry Frank told me that Tiny went out there and qualified and sat on the pole. 'Cause of the new tires. Larry said Tiny took his tires off and lent them to everyone to qualify with, and Larry said he went out and broke Tiny's time and sat on the pole with Tiny's tires. They were like that.

"Wendell Scott's widow told me one time at a race Wendell didn't have any tires, and at the time Tiny was doing pretty well, and Tiny told me he went to Goodyear and bought Wendell a set of tires, and that's the only race that Wendell Scott ever won.

"Tiny said that at the next race Wendell's car was really nasty. Tiny said, 'Wendell, why didn't you at least wash it?' Wendell said, 'I wasn't about to touch something that ran that good.'

"Tiny and Cale Yarborough also were close. Cale was a nut. I'm telling you, they were all nuts. Cale was a daredevil. As a boy he'd catch water moccasins in the river with his hands. He'd wrestle alligators or jump off a high bridge into the Pee Dee River. Cale just had no fear. None whatsoever. I asked him one time, 'How did your mother keep from pinching your head off the day you were born and flushing you away?' I told him, 'I could not have lived with a kid who acted like you did.'

"Cale was like a young Tiny, a miniature Tiny. They were both daredevils. It was like, If you can do it, I can too. And they would. Whatever. Mostly what I witnessed was Tiny and Cale wrestling and scuffling around with each other. I know one time they were riding together going to a race somewhere in Tennessee, and Cale was saying, 'I wish I could see me a bear. I'd get out and wrassle it.' And Tiny loved to tell this story. He said Cale had no more gotten this out of his mouth than they came upon a bear.

"So Tiny stopped the car and throwed Cale out in the bear's face, locked the door and took off. The bear raised up and went 'Rrrrrrrr,' and Cale was running beside the car yelling, 'You big son of a bitch.' Tiny was just laughing like hell at this bear chasing after Cale. Tiny said Cale was keeping up with the car.

"Another of Tiny's friends was Buddy Baker. Buddy too was a big guy and could very well handle himself. One time Buddy and some of the guys went fishing with Tiny. It was so hot the fish weren't biting. Buddy went in for a swim to cool off, and Tiny eased over the side of the boat, swam under the boat, grabbed Buddy and pulled him underwater. Buddy thought an alligator had a hold of him. He almost had a heart attack. Those guys were good friends, but I don't know if they all weren't crazy. To me it was like a gang of pups rolling and hollering and picking at each other.

"They loved to torment Jim Hunter, who today is the president of Darlington, but who back in those days was a sportswriter. He was such a fan of racing, and a lot of times he even put his job on the line, because he was a sportswriter, not just a racing writer. They loved to torment him, and he was such a good sport about it. One time Tiny told him, 'Jim, I'll race you for a case of beer.' Well, Jim had gone to college on a football scholarship 'cause he was so fast. He thought, I can do this. He took the bet.

"They took off, and of course Jim won the race. Tiny was just loafing behind him. Jim said, 'I won. I won.' Tiny said, 'Go buy the beer.' Jim said, 'No, I won.' Tiny said, 'I didn't say anything about who won. I just said I'd race you for a case of beer.'

"Later Jim was PR guy for Talladega. He had to go to the airport to pick up Tiny, Cale, and another driver. He was in this little car, and Tiny had to sit in the back because he took up the whole seat. They were going down the road, and Cale said, 'Is this as fast as this thing can go?' So Cale stomped on the accelerator, and Tiny from the back blindfolded Jim, and they were flying down this road. They hit a ditch and went sailing and landed in a field and flattened all four tires. Jim didn't have a jack, so Tiny got out and picked the car up. When they finally got to the track, Tiny and Cale got out and told everyone, 'That son of a bitch tried to kill us. He wrecked. He tried to kill us.' Jim told me, 'They didn't say a word about what they did to me.'

"I know one time a bunch of them were going to Daytona together. On the way down they were listening to the radio, and they heard that there was a bandit robbing people at motels.

"Jim Hunter, Tiny, and Cale would cram as many in a motel room as they could. They'd take the mattresses off the beds and put them on the floor so they could have more sleeping space.

"Jim said that after they arrived at the motel, he was in the shower, and the phone rang. It was Tiny. He said, 'Oh my God, Jim, get over here.' And the phone went dead. Jim said the thing that immediately went through his mind was that Tiny and Cale were being attacked by this robber. He didn't even dress. He put a towel around him and ran to Tiny's room. Tiny's door was standing open. He walked in saying, 'Tiny. Tiny.' No answer. Jim was frantic. 'Where's Tiny?'

"All of a sudden he heard giggling, so he figured, Okay, they are setting me up. He went back out into the hall. In the meantime Tiny and Cale had gone to his room and locked the door. Poor Jim stood out there butt-naked. He was locked out in the hallway with nothing on but a towel, with all these people coming in.

"These guys were just laughing like hell. They thought it was the funniest thing in the world. They were clowns, like overgrown puppies or kids.

"I know one time Cale and Tiny were in the swimming pool, and Tiny kept dragging Cale in and holding him under. Cale said, 'If I ever do get away from you, I will get even.'

"They were sharing a room together. Tiny was taking a shower. Cale got a big trash can and filled it full of ice and put water in it, and he dumped it over the top of Tiny in the shower. Then he took off.

"Tiny came tearing out of the shower after Cale who ran out the door, down the steps and across the parking lot with Tiny right after him. For God's sake, Tiny was naked. I don't know if he didn't care, or if he just didn't think about it. Tiny came up on this little old lady who was just stepping out of her car. Tiny said she was very short. So she was standing there in a state of shock, staring at Tiny, and he tipped an imaginary hat to her and said, 'Excuse me, ma'am,' and stepped around her and kept on chasing after Cale. Cale told me, 'The last time I looked back at that little old lady, she was still standing there with her mouth hanging open!' Those guys were fun. God, they were fun.

"It's entirely different today. Everyone worries about their image. Back then those guys didn't have an image. But they were so fun-loving. I don't really think they ever intentionally hurt anyone. They were just big cutups.

"The only one Tiny didn't like was Lee Petty. He could not stand Lee Petty. But he liked Richard and Maurice. But not Lee. Tiny and Lee had had some run-ins. At one time Tiny had worked for Lee. He started out working in his shop sweeping up for forty bucks a week. Then when he went to drive for Lee, back then the drivers got forty percent of the purses they won, but Lee didn't want to pay Tiny his forty percent. He wanted to still give him forty dollars a week. So they had a couple of run-ins. I don't think Tiny ever forgave him. There was no love lost between him and Lee Petty.

"Tiny also had a few run-ins with Curtis Turner, but Tiny liked Curtis. Curtis was a mess too. Oh God, he was a mess. Tiny and I went to a party at his house one night, and I don't know why but I was highly ticked off at Tiny about something. I walked in, and I was totally not speaking to him.

"Curtis would throw a hell of a party. You're talking people all over the house, on the deck, in the kitchen, just people everywhere. I went in, and I sat at the bar, and this guy came over and started talking to Curtis, who was behind the bar. The guy said to me, 'How long have you known Tiny?' I was mad, so I said, 'Tiny who?' He said, 'Tiny Lund. That guy you walked in with.' I said, 'That's just somebody who followed me in the door. I don't know that guy.'

"We had been there quite a while, and Tiny was having a ball, dancing, slinging the girls to the rooftops. I sat there deadly pouting more and more. And Curtis was taking all this in.

"Curtis saw his opportunity. He said to this guy, 'Why don't you ask Wanda out?' I looked at Curtis like, What are you doing? Anyway, Tiny saw me sitting there with this guy talking to me. Tiny came over and said to me, 'Are you ready to go?' The guy turned around and said, 'Look, mister. Bug out. I'm in the process of asking this young lady for a date.'

"Tiny said, 'That's my goddamn wife. *You* better bug out.' And Curtis thought that was the funniest thing. He said to Tiny, 'That will teach you to pout, Lund. Hell, I lined your woman up with someone else.' Tiny said, 'Curtis, you stay out of this.'

"The poor guy. We really had a laugh at this guy. I have no idea who he was. But it was the way those guys were. If they found an opportunity to get something going or do something to each other, they would.

"I know one time Tiny put a pair of my panties in Bobby Unser's suitcase in Daytona. I didn't know Tiny had done this. But Bobby got home and unpacked and his wife found the undies. How was Bobby going to explain them? And Tiny thought that was the funniest thing in the world. He didn't care what kind of trouble Unser got in. He thought it was hilarious.

"The next year we went back to Daytona, and we had my car and

In 1961, Ralph Moody (left) dared newcomer Fred Lorenzen (right) to drive for Holman–Moody. The talented racer accepted the dare and won a total of 26 races for the Ford team. (DAYTONA INTERNATIONAL SPEEDWAY)

The older drivers resented the success of newcomer Fred Lorenzen.

Bobby Isaac (left) and Jake Elder (right). Elder was one of the most successful crew chiefs in the history of NASCAR, but his fiery temper caused him to move from team to team, earning him the nickname "Suitcase Jake." (DAYTONA RACING ARCHIVES)

From left: Richard Petty, Bud Moore, and Buddy Baker, three of the most legendary men in stock car racing. (DAYTONA INTERNATIONAL SPEEDWAY)

David Pearson
in Victory Lane.
(DAYTONA
INTERNATIONAL
SPEEDWAY)

Bobby Isaac (left) with David Pearson (right). "Bobby and I were real close,"
says Pearson. "I feel like perhaps I was his best friend." (DAYTONA
INTERNATIONAL SPEEDWAY)

Richard Petty has been The King since Chrysler got serious about racing in the mid-'60s. Richard won a total of 200 races — including seven Daytona 500s.

Maurice Petty, Richard's baby brother, built the most winning engines in the history of NASCAR, with cars that won 198 races. Here, he is once again ready to pit for Buddy Baker. (DODGE NEWS PHOTO, COURTESY OF DAYTONA RACING ARCHIVES)

Cale Yarbrough (left) won 83 races as a driver, and Junior Johnson (right) won 50 behind the wheel. When Cale drove for Junior, they won the driving championship three years running in 1976, 1977, and 1978. (DAYTONA INTERNATIONAL SPEEDWAY)

By the time David Pearson retired, the three-time racing champion had won 105 races, second only to Richard Petty. "David was just smooth; a hard driver, but smooth," according to Maurice Petty. (DAYTONA INTERNATIONAL SPEEDWAY)

Tom Pistone began racing in the South with the backing of Bill France, who suggested to the Chicago racer that he write "A Converted Yankee" on his car to keep the southerners from being so hard on him. (COURTESY OF TOM PISTONE)

Wendell Scott was the only black driver to win a NASCAR Grand National Race. Scott started 495 races over 13 seasons. (DAYTONA INTERNATIONAL SPEEDWAY)

Paul "Little Bud" Moore found his competitors to be "big, burly, bad-ass people." He vowed that if he ever let LeeRoy Yarbrough, Tiny Lund, or Bobby Isaac intimidate him even once, he would quit racing. (COURTESY OF PAUL MOORE)

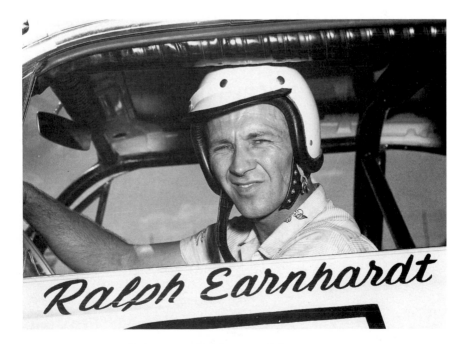

Ralph Earnhardt, Dale's dad, was one of the finest half-mile dirt drivers in the history of the sport. (DAYTONA RACING ARCHIVES)

Bobby Allison won 85 races over a 27-year career. "He was a thorn in our side," says Maurice Petty.

Buddy Baker (left) with his father, Buck (right). Buddy is ninth on the all-time lists in top-five finishes with 202 and Buck is seventh with 246. (DAYTONA RACING ARCHIVES)

Legendary crew chief Harry Hyde would "get along with anybody well as long as they did their work the way they were supposed to," says Tommy Johnson. (COURTESY OF TOMMY JOHNSON)

Tommy Johnson adjusts Tim Richmond's helmet. Tommy says, "Tim didn't lie to you. He knew how the car felt, knew how much it had left, and what he could do with it." (COURTESY OF TOMMY JOHNSON)

Tim Richmond "was a character in all respects. He wasn't intimidated by anyone or anything," remembers Tommy Johnson. (DAYTONA INTERNATIONAL SPEEDWAY)

Lou LaRosa (left) and Dale Earnhardt (right) were together when Dale won Rookie of the Year honors in 1979. Dale told LaRosa, "That ain't shit. I don't care about that. I want to be Winston Cup champion next year." And he was. (COURTESY OF LOU LaROSA)

Richard Childress started out driving his own car on a shoe-string budget. Today he owns one of the biggest and strongest Chevrolet race operations, with Dale Earnhardt behind the wheel. (DAYTONA RACING ARCHIVES)

Dale Earnhardt (left) and Lou LaRosa (right). Lou claims that by 1985, Dale had "mellowed from being a smart-ass to being a mature person who used his head driving. He had learned from his mistakes." (COURTESY OF LOU LAROSA)

Dale Earnhardt (left) and Neil Bonnett (right) were close friends. (DAYTONA INTERNATIONAL SPEEDWAY)

Danny "Chocolate" Myers, the son of Bobby Myers and the nephew of Billy, is gasman for Richard Childress on Dale Earnhardt's pit crew. He says, "In a hundred years from now, they're going to look back and say Dale was the greatest driver that's ever been."

Alan Kulwicki. "I thought Alan was a good guy, "says Paul Andrews. "But I found out that if you told Alan you could do something, you'd better be able to do it."

The sponsorless Alan Kulwicki with his Army car. Kulwicki, who refused a million-dollar offer to drive for Junior Johnson, shocked the racing world by winning the championship on his own in 1992. (DAYTONA RACING ARCHIVES)

Says Jake Elder of Davey Allison (pictured): "The year Davey was killed something was bothering him. I was going to sit down and talk to him one day about his problems, but I never did get to the point."

In Michigan, Clifford Allison was killed in practice before the Busch race. Says Liz Allison, "I remember Davey telling me that Clifford had more born talent as a race car driver than he felt he himself had." (DAYTONA RACING ARCHIVES)

Lou LaRosa on Darrell Waltrip (pictured): "He is a person who's implacable, who has his own ideas and is stubborn. The other problem is that he's easily deceived."

Jeff Gordon. After attending Buck Baker's driving school, Jeff abandoned hopes of Indycar success for the dream of a NASCAR championship.

Davey Allison in Victory Lane. Despite the smiles, his final year was nightmarish. (DAYTONA RACING ARCHIVES)

Liz and Davey Allison. Says Liz, "I want people to know that Davey was truly an exceptional person." (COURTESY OF LIZ ALLISON)

we were driving down the street, and Bobby Unser came up and ran into the side of the car, just knocked the hell out of it. We stopped, and Tiny said, 'Unser, what in hell do you think you're doing?' Unser was just laughing like hell. He said, 'Why are you worried. It's a rental.' Tiny said, 'No, this is Wanda's car you just knocked the hell out of.' Unser said, 'Get it fixed. I'll write you a check.'

"We were staying at the Holiday Inn across from the speedway. How Unser did this I'll never know, but he convinced the man at the front desk that he was Tiny's brother and that he was bringing Tiny some parts for his race car. He said he didn't have credentials to go to the track and needed to leave them in Tiny's room.

"They gave Bobby Unser the key to our room, and he went in there and filled everything we owned full of shaving cream. He put shaving cream in the pockets of everything and in our shoes.

"When we got back, I was furious. I said, 'Tiny, we have to go to this event tonight. My shoes are full of shaving cream. You might think it's funny, but I don't.' Tiny didn't get mad. He thought, Oh, that's the funniest thing that ever was. He felt Unser should have done it to get even for the panties the year before. It was no big deal to Tiny.

"They were terrible. They were *all* terrible. But they all had fun. They really, really had a good time. Can you see the drivers doing that today? I can't. But I'll tell you, they are really missing out on a lot.

"The last couple years Tiny drove he was in the Grand American circuit, which was like the Busch circuit today, only this was Camaros and Mustangs, that type of car. They would race on Saturday before the big race. The circuit came in '67 or '68, and Tiny drove for Big Bud Moore. Big Bud had Mustangs and Mercury Cougars. Tiny had driven for Bud in both Winston Cup and Grand National, but Bud called Tiny and said, 'Tiny, I'm losing my financing. I can't afford the Winston Cup. I'm going to run the little cars in Grand Am, and you're welcome to come along as my driver.'

"Tiny said, 'Bud, I really appreciate that, but I really don't want to run that circuit.' So Bud got Parnelli Jones and used Dan Gurney a couple of times.

When Tiny couldn't afford his own Winston Cup car, he joined the little Grand American circuit, which ran seven years, and Tiny was the champion four of the seven years. Out of 109 races, he won 49.

"When he was running that circuit, he was a hotshot. He was the Richard Petty of the circuit.

"I'd always fix food to feed Tiny and the crew, and I can remember one time after a race, he came over and asked if I could fix Richard Childress and his crew some sandwiches to get back home on. So I did. Richard ran on that circuit also. He was very good on that circuit. To this day when I see Richard Childress, he's very friendly, very nice, very cordial. I don't think he ever forget that either.

"The fans couldn't support the Grand American circuit so NASCAR was going to break it up in 1971, but these drivers had money tied up in the cars. In order to keep these guys from losing their money, Big Bill France decided that the small cars could run with the big cars on the short tracks. Actually, the Winston Cup drivers didn't want this. They didn't want these little cars to be able to run against them on the short tracks. But Big Bill made the rules. Big Bill knew it was a mistake to start with, but he did it because these guys had money tied up in these cars and he was giving them the opportunity for the remainder of the year to make as much money as they could so they wouldn't be left holding the bag with the equipment.

"Tiny won a race at North Wilkesboro, and he won his last Winston Cup race at Hickory, both in little cars, in a Ronnie Hopkins Camaro, but NASCAR didn't give him credit for either win, and that was ridiculous.

"In '74 and '75 Tiny ran a late model Sportsman, which would be considered the Busch Series today. In '75, Tiny only drove in one Winston Cup race, and that was Talladega. A. J. King out of Sevierville, Tennessee, came to Tiny and asked Tiny to run his car in the race. Tiny was like, 'I don't know. I haven't driven Winston Cup in a couple of years.' King said, 'You can do it. You can handle it.' So Tiny agreed.

"I will never forget the day that he left. He was going to Hickory to run a late model Sportsman race. He was running for the championship, and that year his competition was L. D. Ottinger, who had so many more cars and engines.

"When Tiny was leaving, he said to me about Talladega, 'I really don't feel good about this ride.' I said, 'Then why are you doing it?' He said, 'Because I gave the man my word.' It came back to haunt me later. If he didn't feel comfortable, then why did he do it? I don't care if he had given him his word. But Tiny was that way. If he told you he'd do something, he would.

"I didn't go to Talladega. I went to quite a few races, but there were quite a few I didn't. Transportation was one reason. He and his crew was taking his late model Sportsman to Hickory to race, and after the race he flew to Alabama with Bobby Allison. That's one reason I didn't go: Bobby had a small plane. I knew that Tiny would be flying back with Cale to Timmonsville, and then I was supposed to drive up to Cale's house to pick up Tiny. And it didn't work out that way.

"Another reason I stayed home was my back had been hurting. I was thinking I had pulled a muscle, which later I found out I had a kidney infection and kidney stones.

"That Sunday morning I was talking to a girlfriend of mine named Amelia at Monk's Corner. I said, 'I don't know what's wrong with me today. Ordinarily I'm a very uplifting person. Hardly ever do you see me depressed. I don't know what's wrong with me.'

"She said, 'After you drive into town, meet me here at Monk's Corner, and we'll drive to Charleston, go out to lunch and see a movie.' So I did.

"I drove to Monk's Corner, and we went to Charleston. The Talladega race was on the radio, and I reached over and turned it off. Amelia looked over and said, 'Why did you do that?' I said, 'I have no idea. I just have the funniest feeling something is going to happen to somebody I care a lot about, and I don't want to hear it on the radio.' But I didn't think Tiny.

"But I had this really strange feeling.

"Big Bill France called Tiny's mother and told her that Tiny had gotten killed in an accident. I don't blame Ma Lund. She really wasn't thinking, but she gave Big Bill permission to announce that Tiny had gotten killed. And so Tiny's lawyer heard it on the radio. He called the Fish Camp to ask, 'Where's Wanda?' Being under tremendous strain, Ma Lund said, 'I don't know.' She knew where I had gone, because she was baby-sitting our son Chris. She just couldn't think. Tiny's lawyer asked her, 'Does Wanda know yet?' She said, 'I don't think so,' so he called the radio station and asked them to take it off the air because I hadn't been informed.

"My girlfriend who I was with that day was the secretary of the sheriff of Berkeley County. Amelia's sister called the sheriff, and they put an APB out on our vehicle. Of course, they found mine at Amelia's house. When we got back, there was a note on it to call the Fish Camp.

"When I did, two or three people came on the phone and asked, 'Where are you?' Just asking weird questions. I said, 'I'm in town. What's wrong?' I just had this awful feeling something had happened to Chris, our five-year-old son. I said, 'What's wrong with Chris?' Nobody was saying anything.

"Finally, Tiny's mother picked up the phone and right out of the blue said, 'Wanda, Tiny's dead.' I remember I just went to my knees screaming. Because Tiny had me so convinced that he was invincible in a race car. He would always laugh and say that when it was time to go, he hoped it would be in a race car or out there on the lake fishing.

"For a long time I was very bitter at Tiny. I felt, Look what a mess you left me in. I have a five-year-old son to raise alone. You knew this could happen. You had me convinced otherwise.

"I was so bitter at him for so long. For a long time I'd have dreams that I was talking to him. I'd say, 'You son of a bitch. Look at what you've done to me.'

"Tiny died in '75, and in '78 I moved back home to Haywood County. I never did get over being a hillbilly. I love these mountains. I got a job at Dayco. They make racing hoses and belts. A man named Buddy Early worked there. He was dating a girl who worked in my department, and on breaks he would come down to see her. When Buddy and this girl broke up, he asked me for a date, and so we went out. We dated for over a year before we got married.

"I don't think I really healed completely until I went back to the racetrack in 1992. Larry Frank was the one who got me to do it. He kept calling, and he said, 'Wanda, I'm racing in this Legends race at Charlotte.' I said, 'Larry, you're nuts. Do you know how old you are?' He said, 'Wanda, I want you to come watch me race.' I said, 'I don't want to come watch you race.' Because after Tiny's death I had never gone back to another race.

"He'd call and call, and finally after calling five days in a row, on the last day he called and said, 'That big son of a bitch is not here to watch me. And you're the next best thing. I want you in my pit.'

"I thought about that for a minute, and I thought about how Tiny really loved Larry Frank. I said to myself, I can do this for Larry.

"So I went to Charlotte, and for about ten minutes I was a nervous wreck, and after that people like Glen Wood, Little Bud Moore, Richard Childress, Buck Baker, all these people started coming over, and it was like everything fell away, and it seemed like within a ten- or fifteen-minute span I had never been away. I think what helped me the most was seeing race fans again who would talk to me and say, 'We loved him too.' One time a guy said to me, 'I can't think of anything more wonderful or exciting than to say you lived your whole life exactly the way you wanted to, and Tiny had.' I thought about that a few minutes and started laughing. I said, 'You know, he did. The son of a bitch did it all his way, didn't he?' And I thought, He deserved it. Tiny was a hell of a guy. And after that I was fine.

"After I went to Charlotte, Don Naman called from Talladega. Don is the director of the Hall of Fame and Museum. When Tiny died, Don was the promoter of the Talladega Speedway. I had known Don for years. He said, 'I understand you went to Charlotte.' I said, 'Yes.' He said, 'I want you to come to Talladega.' I said, 'Don, there is no way I'm coming to Talladega.' He said, 'Now Wanda, listen. I want you to come down to the Hall of Fame. The induction ceremonies are a lot of fun, and I really think you should come.' Don said, 'Wanda, this is like riding a horse. When you fall off, you need to get back on. We will pay all expenses. You come down, and if you're not happy or having a bad time or you can't handle this, we'll understand if you leave.'

"So Don talked me into coming down to Talladega. Since I wasn't there when Tiny was killed, I don't know where on the track the accident happened, and I don't want to know. When I got down there I really had a good time. So since then I've been going to as many races at different places as I can.

"That night at Talladega, Davey Allison was at the induction ceremony, and I went over and reintroduced myself to him. He started laughing. He said, 'Wanda, do you remember when I was a little boy, you told me my mommy should tie me to a tree?' He said, 'I never will forget you telling me that. Why did you tell me that?' I said, 'Because you were the most . . . ' Davey was a little spitfire who'd dart here and dart there. He was so inquisitive, so nosy, about this racing. This was before wives and children were allowed in the pits. The wives all tried to pitch in and watch each other's kids. Davey got away from me and ran in front of a car, and when I caught him, I wanted to shake him, and I told him, 'Your momma should tie you to a tree.' He never forgot that.

"I still have a lot of friends in racing, and I've made a lot of new ones. I don't know, but in a way, it feels like going home."

32

THE TRAVAILS OF HARRY HYDE

TOMMY JOHNSON, LIKE HIS UNCLE Harry Hyde, grew up in rural Kentucky. Tommy was just a boy when Harry, who was sixteen years his senior, owned a junkyard and salvage business in Louisville. Hyde then moved to Charlotte, where he began working with Bobby Isaac for car owner Nord Krauskopf in 1969. As soon as Tommy was old enough, he began working with Hyde, one of the legendary chassis builders and setup men in the sport. From 1969 until Hyde's retirement in 1991, the two worked closely together. Johnson recalled the teams and individuals they worked for and with, especially a relationship with owner J. D. Stacy, which soured and led to a series of lawsuits that Johnson says almost ruined them.

But Hyde and Johnson bounced back, and in 1983 Tommy Johnson was the first person hired by newcomer Rick Hendrick. Harry Hyde, who was distrustful of new owners with the gift of gab at this point, signed a deal with Hendrick in which he agreed to work the first year for nothing. Hendrick on his part had to provide Hyde with first-class equipment and give him one hundred percent support. Each upheld his side of the bargain, and in 1985 driver Geoff Bodine won a race at Martinsville, the first win for Hendrick Motorsports and the first win for Hyde and Johnson since 1977. Harry Hyde was back on top again.

TOMMY JOHNSON: "I was born in Brownsville, Kentucky, the same place as Harry Hyde. I knew Harry all my life. Harry was my uncle. My mother and Harry were brother and sister. I was born in '40, and he's about sixteen years older than I was. I grew up around him as a kid after he came back out of the army in '46.

"From the time I was seven or eight, Harry and his older brother settled in Louisville, Kentucky, and went into business. They had a salvage yard—back then it was better known as a junkyard—and an automatic transmission shop. Periodically during the year we would go to visit my uncle. It was only a hundred miles. Of course, I wanted to spend time in the junkyard. 'Cause both sides of my family were automobile people—mechanics and salvage yard people. I had no interest in play. I just wanted to see the race cars and look at everything on them.

"I started racing when I was fourteen at small tracks in Kentucky, in and around Brownsville, Bowling Green, Russellville, Morgantown, and Owensboro. I began working with Harry some in '64, and then in '69 I moved to North Carolina and went to work for him full-time. From '69 until I retired in 1991, I never worked for anyone but Harry. I spent more time with Harry than I did with my own family. We were more like brothers. Back then you ran fifty-two races a year. You were gone from home a lot. We spent a tremendous amount of time together.

"In '64 we started with Sam McQuagg, who was from Georgia. We were sponsored by K&K Insurance. Nord Krauskopf was in the racetrack insurance business. They started a team in Louisville at Harry's shop.

"Nord Krauskopf was a very wonderful man. Whether it was his insurance company or his race team, he was really good to his employees. He was a wealthy man, but he never let the money and power take away his feelings for his employees and his love for racing. He came to all the superspeedway races and occasionally the short tracks. He would talk to every crew member at the track, want to know about their family. He was a really good man.

"We had limited success with McQuagg. They didn't run a full schedule until '67. Nord and Harry ran Chrysler cars, and in '69 ran sixth in the points with Bobby Isaac.

"Other than with his family, Bobby Isaac was pretty much of a loner. He would occasionally take the guys out to eat when we were out of town. He'd come to the shop and speak to the guys, but he was not a man with a lot of conversation. The biggest reason was that Bobby didn't have any education. His wife, Patsy, taught him to sign his name. Bobby had a feeling when he talked to people that he was not talking right, so he did not have a lot of conversation, but he really spoke well. He was a nice guy. He was friendly in his own way. He wouldn't hurt your feelings for anything. But more or less, Bobby was a loner. His closest friend was David Pearson. About any time he went anywhere or when he played golf, he went with David.

"Bobby and Harry got along well. Harry would get along with anybody well as long as they did their work the way they were supposed to. A guy didn't have to win every race, but if Harry set the plan and the driver followed the plan, then Harry had no problem with him. The only time Harry had a problem was when a driver deviated from the plan. Of course, caution flags and things like that might change things, and then Harry would adjust the plan, and the driver would go with it.

"We had only been in North Carolina since '68. We moved from Louisville because Charlotte was the center of racing and because the parts were here, and it was easier to maintain automobiles here. Harry put the team together in '68, and we had myself, Harry Lee Hyde, Harry's son, Robert Gee came in June of '69, Ray Fox Jr. came in November of '69, and Buddy Parrott went to work for us after the '69 season was over, and he completed the team. We only had four people plus Harry at the time. Bobby finished second or third in '69, won a lot of races, and then in '70 we jelled and won the championship. We won eleven races that year.

"The last race of the '70 season was at Rockingham. All we needed was to finish somewhere in the middle, but after a hundred laps the differential went out. Bobby came in, and we changed it, and it just happened that a long caution fell, and so we didn't lose very many laps, and we ran another hundred or so laps when it went out again. We discovered that the rear end pump went out, but that was too much trouble to change, so instead we put in another differential in order to finish the race, and that's what it took to win that points championship. It wasn't by many. We beat out Bobby Allison for the title.

"We were happy we won, but it only paid $30,000. Everybody on the team got a diamond ring. There wasn't much fanfare other than a dinner in Daytona. We got a silver chalice from Nord Krauskopf. Wicks Oil Filters was the sponsor of the championship back then, and we got an Elgin watch that said, Grand National Champion 1970. I still have mine.

"Bobby Isaac left us and went to drive for Bud Moore. I don't know why Bobby left. In 1973, in the middle of the race at Talladega, he pulled into the pits and said he was quitting. He said that someone told him to park the car and get out or he was going to get killed.

"And after Bobby, Buddy Baker came, and that was the first time since I had been there that I worked with a driver who was really personable with the team. Very few days went by that Buddy wasn't at that shop. And when we'd be out of town, he'd always go eat with the guys, and there'd be a lot of laughing.

"From the day Buddy started with us, we sat on the pole, won some races, wrecked cars, blew engines. His goal was to sit on the pole wherever he went. But Buddy was a very nervous guy at the racetrack when it came time to qualify, and just before a race. You had to keep Buddy away from the other drivers. Harry or I would have to take him in hand and walk with him, talk with him, because he was in another world worrying. Other drivers liked to talk to him and throw in negative comments like, 'It's a little slick in turn four,' or 'So-and-so wrecked over here. Watch out for that place,' and they would affect Buddy. If you didn't keep him away from them, he would go and mess up, because they had put these things in his head.

"During qualifying, a driver might say to him, 'Last time I ran it in such-and-such seconds.' Buddy hadn't run that fast, and we had timed the other guy and knew he wasn't telling Buddy the truth, and we'd tell him that, but Buddy would try too hard and mess up. So we learned to keep him away from them people for about an hour before qualifying. Buddy was a big fisherman, so we talked about fishing. Buddy fished a lot with Tiny Lund. We'd walk up and down pit road, wherever the other people weren't, and try not to talk about racing. If they were there, we'd walk and talk in the garage area.

"We had good cars with Buddy. With Robert Gee in charge of the body work, we took a lot of care making our cars, especially on the speedway cars. We didn't weld the door and fenders together. They had to be bolted. We took care to align the sheet metal, to have a slick paint job, to mount the windshield as flush as we could, and we sealed all the cracks. That was something people didn't do back then.

"Harry was a perfectionist, and we took great care to seal up the front end of the automobile and the grill area. Instead of leaving the front end wide open, we would adjust the amount of air that could come in from behind, allowing only what we needed to run cool. That contributed to our success back then, especially on the speedways. Plus we had good engines. We were miles per hour faster than other people.

"Back then everybody worked hard. You didn't have the media, the press distracting you. The media would interview the crew chief and the driver. They didn't mess with the actual mechanics or talk about them much. Today, the press will take a story from about anybody that works for them to find out something.

"In '74 Buddy left and went to Bud Moore. Nord and NASCAR had a run-and-gun battle as far as the rules. NASCAR was coming up with restrictor plates on the hemis, trying to get rid of the big motors and get the little ones in. Nord said, 'We're just going to quit NASCAR and run USAC and other circuits.' This was right before the World 600, and Buddy wanted to run NASCAR, and Bud need-ed a driver, and so he went to work for him. We didn't run anymore NASCAR races in '74.

"Chrysler wanted us to race at Pike's Peak. They were coming up with a new medium-sized kit car. Ford had set a record out there, and so we did the prototype kit car for Chrysler and hired Bobby Unser to drive it. We went to Pike's Peak and spent a month out there testing— we had to drive up the mountain, which is 13,000 and some feet high. They do it every year on the Fourth of July. You take off from the bot-tom, and it's 80 degrees, and when you get to the top it's in the low 30s and snowing and sleeting most of the time. It was something dif-ferent, and we enjoyed it, and then we went right on and broke the record, and it stood for a lot of years for a stock car.

"We then ran some USAC races in Milwaukee and Michigan with Bobby Unser on round tracks and won some races.

"In '75 Harry hired Dave Marcis to drive. He was a down-to-earth guy. He wasn't a golf player or a fisherman or nothing. He seemed more a farm boy to me than anything. Dave won a race, sat on poles, and finished second in the points to Richard Petty, and then in '76 Dave won three more races before Nord sold the team to J. D. Stacy, who supposedly was in the coal business. And Marcis and Stacy didn't get along, and so Dave went back to his own deal, and Neil Bonnett came in. Neil had been a short track racer. We had known him. He ran a car in the Sportsman division for Bobby Allison. Neil had run three or four cars in Grand National, and Harry had his eye on him because Bobby had tutored him, and he was a good driver. And Neil was probably the most happy-go-lucky driver we had. Neil Bonnett would lay down on the trunk lid of a car he was working on and go to sleep while you were getting ready to qualify. If it wasn't too hot, he might lay down on pit road and go to sleep. He didn't have any superstitions, things didn't bother him, he didn't let people upset him. You couldn't rattle Neil, and it got to where they didn't mess with him.

"Neil won two races in '77, didn't run too well in '78, but there was a reason for that. I don't like to talk about it, but J. D. Stacy was a bad actor. Stacy was a promoter of anything he could make a dollar out of. He had a lot of leases on coal property in Virginia and West Virginia. Somehow he got some big companies to go in with him. But eventually they pulled out, and the money quit coming in, and he quit paying us. We had bills and obligations, and he didn't pay the bills. Harry had built his race shop with his own money, but the sheriff put a padlock on it. Stacy was trying to say he had given Harry the money to buy the shop and argued the thirty-eight acres Harry and I owned near the shop also belonged to him. He sued us in thirteen separate lawsuits, and we never, ever lost a single case. Everytime we'd win one, he'd bring another lawsuit. Harry and myself together spent $235,000 defending them to keep what was already ours. But that was Stacy's mode of operation.

"And it broke Harry. Broke both of us. We borrowed all the money we could from family and real close friends, mortgaged everything we could mortgage. If it hadn't been for friends back then, we couldn't have made it. When we finally got the case in federal court in early 1982 in Winston-Salem, he was finished.

"And what hurt more than the money, two people who Harry had been loyal to for years really sold us out. They went on Stacy's side. Harry had taken care of them as he did his own sons, loaned them money, gave them things, and that hurt Harry terribly. Harry was the kind of guy who believed if you had a personal or family problem in which money could take care of it, Harry would loan you the money at no interest or give it to you to keep your mind free to work in the shop. Harry had maybe a sixth-grade education, but he was very wise and very smart. You didn't have to tell him your problem. After it bothered you for a day or two, he could figure out something was wrong. He would take you off to the side and talk to you in confidence. 'What can I do to help?' Harry treated every man who was with us equal to the way he treated his own son or myself, his nephew.

"And so while we were having this trouble with Stacy, our team was in turmoil and wreck. Everybody knew what was going on, and then the law came in and padlocked the gate. One morning the sheriff and his deputies came in with papers and said, 'Take your personal toolboxes, nothing else. Out the gate. We're padlocking the place.' And they shut it down, and it was tied up, and we couldn't work in it until 1980.

"In the meantime we rented Robert Gee's shop. And in 1979 we went to work for a guy named Tighe Scott for two years. He had been a modified driver, and he was successful at that. His family owned Scotty's Fashions out of Pennsylvania, a really terrific family. Tighe was a happy-go-lucky person, wrecked a lot of cars, had minimal success, but it didn't seem to disturb him. He couldn't seem to master the asphalt tracks in the South. After two years his dad called it quits. His dad said, 'Harry, shut it down. Give everybody a month's salary.'

"When we were working for Tighe Scott, this young eighteen-year-old kid by the name of Jimmy Makar was hanging around Robert Gee's shop, and he went to work for us, and he worked through all this period.

"Next we went to work for Warren Fabricating out of Ohio. John Anderson was the driver, and then they let John go, and he was replaced by Donnie Allison. He was driving an Oldsmobile for us when he got hurt in the World 600. Donnie was a worker-driver. He worked hard on the car along with us. But the car didn't have any down force, and the crash was a bad one, and that ended our deal with Warren Fabricating.

"Around January of 1982 a guy by the name of Mike Lovern came along out of Virginia, and he had a sprint car driver by the name of

Tim Richmond who he wanted to start a team. We were to go to Daytona in February, and there wasn't anybody but Harry Hyde and myself. Harry had leased out the engine shop. We got back in the shop, and this guy Lovern arranged to buy engine parts from Jack Roush. We went to Daytona with one engine. We hired Norman Negre, and Norman and I went to the Hutcherson-Pagan shop and we built a race car over there from the ground up. We hung the sheet metal, brought it back over to Harry's shop, did the body work, put the engine in, got a U-Haul truck with a trailer, and we were in Daytona in thirty-nine days from scratch!

"But we didn't make the race, because we didn't have a parts supply to work out of. Back then you couldn't buy good carburetors at the track like you can now. You had to build one. But we only missed making that race by four one-thousands of a second, and we ran in what they called the consolation race, and we won that with Tim Richmond.

"We loaded up, came back home, and we ran Rockingham, and that was the end of that deal. Lovern was spending money he was making on a book, and that went kaput. So Tim left and went to drive for D. K. Ulrich, and from there he went to the Old Milwaukee team of Raymond Bealle.

"After the Mike Lovern deal ended, Jimmy Makar left and went to the Levi-Garrett team whose original driver was Johnny Rutherford, the Indycar driver. Makar joined Buddy Parrott, Larry Regan, one of our older mechanics, Robert Gee, and Ray Fox Jr., five of our former employee who started the team. A guy by the name of Eddie Gibson promoted the deal. Eddie was a deputy sheriff of Mecklenburg County, North Carolina, and how he made that connection I do not know.

"Around May or June of '82 two men came into our shop. They had a sixteen-year-old kid with them by the name of Bobby Hillin. His dad and granddad were in the oil business out of Texas, and they wanted this kid to run NASCAR. He had two years' experience on a one-third-mile track in Texas. They had money, and they put it in the bank, and so Norman Negre and I went back to Hutcherson-Pagan's to build another car, a Buick, for Bobby Hillin. We were going to try to run five races that year so we could run for the rookie of the year. Remember, this was a sixteen-year-old boy fixing to get out of high school for the summer. First we ran at Wilkesboro, and then we ran at Daytona on the Fourth of July. And we made the race. He finished twentieth. In 1983 we built two cars and had four or five engines. They had the money allotted. We were pretty careful after the Stacy deal to check people out before we would go to work for them, to find out if their money was real and where it was coming from. All those years Nord Krauskopf was advising Harry on that. He still came to see us, still was a friend after all those years. Hillin ran in twelve races in '83. His best finish was eleventh at Dover.

"In August of 1983 Rick Hendrick began talking to us about building him one car to do some testing to see what he wanted to do. Dale Earnhardt did the testing. We built a Monte Carlo, and the first time we tested the car in Charlotte, Dale was impressed with the car.

"I had raced against Dale when I was a kid running dirt tracks around Charlotte. When he started, Dale was like everybody else back then, a crazy teenager. Wasn't nothing serious to him except when he buckled into that car. He buckled in to win the race. The first car he ever drove was a pink '55 Ford. It belonged to his father-in-law, who I always called Mr. Oliver, and his brother-in-law. They've been friends of mine since 1970, when I started racing short tracks. Dale was a young man who liked to race, and nothing else really mattered, just a crazy teenager like the rest of us. No different than any other guy.

"Then we started with Rick, and I was the first person ever on Rick Hendrick's payroll. I went on it in December, along with D. J. Deland and Harry. Harry worked that first year for nothing for Rick Hendrick. All Rick did was pay the expenses on the shop and all the bills, and he paid Harry $900 a month rent. Harry never drew one nickel. Harry told Rick, 'You give me the parts to run with. Get me a good driver, and I'll work for nothing the first year.' And he did.

"Harry wanted a shot at one more winning team with good equipment and a good driver. He told Rick, 'I will sacrifice my salary if you will give me one shot at it. But the minute you back up on me, I am going to quit. You can move it out of here.'

"And that was their agreement, and they both held up. In January 1984 Rick and Harry hired Geoff Bodine. Geoff had raced under the Gatorade sponsorship up in High Point, had minimal success. Harry called him and talked to him, told Geoff he was forming a new team. In January 1984 it was announced that Geoff would be our driver. We had one car, and we were going to run twelve to fifteen races, but in order to make a bigger hoopla in front of the press, we told them we were going to run a full schedule.

"We had to build four cars in a hurry. We had to be ready by the Daytona 500. At the start there were only four of us working in the shop, and then we hired a few more from all over the country, young guys who we didn't know but who were looking for work.

"Our first race with Bodine we finished eighth in the Daytona 500. That first year I wouldn't ask for anything any better in a driver or a person. We finished in the top ten at Richmond, a top ten at Rockingham, did okay in a couple of races, crashed early in Darlington, and then at Martinsville, Geoff won his first Winston Cup race, and looking back, winning that was an elating experience. Remember, we had not won a race since Neil Bonnett won two races in 1977. We had been used to winning, and all of a sudden it had shut off. This was now 1985, eight years since we've won a race. That's like making a man do without a certain kind of food he loves. And all of a sudden you give him all he wants of it. I don't think there was a man there who didn't have a tear roll down his cheek. I know I did. Kathy Bodine, Geoff's wife, did a lot of timing and laps, and she stood on one side of Harry, and I stood on the other while I timed either the car coming up behind us or a car we were chasing to compare times to see how we were doing. Harry timed our car. So Harry, Kathy, and I worked real close together during the race.

"Kathy Bodine and I just boo-hooed. It was a very elating feeling. As far as the tear part and the feeling, happiness is 180 degrees from sadness, two opposite deals that both bring tears."

BUDDY BAKER

33

RECORDS AT BREAKNECK SPEED

B Y 1976 BUDDY BAKER HAD BECOME known for his fast times on the superspeedways. In May of that year at Talladega, he set a new all-time record for completing a 500-mile race, completing the circuit in 2 hours, 56 minutes, and 37 seconds. His average speed was 169.887 miles an hour, breaking A. J. Foyt's old record of 161.550 miles an hour, which was set in the 1972 Daytona 500.

But Baker's most important goal, that of winning the Daytona 500, continued to elude him. In 1976, an engine blew. In 1977, he finished third to Cale Yarborough. At the end of the season he left Bud Moore and went to drive for M. C. Anderson, figuring that M. C. would be the better bet for the 1978 Daytona 500. In that race Baker led with only a few laps to go, only to see Bobby Allison, in Bud Moore's Ford, win the race when his engine blew up. During that season Anderson's engines tended to give out more than not, and Baker left there and joined the team owned by Harry Ranier. For the seasons 1979 and 1980, the combination of Baker and Ranier was outstanding.

In 1979 Buddy Baker won seven poles and three races on a team that featured crew chief Herb Nab and engine builder Waddell Wilson. The three men, all spirited and opinionated, at times fought bitterly. Then in 1980 Baker finally

285

captured his long-sought grail, winning the Daytona 500, once again breaking the record for the fastest speed ever record in a 500-mile race, 177.602 miles an hour. He completed the race in 2 hours, 48 minutes and 56 seconds this time.

But the friction among the Ranier crew was escalating, and at the end of the year Baker went to drive for Hoss Ellington. It seemed that Baker led almost every race he ran for Ellington, but the engines never would hold up to the finish. In the middle of 1982 Baker got in a spat with the race team's sponsor, and he moved on, going back to Harry Ranier a second time only to finish out the season. When 1983 began, he was driving for the Wood Brothers. Once again he was leading races but not winning them, though he did beat Cale Yarborough to win the Firecracker 400, Baker's final Winston Cup victory.

BUDDY BAKER: "In 1976 at Daytona, they caught Darrell Waltrip, A. J. Foyt, five or six of them using nitrous oxide, which gives a car an extra burst for a short period of time. Everybody pretty much knew they were using it. It was pretty obvious when a car goes out in practice and does, say 190, and then it goes and qualifies at 198. You knew what was going on. I wouldn't use it. If you look at my career, you'll never find that I was involved in anything like that. Didn't have to. Didn't have to.

"There was conversation about it, and the way NASCAR polices things, once the word started going throughout the garage area, the people who had it began getting really nervous about it. Some of them used it anyhow, and they got caught.

"At the end of that race it was Richard Petty and David Pearson again fighting for the lead, and again crashing, and Richard stopped just before the finish line, and David was able to keep his engine running and win.

"In May of '76 at Talladega I set the record for a 500-mile race. At Talladega and Daytona, if my car held together, I pretty much had a shot every time I'd go there. That's not bragging. That's telling the truth. Matter of fact, I could give them a pretty good run right now. I was testing with Rusty Wallace at Daytona [in January 1997], and I wasn't that bad. I can still run fast.

"When I went back to Talladega in August, I was leading the race, but with three laps to go I ran out of gas and had to coast into the pits. I had such a lead I still only finished twenty-nine seconds back behind Dave Marcis.

"That really made me mad. Because I had an opportunity to stop on a caution not too many laps before and had a discussion about it, and they said I had plenty of fuel. They told me, 'Don't worry about it.' So when I ran out, I got pretty aggravated.

"That year, '77, Janet Guthrie drove in a bunch of races. I'm going to tell you something: I've heard stories about these other women drivers, but pound for pound, Janet Guthrie was by far the best I've ever run against. Oh yeah, she could drive the heck out of the car. She wasn't a chick. She was up in her early forties, which is kind of a wind-down time for a lot of athletes, and buddy, I'm going to tell you, I was racing at Ontario, and I thought I was running for the lead, and they gave me a board from the pit with an arrow and number 68 on it, and I laughed. I thought, What a joke. And then I realized it wasn't a joke, it was Janet up front, the only time a woman ever led a NASCAR race, and I had to run like heck to catch her. Let's face it, who would ever give her a chance in a world to even make the race, and she was leading it! She was in several races I wasn't in, and I watched what she was doing, and she could drive. That wasn't a joke. That was for real. That was a time when equal rights wasn't even in the picture. Her sponsor was Kelly Girl. You get the picture how the other drivers felt about her being there. But she just stuck right in there with them. I'm not saying she was Cale Yarborough or Richard Petty by any means, but whether they admitted it or not, she had the admiration of most of the drivers.

"At the end of '77 I left Bud Moore and went to drive for M. C. Anderson. That didn't have anything to do with Bud. Bud was like a dad to us. Bud was always good to me. But when I talked to M. C., it was an immediate friendship between the two of us. If I had to come right out and say what my ultimate goal was, it was to win the Daytona 500, and I didn't think I could do it with Bud, and I thought I could with M. C.

"M. C.'s crew chief was David Ifft, probably the most underrated crew chief in all of racing. If I had a race team right now and only had five days to go to Daytona and run up front, I wouldn't hesitate to call

David. A lot of people don't know that because he's so carefree and misunderstood as far as people saying he clowns around too much. He may clown, but he gets something done. I can tell you that.

"David was a gymnast when he was young, and he'll walk into a restaurant and act like he tripped, do a triple end over end down the stairway going into the restaurant. It would look like he broke his back, and he'll act like it did. Everybody goes, 'Oh God, David's dead.' The first time he did it in front of me, I thought, Jesus, God, I lost my crew chief. He killed hisself. When I got over to him, he said, 'You'll get used to it.' I said, 'You son of a gun.'

"He's that type of fellow, but he also had his serious side. He and Benny Parsons had good success together. He and Darrell Waltrip ran very well together. When he was a young boy with Bud Moore he was a good mechanic, and then he just got better and better. What a great coach. If I had a young driver, David would certainly be the guy. He's the type to bring a guy along slowly, and if the car is a little bit loose, he'll tighten it up a bunch to make sure he takes care of the problem, instead of letting the guy hurt himself.

"The funny part about leaving Bud and going to M. C., I had almost a lap lead on Bud in the Daytona 500 in '78, but with three laps to go I blew up, and I watched Bobby Allison win it in Bud Moore's car.

"It would have been a storybook first race out of the box with M. C. Anderson. We had our engines built in Virginia and sent down to us. I was heading toward the finish line, only a few laps to go, and I already was counting my money. I said to myself, This one is mine. This car is so good. No way anything in the world anything can—And about that time, with three laps to go, I was going through the dogleg and *pooooof*. I watched the number 15 Ford I had left the year before win the Daytona 500. If you don't think that don't make you feel like the tiger bit you. Oh, wow.

"Richard Petty said that if I had finished the last fifty miles of the races I was leading, he said, 'Forget about it. You'd have some record.' That's why they said I was the official dyno for NASCAR.

"In April of that year at Darlington I had the win, until Dave Marcis spun me out. I was out and gone, and Marcis slid up into me or whatever happened. We made contact coming off turn four, and it's the tricky part of the racetrack. It's a place where you can't get mad if something happens because all you have to do is slip a little bit, and it's over with. On the caution lap, I rammed Marcis's car. I look back at some of my temper tantrums, getting mad and showing off, and I kind of want to slap myself. But that's also what drove me. As I mellowed as a driver, I mellowed as a person, and thank God for that.

"Then in May at Talladega I had the lead in the last lap and finished second to Cale. Let me tell you about that. That's a good story there. This was when I found out I was as good as anybody who ever drove there.

"We went down there with three engines ready to run, and for some reason the engine builder had not shaved the grates in the oil pump, and we lost all three motors. I called up M. C. and said, 'M. C., I've cost you a fortune this week. We'll just load up and come on home.' M. C. said, 'We didn't take that car there to load it up and come home. You're racing no matter how much it costs.'

"Sparky Nolles from North Carolina had a motor in the back of an El Camino. He said, 'Buddy, this thing won't run. It absolutely won't. It's about thirty horsepower off but it will run all day.' I said, 'Thirty horsepower off? Well, then it's not a problem.' I was just cutting up.

"We put that engine in the car and led the lion's portion of the race. Cale passed me on the last lap.

"When the race was over, Sparky came over and said, 'I'd like to build you a real motor one time.' That thing was a slave motor, just something to fill in in case all else failed, and yet we were able to finish second. Yeah, we lost the race, but in a way we won the race.

"For the rest of the season a lot of times the engines blew up. Like I said, if I finished I had a good shot at it. Too often we didn't finish. It got so serious that the engine builder was named 'hand grenade.' I don't want to say his name [It was not Lou LaRosa], because he went on to make a pretty good engine builder. Sour grapes are not on the agenda, because he was doing the best he could do. Quite frankly, building the motor for me at that time was pretty tough, because I ran it wide open all day and didn't leave anything to put up at the end. Still, I was very frustrated, with the engines blowing up, with trying so very hard, and though the guys were very nice and the guy building the motors was very nice, they don't pay me to be nice. I needed to try to get where I could win, so I went over to Harry Ranier's team.

"Harry had a coal mine in Kentucky and did very well with it. This guy is a racer through and through. His father loved racing. That's where Harry got his beginnings. One time I drove for Harry's father way before Ranier had real money, and Harry was my gas man.

"We had a Monte Carlo for the short tracks and an Oldsmobile for the major speedways. I had almost a career season in '79. I won the first Busch Clash ever. In that race Darrell Waltrip and I almost lapped the field. Darrell made a pullout on me and lost about seven car lengths when he dropped out to pass. From there, it was over. Darrell said, 'From then on all I was hoping was that you didn't get away from me.' That's what kind of car that was. I'm certainly not making fun of the blind, but I told someone about that car, 'With curb finders on the side, Ray Charles could run second in that son of a gun.'

"I sat on the pole, won the 125, and the morning of the 500 they repaired the bumper and didn't unplug the ignition in the car, and it burned through and knocked out the primary. On the first lap when it started up to speed, it started skipping and popping. We thought something had happened to the motor. Everyone got excited and frustrated, including me, trying to diagnose what went wrong, and they plugged the same ignition system right back up, and of course, it wouldn't crank.

"When we got home, one of the mechanics got in the car, switched the ignition over, cranked it up, and it was perfect. I mean, I could have been two laps down and made them up. That's how good that car was. That was the most disappointing thing that ever happened to me. That car was SO good.

"Herb Nab was the crew chief. Man, he was something. Look at how many races Herb won with so many drivers. At one time he and Junior Johnson had the world. And before that, when he was with Freddie Lorenzen. He was so talented. He had his own ideas, and the one thing that was kind of tough, he had set up so many race cars that sometimes in between the conversation and the race, things got changed to his way. Sometimes it was great, and sometimes it wasn't. The victories, the talent, spoke for itself, and it was gratifying he was part of the team and certainly a highlight of my life, but the only thing, sometimes he had his own opinions, and that was the way it was going to be.

"Waddell Wilson was the engine builder. I have articles where they said that motor sounded like a band of angels singing. It would *go*. It was obvious to everyone that if I didn't have a problem, the rest of them would be racing for second.

"With Herb, Waddell, and me, the only thing missing was an ignition cap! You talk about three headstrong people. There was some friction, but there was admiration for what each of us did for the team. I won't tell anyone there wasn't friction. It's hard to explain. Each of us being as proud as we were about what we could do, sometimes you get into a situation where the others might have expected a little too much from you, or you of them. Sometimes people tried to do other people's jobs. And if you have a chassis man as good as Herb Nab, he ought to be left to do the chassis. If you have a guy as good as Waddell Wilson in the engine room, then other people shouldn't try to mess with his carburetors.

"We were tied with Neil Bonnett for the most poles, and so when we went to Atlanta in March of '79, we took the Oldsmobile, our dominant car, because you got $75,000 for winning the most poles. Then in the race the car lead for twenty-five, thirty laps and I'd use up the tires because it had a lot less down force and was a lot looser race car than you need for Atlanta.

"And the strangest thing: I had managed to stay in the lead lap all day long, but about twenty laps from the lead, I was very, very close to getting lapped when they threw a caution. I said, 'We just won the race. Get ready. Four tires.' I knew. When they threw the caution, I said, 'We got lucky out here guys. Not only did we win the pole, we just won the race.'

"I came in, and they put four tires on the car, and after starting in third, I won it a full straightaway ahead. I hadn't used up the tires yet.

"In '79 I won seven poles and three races, and going into '80 I felt pretty good about everything. I had almost a sixth sense that when I went to Daytona in 1980, the rest of them were in trouble. I had won a bunch of races but never the Daytona 500, and that was where I was aiming. I had been driving for twenty years and had never won it. Every once in a while I said to myself, Maybe that's the one you aren't supposed to win. Because it was obvious on the major speedways that at Talladega, which was the sister track to Daytona, that I could take a slim bicycle and run in the top four. But then again, think of how many top fives I had at Daytona. It wasn't that I was coming home with an empty sack every time. I mean, there was the Daytona when the accelerator broke. I had a flat tire one time leading the race with six or seven laps to go and the second-place car was all the way on the front straightaway behind me. And you feel the tire going down, and you say, 'Guys, we're in trouble.' And there was the time I broke a timing chain with the race absolutely in the bag, with me sitting in the car practicing my speech, 'I want to thank Goodyear . . .'

"So when I went to Daytona in '80, the only thing that mattered was winning the Daytona 500, not the 125 or the Busch Clash. In '79 we were running five, eight miles an hour faster than anyone else in practice, in qualifying, and all it got us was trouble. I had so much trouble all through '79, because the car was so dominant that people thought I was cheating, though the fact was, we had the best team. We had everything working for us. And all year long we were subjected to a lot of checking of our car. People would come over and look at it, almost measure it to see why it was running as well as it was.

"Quite a few times in '79 I'd start out to practice, and the NASCAR inspectors would say, 'We want to check something else on the car. Bring it over.' Why put yourself through such misery?

"So in '80 at Daytona, we were smart enough to realize that to win practice was not important, so during the Busch Clash, the 125s, I just kind of laid low, rode it out, finished in the money slots. When they dropped the green at the 500, I told Waddell Wilson, 'I'm heading South.' [Baker won in the fastest speed ever recorded for a 500-mile race, 177.602 miles an hour.]

"And when I won, oh man, that was it. There is nowhere to go from there. To me, that was my lifetime goal. And once I got there, I really didn't know how to react. I had waited so long it was almost a shock to me that things went as well as they did all day. I never was much under the car. The car was so dominant. Not that it was a piece of cake. You still have to drive it. But it was a very, very dominant race car.

"In '80, everyone was surprised that Dale Earnhardt had run as well as he did, winning the racing championship. But it really wasn't his second year at all. He had raced a bunch. But he was still learning. When we beat him at Talladega, he was twenty-eight seconds in the lead when I came out of the pits, and I ran him down and beat him. It wasn't like he was ironing us out every week. He still didn't know a lot of things about drafting, how to use the slower cars to draft off. It's like being a great pilot who has only driven a single-engine airplane and all of a sudden someone says, 'Here's your Lear[jet].' When you get to Talladega and Daytona, you better know what you're doing. A lot of people think that short tracks are harder to run. You ever heard of a driver when he leaves the dirt and goes to Daytona, doesn't say, 'Man, I got a lot to learn'?

"If it had been the same Dale Earnhardt we see today with a twenty-eight-second lead, he'd have a thirty-six-second lead when it was over. There is a technique to drafting that he knows now that makes him the dominant force when he gets to Talladega and Daytona.

"In '80, friction was growing on our team. They added another mechanic to help Herb, Jake Elder. They had dual roles. Jake was very, very talented. We were having problems at Daytona when we first got there with people arguing. Jake said, 'Take everybody to lunch. When you come back, it'll be fixed.' Well, that's exactly what we did, and it was fixed. But you could tell there was a lot of friction. Even though we had a car that was that good, way back in the year I knew it was pretty much over.

"That year I won Daytona and Talladega in May. After winning at Talladega I was up in the press box, and then I walked down across the racetrack, and a guy came up to me and said, 'What's this I heard about somebody else going to be in the 28 car next year?' I mean, I had just won the race. I replied, 'Hey, I don't know. That's their choice.' I went over and talked to Ranier, and he said, 'We talked to another driver.' I said, 'Oh, okay.' And from then on the balloon was gone. Right now Harry is one of my best friends, but at that time he saw that Waddell and I were having problems, or Herb and Waddell — as a matter of fact he fired Herb that year. A team has to have harmony, and for some reason it had gone. And so at the end of '80, I went to Hoss Ellington.

"That was a good time in my life, because I had achieved some of the goals I was looking for, and the pressure was never on me at Hoss Ellington's. It was a good time. I left a race car that was quite fast and got in one that was quite fast. I liked everybody. I liked the people working on the car, the whole bit. And we had some great moments. It seemed we led every race [Baker led nine of the sixteen races he entered] but durability sometimes wasn't there. But it wasn't lack of effort. Look at what our engine builder Runt Pittman, who is with Sterling Marlin now, has done.

"I quit Hoss Ellington during the '82 season. It was another one of those situations where I was fixing to walk out the door with my suit-cases to go to an obligation, and I was asked to do something, and I said, 'I've made plans already.' And it wasn't Hoss Ellington; it was the sponsor, Uno. I said, 'I have made plans. I can't. And in the future I would like you guys to let me know at least a day ahead. 'Cause if I tell you I'm going to do something, I'm going to do it.'

"They wanted me to cancel the promise I had made to one of my other sponsors, and I wouldn't. They said, 'If you can't make certain things, we might oughta look around.' I said, 'Well, good, that's the thing to do.'

"It was a misunderstanding that escalated. Once you have made an obligation to someone, I don't care whether it's a money-paying appearance or not, once you give your word, I don't have a choice.

"I went on and drove that weekend for Hoss at Pocono, and we fell out, and as I got out of the car, I shook Hoss's hand and brought all the crew over and said, 'I just want you to know it's been a fun time, and I've really enjoyed racing with you guys.' It was pretty much done.

"About that time Ranier fired Benny Parsons. He was leading a race at Talladega near the end and was passed by Darrell Waltrip and Terry Labonte. Let me tell you, Talladega is a pressure cooker, and you can give everything you've got, which I'm sure Benny was doing, and still lose. There are two sides to everything—with internal problems you can't blame Benny Parsons for everything. But Ranier felt he was the wrong guy for the car, and he hired me back, and people are exactly right: you never go back. You just don't. I drove for them a little while, but the chemistry was never right. Sure I almost won Talladega for them, but I almost won Talladega every time I went there.

"When I went back to Ranier, that was over with before it really got started. When I went, I didn't expect to stay. It was pretty mutual between everybody that we were going to just try to finish the year out.

"Then in '83 I was hired by the Wood Brothers. All my racing career Leonard and Glen Wood were my foes. We fought it out. When Cale was driving for them, when David Pearson was driving for them, that was *the* car. When David was in their car, whether he was a lap down or not, so long as he was in the race that car was in con-tention. On major speedways they were supergood, but when I went there they had gone into a slump. They were in a decline as far as their dominance on the superspeedways, and I can tell you this: as far as setting the car up to feel right, Leonard Wood was as fine a setup man as anybody I ever drove for. That race car had such a quality feel.

"We started the '83 season running third at the Daytona 500. I had the lead with twelve laps to go. Cale came by and passed me. When you're in that position you do everything you can do without wrecking both cars. Remember the two races with Richard Petty and David Pearson where they wrecked. You don't cut these guys off. Not to the point of wrecking. If you do, as we saw, that's exactly what you're going to have.

"I took as much racetrack as I could take without killing us both. When I got to that point, I had run Cale over to the grass down the back straightaway. I did everything I could short of try to wreck him. I know if it had been in reverse, Cale wouldn't have wrecked me either.

"Cale had some help. He had Joe Ruttman cutting up under him, and the two cars drafted by together. Cale would have never made it by himself.

"Cale dropped back going into turn one, and that gave him a tremendous vacuum on the back of my car pulling up with Ruttman pushing him. And what happened, Ruttman pushed him right by me. And that also helped Cale because I was coming back like a son of a gun. As I was saying, 'Okay pal, I'm either going to win or you're not going to finish second,' Ruttman went on by too. I dropped all the way to third. Ruttman was driving for the 98 team. We almost welded those two cars together off turn four. Without him, I could have caught Cale back. He was nursing a car that was overheating a little bit. Everything had to work as it did for him to win.

"You have to give Ruttman credit. He's overlooked as far as talent. Ruttman was a lot better than anyone ever gave him credit for. In my opinion he may not have been as good as Richard or Cale or Bobby on a week to week basis, but he would have won some races had he had topnotch cars.

"On July 4, I learned my lesson well from Mr. Yarborough, and I won the Firecracker 400 at Daytona. See, these were nonrestricted cars, so leading that thing was like the kiss of death with eleven laps to go. I was just sitting there behind Terry Labonte, waiting, thinking, Okay, we played chess long enough. I have the perfect move. You couldn't have thrown dynamite at me to make me move.

"All of a sudden, with just over a lap to go I was passing Terry. I didn't want to do it, but he had run out of fuel.

"I can't say there was a lot of cheering when I won. The Wood Brothers are like the Green Bay Packers. At one time they were the best, and even though they had gone through tough times, when they won again, it was like they were the Green Bay Packers again. They had a pride that they expected to win every time, so when you won, there was no, 'Gee, that's the greatest win we ever had.' Nah. They expected to win every week.

"Unfortunately, we had a series of problems which prevented me from winning a bunch of races with those guys. In late July I was leading the race at Talladega, and I had run about seventy miles and didn't know I didn't have any brakes on the car. If they had wrecked in front of me, that would have looked like a plane crash. But I didn't know it until I started to pit. They said, 'Come in for four tires,' and I started down pit road, and the brake petal went right up under the dash.

"I had to go back around, turn the switch off on the back straightaway, and then coast in. They met me in the pit road, and I was down to a crawl, drove all the way down, and stopped. But we had a really good race car until then.

"In November in Atlanta, I was running second to Bobby Allison. Neil Bonnett was behind me when Bobby blew a tire and hit the wall. With only a few laps to go, Neil passed me for the win. I can only tell you that any time you lose the lead at Atlanta, it's because you're out of tires. Atlanta is like a bowl. You're the rabbit that everybody has been chasing. The guys behind you are taking it a little easier getting in the corners and drafting back up on you in the straightaways. Once you start skating across the racetrack, you say to yourself, 'I'm out of tires.' That's what happened to me when Neil passed me that day.

"Boy, Neil Bonnett was so talented, but he got hurt a bunch. He broke his leg at Charlotte, had a bad injury at Darlington, and one time leading the race at Martinsville he broke his thumb. He said it was pointing back at him. He was a good race driver, but his seventeen wins do not tell you what kind of a race car driver he was. Neil

Bonnett ran wide open, half-turned over all the time. That was his style, and that takes away from you sometimes.

"I feel like I knew Neil quite well, because he and I broadcast together for three years. After his crash at Darlington, he sat out those three years. People say he never should have gone back to racing, but I can tell you why he did it. All the time he was broadcasting, he was testing for Dale Earnhardt, and he was running lap times that were as good as anybody. He told me, 'This is what I'd really like to do.' TV was just a sidelight for him. When he got healthy enough, he said, 'I'm going back out there. I haven't done the things I want to do yet.' We talked about it, and I said, 'Neil, you are so good on TV.' He said, 'Buddy, driving is what I want to do.' I said, 'Well then, go for it.' And while he was testing for the Daytona 500 in '93, he crashed and died. I've often said, it's not how many years you are here, it's how well you've lived the ones you're on."

34

THE EMERGENCE OF DALE EARNHARDT

IN 1975 LOU LAROSA LEFT THE DiGard team and went to work for Smokey Yunick, known for his engine building and mechanical genius. LaRosa received an education. But Yunick was no longer racing, and LaRosa's goal was to build engines for Winston Cup cars. The next year he was hired by M. C. Anderson of Savannah, and soon thereafter moved to Charlotte to work for the Rod Osterlund team with crew chief Roland Wlodyka and driver Dave Marcis. At Osterlund, LaRosa learned engine building from Ducky Newman. When Newman left the team in 1976, LaRosa was named chief engine builder. Only a few years earlier he had been sweeping floors at DiGard.

In 1979 Osterlund gave LaRosa and Jim Delaney the choice of three drivers: Cale Yarborough, David Pearson, or an unknown youngster by the name of Dale Earnhardt. Even though they knew the aggressive youngster would crash a lot, they picked Earnhardt, who won Rookie of the Year in 1979 and won the Winston Cup championship in 1980 in only his second year as a driver. Earnhardt's two years together with Osterlund were memorable.

After Wlodyka fired crew chief Jake Elder, the team suffered. The outspoken, apolitical LaRosa was so upset that he quit. He would team up with Earnhardt again later.

299

Lou LaRosa: "Through Mario Rossi I had gotten to know Smokey Yunick, whose garage, The Best Damn Garage in Town, is still in Daytona Beach. In 1975, I went to work for Smokey. This was another dream come true for me, because he was the winning car owner of the first stock car race I ever saw. I was watching *Wide World of Sports* on TV in 1962, and Fireball Roberts won the Daytona 500 driving a black-and-gold '62 Pontiac. We just had a little twelve-inch screen. Chris Economacki did the announcing. They showed Fireball coming into victory lane, the pipes coming out the back of the car. Up to that time I was into drag racing, and I had never seen anything like that car. It was Smokey's car. Well, thirteen years later I went to work for that man, and he paid me money. I'd have worked for him for nothing.

"Smokey was a super innovator. He was working on a submarine motor for one of the Florida universities. The motor took hydrogen out of the water and used that for fuel and turned it back into water. Smokey worked on Indy cars. He made his own manifolds. When I worked for Mario, he taught me a lot. What Smokey taught me was patience and to think things through. He'd work on a box manifold, and at the time everybody said the box manifold was crap, and it was at the beginning. Every day he worked on it, patiently and diligently, running it down, taking it off, putting it up, working on the airflow. Everyone said he was a son of a bitch when he was racing, that he'd come in and kick over the toolbox, but when he worked with me, he was one of the nicest. People bad-mouth him, but in his day and later, the man was brilliant. He was truly, truly brilliant.

"Back then nobody got into his shop. The walls were painted black, the doors triple-locked. Being let in the shop was an honor. To do work for him was a double honor. I was a peon, an apprentice. At the time he was building motors for Sportsman and Winston Cup cars. The thing I liked about him, I paid my dues working for him as an apprentice Monday to Friday from eight to five. In addition, on Monday, Wednesday, and Friday, if you wanted to come back at six and work from six to twelve for no pay, that was the fun time. That's when he'd do experiments, and that was learning. I thought the world of that. We were experimenting on carburetors, airflow, manifolds, motors. But it wasn't for a customer. It was for him. It was his time. You wouldn't be under a deadline of the next race.

"Smokey was always into something. He had his own helicopter on the back pad, and sometimes he would fly off to make connections for Bolivia, where he was part owner of a gold mine somewhere. Smokey was always into something. He's a brilliant person, a fun person, an intelligent man, and I learned from him.

"I worked for him for a little less than a year. I really wanted to get back in racing, and David Ifft called me. David had left DiGard and gone to Savannah, Georgia, to be the crew chief for M. C. Anderson in '76. Anderson was a contractor, built roads and airports, an old country boy who made a lot of money, liked racing. He hired Sam Sommers, a local hero who had run on a lot of dirt tracks, won, and was in a bad wreck at Daytona in a Sportsman race when he hooked the wall, spun and T-boned Don McTavish, an up-and-coming driver who was killed. I remember a picture of the wreck from the sixties. The whole front of McTavish's car was gone, and he was hanging out the front of the car. Sommers had never made it to the top, and M. C. was going to give him his chance, and David was going to be the crew chief.

"That pairing didn't go over too well. David didn't like Sam, and Sam didn't like David. The team was running a limited schedule, had no sponsor. I was hired to do mechanical work, to work on the car, and that was a plus, because it added to my knowledge. But that wasn't going anywhere, and I came up to Charlotte to work as the assistant to my old friend Ducky Newman, who had gone to work for Rod Osterlund as the chief engine builder. I was to be Ducky's assistant.

"Osterlund had two cars, the 2 car with Dave Marcis and the 98 car driven by Roland Wlodyka. This was 1976. Marcis had finished second in the points in 1975, but he didn't win with us. And once again, the situation turned into Byzantine politics. Roland really didn't like Marcis, and Marcis didn't like Roland. Roland, who was Marcis's crew chief, wanted to be a driver. In '78, Marcis finished fifth in the points, he ran fair, but it wasn't as good as Osterlund expected. Osterlund was another visionary. He saw racing growing big. He was the first to have a team rig, way before Petty. He was one of the first to put in a big machine shop, an engine room, the first to hire a first-class surface plate man to build cars.

"Roland was a hardheaded Polack who had his good qualities, but at the end of the year they fired Marcis, and Ducky took a better offer from M. C. Anderson, from where I just came. M. C. was going to put in his own engine room. Benny Parsons was going to be their driver. David Ifft wanted me to come back too, but I had just left there, and I didn't want to go back—I didn't like Savannah that much. It was too hot—even though I liked David, liked Benny, and loved Ducky. Of everybody, Ducky was really my mentor. He was part of that closed circle of southerners, and for him to take me in and teach me, that was special to me. Ducky took the time to teach me the Winston Cup way. People don't think Ducky Newman was a great engine builder, but Ducky could assemble motors, do the machine work, run the dyno, and he was great to me. During that season together at Osterlund's, Ducky and I must have built a hundred motors. We built them for Marcis and Roland, and after Harry Hyde fell out with Boss Hogg, J. D. Stacy, with Neil Bonnett driving, Stacy hired us to build his engines as well. Then at that time Humpy Wheeler of the Charlotte Motor Speedway asked us to build engines for a car for Dale Earnhardt, so we were building motors for four different drivers.

When Ducky went to M. C. Anderson, at the end of '76 I got my first opportunity to be the chief engine builder. I wasn't quite ready for it. When I was named, Richard Petty was quoted in a magazine saying, 'It's very easy to be an engine builder in Winston Cup racing. They hired someone who was a floor sweeper, and now he's chief engine builder.' He didn't mention me by name, but I guess that quote was directed at me, 'cause I had been sweeping floors in Daytona, and now three years later I was chief engine builder. I'll never forget reading that, but it didn't bother me because the hardheaded Italian in me said, I'll show your ass who's a floor sweeper. I'm not the sort of guy to make quotes, to make promises. It's: I'll show you what I can do. That's the true proof. To do it.

"At the time Rod Osterlund was sitting in San Jose, and he told Jim Delaney and myself that we could have as our driver Cale Yarborough, David Pearson, or Dale Earnhardt.

"Cale wanted to leave Junior Johnson, wanted to run a limited schedule cause he was getting burned out. He wanted to spend more time with his family. His daughters were growing up. Pearson, who was driving for the Wood Brothers, also wanted to run a limited schedule. Earnhardt, who was full of piss and vinegar, was unknown. We had been impressed with the way Dale had run with our motor in the World Service Life 300 at Charlotte in a Sportsman car, and how he ran in Ontario and Atlanta, and we chose to take Dale. Jim Delaney said, 'We'll take him, but the son of a bitch will tear up a lot of equipment learning.' And he did.

"There were a ton of drivers as good as him at the time. We ran for Rookie of the Year. In '79 he had a stellar field of competitors. He ran against a great driver, Harry Gant. If Harry had started earlier, he'd have kicked everyone's ass. Joe Millikan was in that field. We started and ran at Riverside, finished that race, and we went to Daytona.

"We qualified terribly because we had an old '78 Buick squareback. The hot car was a 442 Oldsmobile, which was a good three to four miles an hour faster. Dale started way back, came to the front, and son of a bitch if Dale Earnhardt didn't lead that race! I believe we could have won that race. They called him in early for gas, and he lost the draft. He got pissed. He dumped the clutch, revved it to 9,000 rpms, and broke a valve spring when he left the pits. It was a lack of experience, plus being pissed and hot. He finished eighth. It was an outstanding start for the boy.

"Dale was cocky. He was a smart-ass, which is great. I compare good drivers to navy fighter pilots coming off aircraft carriers. If you ever meet a navy fighter pilot off a carrier, they are young, cocky, and aggressive. You've got to be aggressive. The cleaned-up image they have today for the drivers is bullshit. 'A guy bumped me, but that's okay, I love him anyway' is bullshit. A race car driver is like a boxer. How can you be a timid boxer? How can you be a timid judo expert? You have to be aggressive, determined, and focused. You don't win races if you're not.

"I really liked the kid. Dale was a smart-ass, aggressive, cocky. He didn't give a shit, he was going to the front. A hundred miles into a race he'd take a chance, pass on the outside when he didn't have to. One time at Martinsville he tried to pass twelve cars the first lap, and he took out the whole field. It was immaturity, a lack of experience.

"You got to remember, Dale came from a racing background from his father. His dad Ralph had died in '73. I never met his dad. His dad was a winner from the git go. His dad actually supported the family by racing a Sportsman—unheard of. Back then you raced three, four nights a week. Dale was around race cars his whole life. So he thought, even though he was young, that he knew everything. From drivers you always get that: 'The motors don't run' shit, or 'The car doesn't handle,' but in '79 we had a good relationship.

"Our crew chief that year was Jake Elder. Jake was a big help to Dale. Jake in his day was a top crew chief. Like Herb Nab, Jake was good. Jake had a lot to do with a lot of drivers winning their first race. Dale was a hardheaded son of a bitch. We went to Martinsville, and Dale would say, 'Goddamn, I'm driving this son of a bitch, and it won't go at all.' Dale was used to driving a car hard. He'd brake late, wait for the car to get stable and take off.

"Jake would say, 'You're driving it too hard. That's the trouble. Let the car carry you, and save the brakes. Don't get the car upset.' Jake calmed him down and talked him through it.

"If Jake hadn't taken Dale under his wing, if Jake hadn't been that capable fatherlike figure, Dale might not have made it, or he might have floundered a few more years. 'Cause you have to have the trust of your crew chief. Don't forget that these drivers are running 200 miles an hour, shit is happening so fast, and you need a calming influence to tell you everything's okay. And that's what Jake did. We ran decent, usually finished, and lo and behold, in April of '79, Dale won his first race at Bristol.

"I was the chief engine builder and the jackman. Dale was battling Darrell Waltrip and Bobby Allison down to the end, and the thing that stands out in my mind, Darrell claimed his lug nuts were loose or some other bullshit, but we kicked his ass, won the race. And what was great to me, David Ifft was there with Benny Parsons and Ducky Newman, and they had a giant bottle of champagne, a magnum, which they had brought because they thought they were going to win. But after we won, they came over and gave it to me. Ducky congratulated me, and that's a great thing, to have your mentor say 'Congratulations.'

"The win pumped everybody up. We didn't have a sponsor. The money was coming out of Rod Osterlund's pocket. We were happy for Rod as well as for ourselves.

"The next week we went to Darlington. Everybody was on a high. We went out to practice, and some son of a bitch didn't put the hood pins in, and the hood blew back and smashed the windshield. We struggled through that. In June Dale won his first pole, at Riverside,

California. Everybody said, 'He can't drive a road course,' but he sat on the pole, which was great.

"Then in late July at Pocono, he lost control, the car spun backwards, and he hit the retaining wall on the driver's side, and it knocked him unconscious. Dale broke his sternum and his collarbone. He's lucky he wasn't killed, 'cause that's how Joe Weatherly was killed in '64 when he hit the wall at Riverside. The walls were made of boilerplate at Riverside, and it was boilerplate at Pocono.

"They had to airlift him. I remember him telling me that he woke up on the helicopter going to the hospital. He told me he opened his eyes, and all he could see were clouds as he was flying through the air, and he thought he had died and gone to heaven.

"So now we've lost our driver, a bad deal. I'll show you how funny life is. Dale was running for Rookie of the Year. To replace him, I went to interview the two drivers we could have had at the start of the season, Cale and David Pearson. Around that time David had had a falling-out with the Wood Brothers. They were having an ongoing feud, and he left the pits at Darlington, and they didn't tighten the left-side wheels. They said, 'Whoa,' and he thought they said, 'Go.' That was the end of their relationship, which had been great for years. I know they were friends. But all good things end. Stuff like that happens.

"We took David over Cale mainly because Jake had worked with Pearson in the sixties as his crew chief at Holman-Moody. Again, I think the world of Jake Elder. People can talk trash about him all they want, but he won the Daytona 500 with Mario Andretti. He had won racing championships with David Pearson.

"Jake and Pearson had a great relationship. Pearson would give Jake shit, and Jake would give it back. They went back to when they were kids, and they resumed it many years later.

"Pearson was a great, great, wonderful driver. After we took him, right off the bat, his ego—and ours too—was that we wanted to run well to show the Wood Brothers.

"The first race after Dale got hurt was Talladega. David finished second in qualifying and came in second in the race behind Darrell. The clutch went out on the end of a restart, and Darrell Waltrip beat us. We would have won.

"The next race was at Michigan. David practiced two laps, and he told

Jake, 'Blow the right rear tire up.' They were staggering the car. They practiced another lap, adjusted the tire again, and David said, 'We're ready.' He went out and sat on the pole. I was like, Holy shit, man.

"We went to the Southern 500 at Darlington. Darrell Waltrip will tell you he should have won the race, but David was running first or second all day. Darrell passed him and spun out, and we won the race. This was a big moment for me personally, a great moment, one of the highlights of my life, because three years earlier I was sitting in the grandstands under the shade coming out of four, watching as a spectator. When you leave the Darlington track, there's a list of winners going back to 1950 when Johnny Mantz won in a Plymouth, and he won because his tires didn't wear out. And whose name was on there just about every other time? David Pearson, David Pearson, David Pearson. And here it is, three years later, and my engine wins the Southern 500 with David Pearson. I thought, I can't believe this is for real.

"And after that race Pearson gave Jake Elder hell because he didn't have any water during the race. The radios had gone out, which they used to do, and the tube had pulled out of his water bottle so he couldn't get any water, and he gave it to Jake. And that day it had to be 150 degrees in that car. If you looked at us, we were dead just standing in the pits. I had an ice bucket on my head. And here David ran the whole race, and he looked like he had walked out of an air-conditioned room! Unbelievable.

"I said, 'David, I know our car was running quicker, yet Waltrip was able to pass us. Why?' David said, 'At Darlington you don't race the other drivers. You race the track. You set a pace where you're comfortable. If you drive faster than that, this thing will jump up and bite you, and you'll crash.' He said, 'What did Waltrip do?' I said, 'He crashed.' David said, 'There you go.' That was David Pearson telling you how to win the Southern 500.

"This gets better. We went to Richmond in September. Dale hasn't healed up. He was about 60 percent, but the hardheaded son of a bitch wanted to drive anyway. After David had won, I know it had hurt Dale's heart that Pearson had won in the car and sat on the pole, 'cause that was his ride. He didn't wish David bad, but he wished that he had done it, and he was going to prove a point, and that son of a bitch came back and he sat on the pole at Richmond and I was amazed.

"Dale'd been out five races, out two months. The boy was laid out, and he was hurting. He was in pain. 'Cause I went to see him. He lived in a little shack on Sugar Creek Road. He and Teresa had bed-sheets up for window curtains. Dale wasn't always rich and famous. And he was lying on a mattress on the floor with a plywood board under it, and he was in tremendous pain.

"He'd drive five or six laps in practice, and he'd be all over the track because he was hurting. He'd have to come in, because he couldn't turn that wheel. People don't realize when you go in a corner at 150 miles an hour, it's like somebody has thrown you against the side of the wall. You get aches and pains when you're healthy. There was no power steering back then. After a race, you'd see drivers laying on the ground, exhausted. 'Cause the cars didn't handle. They'd jump all over.

"And what did Dale do his first race back? He sat on the pole!

"I said, 'Dale, what do you think about the motor?' He said, 'It sucks. It's got no power.' And here we had sat on the pole.

"We got Bill Elliott to be a relief driver. We were running Chevrolets at the time instead of Fords. Bill got in the car, tested it. I said, 'Bill, what do you think of the motor?'

"Just like that boy from *Mayberry, RFD*, he said, 'Gol-lee, that thing sets you back in the seat. When you come off the corner, it feels like it gains fifty horsepower down the straightaway.' And here was Earnhardt saying that the motor sucks.

"The last race of '79 was in Ontario. We finished ninth and won Rookie of the Year, despite Dale laying out, to show you what a good year we had. Even though he missed five races, Dale still finished seventh in the points overall. Richard Petty won the championship, his last one, by ten points over Darrell.

"I'll never forget leaving the track and seeing a big billboard they had out there that said, 'Congratulations Richard Petty, Winston Cup Champion; Dale Earnhardt, Rookie of the Year.'

"We got back to the motel. We were up on the second-floor balcony, me, Dale, and Jake, and I said, 'Man, I'm really happy that we won.' Dale said, 'That ain't shit. I don't care about that. I want to be Winston Cup champion next year.' And he walked off. Jake said, 'Boy, we've got our hands full with him next year.' Dale wasn't going to be content running in the back. He wasn't going to be Mr. Nice Guy. He was going to win, and he didn't give a shit. It wasn't, 'I won the rookie, and I'm going to sit on my fat ass and rest on my laurels.' Dale was going to be champion.

"We went to Riverside to start the '80 season and finished second to Darrell. I built an engine for Dan Gurney, who came out of retirement for the race. Dan was one of my all-time heroes growing up. He was running great until he tore up the transmission.

"We went to Daytona, and son of a bitch if Dale didn't go out and win the Busch Clash. A sophomore won the Busch Clash! I almost fell over. I couldn't believe it. That meant a lot to Rod Osterlund, because he didn't have a lot of money. He was on the ropes. The $50,000, or whatever he won, carried the team. We went on that year, and in 1980 Dale won five races and won the Winston Cup championship by nineteen points over Cale Yarborough. That had never been done before, winning the rookie of the year and the next year winning the championship.

"And then in the middle of the year, the team got involved in politics, and to show you how stupid people are, around Charlotte in May, Roland fired Jake, and Osterlund agreed with it. They said, 'Doug Richert knows all the setups.' Doug was just a kid at the time. I said to Roland, 'You stupid son of a bitch. It ain't what's on paper. It's how Jake arrived at the conclusion.' Jake had experience. Like when we won the Southern 500 with Pearson, we didn't race on Sunday, the track was closed, and it had rained. Jake came back and changed all the setups on the car. I said, 'Why, Jake?' He said, 'It's because of what happened to the track over the weekend.' Jake had a feel from experience of what the track was going to be like, what the tires were going to do on it, what effect the heat was going to have. Jake would know.

"Roland fired Jake because he was hardheaded, hard to get along with. But if you're in a leadership position, you have to lead. Lead, follow, or get the hell out of the way. I was like that myself. I believe in this: If you are going to give somebody responsibility, then you have to give him the authority. The wannabes, would-bes and neverwuzes always can do it better, cheaper, quicker. But they never do. They never will. As the leader you have to make a determination that 'I'm going to go with this plan right, wrong, or indifferent.' You gotta have a plan in your head. You gotta execute the plan. You can't have every Willy Nilly telling you, 'This ain't right,' changing your mind. Now

Jake was hard to get along with. He cussed, swore, but I told them, 'You're making a mistake letting him go,' and if you look at our performance after Jake left, we went from the front of the field to the back of the field. But we still won five races and were able to win. And at the end of the year, my turn came, again because of Roland.

"During that '80 season I'd be working in the shop until eleven at night, along with my wife and Jim Delaney. We lived there. And where was the rest of the help? They left at five, couldn't stay for one reason or another. But come the next year, those same guys had belt buckles that said 'Winston Cup champions' on them. I didn't see those people there in the middle of the night. All them would-bes, wannabes, hangers-on, leaches, they weren't there. But when it came to winning time, they were there to pump Earnhardt. What you find in racing it's CYA, cover your ass, every man for himself. Holding on to your job is more important than speaking the truth. But as far as I'm concerned, racing is only a sport. Yes, it's important to do well at what you do, but you gotta have loyalty, you have to say what you mean, mean what you say, and stick by the consequences. Anyway, I told Roland to stick it up his ass, and I left and went back to M. C. Anderson."

35

HARRY HYDE AND TIM RICHMOND

CAR OWNER RICK HENDRICK IN 1986 hired one of the most flamboyant and talented drivers ever to race on the NASCAR Winston Cup circuit. His name was Tim Richmond, and from the time he began driving the Chevy numbered 25 under the direction of crew chief Harry Hyde, Hendrick's race team became a force.

Behind the scenes, Tommy Johnson, Hyde's nephew, watched the relationship between the mercurial Richmond and the exacting Hyde grow. Once they began to understand each other, the wins flowed, seven in all as Richmond finished third in the points behind Dale Earnhardt and Darrell Waltrip. It was to be Richmond's greatest season.

That winter he ended up in the hospital. He had a serious illness, but no one on the race team knew exactly what. He returned to the track in June of '87, won the first two races he entered, then fell ill again. After he disappeared from the racing scene, it was revealed that he had contracted AIDS. According to his friends, he had a thing for prostitutes, along with his other romantic entanglements. Tim Richmond died on August 13, 1989. Tommy Johnson, who admired him greatly, will never forget him.

TOMMY JOHNSON: "We won three races in 1985, Martinsville, Nashville, and the final race of the season at Riverside. But in the second season, Geoff [Bodine] changed. We started the season winning the Daytona 500. But Geoff manipulated the power around to where he was the one who called the shots on the car, what setup went under it, and then Harry and Geoff got to where they totally could not get along. Meanwhile, Rick hired Tim Richmond to run a second car for the rest of the 1986 season. Everybody said *that* wasn't going to work, because as nonchalant as Tim was, the flamboyant cat, the partyer, they predicted that he and Harry would not get along.

"And from the beginning they did. It's a myth that they didn't. Always Harry tried to get to know his driver, not personally, but in terms of 'How do you like the race car?' or 'What do you like the race car to feel like?' And it took about six months for Harry and Tim to reach an understanding. They had to sit down and discuss things in order for them to understand each other.

"Two people discussing strategy do not understand each other to start. They think they do, but it takes people a period of time to get to know each other so they understand. They *hear* each other, but the understanding is not there. So Tim had to try to understand the questions that Harry was asking him. Harry had to try to understand the answers Tim was giving him.

"So Harry and Tim *never* had a verbal argument. Nobody got mad. But Harry would get very frustrated, because he could not understand what Tim was telling him he wanted. But that understanding came about in June at Pocono.

"From the time they unloaded the automobile at Pocono, that understanding jelled. We were quick off the truck. We were on the pole for the race. And we won the race. And after that, there was never any confusion of understanding. I worked on the car. Harry wrote the figures down. Tim had to translate to Harry what 'I want the car to feel like.' It wasn't, 'I want this spring, this shock, this sway bar.' It was, 'I want the car to do a certain thing when I get into the corner,' or the middle of the corner or off the corner.

"And Tim was the kind of guy who had feel for an automobile. He could point to a spot on the racetrack and say to Harry, 'This car is doing this—right there.' He'd mark it, actually put a black mark on the wall where the car was doing something. Tim would say, 'You fix it for me where it won't do that, and I'll show you the improvement on the stopwatch.' And he could do exactly that.

"Everyone said that Tim and Harry didn't get along, but what would really happen, Tim would go out and practice for three or four laps, and he'd come in and say, 'Get it ready to qualify. Cover it up.' And that would make Harry absolutely furious. He'd say, 'Tim, So-and-so is two-tenths seconds quicker than we are.' Tim would say, 'It don't make no difference. We got it.' And off he'd go. He'd go to the camper, lay back, walk around and talk to everybody. I think he was using head games on everybody. But Tim would not get back in that car. He'd say, 'Harry, it don't need it. We got it.' Tim never said, 'I got it.' It was always, 'We got it.' Harry'd say, 'Tiiiiiiiiiiimmmmmm. So-and-so is running faster than you.' 'I don't care. We got it.' And Tim didn't lie to you. He had it, and he knew it. he knew how the car felt, knew how much it had left, what he could do with it. Over the years we had some drivers on a scale from one to ten I would rate a seven or eight. Tim was the only ten we ever had.

"Tim was a character in all respects. He wasn't intimidated by anyone or anything. He wasn't moody, didn't go from feeling good to feeling bad. Tim Richmond was the same every day. He'd take us out to eat all the time. We'd be working feverishly at the shop, and at lunchtime Tim would come strolling in, no socks, a pair of loafers, pair of shorts, and in would roll a big catering truck and unload food and set up tables. 'All right, boys,' he'd say, 'time to eat.' You never knew when he was coming. He didn't give you a warning. He just would roll in at fifteen to noon. 'All right, boys, I'm cooking today.' And if we were out of town, he'd come strolling into the restaurant. He'd say to the waitress, 'That table over there. Give me the check for it.'

"As I said, we didn't win our first race until June at Pocono. Then we won Daytona, Pocono again, Watkins Glen, Darlington, Richmond, and the last race of the season at Riverside. When Tim Richmond decided to go, the competition was over with. He kind of played a game during every race when he was running up front. He was smart enough not to use the car up until the very end of the race; in the last five laps he had no mercy on it. He figured if it lasted that long, it was time to use it up to win the race. On the road courses the last five laps he was so abusive, he would take it to the limit, wiping the decals off the quarter panel against the wall but not wrecking. He constantly was at the ragged edge. He'd go to it, but didn't step over it. He wasn't idiotic, didn't overwind it, throw the engine apart, strip the gears, but he used up every bit of that car. He learned that from sprint cars and from driving Indy. There's a fine line to which you can go, and Tim took it to that. It was hard to watch sometimes, and you were afraid he'd stuff it, but after a while you began to trust him.

"We won seven races in '86, but Dale Earnhardt won the points championship. Earnhardt was also winning races, and he was a very tough competitor, like he's always been. You will not find the Richard Childress team off but about one out of every fifteen or twenty races. They will be in competition for the first three positions most of the time. I don't care how bad the car is off. Through pit stops, caution flags, through hard effort in driving, one way or another Earnhardt and that team will get it to the front. And Tim and Earnhardt were very competitive.

"After the Riverside race in November, Tim wound up in the hospital. Some people said he seemed on drugs, but that's hindsight. We didn't think there was anything wrong. Tim Richmond was our driver, and every man in the shop loved him. We were dedicated to that race car for Folgers and Rick Hendrick and Tim Richmond, and we couldn't see it if it was happening. And that's all I know about that.

"We had a pool party at the motel the night before the Riverside race. He was out there. He didn't drink anything. He was just walking around. I know Tim wasn't drunk. And Tim didn't need marijuana or cocaine. He admitted that back in '82 and '83 he had done it, and I couldn't absolutely swear he wasn't doing it at this time, but as much as you travel, eat, share fellowship, bull around with someone, you're only away from each other a short period of time, and Tim would be in the restaurant late at night, or he would walk through the bar where we were at and have a beer or a drink, and then Tim would show up at the track at eight—so in that eight or so hours of the night people can do a lot of bad things, and eventually it will show on them. I'm not saying that Tim Richmond wasn't guilty of what killed him. I'm not saying he was lily white or he could walk on water, but I can say that I do not know in what fashion this happened. I never did know, and I don't really care to know.

"But as a driver and a person with personality, Tim Richmond exceeded everything I could have wanted. He never mistreated people. He treated his own team like family. Whatever you wanted or needed, Tim would help you out. He was just a good guy. What he did with his personal life was his business, but this time it was devastating. I'm very sorry, but it hurt everybody that this happened. It almost wants you to get mad at him for doing it, because we were enjoying success and happiness in all modes, and then this happened and took it away. You wanted to get mad at him, but he was the type of person that you can't do that.

"When he went into the hospital the first time after the Riverside race, he tried to portray the feel-good deal you always knew before. And he did a good job at it, but you could tell that Tim Richmond's strength was not there. His personality remained, he had the same flamboyance, but he no longer had any strength.

"In June of 1987 Tim felt well enough to drive again, and when we went back to Pocono for his first race, he won the race, and you could not tell the difference. He also won the next race at Riverside. I walked up to the car in the winner's circle—I was generally the first guy to the car because we had to tape the speakers to his ears, and it was my job to untape his ears after we got his helmet off. He looked up at me, and he said, 'You can't tell me this is easy to do.' He was laughing. He put his hat on crooked and turned the bill up. And that's the way he got out of the race car. Even then, you couldn't tell there was anything wrong with Tim Richmond.

"After Riverside, Tim started doing public appearances again, and he wasn't getting enough rest. I guess maybe he knew it wasn't going to be very long, that 'I'm going to do it to the end, and when it happens, it'll happen.' I knew he knew [he was dying]. Of course, he had to know. Everybody thinks they are going to fight that deal [AIDS] off, but very few people have won that fight. Everybody thinks once they get into remission, even though it's still there, it's not going to come back but that it's going to get better. So I think Tim was taking it right to the end the best he could do.

"Tim drove one more race, at Michigan. He was late getting to the car to qualify. We pushed the car out of line and sent someone to get him. He didn't qualify well. And on race day, when I put him in the car, he was just not the Tim Richmond that we knew. We only ran about half the race that day, and shortly after that Tim went back into the hospital. Harry and I didn't go see him, only family and Rick Hendrick. Tim didn't want people to see him under those conditions. That was his request.

"The rest of the year was hard, because Harry was having a political struggle with the rest of the Hendrick Motorsport team. Harry was supposed to be the crew chief and the team manager, but more of the people working there didn't paid any attention to him, didn't do what Harry wanted. I was shop foreman, and I worked there and handed out orders, and people were ignoring us. There was a lot of disturbance within the team, and we weren't enjoying success. I got tired of the power struggle, and I told Harry, 'I'm not going to work under these conditions. I'm leaving.' So I left and went to work for the Stavola Brothers, and in December of '88 Harry joined me. And in August of 1989 Harry got a call from Jimmy Johnson, Rick Hendrick's general manager, to tell us that Tim had died. Even though we knew it was coming, it was still hard to deal with.

"They had a memorial the next day at the Charlotte Motor Speedway, and we went over there, and it was very hard. You felt like Tim was a close member of the family. He had so much talent, and now it was gone.

"Tim Richmond touched a lot of people's lives. He was close to so many of the team members who worked for him. The big room at the speedway was full for the service. People were standing outside in the halls.

"And after he died, it was like he never existed. You know why? Some people think if they write about somebody who had AIDS, you're going to go to hell. That's the appearance it gives to me. 'We don't want to touch this.'

"But there are a few people who will write about him, not because they were close to Tim Richmond but because of who he was and what he was and what he brought to racing.

"Every race driver has something controversial about them. Look around. But I was watching Benny Parsons on TV, and someone called in and wanted to know why racing had become the number one spectator sport, and the caller said, 'With all the short tracks and the thousands of drivers, how many of them do you read about in the papers who are dealing drugs or taking drugs? How many have been arrested for child abuse or assault and battery? This is the cleanest family-oriented game you can go to.' And he said, 'No wonder it's the number one spectator sport.'"

36

CALE AND MORE
ABOUT DALE

IN 1981 LOU LAROSA RETURNED
to his friends Ducky Newman and David Ifft
to build engines for M. C. Anderson. Cale
Yarborough was the team's driver, and it was from
this vantage point that he got to see up close the
greatness of Cale Yarborough.

The next year there was conflict on the team,
and after 1983 LaRosa left, undecided as to
whether he should stay in racing. He was told
by friend Ricky Rudd that his car owner, an
independent by the name of Richard Childress,
needed help. At that time Childress wasn't competitive. He ran a low-budget race program, and
Rudd was upset that Childress's engines blew up
more often than not. When the head engine
builder was fired at the end of 1983, LaRosa got
the job.

After LaRosa was hired, Childress brought
Dale Earnhardt back to drive for him. LaRosa
had been upset that Earnhardt had left Childress
after their two years together, and when
Childress took Dale back, LaRosa considered
quitting, but Earnhardt called LaRosa and asked
him not to leave.

After the Childress race team finished fourth
in the points in 1984, the car owner built his own
engine shop. Everything was going smoothly.
Everyone was getting along.

In 1985, the team seemed jinxed. Motors

started breaking in midrace. No one was happy, but no one called for heads to roll. The team learned from its mistakes, and in 1986 Dale Earnhardt won his second driving championship running Lou LaRosa's engines.

In 1987 the team was at its apex. RCR won eleven races and another championship. Lou LaRosa was named Engine Builder of the Year.

And then in 1988, according to LaRosa, things started to change. Beginning at Daytona, other crew members were harping about his motors behind his back when, says LaRosa, the car didn't run well because the chassis design created too much drag for success. LaRosa also discovered that as the Childress race team grew, the family atmosphere and closeness among everyone was disappearing and a more businesslike, employer-employee relationship was developing. It got so corporate, says LaRosa, that when he wanted to see Childress in his office, he had to make an appointment first.

By then, Lou LaRosa was disgusted, not with the win-loss record, but with the way things had changed. Racing had become big business. Side interests, including the souvenir sales and merchandising, were just as important as racing. To a pure racer like LaRosa, who was looking for the same dedication from his crew that he himself was giving, this was not racing the way he remembered it. And the harder he worked his men, the more they resented it.

LaRosa left in 1988, mourning for the good old days, when all the members of the race team, including Richard Childress, would go out to dinner together. He was happy that Dale would go on to win several more championships, but just as glad no longer to be part of it.

LOU LAROSA: "Going back to M. C. Anderson in '81 was a hell of a deal. We were going to run a limited schedule. I was back with my friends Ducky Newman and David Ifft. And we had Cale Yarborough as our driver.

"I liked Cale very much. He didn't party. He was real quiet, real reserved. But when I got to know him, I saw he had a dry sense of humor. He could be really funny.

"We won some races in '81, and some races we ran terrible. We went to Pocono, and man, we ran tenth all day. We couldn't run at all. And with about five laps to go at the end, the caution came out, and Cale came into the pits and got four tires.

"We were fourth, and then third, and then second, and Cale passed Darrell Waltrip, came around one more lap and won the race. So we thought. 'Goddamn, this is great.' We went to victory lane, and NASCAR came over and said, 'Get out of victory lane. You didn't win the race. Darrell did.' I said, 'How did Darrell win this race?' They came up with some hokeypokey that while we were in the pits Darrell came around under the caution and lapped us, so all we did when we came from fourth was unlap ourselves, so instead of finishing first, we were awarded fifth. And that was bullshit, because under the caution it had to take three minutes to go around once. They kicked us right out of there.

"The next race was at Talladega, and we flew with Cale in his plane. Waiting for us was a little four-cylinder Chevette. There were six of us, Cale, David Ifft, myself, all 200-pounders, with the luggage. Cale was driving, and he floored it, and it kind of sat there and chugged along. Cale said, 'Look, Lou.' I said, 'What is it?' Cale said, 'That's your motor at Pocono.'

"Let me tell you how great Cale was. At the Firecracker 400 in July, Cale sat on the pole and won the race. That was one of the great races I was ever part of as Cale and Harry Gant battled for it. That track was just as greasy as it could be in July. Back then, those cars were off the ground, didn't have the spoilers they have today, and as they came by, Cale and Harry looked like they were dirt-tracking it at the end coming off the corner. Cale drafted past Harry with a lap to go and beat him by two car lengths. I said to Cale, 'I can't believe we won it.' Cale said, 'We were going to win it or we were both going to be hanging over the fence post.' That's how great he was, never giving up, driving sideways. He wasn't afraid of anything, wasn't cautious, a great driver in the mode of Pearson and Earnhardt. We won by a whisper, two great drivers side-by-side, dirt-tracking it at Daytona.

"I returned to M. C. in '82, and that year he hired three men, Harold Elliott, Tim Brewer, and Eddie Thrap who had worked for Junior with Cale, had helped win his championships. Harold was an engine builder, and I knew this wasn't going to work because you can't have two engine builders any more than you can have two crew chiefs. Needless to say, there was feuding.

"We started the season with my engine, and we qualified third. The only car running a little faster was Bobby Allison's, and not by much.

But M. C. got it into his pea brain that Harold was going to bring down a better motor. Where was M. C.'s loyalty? There was none. M. C. was like other owners who are bullshitted by the latest tip of the week. In Winston Cup racing you have to have a plan, and you have to stick with it. This is what I learned from Ducky Newman. The first rule of Winston Cup racing: You got to finish races. I go back to when these other people were doing tricks to the engines at DiGard. When you're doing tricks, you trick yourself right out of the race. I'm talking about long races, not qualifying. Usually when you trick up a motor, you trick yourself right out of the race. A motor is a constant that has to run. At DiGard, they tricked their engines up with lightweight pistons, different rods, cut-down parts, stuff that was good for drag racing, good for qualifying, wonderful in fact, but not for five hundred miles. The engine has to run. You never adjust the motor. You can't put a wedge in a motor. You can't change the camshaft or the manifold. You can't put more compression in it or put a different stroke and bore. During the race you are stuck with the basic motor combination. Crew chiefs can change tires ten times in a race or adjust the wedge or change the track bar, and if they hit it, everyone says what a hero they are. So they can bullshit about what they can do. You can't do that with a motor. Either it runs, or it doesn't.

"They rushed Harold's motor down to Daytona, worked on it until the race, put it in the car on Saturday, and right from the git go that motor had an oil leak. The oil blowed every friggin' way, Cale almost lost it, went into the corner, the car got sideways, and Cale was driving blind. He was lucky not to wreck the car.

"We put my motor back in the car, and we ran second in the Daytona 500 to Bobby Allison. And that was the race where Bobby Allison hooked his back bumper, and it was only held on with pop rivets, and it came off, and that car ran better with the bumper off! Anyway, we finished second, and then we got into the feuding heavy, and my old self, I won't kiss your ass for love or money or a job, so we split in the middle of the season. M. C. said if I left he would pay me for the rest of the season, and he didn't keep his word. I had a wife and a one-year-old and no job. And it turned out to be a great break for me, because the next team owner I went and worked for was Richard Childress.

"At the time, the middle of 1982, Richard Childress was a nobody.

He was an independent driver like J. D. McDuffie, Dave Marcis, Jimmy Means, and Wendell Scott, low-buck, back-in-the-field cars. During the seventies he drove Grand American cars—Mustangs and Camaros—at Bowman-Gray Stadium in Winston-Salem.

"For a while Childress had Dale Earnhardt driving for him, but Dale left Childress and went to drive for Bud Moore before I went to work for him. In the middle of '81 Earnhardt was driving for J. D. Stacy, Boss Hogg we called him because he had a cigar like the guy in *The Dukes of Hazzard*, but Stacy told Earnhardt in essence that he didn't care whether Dale stayed or left. Stacy had Joe Ruttman, and he told Dale, 'Drivers are a dime a dozen.' So in July, Earnhardt left Stacy and went to drive for Childress in a deal put together by Junior Johnson, who advised Childress that he'd be better off quitting driving and being an owner.

"Dale took some people from Stacy's shop, went to Childress and stayed the rest of the '81 season. Based on assurances that Dale was going to stay, Childress bought all sorts of equipment.

"Then with no notice Dale upped and quit and went to drive for Bud Moore. Now Childress was sitting there with no driver, no sponsor, no nothing, just a nickel-and-dime organization. Luckily, Richard got Ricky Rudd to drive and Piedmont Airlines as a sponsor, but they had a lot of motor trouble and other trouble.

"When I left M. C. Anderson in the middle of '82, I was helping some people on the side, and I was debating whether to stay in racing or get out, when Ricky told me, 'Richard might need some help up there.' Toward the end of '82 I went to see him. Bill Carter was the engine builder. Ricky had won at Riverside, but their engines blew up in more than half the races. In defense of Bill Carter, you have to remember that Richard didn't have an engine room per se. He didn't have top-quality equipment. He used parts over and over and over again, so Bill had to use crap parts, which wasn't his fault. He didn't have boxes and boxes of pistons and rods and what-have-you that they have now. So Bill more or less was stuck, and some of his help wasn't very good either. Also, he tried stuff more suited to drag racing, put the engine on its edge, and the engine would blow up.

"In '83, Bill's downfall came at Riverside. Childress needed to finish the race to earn about $50,000 in incentive bonuses, when the motor blew up, and it shouldn't have, and they didn't have a viable spare, so at the end of '83 Richard got rid of Bill, and he got rid of Ricky, and he got rid of the Pontiacs. Dale Earnhardt, meanwhile, had become discouraged driving for Bud Moore because they fell out of half the races in '82 and '83, and so in '84 I joined Childress's team as the head engine builder. Again, I was working for a team that had nothing. Childress had *nothing* at the time. Everything came COD. When parts came in, his wife would have to pay with a check. You had to call her to get the parts. RCR wasn't like it is today, with ware-houses full of parts. And this forced us to work late hours, because when a part finally did come in, you had to get to work.

"Dale called and said, 'If I come, are you going to leave?' I didn't have animosity toward him, but when the deal happened at Osterlund at the end of '80, I didn't feel he was loyal to me, so I said, 'Probably.' Dale said, 'Stay,' and I said, 'I'll probably stay.'

"Around the time Dale decided to join Childress, one of the top officials of Chevrolet said to me, 'How well do you think you're going to do?' I said, 'We're going to run for the championship.' He said, 'You aren't gonna win any championships. That's Junior's territory.' Chevrolet thought a lot of Junior Johnson at the time. Junior had won with Cale in '76, '77, and '78, and then in '81 and '82 he won with Darrell Waltrip, the fair-haired boy.

"We started off '84 running well. We won two races and finished fourth in the points, where before with Bud Moore Dale was back in eighth. At the end of the season Dale said to me, 'I'm glad you stayed. You built my confidence back up,' because with Bud he was blowing up, and drivers wonder, Is it me? But it wasn't him. Not at all.

"Richard had a little old shit shop on Gum Tree Road in Winston-Salem, and at the end of '84 he said to me, 'What do you want?' I said, 'I'd really like my own engine room, separate from the chassis depart-ment.' 'Cause the dust from the machine shop would get into our engines. So at the end of '84 he built me a beautiful, self-contained shop for my engines.

"Richard treated people right back then. We were a very close-knit team. While we tested for Daytona in the beginning of '85 we would all go to a restaurant, Dale, Richard, and a bunch of us other guys. One time Richard went to the bathroom. He had left his suit jacket on the back of his chair, and while he was away I took some anchovies—stout-smelling sardines—and put them in the inside pocket of his jacket. It really smelled, and he never could figure out why. The next day when I went to the bathroom at the same restaurant, I left my coat, and while I was away they loaded my pockets with knives, forks, and spoons. When I went to put the coat on, it must have weighed five hundred pounds. They told the owner I was trying to steal the silverware. They fell all over the floor laughing. We were like a small family.

"In '85, Dale won four races, and then my turn came. Everything in a motor that could break did. It wasn't because Richard didn't spend the money on the parts. He did. A cloud hung over us like we were jinxed. Parts you wouldn't dream of broke. Oil pans. Timing chains. But through it all—and this was a plus—you learn from your mistakes, and I learned more about engines and durability that year than I ever had working for someone else. It's a learning curve. I've learned a bunch.

"We ended up the year with things shaky. Dale wasn't happy, and Richard Childress wasn't happy. But there was no politics, no back-stabbing. Richard decided, 'It was a bad year. We'll tough it out and start again next year.'

"It was at the end of '85 that Richard decided to build a new shop he has now in Welcome, five miles away. During the winter we not only worked on the cars for the next year, we also worked on the plans with him for putting up the building.

"Well, come '86 we moved into our new shop, won five races, and won the racing championship. Richard had never won a championship, and everyone was elated. We had a great, great sponsor in Wrangler, a privately owned company run by a wonderful man and his wife. If you blew up or if you crashed, it didn't matter to him. There was a lot of comradeship in '86. The team was tight. And Dale was wonderful. He really matured. He mellowed from being a smart-ass to being a mature person who used his head driving. He had learned from his mistakes of rushing to the front early and crashing, of getting into trouble, to knowing when to lay back. People look at him now and say, 'He isn't the driver he used to be.' But that's maturity. He knows not to take a chance. It's not that he's afraid. He knows that it's foolish to take a chance a hundred miles into the race, to pass on the outside when you don't have to. What's the difference whether you're third or tenth one hundred miles into a race? It doesn't matter. When he was driving for Osterlund, Dale won on aggressiveness. Now he was winning on intelligence, maturity, and thinking.

"Another thing Wrangler did, they took Earnhardt and Childress and sent them to Winston-Salem to learn how to speak, because they figured they were going to have to represent them in public speaking. They didn't want this redneck image. And that really helped Dale.

"Everyone had the impression that Dale didn't like people, wouldn't talk to them. But talking to people wasn't Dale's thing, especially if he didn't know you. If he knew you, he'd hang around. He's become a good spokesman, outgoing, and he'll take the time to sign autographs. That was the example set by Richard Petty. It didn't matter if Richard won, lost or drew, two hours after the race, or twenty hours after the race, Richard would sit there and sign autographs. That's why people liked him. Dale just wouldn't, especially at the beginning, and that's how he got a bad rap that he wasn't friendly.

"In '87 we were at a pinnacle. We won eleven races including Rockingham, Richmond, Darlington, North Wilkesboro, Bristol, Martinsville, Michigan, Pocono, and then three in a row—Bristol, Darlington, and Richmond.

"His most famous win that year was the Winston at Charlotte, the famous pass on the grass where he and Bill Elliott hit. Elliott dived down low trying to pass, and Dale steered left to block him, but they touched, and Dale went skidding across the grass, stayed on the throttle, pulled it around until he got back onto the track—holding the lead. That was a highlight. Sam Bass painted a picture of it. You couldn't have done it any better.

"By the end of '87 we won everything you could have won. I won Engine Builder of the Year, and I should have won it in '86 too, and the only reason I didn't was because Randy Dorton, who I like a bunch, ran the entire Hendrick shop and was allowed to take points from both the Tim Richmond and Geoff Bodine cars. In '87, they changed the rules so that you could only take points from one car, and so I won, and Dale won every award that was given, plus millions of dollars. We won back-to-back championships in '86 and '87. You'd have thought everything was going smoothly. Everything should have been beautiful.

"But in '88 internecine politics became too much for me to take. It started at Daytona. We took two cars, one for the Busch Clash, one for the 500. The 500 car had to be five miles an hour slower than the Busch Clash car. The 500 car would not run a lick. At breakfast in the morning, I could see that the crew chief, Kirk Shelmerdine, and some of his nitwits were starting to suck up to Childress, complaining about the motors. I heard, 'Motor, motor, motor, motor, motor.'

"We took the motor out of the 500 car—the so-called 'slow' motor and put it in the Busch Clash car, and it ran just as fast as anybody. Later we learned the truth: The 500 car had so much down force that where Bill Elliott was running 210 miles an hour, their car had so much drag, it wouldn't run. Here were these lying sons of bitches knowing that that car had all this drag built into it saying that my motor didn't run.

"After that motor won the Busch Clash, they took it out. I said, 'Let's run the Busch Clash car in the 500. They said, 'What if we wreck it?' I said, 'If you wreck it, what's the big deal?' So we ran the car that didn't have all that down force, and it ran fine.

"Another problem I had with Richard was over using the new tire that came in, Hoosiers. Bill Elliott and Rusty Wallace were kicking ass with them tires. We were running in the back. We rented a motor to Bob Whitcomb and Tri-Star, with Ken Bouchard driving. He was running on Hoosiers, and he went by Dale like Dale was standing still. Here we had a chance to win our third championship in a row, and I said to Richard, 'We need to get Hoosier tires.' We were running Goodyears, and they weren't competitive. 'Oh no, we can't do that.' I said, 'Rusty Wallace is running them. Bill Elliott is running them. Other people are too, and they're kicking our ass.' Richard wouldn't switch.

"And about that time Pontiac came out with a Brodix cylinder head, which was a good twenty-five horsepower better than the Chevrolet cylinder head we ran. I said, 'We need to put these Brodix heads on.' Richard said, 'Oh no, we can't do that. If we do, we'll lose our deal with Goodwrench,' which makes the Chevrolet parts. The Chevrolet man told me, 'They ain't gonna be better.' The bottom line was that they weren't going to let me use something that wasn't made by Chevrolet. Instead of Chevrolet getting off its ass and saying, 'We're getting beat. We need to get to work,' they were still saying, 'Our parts are the best.' That's why Chrysler dominated in the seventies. You have to be in the forefront. Chevrolet was fat, dumb, and lazy, had no competition per se, until this other stuff came along. They weren't the best anymore. Brodix *was* better. They were better, and we were getting outrun. So now we were handicapped by tires and with heads.

"I'm a son of a bitch if Junior didn't put them on Terry Labonte's car, and Terry won the Winston at Charlotte. I said, 'Did goddamn Junior lose his deal? We gotta win with whatever we need to win. We're getting our ass kicked.'

"Earnhardt wasn't happy. Nobody was happy. We were getting outrun on tires and cylinder heads. Another team, I won't say who, let me try a pair of the Brodix heads. We had to work to put them on. The bolts were different lengths, and there were other modifications we had to make, but we fitted them, and son of a bitch if that motor didn't run twenty-two horsepower better than my best motor with the Chevrolet cylinder head.

"Around this time Alan Kulwicki called and asked me to go to work for him. Ford people also called and talked to me, and I went over to Alan's house for a meeting. I didn't know Alan well. I talked to him, and he was real distant. He was talking to you, but it was like he was somewhere else. That's why he had that reputation for being cold. He was just always thinking. It was the engineer in him. He was here, but he was there.

"Alan offered me a lot of money, and at the time I could see that Ford was coming on strong. In '85 Bill Elliott had the only Ford that was strong, and that year he dominated. I saw that Alan and Ford had a good relationship. Alan had a bright future, and you could tell he was driven.

"But when I thought about it, it went back to loyalty. Even though the thing with the tires and the cylinder heads pissed me off, I thought, We'll tough it out. 'Cause Childress had stood with me, had toughed it out in '85 when all those motors broke.

"I told Alan, 'No, I think I'll stick with Childress.'

"Toward the end of '88 Childress came in pitching a fit. Now he wanted me to put the Brodix heads on all the cars. I said, 'It ain't that simple.' Everything I had in stock was Chevrolet—pistons, valves, springs, rocker arms. We bolted them on and ran at Martinsville in September, and we had a problem: we didn't have the right clearance, and the spark plugs closed up. And what pissed me off, here I was struggling in the engine room, running behind, and we were supposed to be the defending champions, and we were running like a man on crutches, on one leg.

"We went to Wilkesboro, where we got rained out. I came into the shop on Monday, and there isn't anyone but me and one other guy in the engine room. I used to send one man, Ed Miller, to the race to take care of the motors. But half my people were at the races.

"I came back that night, and Childress said, 'Why are you all pissed off?' I said, 'All my help is at the race.' Richard said, 'This one has to work with the radio. This one has to . . . ' It was lame-brain shit. I sat there thinking, Son of a bitch. I'm breaking my ass. We have to be in Charlotte for a major race. This is too much between the tires, the heads, and the professional suck-asses on the team—the professional leaches who sucked up to Richard. And Richard was forgetting the people in the shop, the same way it was when I was at Osterlund. We're in the shop working while they're in the bars or in their beds sleeping.

"There were nights when I never went home. Bob Gurrell, the cylinder head man, was there with me when we worked forty-eight straight hours cause we had trouble with a motor, had to get another one, for Talladega. We never went home, never changed clothes, worked all night, finished and sent the motor down.

"Things like that people forget. And I wasn't the only one. The good people do it. Buddy Parrott, Harry Hyde and Tim Brewer have worked many, many all-nighters in their careers. Harry Hyde and Buddy Baker would work all night. Junior would work all night. And nobody would give two shits because that's the way it is. You had to get the car to the racetrack. And I get told, 'You're such a hard-ass, too demanding on your people.' Well, you have to be. We were going into a major race.

"And it was then that Ricky Rudd called me up and said they were having big-time engine problems at Bernstein's. They'd lead, and the engine'd blow up. Would I come?

"And again I weighed all the choices. And the clincher was, here we were getting ready for Charlotte, a major race, and nobody was at the shop. I said to myself, This sucks, and this ain't gonna change.

"And something else was bothering me. In the past Richard had always treated me like we were friends. Then after '87, he built his big shop in Welcome, and he hired Bill Patterson, who was just a parts man, to be his office manager. In '88 it had changed from being a big family to a business, and it was bullshit. Now if you tried to see Richard Childress in his office, you were told, 'You can't go in the office. He's busy.' That's bullshit. If I'm the chief engine builder or the crew chief, I should be able to see him any time. But Patterson was Richard's foil. Patterson fronted for Richard, who seemed to be more interested in his cows, his bulls, building his new house. It was always something. He'll deny it, but it was true. It wasn't that Richard didn't care about your problems, it was that he's got cows, a new home, which he deserves, that have his attention. And this nitwit is taking care of Richard's other businesses. Is there anything wrong with that? No. It's Richard's shop. He can do anything he wants with his employees. But little by little, even though Richard was saying racing was important, it wasn't important—important where everyone lives and breathes it.

"And people don't realize it, but though Richard doesn't know jack shit about motors, he is one of the most knowledgeable crew chief/owners in the Junior Johnson mold. He's a man who can take a wreck, mount a body, smart enough to know when a car doesn't run, and intelligent enough to go back and find out what's wrong with it. Richard is the man behind Kirk Shelmerdine, David Smith, and Andy Petree. He's just got caught up with the money shit and the big bullshit of people blowing smoke up his ass, 'How great thou art.'

"If Richard takes his hand off of it, there'll be no RCR racing. It won't matter if he has a hundred people working for him. He's the driving force behind that team. The success of that team is due a hundred percent to Richard—and Dale, of course. If it's suffered, it's because Richard doesn't have his hand enough into the pie. If he puts it back in again, and if Dale recovers from that terrible wreck he had, the team will run good again.

"But back in '88, Richard had his mind on a lot of other things besides racing. We had major problems, tires that weren't running, people who ain't here, and I wanted some action, wanted dedication from the men in the shop, and all Richard was asking me, 'Why are you pumped up, crazy, and hard on your people?' 'Cause we had problems, 'cause our team was going backwards, and we weren't winning. I thought to myself, Can't you see the light? We're running in the back.

"Richard had treated me good for a long time, but now it wasn't a family any longer. It had become a corporation, with all the corporate crap that goes with it. Richard forgot the, 'Let's go out to dinner, gang.' Now he didn't have time to look at the individual.

"So it was time to get out of there. When Ricky called I said to myself, Piss on them. That's it. I ain't gonna deal with it. Leaving wasn't about money. It wasn't about power. I didn't ask Richard for nothing. I was telling him, 'Your team is running like this, things ain't right, and I ain't staying. Period.' And that was that. I asked him to change things, and he wouldn't. I said, 'You need to get rid of certain people.' He said, 'No, no, no, no, no, no.'

"So I left. Was it right, wrong or indifferent? Doesn't matter, because when I left, they didn't do nothing the next year, and then they won three more championships. Doesn't matter. The things were in place with Earnhardt for that place to win. But was it a happy camping ground? When you have a hundred employees, with a lot of turnover, it becomes like what happens to other teams that were great. It gets so big, it blows up. And it was getting to be a *big* corporate thing."

37

MEMORIES OF RICHARD CHILDRESS

DANNY "CHOCOLATE" MYERS AND his wife, Caron Pappas, live in a Victorian house on the corner of Second Avenue and Vance Street in Lexington, North Carolina. The house sits in a sleepy part of town, with large oaks and stately elms all around it.

For Chocolate and Caron, who has worked both in TV and as a magazine writer and editor, their home has become a NASCAR bed-and-breakfast. Inside on the second floor, Myers keeps a shrine to his late father and uncle, Bobby and Billy Myers, and throughout the house are mementos of a career spent with Richard Childress, Dale Earnhardt, and the RCR racing team.

Myers, a mechanic and the gas man for the Richard Childress race team, is one of the most easily recognized crew members in NASCAR. A bulking man with a bushy black beard, he looks like Paul Bunyan in black when he puts on the Goodwrench pit crew uniform. When NASCAR raced in Japan in November of '96, he was mobbed for autographs.

Myers grew up with Richard Childress in Winston-Salem. They sold programs together as boys at Bowman-Gray Stadium. When Childress started running Camaros in the Grand American series in the late 1960s, Chocolate was his crew. Childress continued in racing, advancing to

Winston Cup, but Myers lost interest and dropped out to work as a mechanic for a mobile home dealer in Winston-Salem.

In 1983 his interest was rekindled. Watching a NASCAR race on TV, Myers realized that he knew many of the crew members he saw on TV. Not wanting to be left out, he asked Richard Childress for a job, was hired, and has worked for RCR racing ever since, helping the team to six Winston Cup racing championships in fourteen years.

The credit, says Myers, has to go to Richard Childress.

DANNY "CHOCOLATE" MYERS: "A lot of people don't know that my real name is Danny. The name 'Chocolate' was given to me by this wonderful Little League football coach I had, Henry Ford, a great guy in town. Passed away a few years ago. I always stayed out in the sun in the summertime, and myself and my brother had very dark complexions, and one day I went out for a pass, and the coach hollered, 'Catch the ball, Chocolate Drop,' and it stuck. They've called me 'Chocolate' ever since. Another time the coach said to my brother, 'Hey, Pancho, run,' and he's been Pancho ever since.

"One time my mother went to a PTA meeting. She told the teacher I was in her class. The teacher said, 'What's his name?' My mother said, 'Danny Myers.' The teacher said, 'I'm sorry, the only Myers I have in my class is Chocolate Myers.' So they've called me Chocolate for quite a while. And I kinda like it.

"When I was growing up in Winston-Salem, one of the boys I knew in town was Richard Childress. He's a few years older than I am, and we would sell programs and peanuts and popcorn together in the grandstands of Bowman-Gray Stadium. If you were a kid and wanted to make a buck, they'd strap a big old thing around your neck to hold the programs, and if you sold a program, you got a nickel. And we were not doing it for the fun of it, but for that nickel. We were both from the same side of town.

"I hung around Bowman-Gray Stadium, and around 1969, NASCAR came out with the Grand American series. The factories were introducing Camaros, Mustangs and Barracudas, and they were wanting to get into that market so they started a series for them, and Richard Childress built himself a Camaro. Ernie Shaw, another guy in town, built a Mustang. One day Childress said to me, 'What are you doing?' I said, 'Nothing.' 'You want to go to Daytona?' 'Sure.' So we took that Camaro and welded roll bars on it and put a decent motor in it, went to Daytona and raced that Camaro for fun.

"When we got down to Daytona I ran into Bill France Sr. He and my dad were buddies. I had gone down with fifty bucks in my pocket for two weeks. France walked up to me with a factory guy from Ford. France said to me, 'Danny, this guy here was a real good friend of your dad's.' I shook the man's hand, and he slid something into my hand, and after they walked off, I looked, and it was two hundred dollars. I went over to Richard and I said, 'Childress, we got money! That guy gave us two hundred bucks!'

"Childress qualified good and ran pretty good. Childress had a '52 Ford truck, and it had two ramps welded on the back of it, and we put the Camaro on the truck and went to Richmond, Virginia, to race. We were running pretty good, and then something broke, and we didn't finish that well. After the race we got the race car loaded on the back of the truck ready to go home, but the truck wouldn't run. There we sat with this truck.

"Childress worked for Douglas Battery, and he had to be at work the next day. I stayed in Richmond with the truck and the race car while Childress got a ride home with somebody. He went to work Monday, worked all day long, got off work, borrowed a two-ton Ford flatbed truck, came back to Richmond that night, and we put the smaller truck with the race car on it onto the bigger truck and came home. That was quite a sight. We still talk about it today.

"A few years later my cousin Gary, Uncle Billy's younger son, was running a car over at Bowman-Gray Stadium, and a guy wanted to know if Gary would drive his Winston Cup car. Gary said to Richard Childress and me, 'It's ready to go. Let's do it.' We said, 'Yeah.' We went to Darlington, but we didn't make the race. So Childress came up with the idea of going to Michigan. He said, 'I'll tell you what let's do. Let's leave a day ahead of time. That way we can get up there early, and we'll get a good spot in the garage,' because at the time they parked you in the order you got there, not by the points standing. So we all left and went to Michigan, got there about two in the morning, and nobody was there. We said, 'We beat everybody.' Daylight came, and we went to check in, and the guy said, 'Where were you guys yesterday?' Instead of being a day early, we were a day late! We ended up parked out on the dirt.

"We made the race at Michigan, and we could only race the car another race or two when the guy wanted his car back.

"And then I got out of it. I lost interest. I was working at a place that sold motor homes as a general mechanic. Then one day in 1983 I was watching TV one afternoon, and a Winston Cup race was on. One of the cars made a pit stop, and I looked at the crew members, and I said, 'I know him. And I know him. And him. And him.' And right at that moment, I said to myself, 'I'm fooling myself. This is what I want to do.'

"The next day I went to talk to a few people about a job. I talked to Childress, but he didn't have anything. He said, 'Check with me later.' About two weeks later, I went back and checked with him, and it just so happened on that day he had bought a bunch of machinery, and he needed someone to clean it up, and I started helping him.

"I've been with him ever since. A couple years after he hired me, he told me, 'I made up my mind I would never ever hire another friend or relative, because every time I did that they thought I owed them something.' He said, 'You're the only guy I ever hired who was a friend of mine who came in here and worked instead of thinking I owed him something.' And it made me feel good.

"It wasn't that long ago when I joined him, but things were so much different. Richard was just getting on his feet. We didn't have anything to work with. If you counted everyone in the shop, we might have had twelve people. When we went to the racetrack, there were a couple people left working in the engine room, but nobody left to work on the cars. You would go to the track, come back Sunday night or Monday morning, and you'd start working on the cars again, and you worked however long it took to be ready to go again. Today you have a shop crew, a weekend crew, and a road crew. Wasn't like that then.

"In '84 Dale came back to Richard with Wrangler as his sponsor. Dale had had Wrangler when he first joined Richard, but then he left to go to Bud Moore's, and when he came back, he still had Wrangler. The Wrangler deal was pretty much Dale's deal. And we went from there.

"We've been fortunate that we have Dale Earnhardt. In a hundred years from now they're going to look back and say he's the greatest driver that's ever been. I thought that before I ever personally spoke to the man. He was tough when he started out. And it's because of his roots. Dale has told us so many stories.

"I can remember being at Bristol testing. We were up there by ourselves, nobody else, just us. Earnhardt ran a few laps, shut it off, and came in. He said, 'The crankshaft is broken.' 'Say what?' 'The crankshaft is broken. I felt it.' I said, 'You felt the crankshaft break?' That seemed impossible. He said, 'Yeah, I felt it. I don't think it hurt anything, but it broke so I shut it off.'

"We raised the hood up, looked at the car, and everything seemed good. 'Dale, turn it over.' He said, 'Don't do that, because I'm pretty sure the crankshaft is broke.'

"We took a screwdriver, stuck it down the front of the engine and pried on the balancer, and the crankshaft sure enough was broke. I said, 'How can you tell that?' And I never will forget Dale said, 'When I was starting to drive, my dad would sometimes make me drive barefoot so I could feel it.'

"One time Dale was running 200 miles an hour at Talladega, and he'd pass someone and say on the radio, 'So-and-so is blowing up. They're about to blow a piston. I smelled it when I went by.' And sure enough, a couple laps later it would be gone. The car would blow up. He's that good. Because of his roots.

"[His father] Ralph never did drive in many Grand National races. He ran at Charlotte a few times, and when he did, he was great at it. And that comes from experience. He raced all the time, and he taught Dale, and he taught him well, but to be able to be taught, you have to want to learn. The two go hand-in-hand.

"Since Dale returned to our team, Richard Childress Racing has won six championships in fourteen years, and that's pretty dadgum remarkable. Not to take anything away from any of the other teams— Junior Johnson was a legend. He had a great team, I'm not saying he didn't, but there's nobody as successful in the history of racing as this team. For this team to have do what it has in the time that it's done it, it's pretty incredible.

"The credit has to go to Childress. Richard is not a man with a college education, and neither is Dale, but they've sacrificed and bared down and not backed up and said they were going to do something and done it, by thinking and planning ahead and doing what's expected of you. The place opens at seven o'clock. You don't come in at ten past. You come at seven. That's just the way it is. The people who aren't successful are the ones who come in when they want. We've put the place first, and it's been successful.

"Childress has always said, 'There is no such thing as good luck or bad luck. You make your luck.' If you're running fifteenth and a wreck happens in front of you, you've made your luck because you should not have been back there. We've been successful, and Richard gets the credit.

"I know the place would have been just as successful without me, but I've been part of it, and it makes me feel great. You say, 'Anyone can be replaced,' but it wouldn't have been just as successful without Richard or Dale. That combination just works well together. They mesh.

"Richard Childress deserves everything he's got. 'Cause he's worked hard for it. I've told people, 'I'm proud of him.' A guy like that has done it on his own. Of course, it helps to have Dale driving. And Dale has done it on his own.

"I love this sport to death, but as I got older, it was beginning to take a toll on my family. I found I had to get off the road. You've heard about the good old days of racing where you eat, sleep and breathe it. That's what you still have to do. We were racing thirty-two weekends a year. We were testing all we wanted to test. We were doing Goodyear tire tests. We were going to the wind tunnel. And most of the tracks opened on Thursday, so you'd be gone Thursday, Friday, Saturday, and Sunday. We go to Talladega on Tuesday. And you were gone. You were gone, gone, gone all the time. It's easy to get your belly full of it. The driver can take his family with him to the track, and so can the car owner. He has that option. But for you to do it, it costs you more than you make. You have to get them there, have a car, get your own room, and while you're there you're working on the car and can't do the family thing anyway. There comes a time in your life when you say, 'Hey, my life is gone. I've lost my family.' And if you want your family, you have to do something. So I went to Richard and said, 'Look man, I want to quit doing this.' He didn't like it. He wanted me to stay and work on the car at the racetrack.

"I took a couple weeks off and just worked on Sundays at the race. I'm the gas man on the pit crew. Then I went back to working seven days a week, and it was hard for me. He finally got someone to replace me, so finally I've gotten off the road. It was a blessing for me to do this.

"Racing is growing so fast, and I'm getting older, and I'm afraid I'm not going to be around for the really great part of this sport. I've got a job. It's a decent living. We're not getting rich. Some of the crew chiefs are making a ton of money, but the guys who are working on the cars aren't getting rich. They're making a living. It's a good living, but there is an awful lot of money out there. I'm not complaining. This weekend a guy put it to me in a way that made me understand a lot that I never thought about before. He said, 'The money in racing is incredible today.' I said, 'Yeah, but it's not trickling down a lot. A lot of people are making a lot of money, and a lot of people aren't.' He said, 'Let me tell you, I grew up in rural Alabama. We had one man in the county who was so filthy rich it was unbelievable. But you know, if it wasn't for that one rich man giving us jobs, we'd have starved to death.' It could be a lot better, but it could be a lot worse too."

38

THE DEATH OF
HARRY HYDE

SOON AFTER THE DEATH OF TIM
Richmond, Harry Hyde and Tommy Johnson left Hendrick Motorsports and went to work for the Stavola Brothers. Driver Rick Wilson ran hard, but crashed a lot. Johnson retired in June of 1991. Harry spent a year and part of a second with driver Chad Little at Harry Melling's shop, and at the end of the 1992 season Harry Hyde retired, bitter that the newer owners and crew chiefs no longer would listen to his suggestions but instead preferred the advice of their computers and high-tech gizmos and gadgets.

Retirement was hard on Harry Hyde, though for the most part he enjoyed watching Robert Duvall play him in the movie *Days of Thunder*. Harry Hyde died in 1996, at the age of seventy-one. Tommy Johnson misses his uncle dearly. But thanks to Tommy, we will always have his memories of Uncle Harry.

TOMMY JOHNSON: "After Tim Richmond died, Benny Parsons replaced him for the rest of '87, and in '88 we had Ken Schrader. Ken won Talladega, and we had some other good finishes, won poles, and then when we went to work for the Stavola Brothers, we had Bobby Hillin. We didn't win any races, but we had some good runs, and then we had some good runs with Rick Wilson. Rick drove really, really hard, to the limit, but if you don't run up front, your chances of having a wreck are really good, I don't care who you are. One little mistake and a whole bunch of cars get taken out. And that happened to Rick a lot.

"In June of '91 I quit, and Harry went on to Melling, with Chad Little. Harry was more or less helping, not really running the team. He was working toward retirement.

"The Robert Duvall character in *Days of Thunder* was modeled after Harry, and he got a kick out of that, but it upset him that there were a lot of things not exactly so, like when Tom Cruise was working out of a barn loft, and no, Harry and Tim Richmond never cussed each other the way Duvall and Tom Cruise did. But they did have a lot of funny things in it that did happen with Harry, like when Duvall told his driver, 'Go up there and hit the pace car because that's the only thing you ain't hit.' That's what Harry told Buddy Baker at Martinsville. In a hundred laps at Martinsville, Buddy had wore both sides off the car, 'cause he burned the tires off. Buddy was a good driver, but not patient enough. He wanted to drive a short track like he did a speedway, wide open, bury you, but you had to take care of the tires and be gentle with them. Buddy was a ball of fire for twenty-five laps until he'd burn the tires off, and then everyone would go by him, and he went from first to last. He was riding on a caution after a pit stop, and Harry told him, 'Buddy, I want you to pull into that left lane, and I want you to pass everybody on through there on this caution and knock the hell out of the pace car.' Buddy said, 'What for, Harry?' He said, 'That's the only damn thing you ain't hit on that racetrack, and I want you to get it!'

"And in the movie, Duvall told his driver, 'No, don't pit. We're all eating ice cream.' That's what Harry told Benny Parsons at Darlington. We were running really good, in the top five, and there was a wreck and Benny got tied up in it, and we came in and put in all new steering components, pulled the sheet metal away, put on four new tires, and he went out there and hadn't run ten laps, and we were forty laps down when the caution came out.

"Benny said, 'Well, Harry, do you want me to come in and pit?' Harry said, 'Hell no, the ice cream wagon came by, and we all are eating ice cream. Don't come in. You have new tires and a tank of gas, and you're running on three-quarters throttle.' Benny said, 'Okay.' He came down the front straightaway and waved. Benny said, 'Well, can

I get some ice cream the next time I pit? I'm pretty hot myself.' Harry said, 'Yeah, we'll have you one ready.'

"A lot of funny things happened. We were at Atlanta with Tighe Scott, and Tighe was really running good that day, running third or fourth behind Richard Petty, been following him for 250 miles, and we were about 25 miles from the end of the race, and it looked like we were going to get a top-five finish. Atlanta is the one track where the crew is able to see the cars. We could see everywhere except where the cars came by the scoring stand, one little blank place in the number four turn.

"Coming into three, here came Tighe sailing right behind Richard, and Tighe went head-on into the wall. We thought he blew a tire. The wrecker picked up the car, brought it in, and Tighe got out of the car. Harry said, 'Tighe, what in the world happened? You blow a tire?' Tighe said, 'No, I was so busy racing I forgot to turn left!' Harry said, 'Tighe, I believe I would have lied to me about that.' Tighe said, 'Well, you asked me what happened.' Harry said, 'Damn, Tighe.' Tighe said, 'Didn't nothing happen to the car. That's the only thing I can think of.'

"Harry and Tim would kid. Tim Richmond never talked about racing during the race. Harry would kid Tim about his girlfriends. 'When are you and Julie going to get married? Have you proposed yet?' And Tim would be right in the middle of a corner, leading the race, and he'd say, 'Now Harry, next race we go to, we need to try so-and-so like we did on this car.' They'd be discussing the next race during the present one.

"Most of their talk didn't pertain to the race, except when it was time for Tim to pit. 'Tim, we're going to pit this next lap.' 'Okay, I'm bringing her in,' and Tim would tell Harry where he was at. 'I'm in turn three, turn four, I'm coming onto pit road.' 'Cause a lot of times the pit crew can't see, and Harry would stand on the pit wall and say, 'You're coming down pit road. Move over to the left but don't get in the pit stalls. Do you see me? Come at me. Come on. Come on. Pull in.'

"And after Tim pulled in, during the pit stop Harry would see everything that was going on, and he'd say, 'Get ready, Tim. When I say, 'Go,' you go. And when Harry gave the word, Tim would go.

"Among the crew chiefs, the most famous were Harry and Junior Johnson. Junior was an owner-chief, and the minute he stepped away from his team, it went down. There are people who know how to run a team and people who know how to run a race car. One makes the cars, the other runs the race. And today those people are kept separate. You don't see much of that in one person today.

"In the end, Harry retired for the same reason I did. Harry was working in an advisory capacity more than anything for Melling. Harry had every race he went to recorded on 3-by-5 cards and on notebook pages going back to the forties. Every lap was recorded and timed, and he wrote what happened to the car, how it qualified, how it finished and who drove it, with a note at the bottom on what was wrong with it and what should be changed. And he had a book for each racetrack. When it got time for a race, he'd pull all the cards out and go back four or five races and study them. He knew the history of these tracks, and what the cars should run as far as motors, gears, suspensions, and he would sit down with the crew chief and driver and say, 'Okay, here's what we got. This worked good for this driver. This driver didn't like it.' Harry could relate one driver to another, the kind of setups they liked, and how they drove the car.

"But with your younger crew chiefs coming along, everything that comes now is technical. Harry never did refuse that. He went along with it. He could separate the bad from the good after it had been used. He had nothing against technology, was absolutely for it, and he'd say, 'Here's what we need to try to do for a base,' especially if he had a new driver. 'Let's start off with this, and then we can change it.' For years Harry worked off percentages and figures. That's the reason he was successful. It was not a hunt-and-peck system. But the younger crew chiefs and even the younger drivers didn't want to go along with that. Over the period of the last three or four years Harry was in racing, he would say, 'I'm butting my head against a wall and being ignored.' And finally he said, 'I've started and set up enough teams that I'm not going to do another one, so I'm quitting. I have butted my head against the wall since 1990. I'm not going to build any more race teams for anybody and train any more people. I'm too old.' He said, 'I'm just not going to do it any more. I quit.' And he said, 'Tommy, you're going to have to help me, because you've been through it.' I said, 'Harry, it was a little easier for me than it was for you because my whole life has not been devoted totally to racing like yours has. I've had other things to fool around with, my house, my family, going up to the lake, fooling with street rods.' I said, 'But you, your outlet of work and relaxation was racing. I'm not going to tell you it's going to be easy.' And he dreaded the thought a full two months before he retired. Constantly he would ask, 'What am I going to do?'

"He liked to fish a little bit, and he bought himself a boat. He put the boat in Swanee in Florida. He had a good friend by the name of Buddy Ward, and he and Buddy toughed it out. Buddy had been a short track driver, and they had remained closest of friends, and two or three days a month, usually on weekends, Harry would go fishing. My wife, Sherry, and I sometimes would go with him, but I could see missing racing so bad was wearying him.

"His wife was very sick, and Harry was afraid he wouldn't have enough money to take care of her. She needed round-the-clock care and had large doctor bills. And around that time, he thought he too was feeling sick—he had a constant hurt in his stomach—and he went into the hospital for three days and had a total, complete physical, MRIs and everything. And they couldn't find anything wrong with him, with the exception that he was having a hard time dealing with his retirement.

"But from the day he retired, Harry never went to another race. Everybody we had ever worked for called him and asked him to fly with them and see a race. Harry would thank them and say, 'I'll think about it,' but he never would go to another race. He watched them on television. If it wasn't a good race, he'd turn it off and go to sleep. But he had a hard time separating, because he had devoted himself to racing since 1946.

"After the physical the doctors told him he was as healthy in all respects as a forty-year-old man. They gave him some medication for his nerves, and that worked, relieved the pain, and it went away. He got to feeling better, and he was running back and forth between Charlotte, where he was looking after his wife, and Louisville, Kentucky, where he owned some property.

"About four weeks later, Harry called up a friend of ours who worked for Harry on some race teams by the name of Kenneth Claybourne. Kenneth is a good carpenter along with being a good fabricator and body man, and Harry, who didn't trust many people, called him and said, 'I'm fixing to take off, to go fishing, and I'm going to do some traveling. I want you to do some repairs to my home. Come over here and live in it.'

"Harry lived right next door to me, and on a Monday morning I walked over to his house about eight o'clock. Harry and Kenneth were standing by his house, and Harry was hitting his chest. He said, 'My chest is hurting, Tommy.' There have been a lot of heart problems in my family and Harry's family. I think Harry knew he was having a heart attack. But he didn't want to admit it. From experience with my father and uncles and a few friends and watching TV, I started asking him some questions, and it took me about thirty minutes to talk him into going to the hospital. I took him to University Place right down the road. And he was having a heart attack.

"At University Place, he got on a helicopter to go to the Carolina Medical Center where they have a top cardiac ward and all the specialists. The last thing he said to me was, 'I'll see you downtown.' Well, we never got to see him alive anymore.

"We got there about a quarter to nine, and somewhere around 12:15 Harry passed away. Harry had had a heart attack, but the doctors think a blood clot is what actually killed him.

"Harry had lived his life and enjoyed what he did the way he wanted to do it. He was successful in what he did, and that's the end of a life story of seventy-one years. And we all miss him."

39

THE DEATH OF
ALAN KULWICKI

PAUL ANDREWS BECAME A WINSTON Cup crew chief as a result of a chance conversation. After moving to St. Louis as a youngster, Andrews in 1977 got a job fixing vacuum cleaners for a man whose son, Rusty Wallace, had a passion for stock car racing. After work, Andrews helped Wallace with his car, and for seven years raced throughout America's heartland running mostly on the Midwest USAC circuit. In 1984 Wallace moved to North Carolina and Winston Cup racing, and Andrews moved to Louisiana to run Rusty's Sportsman equipment for driver Nicki Fraisson.

In 1986 Andrews quit the race game altogether. He had a wife and two infant sons, and he moved to Tulsa, Oklahoma, to live with his mother, with whom he had fought his whole life, to sell real estate and build race cars at night.

At the Winston Cup banquet after the 1986 season, Rusty Wallace was sitting at a table next to Alan Kulwicki, an independent car owner who asked Rusty for some advice on who he might suggest for a new crew chief. Rusty suggested Paul Andrews.

Around that time Andrews and his mother had another blowup, and Andrews was ready to return to racing. For the next five years he would experience the intensity, quirkiness, and perfectionism of owner-driver Alan Kulwicki, who started with little more than a dream but who with Andrews's guiding hand implausibly, wonderfully, won the 1992 Winston Cup driving championship.

Paul Andrews and Alan Kulwicki were on top of the world. They were enjoying the perks of being the defending champs—the media attention and the showering of affection by the fans. Just a couple years before, Alan Kulwicki had been laughed at by the racing world for turning down car owner Junior Johnson's offer of a million dollars to drive for him. With his championship in 1992, Kulwicki proved his mettle and earned the respect of the entire NASCAR family.

The following year began with a string of top ten finishes, though no wins, but neither Kulwicki, Andrews, nor his race team were concerned. They were in the thick of the race for the points, and everyone was optimistic.

But on April 1, 1993, en route from Knoxville, where Kulwicki was making an appearance, to the small airport near the Bristol racetrack, the Hooters corporate jet crashed, killing Kulwicki, the pilot, and two Hooters executives. For Paul Andrews, Kulwicki's crew chief, it was a nightmare.

Hooters made things harder for Andrews and the crew when the company abandoned the team, angered that Kulwicki's father wouldn't hire driver Loy Allen Jr. and also sell the race team to Allen's father. The team was sold to Geoff Bodine. To this day Andrews misses one of the finest and fiercest competitors NASCAR has ever seen.

After Alan died, a friend gave Andrews a bronze plaque in Alan's memory. On it was a quote from Alan: "Obstacles are what you see when you take your eyes off the goal." Before Andrews left the Bodine team, the plaque used to sit in a prominent place in his office, which once had been Kulwicki's office. When I mentioned the plaque to Andrews, Paul said, "He would say that occasionally." You could feel the pain and the loss in his voice.

PAUL ANDREWS: "I was born in Bangor, Maine, on May 25, 1957. My parents divorced, and when I was twelve months old I moved to Pineville, Louisiana, to live with my mother's parents, who raised me. My mother had other things to do, apparently. She left me with my grandparents, and they raised me my whole childhood. When I was ten, we moved to Monroe, which is in northern Louisiana, and my grandfather began working for his son who owned restaurants. I went to work with him and did that for a long time.

"When I finished high school in Monroe, I figured it was time to make a change. There wasn't anything for me in Monroe. The plan was for me to live with my mother in Knoxville, and after a few months move with her to St. Louis. Which I did, but she and I did not get along very well.

"I was young and set in my ways and thought I knew everything, like every child does. I was not the easiest guy to get along with. We didn't hit it off too well. We ended up splitting up our relationship in St. Louis. I was working for my stepfather at the time. He managed a motel and I worked in its maintenance department.

"We had a vacuum cleaner that needed to be repaired, and I went to O.K. Vacuum, which happened to be owned by two brothers, Gary and Russell Wallace. Russell is the father of Rusty Wallace. Generally all the motel did was send the vacuum out for repairs but I went there just wanting parts, not wanting it repaired, because I knew it was pretty simple, that I could do it.

"I got to talking with Gary, Rusty's uncle, about vacuum cleaners and different subjects, and before I walked out the door he offered me a job working in the repair shop of his store.

"I worked there for about a year and helped them move into their new, bigger facility. Rusty was there, and we worked pretty close together during the move. We got to know each other pretty good. He had been racing all his life really, in motorcycles and stock cars, which he raced as a hobby in the St. Louis area. He had a small race car business that he ran at night where he built chassis and race cars for other people, just doing anything to make a couple of bucks so he could go racing.

"I really knew nothing about a race car, but I got to know him, and I went with him and started helping out. Turned out I had a pretty good talent and was able to pick up things quickly and do them pretty easily once I figured them out.

"So for a year I worked for O.K. Vacuum during the day, and at night worked with Rusty, until Rusty saw he had enough business on the side to make a living, so he quit O.K. Vacuum and went to work full-time for himself. I and a couple of good friends would come over and pitch in and try to make things work so he could go racing on the weekends.

"The first racetrack I went to with Rusty was in Pensacola, Florida, the Snowball Derby, in December of 1977. That was a big race for us, the biggest race of the winter. We wrecked. At the start we also raced in Springfield, Missouri, a couple hundred miles from St. Louis, and in Fort Smith, Arkansas.

"I ended up going to work for Rusty full-time. I was his first full-time employee. It was between me and Jeff Townsend, another boy doing the same thing I was doing, also working at O.K. Vacuum, but he wasn't ready to make that move. I felt I had nothing to lose going to work for a guy building race cars. People would say to me, 'What are you going to do when you get old? How long are you going to mess around with these race cars? When are you going to get serious about life and go to work? Now I got people beating on my door begging me to hire them so they can get into this business.

"Rusty and I had a lot of success during the ten years we ran together on the short track circuit. We went all over the place, as far south as Miami, north to Canada, west to California where we raced at the Ontario Speedway. We ran the USAC circuit, won Rookie of the Year, and the same year almost won the points championship. A. J. Foyt beat us out by a little bit.

"USAC, though, was going by the wayside. It was getting harder for them to draw cars. Winston Cup was getting larger, and some of the bigger USAC teams were going there. A. J. ran in both USAC and NASCAR, and so did Rahmoc. The fewer cars that enter, the more it drives the cost up, and it became harder for the lower-budget guys to make the race, and the quality of the cars went down, so USAC kind of fizzled out. We went from there to ASA, lighter-weight stock cars with smaller engines, and we won the championship in that division, and after that Rusty was offered a ride by Cliff Stewart to drive his car in Winston Cup.

"Rusty was a little edgy about making this move to North Carolina and driving this guy's car, and he didn't want to drop all his ties to his short track operation. You couldn't blame him. We knew a guy named Nicki Fraisson out of Gonzalez, Louisiana, who wanted us to move our short track operation to his shop and run a limited schedule, so that's what we did. I moved all of Rusty's equipment down to Gonzalez, which is dead in the middle of Cajun country, in between Baton Rouge and New Orleans. Rusty and Nicki pooled their resources, and we ran a team for two years on a limited schedule, and it was real successful. We ran a lot of Southern races on the All-Pro circuit and also went to Milwaukee a couple of times and ran up there.

"I got tired of the racing deal. I had a wife and a one-year-old son when I moved to Louisiana in '84, and I had another son while I was there, and I guess I got worried about what I was going to do for the rest of my life. Right after the Snowball Derby in '86, I moved to Tulsa with my mother and give her another try, and I went into the real estate business.

"I needed to make money right away, and when I moved to Tulsa I met a guy named Raymond Patterson, a tire dealer who built race cars. I told him I just wanted to work at night, which was good for him. I helped him out, and he helped me out. I was able to get money in my pocket, which was what I needed. I did that for two years.

"Rusty, meanwhile, was in good shape running NASCAR. He had moved on to Blue Max. He called me up a couple of times but I told him I was done racing. I had a setback when I slipped on the ice, broke my leg and was laid up on my back for a few months. That was around the time I got a call from Alan Kulwicki.

"Alan and Rusty had been sitting together at the Winston Cup banquet in 1987, or at least that's what they told me. Alan was telling Rusty all the problems he was having with his race team, and Rusty said, 'I know the guy who can help you out.' He was talking about me.

"Alan called me on the phone and wanted to know if I wanted to move to North Carolina and be his crew chief. I said, 'That's a pretty big move for us, a big decision.' He offered me as much money as I was making in Tulsa, with the potential for a lot more.

"It had been a rough two years in Tulsa, though at the time he called I was back on my feet and things were looking up. But I had had another big run-in with my mother, and my wife and I felt like it was time for us to go back to something we knew well, which was race cars, so that's what we did.

"Alan flew me into Charlotte for an interview, and we talked and spent time. I stayed at his house and went out with him at night, just had a long weekend together. I knew what Alan was about, because I had called Rusty and we talked about him. You always hear the bad stuff about somebody when you hear the rumors. There was even talk on the ASA circuit about how Alan was demanding and hard to work for—some people said impossible to work for—but when I went to talk to him, I didn't have that in mind. I talked to Alan Kulwicki, just Alan Kulwicki, not Alan Kulwicki the tyrant. I kept an open mind about it, and he even brought some of that stuff up. And I thought Alan was a good guy. But I found out that if you told Alan you could do something, you'd better be able to do it. That's the problem with a lot of people, especially ones trying to get into this business. They'll tell you anything in the world just to get hired. If you told Alan you could do it, and you got there and he saw you working and he could tell you couldn't or hadn't done it, or if you tried to con him or tell him lies, that's when you had trouble with Alan. If you were truthful with Alan, you didn't have any major problems.

"We moved our family to Charlotte on January 1, 1988. We came down in a Ryder truck, pulling a minivan behind the truck, me, my wife and my two boys. Alan had signed Zerex as a sponsor, the biggest contract he ever signed. Alan was really excited about the upcoming year. He had a big tractor-trailer, which was something he hadn't had, and at the time there weren't that many of them around, not bad for a small operation.

"We worked in a little shop that we rented. We rented motors from Prototype Engineering in Chicago. We only had two cars from the year before, and when I arrived, he also had two brand-new cars for a total of four. We had five or six employees, and he had a lot of volunteer help. A lot of people were just wanting to help on the weekends. Others would come down and volunteer a little bit at nights. They'd come down and clean up a little bit, and you'd take them to the racetrack on the weekends, and they'd love that. A lot of teams won't hire volunteers, because you can't control them. But we did what we had to do to make things work.

"Alan was really nice to me. I guess he was being careful. He'd say, 'Why are you doing it like this?' I'd explain the reason why, and once he heard the explanation, he'd say, 'Oh, that makes sense.' You weren't going about it the way he would have, but he saw the end result was going to be the same. And once he gained trust in you, the questioning went away.

"There were people he didn't trust, and no matter what it was, he'd let them know about it. If you'd do something wrong, he'd scream at you. Especially if you did something wrong and you knew better. Even then, this business can't tolerate that kind of stuff. You can't let it happen but once because a mistake can put a race in jeopardy. For instance, people have left lug nuts loose on pit stops. After a pit stop, Alan would feel a small vibration, and I'd ask the three tire changers who put on the wheels, 'Did everybody get the lug nuts tight?' And everyone would say, 'Yes.' After a few minutes Alan could feel the vibration getting worse and he would say, 'Are you sure?'

"And then we would know. Alan would have to come in on the green and by then you'd have to change the tire, because it hollows out the wheel so bad if you don't change it, it will break. And if you don't know which tire it is, you have to change all four, so it's a disaster. So people have to be aware of what they are doing and how they are doing it. That's why the part-time people don't work out very well.

"The better quality of people who Alan got, the less people he started losing. When you let anybody in to work for you, you don't get anything. They're going to go out the door as soon as they get there. In our old shop there was one guy Alan hired, let him come in and work for us. Alan told him what he was going to do and how he was going to do it. We were all working hard. There wasn't any slacking off. We hired him in the morning, and he went to lunch, and he never came back! About a year later, a guy calls and says, 'You probably don't remember me, but I worked for you about three hours.' I said, 'I remember you. We still talk about you.' He said he was afraid it was too much work and he couldn't handle it, so he left.

"We had a pretty good year in 1988. We had some poles, had some good runs, and also had bad runs, motor failures, crashes, which is pretty normal in a season. We went to Phoenix, the next-to-last race of the season. It wasn't a brand-new car, but it was a real good one, one of the cars we had been running throughout the year. Things fell our way, the pit stops were good, and we ended up winning the race. Terry Labonte was second in one of Junior Johnson's cars. Winning that first race was one of my most memorable moments.

"For some time Alan, myself and Tom Roberts, our PR man, had been talking about what we were going to do when we finally won a race. Alan came up with the idea of his famous 'Polish victory lap,' which he drove around the track clockwise rather than counterclockwise as is the custom. He said, 'This is what I want to do. What do you think NASCAR's reaction will be?'

"I said, 'I don't think they'll like it much, but the race is over. What are they going to do? If they fine you, you'll have a little money from winning the race.'

"So we got the checkered flag, and Alan said, 'Should I do it?' Tom Roberts had already come over to the pits. He was listening to us talk on the scanner. He said to me, 'Tell him to go for it. Tell him to do it.' So he turned around, and he did the famous Polish victory lap.

"We were afraid of what Dick Beaty, the director who ruled with a firm hand, was going to say, but everyone was so happy to see us win that he just said, 'We didn't really care for that, so please don't do it again.' But when Alan did his Polish victory lap, the fans went crazy. Nobody had ever done anything like that before. A few days later Alan said, 'I'm not going to ever do that again until I win the championship.'

"In private, Alan was really appreciative of the people who had stuck with him, stuck by him, the ones who had faith in him.

"In 1989 we didn't win any races, but we had a real good year. Alan had big plans. We built a new building, and we moved in early in '90, and right after that Zerex decided to back out as our sponsor. They got bought out by a major corporation, and they really didn't want to be in racing.

"We went through the whole winter without a sponsor. Luckily we had a good amount of cars and we had a real good group of guys, so everyone knew we were going to do good in '90, even if we didn't have a sponsor. And it was at this point that Junior Johnson offered Alan a million dollars to drive for him. Alan was counting on Maxwell House sponsoring us, but then Junior decided to form a second team, and Junior ended up getting the sponsor, but Alan didn't accept the ride.

"Alan didn't talk about Junior's offer at first, because he didn't want to scare any of us away if he didn't take it. When he finally told us about it, he said it might be a pretty good deal, that Junior had offered him anything he wanted, control of what was being done to the cars, whatever Alan wanted to make the cars work, that as long as it worked, Alan could keep doing it. And of course, lots of money too.

"But Alan thought it would be better here. He didn't feel that going to Junior would be a long-term situation for him, and he was building something that he felt was going to lead to a championship. Alan had been building it two years before I arrived, and for him to walk away from it meant he was destroying everything he had built. Alan had a vision. He knew he could win his way so I wasn't surprised when he turned down Junior because I knew Alan pretty good and knew where he was coming from and knew what his thoughts were. The people who knew Alan knew he wanted to do it his own way. Alan was focused. He wouldn't get off the beaten path. He was going to stay on that path, and that path was to win races and ultimately win the championship.

"We watched our spending throughout the winter. We moved our motorshop near Charlotte, renting a building from Stavola Brothers five miles down the road. So Alan was putting out a lot of expenses. We didn't buy any new cars, but we had a good amount of cars. We redid everything necessary, made everything fresh, didn't cut any corners in that area, spent what we needed to but didn't spend extra money. We didn't have a lot of employees, but the ones we had were real good. When we lost our sponsor, we didn't lose anybody, and that's saying a lot for the people we had, and that's saying a lot for Alan.

"Everyone worked hard. There was no time to slack off. And you not only had to work hard working for Alan, you had to work efficiently. Alan was very efficient with his money and with everything else he did in life. He was a *very* efficient person, which is why he got as far as he did with what he had.

"He was also very focused. Before qualifying he'd go into his street car in the infield and listen to rock 'n' roll music—I can't remember the band, but he listened to this one album, played it really loud, and he'd be totally focused on that and he'd get out and walk straight to the race car, get into it and go and qualify, and he'd usually qualify pretty good. He sat on a lot of poles.

"Another thing, Alan was kind of quirky with autographs. If you came up to him right in the middle of practice and asked for an autograph, he'd be short with you. 'I'm working right now. Leave me alone. Come back later.' Not because he was rude, but because he was concentrating on what he needed to do, what he needed to do to make the car run faster.

"Alan was also a very particular person. He was particular as far as the type of woman he wanted to date. They were all beautiful. But Alan wanted the perfect woman. She had to be the right height, small.

Couldn't be taller than he was. She definitely couldn't smoke. After he dated one a couple of times, it looked like they were getting along fine, and you'd ask him, 'What happened to her?' 'I didn't feel that it was going to work out, so I told her we weren't going to go out anymore.' He was so particular.

"We started out the '90 season unsponsored. We were scheduled to run in the Busch Clash and the Daytona 500, and R. J. Reynolds wanted to pay tribute to the military in the Gulf War, and they assigned five cars one branch of the service. They asked us to represent the army, and the car was all camouflaged up. It was a pretty neat deal though only for the one race.

"We finished eighth at Daytona, and with AK on the car finished fifth at Richmond, not so good at Rockingham, and then we went to Atlanta and sat on the pole. Hooters restaurants, meanwhile, had sponsored another car that didn't make the race. Here we were sitting on the pole without a sponsor, something that didn't happen very often, and that turned everyone's head. That's when Hooters approached Alan to be his sponsor for the Atlanta race, and Alan didn't want to do it. I don't think it was a secret. It wasn't an image Alan wanted to have, not even for one race, but on Sunday morning they finally talked him into it, probably by throwing money at him. 'Cause that was a weak point for him. He had run three races pretty much out of his pocket, so he couldn't go much further without a sponsor, so Hooters got him to commit to a few races, and he got Hooters to pay him more than they wanted to pay. So we ran three races with Hooters on the car, and then went three more races, and then they renewed for the rest of the year, and before the year was out, they had signed a multiyear contract. And while they were sponsoring Alan, Hooters expanded more than they ever did before. It was really good for their business.

"We finished 1991 really strong. We won Bristol in August, and at the end were thirteenth in the points. I knew how strong we could be, and I made a statement, 'We're going to have an excellent year in '92. We're going to run in the top five in points in '92.'

"We came out strong, ran real good, and all year long ran in the top five. Alan was strong, and Davey Allison. Dale Earnhardt, who won the championship in '91, was having a bad year. That was a big year for radial tires, a big transition for a lot of people. We spent a lot more time on radial tires that year, raced them more, 'cause the advantage of radial tires was that they didn't change much throughout the run. You had to drive them smooth, and that's why Alan did so well on them. Alan wasn't a beat-bang driver, he was smooth, and that was another reason we did so well. But when the radials first came out, they were tricky. It was hard to control them, and the driver's ability to work with that car during practice in order to get the car set up meant so much more than it ever did.

"We won two races in '92, and we ran in the top five in eleven races, and had seventeen top-ten finishes. We won the night race at Bristol, and we won in the first Pocono race, and we should have won the second Pocono race, but Harry Gant won it on gas mileage even though we had an excellent car that day.

"After Davey won Daytona, Bill Elliott began the year by winning the next four races. We finished second at Richmond, were top ten in most of the races, and then Dover almost finished us. That year we replaced five clips from wrecks, and all were at Dover. The first race in late May we unloaded the car, and in practice the car bottomed out a crossmember, slid and hit the wall. We ran our second car, and the secondary part of the carburetor hung open just a little bit, and that car hit the wall. I had told the shop to prepare a third car and make sure it was ready to go, and after we wrecked that second car Saturday morning in practice, the third car was there for the final practice. The third car was the one we ran in the race, and we finished twelfth.

"We hung in there through September, and then we just about knocked ourselves out of the points race when we got back to Dover. In practice, again we wrecked our first car. Back then it was a rarity to have a backup car ready to go. Now everybody does it. We unloaded the second car, went out and sat on the pole with that car. And then in the race Alan and Chad Little got together. Chad moved up on Alan when Alan was passing him. It was one of those racing accidents. We ran only ninety-one laps, finished near the bottom, and we lost a lot of points. It sure didn't look good for our championship hopes. Alan told the media, 'This definitely hurt us, but we're not going to give up. We're going to go on and do the best we can.' He never would say we were done for the championship. And that's what we said to him, because after Dover he was devastated. But we didn't give up as a team either. We didn't know we could win it, but we never stopped trying. We weren't going to lay down. We were going to work harder than ever to try to get back up to the top.

"We ran real well those last few races. We finished fifth at Martinsville, won the pole at North Wilkesboro but finished twelfth. When Bill Elliott, the points leader, fell out early, we had pulled to within fewer than 150 points of him. At Charlotte we finished second to Mark Martin, and Elliott again fell out early, and the lead was now less than 50 points with three races left.

"At Rockingham Elliott was fourth, we were twelfth, and Davey Allison, who was second in the standings, was tenth. We were now 15 points behind Davey and 85 behind Elliott.

"The next race was Phoenix. Davey won that race. We finished fourth, ran extremely well, but we had some bad pit stops. I know we had a really good car and should have done better than what we did. And when that race was over, Alan and I had a big fight over the pit stops. The pressure was on. We were all tense. We were back in contention to win the championship, and here we were having bad pit stops, something that can't happen.

"We had made a couple mistakes that shouldn't have happened, and Alan was screaming on the radio, and I was screaming back, 'We're doing the best we can.'

"People's feelings were hurt for a couple of days, but we got back on track. We didn't talk much after the Phoenix race, but when we got back to the shop, we talked about the weekend, and how he was right, and how I was right, and that was it. We never would hold a grudge. That's why Alan and I got along so well—he'd tell me what he thought of what I did, and I'd tell him what I thought of what we did, whether I was right or wrong. If there was an argument, we'd each give our side, and when we walked out of the room, we were done. We didn't concern ourselves about it again. We began preparing for Atlanta, the final race of the season.

"Davey held the points lead going into the final race, 30 points ahead of us and 40 points ahead of Elliott, who finished way back in Phoenix because of engine problems. If Davey finished fifth or better, he would be the champion.

"We were parked near Dale Earnhardt, the points champion the year before, and right before the start of the Atlanta race, Dale came over to us and wished us luck. Alan said, 'You've been in this position before. What should I do?' Dale said, 'You don't change anything. You do exactly what you've been doing all year long. You do what got you here.' And that's what we did.

"Our plan was to be consistent and run the best race we could and not take unnecessary chances, to run a good, clean race. We wanted to run the best we could with what we had. If the car will go to the front, take it to the front. We were going to put it where it'll go.

"That race was also Richard Petty's final race of his farewell tour. That distracted a little from the championship, but not that much. Everyone loves Richard, and it was a good deal.

"We had qualified fourteenth, and we started the race, which was sponsored by Hooters. Davey wrecked early—he was damaged but it didn't put him out, and we were scanning him so we knew about it. After his crash, the first caution came out, and we made our first pit stop.

"We were prepared for this race. We had everything new in the car. Every part of it was brand new. We had had transmission problems at Phoenix and Rockingham, so we made sure we had a new transmission. And leaving the pits after that first pit stop, Alan broke the new transmission!

"It was a combination of the radial tires with more grip, the hydraulic clutch with instant release, and leaving the pits hard. The parts back then were not as strong as they are now. So we broke first gear right off the bat, and we thought we were done, 'cause you can't fix that during the race.

"The broken transmission didn't effect our performance until we came on pit road. We had to leave pit road in fourth gear, because we had broken metal parts in there, and only by leaving it in fourth are you not going to move metal around as much. We could only hope that the loose piece of metal didn't get in there and break the gears in half.

"We had three or four pit stops after it broke. I held my breath all day long. With Davey having wrecked, the points race was between Alan and Elliott. He was strong, but we were too. We were in contention to lead the most laps of the race, and when we did that, we got a five-point bonus. At that point we knew that if we finished second, even if Elliott won, we would be the champions.

"It was toward the end of the race, and we still had one more pit stop to make. We both had to come in for one more splash of gas. We had only fourth gear. We had to push the car out of the pits, which we could do under the rules because of the problems with the transmission.

"We came in. We wanted to make the stop as fast as possible, gas-and-go. We knew how many seconds of gas we needed. The gas man was to count to three and pull the gas can out.

"All seven crew members were across the wall to push the car. They were behind the car, and we put our three seconds of gas in, told him to go, and he eased it off and we pushed the car to give it movement, and he took off. Elliott, meanwhile, beat us out and took the lead. We were second.

"After Alan left, we measured the gas can to see how much gas was left in it, and we determined that we might be a little on the short side, that perhaps we hadn't quite given him enough. Had we waited one more second, we'd have been fine, but at the same time if we had waited much longer, we might have been overtaken by the third-place car. So we couldn't spend too much time in the pits. We knew Alan couldn't get out of the pits fast because of the transmission problem, and all that was in consideration.

"We knew we had led the most laps, knew we did not have to win the race, knew the third-place car was quite a ways back. We'd win the championship—unless we ran out of gas.

"I broke the news to Alan. I said, 'You need to conserve gas every chance you can.' And for the first time there was silence over the radio. He had been really calm all day long and never did want to talk about the championship. But as the race went on, you had to. We told him when he led the most laps. Alan was an information nut. He had to have as much information as you could possibly throw at him. This time, total silence. He didn't say a word.

"A couple of laps later, Alan said, 'Exactly what do you mean by that?' He paused. 'Does this mean we don't have enough gas?'

"I said, 'It's going to be close. You just need to conserve as much as you can.'

"To save gas, you're just really easy with the throttle. You don't go completely wide open going down the straightaways. When you back out of the gas, you roll out easy. Atlanta is the type of place where you never have to lift completely. You just roll out easy and roll right back into it.

"And that's what he did. We didn't have to worry about winning. We weren't going to try to catch Elliott. We kept telling Alan where Geoff Bodine, in third place, was. All we needed to do was finish second.

"When Alan was on the last lap, he didn't say anything that I remember. When the checkered flag dropped, and he won the championship, that's when he asked, 'Did we win?' And I said, 'Yeah, you did. Congratulations.' We all just went nuts on the radio.

"Alan said, 'I'm going to do it again,' recalling his pledge to repeat his Polish victory lap if he ever won the points championship. He spun it around after he took the checkered and did his Polish victory lap going to victory lane.

"And when it was all over, we couldn't believe it happened. Even in New York at the banquet, it was almost like it was still a dream. When Alan turned down Junior's millions, no one thought he could win it. He believed he could and a small group of people who worked for him believed he could. It made us proud of all the hard work you've put in. You feel like it has finally paid off.

"We came back from the banquet, and we made our plans for '93. We were going to work on our weak points, Dover, our short tracks, the road courses, and set our sights on winning the championship again in '93.

"We went to Daytona in '93. We had a really good car, were close to leading the race, and broke a valve. The rest of the day we had to putt around on seven cylinders. After that we had some good runs. We finished fourth at Rockingham, third at Richmond, and after crashing early in the race at Atlanta, we finished sixth at Darlington. We hadn't won any races, but we were ninth in the points, where we needed to be. Things were going well. It was going to be a good year. And being the defending champion was great. Whenever we went out, everybody was timing us. 'What's the 7 car running?' everyone wanted to know. It was a great feeling being defending champion, just as much fun as winning it.

"Our next race was at Bristol. For the first time we were flying to the races in a private plane. In the past we flew commercial jets to the far tracks and drove to the near one. This year Hooters supplied us with their private plane, and before the races, Alan and I would sit in the back and we'd talk business.

"The plane was a Merlyn, sat real high compared to the King Air.

It sat ten. Felix Sabates was a close friend of Alan's, and he gave Alan business and general advice, and he told Alan, 'You're going to get killed in that Merlyn. Those things are terrible. You have to get out of that plane. They're junk.' Felix was serious. Ironically, Hooter's pilot loved that plane. He thought it was the greatest plane ever for that size, thought it was the best plane on the market. He did not like the King Air, which is the popular plane for its size.

"Our original plan was to fly from Charlotte to Knoxville, Tennessee, where Alan had to make an appearance. From Knoxville it was only a short distance away from Bristol. Alan said, 'You guys come with me.' And that's what we were going to do.

"And then we got to thinking about our pit stops. They had been okay, but they needed some work. I got talking to the guys. I said, 'The cars are done and they're looking good. Why don't we spend a couple of hours working on the pit stops this afternoon, and then we'll drive to Bristol. We can still be there by ten o'clock. So that's what we did, and that's the only reason that plane wasn't full.

"We drove to Bristol and got to our motel. I arrived at about eleven. There was a message to call somebody at the small airport in Bluntsville, Tennessee, where Alan was scheduled to arrive. It was an emergency, the note said. I called, and one of our weekend guys was at the airport. He already knew what had happened. He said, 'I have some terrible news.' I said, 'What's that?' He said, 'Alan's plane went down.' I said, 'Is everybody all right?' He said, 'Well, they won't tell us. But it doesn't look good.' He never would say Alan was dead. That was the worst part of the deal.

"Immediately three or four of us went to the airport. There was a huge crowd. The plane had gone down almost two hours earlier.

"The police were there. I could not comprehend what had happened. I hadn't seen a news story. I could not comprehend how bad the crash was, and I was still hoping for the best. And the authorities never would say what was going on. They'd say, 'The plane went down, and it doesn't look good. We can't tell you anything other than that.' They didn't tell us that when the plane went down it erupted into a ball of flames, and that everyone on board was killed. They didn't want to say someone was killed without knowing exactly who was on board. In my mind, it was wrong.

"At two o'clock in the morning they finally told us there were no survivors. I never went to the site. To this day I haven't been to the site. The motors died. Apparently the pilot didn't de-ice properly, and it stalled the motors completely out. Pilot error. That was a horrible deal. Dale Earnhardt's plane had landed right in front of Alan's, and as they were taxiing in, apparently everyone in Dale's plane could hear the cries across the radio waves as Alan's plane was going down.

"Alan not only was my friend, but he was the man who paid my salary, and now he was dead. With me being the crew chief and now the guy who had to make the decisions, what do you do at that moment? The next day, what do we do?

"We spent half the morning meeting with NASCAR trying to figure out what to do. Nothing like this had ever happened in the NASCAR family. It was new to everybody. It was a tough situation to get through, and Felix Sabates helped us get through it. He told us to go home and get ready for the next race, to figure out what we were going to do for a driver. He helped us make that decision not to race at Bristol. We talked with Don Hawk, who had been brought in the first of the year to be the team manager and also handle Alan's souvenir business, along with the huge overflow of calls and potential sponsors. We all decided to go home.

"Luckily there was a week off after the Bristol race which gave us more time. The Bristol race was the first Winston Cup race I ever watched on TV since I'd been in Winston Cup racing full-time. I couldn't even watch it. I taped it and watched it later. I was devastated, crying. I'm a pretty emotional person as it is. It was tough, and it's still tough. It's the hardest thing I've ever been through in my life. Never been through anything like that with another family member, and I felt Alan was a family member.

"We went through the funeral, got through that mess. We had gone to Milwaukee, where he's buried, did services there, then came back here and had services here, and then had a small reception at the shop. Bob Brooks, the CEO of Hooters, had come down. Bob lost his son, Mark, in the accident, as well as his pilot and one of his marketing executives. So he had total devastation.

"Felix Sabates, Jerry Kulwicki, Alan's dad, and I talked with Bob Brooks about who would replace Alan in the car. We wanted Jimmy

Hensley. We felt he was a good, capable driver, and Alan thought well of him, because Alan had once made a comment to Felix that he thought Jimmy would do well if he had a good car.

"Brooks wanted Loy Allen. At the end of the conversation at the reception in the shop Bob Brooks set out the bottom line when he finally said, 'If you want to continue the Hooters' sponsorship, Loy Allen is my driver. If you do not put him in the car, you will not have a sponsor.'

"We wanted to test Loy out to see if he could do it. At the time he had never been in a Winston Cup race. We said, 'Let's take him to a few races. Let's run him five races,' cause if he ran five races he could still run for Rookie of the Year the following year. 'We'll go test with him and put forth a good effort for him and give him a good, fair shake.' But that wasn't the way Bob wanted to do it. Bob wanted Loy Allen to be the driver, and the other thing he insisted upon was that Loy's father buy the team. And that was not the way we wanted to do it.

"We put Jimmy in the car, and we didn't win any races, but we ran respectably, finishing most of the races we ran.

"We had different people wanting to buy the team. Ricky Rudd was interested, Brett Bodine, and Geoff Bodine, and a lot of other people who were only interested in buying it so they could liquidate it and make money. But that's not the way Jerry Kulwicki wanted to sell it. He wanted to sell it to someone who would own it and run it in the proper way and keep everyone together as best as possible.

"Geoff Bodine convinced Jerry that he would be the right one to buy it. At the time Geoff was with Bud Moore. Before the year was over, we went to Dover with Geoff in the car, and he ran in the final six races. It made Jerry and everyone else happy, and it was a good deal for everyone."

40

DISTURBING MEMORIES

WHEN I VISITED JAKE ELDER AT his race shop on Zion Church Road in Concord, North Carolina, he was just another mechanic working for the Filmar Racing team, owned by a Nashville businessman with Kenny Wallace behind the wheel.

During his illustrious career, Elder had worked for most of the powerhouse race teams: Holman-Moody, Osterlund, J. D. Stacy, DiGard, and Robert Yates among them. He's with the fledgling Filmer team now, and it is no longer easy for Elder.

Several years ago Elder suffered a stroke, and only recently has he been able to get back on his feet. Still a tough old bird, Jake Elder gets up every morning and heads to work. Cars, after all, are what he knows.

Elder's list of drivers is most impressive. He has been crew chief for Dale Earnhardt, Terry Labonte, Darrell Waltrip, Ricky Rudd, Bill Elliott, and Davey Allison. He talked about them, and was moved when he recalled his conversations with Alan Kulwicki. When he worked for the Robert Yates team, he said, the late Davey Allison really knew his stuff. His affection for Davey was obvious.

The time has passed for a whole generation of crew chiefs and engine builders, including Harry Hyde, Robert Gee, Herb Nab, and Suitcase Jake, who has survived them all. He may be getting old, but he'll never give up the fight.

JAKE ELDER: "After quitting Holman-Moody, I jumped from team to team. One of those teams I worked for was owned by Rod Osterlund. When Osterlund told me they were going to hire Dale Earnhardt, I knew I was going to have a fine race car driver. In '79 we were in Riverside, California, and that's when Dale sat on the pole for the first time. At that time he wasn't claiming to be a good road course driver, which he'll tell you right now. I don't know how he did it. He just manhandled that car. He got more out of the car than what the car was capable of doing. He was that good. He'd drive out of shape, the car would be sideways, and it didn't bother Dale.

"Osterlund sold out to Jim Stacy. He had four or five cars in a race that said 'J. D. Stacy' on them. I thought, The publicity isn't helping him none. I couldn't figure out what his deal was. But we went on like that a couple years, sponsoring different teams. I had Terry Labonte. We had a black car with 'J. D. Stacy' on it. Terry was very quiet. He was an easy guy to work for. Couldn't tell what Terry could do, whether he was doing all he could or whether he was holding back. Terry is like that today. He don't show everything he's got until the time comes. I worked for Terry two other times as well. Terry is a good race car driver. And now that he's won a second championship, he'll get a lot more credit than he got, cause he's a better race car driver than people give him credit for.

"And after I left Stacy, I went to work at DiGard for the Gardner brothers with Darrell Waltrip. They were what I call overbearing people. Jim wasn't all that bad, but Bill, he was from up North, and he's one of them who kind of wants everything done right then, no matter what you're doing or what you're saying. He was just a hateful person. Bill was a northerner, and like all northern people, his attitude was different from the people down south. Like he wanted you to win a race today, and sometimes you do and sometimes you don't, but if you didn't, he'd get hot and mad. I didn't like him. I don't think nobody liked him.

"Darrell Waltrip drove for them. At the time they were calling him 'Jaws,' because he wanted to win and he wanted everyone to know that he could win. Darrell would talk a lot. And I used to get on him bad about that talking all the time. He'd say, 'I'm going to do this, and I'm going to do that. This driver ain't as good as I am.' He talked about Cale a little bit, and that's when Cale called him 'Jaws.' Darrell didn't really like that business of being called 'Jaws.' But hell, he went about his business, and he won a lot of races, ole Darrell did. He made a lot of them old-timers mad. Darrell was an aggressive driver. He would take a lot more chances than the rest of the drivers would take, because he was young and he knew he could do it and get away with it. He'd pass to the inside, pass to the outside. There was a wreck at Darlington, and the road was plumb blocked, and Darrell came through that son of a bitch and drove right through that wreck, and how he did it I don't know. I couldn't believe it. But he drove through that wreck, and he won the race. I said, 'Well, he must be that good.'

"The Gardners wouldn't let Darrell out of his contract. One night in Atlanta I was in my motel room and Darrell was in the room right beside me, and he was on the phone with Bill Gardner, and he called him everything but a white man, know what I mean? They never could see eye to eye. Darrell used to tell me, 'I gotta get out of this contract.' He said, 'I know it's going to cost me a lot of money.' So his father-in-law bought him out of it.

"When Darrell quit, Ricky Rudd started driving the car, but things weren't working out right, so I left and didn't do nothing the rest of the year. I worked for Terry Labonte some, worked for Darrell again, then Terry, who was driving for Billy Hagan, who wouldn't let me do what I wanted to do because it seemed like he was holding back on the money.

"I worked for a lot of teams that year. In 1981, I helped Bill Elliott sit on the pole at Darlington, then I sat on the pole at Texas with Terry Labonte, and then I sat on the pole with Darrell. Three poles in one year with three different drivers. They used to call me 'Suitcase Jake.' I had a lot of fun out of that.

"I remember Alan Kulwicki—he was sort of a tricky person—he'd trick you into a lot of setup talking. Me and Alan talked a lot. I'd be at the racetrack working, and he'd come to me, and he'd always stand off to the side when he wanted to ask me something. Me and him were pretty close about talking to each other about chassis work. He'd ask me what I thought about this, or what I thought about that, and I'd tell him, and I'd think, I want to see what he does. I'd watch him.

And I must have told him right, because I'd never see him again the rest of the day. He was a strange man, but he was a fine person.

"After I left Billy Hagan, I went to work for Robert Yates in '91. I worked for Yates twice. I've known Robert a long time. When I first joined Yates, Davey Allison was the driver. He was young. Davey had a real good feel for a race car. Davey would come in and tell you about what spring he wanted you to change. He was getting real good with chassis work, cause he learned that from his daddy, all the places his daddy run and he went to and drove. Davey, he never forgot it, and he'd go out and make a run and come back in and say, 'I want to work on this. I want to work on that.' Sure enough, before long, he'd hit it, find the right combination.

"We won five races in '91 including the World 600. He just kept saying, 'This is a good car.'

"The year he got killed something was bothering him. I don't know what all Davey's problems were. I was going to sit down and talk to him one day about his problem, but I never did get to the point. Was his family like he wanted it? What was going on? He did a lot of what I call foolish things. He got that ole' helicopter. I said, 'What the hell do you want that thing for?' Davey said, 'I like to fly. It's a lot of fun.' What can you say to a driver making money and winning races? What can you say? You can't tell him no, tell him he's doing crazy things. Cause Davey was a good race car driver. He was a likeable person, friendly. Neil Bonnett was the same way, a likeable person. I don't know what happened to Davey, but if he was here today, the people would take notice, wouldn't they? He'd be winning a lot of races.

"After I left Robert Yates, I more or less didn't do nothing for a couple of years. Then for a year I worked on Hank Parker's car for David Bonnett, Neil's boy, but I saw that wasn't going to get nowhere. I was spinning my wheels. He might have been a good race car driver, but it was going to take him twenty years to be one. I said to myself, I ain't got that many years to fool with it.

"Today I work for Filmar Racing. Kenny Wallace is the driver. Mr. Filmar is out of Nashville, used to own a credit card business. I'm a mechanic, got to do everything.

"Racing isn't the same as it was when I started. What's changed? Everything. You got high-buck stuff now, transporters. You got all these high-buck people with computers. Used to be you could go to the racetrack with three or four people. Now you got one man to look at just the shocks. A man to work on the air pressure of the tires. That's all he does. Today you got to have a specialty man for everything.

"The car manufacturers are big into it, and you have these big sponsors, five-million-, seven-million-dollar sponsors, so you might as well spend the money. You might as well buy the best. These chief mechanics now make $250,000 a year. Years ago, why you were lucky to make six hundred dollars a week. Things have really changed, and changed bad. Like they go and race in Japan. Who in the hell ever dreamed about them going over to Japan racing? I mean, it's all different. Like now, Bruton Smith built a big, nice track in Texas. Just a lot of things are not like they used to be. Now it's all big tracks. You ain't gonna see no Martinsvilles, 'cause there ain't gonna be anything but superspeedways. That's just the way it's gonna be.

"Racing has been good to me. I wish I hadn't gotten sick when I did. About three years ago I had to have an angioplasty on my heart. So that set me back a little bit. It's no good when you can't do what you want to do. Then I had to have an operation on my carotid artery on my neck. So that set me back awhile. I got dizzy all the time. The doctors say that's something I have to live with the rest of my life. I get used to it. Some days it's worse. When it's cloudy and raining, drizzly outside, I'm more dizzy than on days when it's real clear. It's something I have to live with. Six months ago I was real bad. I'd stagger around 'cause I couldn't get my balance right. I'd try to work, but for a while I couldn't. I can't think like I used to. The dizziness has a lot to do with it. I'm getting a little bit old."

LIZ ALLISON

41

THE DEATHS OF CLIFFORD AND DAVEY

WHAT JAKE ELDER AND A LOT OF other people close to Davey Allison didn't know was that Davey and his second wife, Liz, were having serious marital problems, major rents in the fabric of their lives. The worst was that Davey had had an affair with a young woman who accused him of fathering her child. Another was that he and his first wife, his childhood sweetheart, a girl he had known since elementary school, had begun seeing each other again, though friends say the relationship was more an attempt on Davey's part to patch up bitter feelings than it was to rekindle a romance. Either way, Liz knew of both the affair and the reconciliation, and she was irate and resentful.

Perhaps in self-defense, Liz began a relationship with country and western singing star Joe Diffie. Bobby Allison, for one, has never forgiven her for it, and close observers say that Bobby's antagonism toward Liz in part caused the breakup of his own marriage. Friends say Bobby had been closer to Clifford than to Davey, and after Clifford died, Judy Allison pleaded with Bobby to embrace Liz for the sake of the grandchildren. To no avail. They say Judy held Bobby's intransigence against her husband, just one of the issues that broke them up.

Davey did not name Liz as the executor of his

estate, but instead named a cousin. Friends say that if Davey hadn't died, divorce would have been a real possibility.

After Davey's death, Liz allowed Diffie to stay in her home in Hueytown. This did not sit well with the Allison clan or with Davey's old friends who saw Diffie driving around in Davey's pickup, further angering them against Liz.

Stung by the criticism from both Bobby and Davey's friends and fans, Liz now lives in Nashville, Tennessee, where her relationship with Diffie continues. In looking back on her marriage to Davey, perhaps the remorse for what could have been or perhaps her denial to help mask the terrible pain she feels over Davey's death causes Liz Allison to ignore or skip over the discord and instead to concentrate on what they had together when things were good. She has gone through much. That is her prerogative.

LIZ ALLISON: "I was born in Augusta, Georgia, on June 7, 1965. I had a pretty normal childhood. My parents divorced when I was young. They had a good divorce, if you can have a good divorce. My mother raised me. I grew up in North Augusta, South Carolina, and then in the ninth grade, when I was fifteen, I moved to Clinton and lived with my dad. I finished school there, and then moved to Charleston and started working as a customer service representative for Eastern Airlines.

"A girlfriend of mine was engaged to the son of the owner of the Somerville Speedway. I went as her guest to the race that night. This was August of 1988. They were having a memorial race for Tiny Lund, and Wanda was there and Davey was there, and we met.

"At the time I didn't know much about racing. I knew a little bit. I knew of the Allison family and Richard Petty. The thing I remember most about that first time that I met Davey, it was burning hot in Charleston, just scorching. We all had on shorts and T-shirts, and sweat was rolling down our heads, and he was wearing black corduroys and a flannel shirt. And I looked at him and thought, What a geek! I mean, that was the first thing I thought. What a geek! He was just like, 'Hey.' He had no idea that he was completely backward. He was dressed for the fall. People would look at him. He didn't care. He was the only person I ever knew who in the middle of the summertime would still be cold. His chemistry was completely backward. He did that to himself so he could take the heat in the race car. Luckily for me, his clothing style changed over the years.

"They were racing at Darlington that weekend, 'cause Darlington is real close to Somerville, and I talked to him that night, and he asked me for a phone number, and I gave him my office number. I didn't hear from him for about a month, and then after that he started calling. They were going through a lot of family things. Bobby had had a bad accident, so I didn't see Davey until November at the Atlanta race. Davey invited me to come see him that weekend, and I went, and we started dating steady after that. We married in August of '89.

"When Bobby suffered those serious injuries at Pocono early in 1988, that was a really hard situation for the whole family. Davey had looked up to his dad all his life and always wanted to be just like him. Bobby called the shots for that entire family, from great-grandparents all the way down to the little kids. He had made the decisions for everything, and so when Bobby was injured, they all just stood around. He'd done everything, and they didn't know where to turn or who was going to lead them, and so Davey felt like he had to step into that role. Davey all of a sudden was thrown into the role of 'man of the family,' and it was really hard for him. It was very difficult for him to do that, and it added a lot of pressure to the growing up he was doing at that time. A lot of that pressure he was putting on himself, and some of it was that the family needed somebody to step in and take over.

"In some ways Davey talked about how difficult it was, and in some ways he didn't. He would open up about some of it, how he felt the sense of responsibility. But he never resented it. He was just afraid that he couldn't walk in his dad's shoes. Like I said, a lot of the pressure he put on himself. He wanted to do right by everybody. He was under a lot of stress at the time.

"In '89 Harry Ranier owned Davey's team, and Robert Yates was his engine builder. Robert and Davey had a great relationship. Robert to Davey was like a big brother that he never had. Too, Robert had worked with Bobby in years past, and he was on a great personal level with the whole family, so he was a great support system for Davey through all of this, his daddy's accident, through them starting a new team in '90 with Yates as the car owner. Davey was very close to Robert.

"That year, too, Bobby started his own team, with Mike Alexander the driver. Mike lives here in Nashville. He's a little, teeny guy. His wife's name is also Liz. They had known him for short track racing, and they thought he was ready to make the big step, but it just didn't click for him, and then Michael was in a bad accident at Pensacola in the Snowball Derby, and he suffered some head injuries, and he didn't really fully recover from that. Bobby then hired Hut Stricklin, who was married to Pam Allison, Donnie Allison's daughter. Hut and Davey grew up driving against each other at the BIR [Birmingham International Raceway]. Hut and Pam had dated in their high school years and had gone on and gotten married. They felt Hut was a very capable driver and ready for that step up.

"In April of '90, Neil Bonnett crashed at Darlington, and he was seriously hurt, suffering from amnesia. We went to the hospital right after the race was over and spent some time up there. Luckily for us, we were able to see Neil right away so we weren't quite as shook up over his amnesia as we would have been if we had not seen him first-hand and known the situation. Even at this point, it hadn't hit me or Davey, but we were starting to get a little rattled with some of the stuff going on. When you start seeing people you love and care about getting truly injured to where in his daddy's case it ended his career, you look at racing in a different way. But we still, as hardheaded as both of us were, we still had not gotten it through our heads yet.

"I don't know why Neil had so many serious crashes. Since the time I met Davey, Neil was out of the car more than he was in it. I don't know what it was. Sometimes it's just bad luck. It could be the equipment. It could be the eye of the tiger, when you lose that drive. I'm sure it was a combination of all of the above. But all through '90 Neil suffered from amnesia. It was come and go. It wasn't that he couldn't remember anything and anybody. He was rattled enough to know that at that time he wasn't capable of getting back in the car.

"So 1990 was a very tough year for Davey. It was a big transition year. The sport was and still is changing, a popular sport moving into the big time, big-time money, and things were really changing on the business side. And there was still the stuff at home, his daddy's recovery, and too, Ford was having some problems getting the engine program together. All those things played into it. It was just a lot of things going on that year.

"The thing about Davey, about this time he started making a great deal of money, but it never affected him. Never. I mean, it did not affect him as a person. He was just as tight the day he died as he was before. Believe it or not, that's the truth. That was a big joke in the family. He'd have me clipping coupons out of the paper to take to the grocery store. Which was great. I respected that. He was so responsible that way. That's why we had what we had and were able to give our family what we had. On the other hand, he liked big toys too, like his airplane and his helicopters, and he was able to get those too.

"In '91, Larry McReynolds joined Davey's team. Larry also is from Birmingham, and he also kind of got his feet in the mud at BIR. They all kind of grew up together at that racetrack. Davey had known him for years. I don't want to take anything away from Larry, cause he's great at what he does, but everything was kind of coming together anyway. The engine program was getting there. Yates had hired some great people, and then he brought Larry in, and everything kind of clicked, and in racing that's what it takes. It's the whole package. It all has to click for it to work.

"Ninety-one started at Daytona. Davey had the lead with two laps to go when Dale Earnhardt hit him and kept him from winning. Davey was mad. All the drivers have tempers. They are highly competitive people, so if they think you're keeping them from a win, they're going to get mad. But there were no hard feelings. If the truth were to be known, Davey really admired Dale. He would never admit it, but Dale was one of his heroes. I mean, he admired Dale. Dale no doubt is a remarkable race car driver. They had a funny little chemistry between them, but it was a good chemistry. They were both big outdoorsmen, big hunters. They did some hunting together, some fishing together. It wasn't like they were huge pals who hung out all the time together, but they had a lot of things in common.

"Dale complained that Davey's car was illegal after Davey won the Coca-Cola 600 at Charlotte in '91. I'm not defending the drivers, but for the most part the drivers do not know on the car what's legal and what's not. It's not their concern. Then at Sonoma in June, Ricky Rudd won the race but Davey was given the victory when NASCAR officials ruled Ricky had hit Davey's car unnecessarily while approaching the white flag. The officials called what they saw. Whether somebody thinks it was fair or not, it's also not fair to go on the racetrack and intentionally hit somebody to try to take them from a win. Why did the officials say, 'This race we're going to take away from you, but the next one we won't take it from someone else?' I don't know. Unfortunately, that sort of thing happened a lot, and usually the rulings went against Davey. This one was in his favor. So my feeling was that since the officials of NASCAR were the way they were, by golly, if they said it was supposed to be that way, then it was meant to be that way. 'Cause they don't do that very often. To be honest, I don't know any other time that it happened. But it was clear to them watching it happen and watching the replay that that's what happened, and they made their best call. Luckily for us, it was in our favor.

"Afterwards, Davey felt the controversy took away from his win. Davey felt that Rudd had always been the Superman of the road races and that Davey had really learned how to drive those tracks, so he was disgusted that he had driven such a great race and that his performance was overshadowed by the controversial finish. Though Davey said a win is a win, he was sorry it ended the way it did because nobody had noticed what he had done in the race.

"One of the highlights of the '91 season was at Michigan, where Davey won and Hut finished second in Bobby's car. That was great. Bobby's team had been struggling financially, trying to get things going sponsorship-wise. They had struggled. With Hut being a member of the family, it was just a really neat experience for everybody. Just to see Hut run good was just great, and for him to finish second to Davey, that was a great moment, something everyone of us was proud of. I know Hut would have loved to have won that race, but now he'd probably say he's glad it ended just the way it did. It was pretty neat.

"In October, after winning Rockingham, Davey flew his plane to Phoenix, and on the way had to make an emergency landing when the cabin filled with smoke. I wasn't with him on that trip. But it scared him to death. It was one of those freaky deals. He won at Phoenix, but Dale won the championship. He ended up finishing third in the points, and that was a great year for him. There was no frustration for us at the end of that year, not like it was at the end of '92. It may have been a little disappointing not to have finished second, but we were thrilled with third.

"Going into the Daytona 500 of '92, we *knew* he was going to win that race. We just knew it. The writing was clear on the wall for us.

They had run so good at the end of '91, and everyone felt they were going to take that momentum right into '92, which they did. I mean, Speed Weeks was pretty neat, because we could feel the power. We knew it was there, knew it was going to happen. The reporters were all around Davey. He had all that attention. And Davey, too, he was a pretty remarkable person. He always had this confidence about him, and I really admired that in him. Because nothing got him down. He might get mad and bum for a second, but he basically was very upbeat, a very motivated person, and people loved that energy, so people were around him anyway. But when things were really good, he just beamed. So it was really cool to be around him and experience that.

"I'm prejudiced, and I like to think Davey was good with the press. He took time that so many drivers didn't take, and some of that was overlooked. He could sit and sign autographs and talk to the press for forty-five minutes, and you could get up and leave one person, and they'd bash you. But yes, for the most part the press enjoyed him because of the energy around him.

"And he won that Daytona 500, and he was leading in the points when he lost his grandfather who he loved just before the Bristol race in early April. This was the absolute year from hell in our lives. His grandfather, Bobby's dad, was kind of the ringleader of the Alabama Gang. Everybody called him Pop Allison, and though Davey suffered, he drove at Bristol. I admired the fact he was able to go and run that race and put every emotion out of that car and still drive unbelievably. But there were times I wanted to choke him because of it too.

"He crashed during that race and hurt his shoulder badly, but he went to North Wilkesboro and won it. I wasn't able to go to that race. I had something going with Krista back home and couldn't go. It was a very emotional race. He dedicated the race to his grandfather.

"He was in a lot of pain. It took me a while to realize how much pain he was in because he never complained. He had all these little stimulators strapped on him like you get at the chiropractor and a battery pack to try to keep his muscles relaxed. I thought, If that was me, I'd be in a hospital bed. He was out driving a race car.

"Then came the Winston, the night race at Charlotte when Davey had a bad crash as he was winning the race. The Winston changed everything for him and for me forever.

"We have a first-turn condo at Charlotte, where we were looking down at the race. The children were up there, all the family. With five laps to go, I decided to go down to the infield so I could see Davey when he got out of the race car. At that time he was not running up front. I didn't think he had a shot at winning. But as I got down there, I heard people screaming, 'Davey Allison's won the race.' I thought, What? What's happened?

"Then came the ordeal. The children saw the wreck from up in the condo. He was knocked unconscious, and he had a really weird experience from what happened to him there. He really felt like he should have been killed in that wreck. He really felt he had been given a second chance and at that point it was time for him to get his life straightened out, to get it in line the way the Higher Power felt like he needed to have it in line. That experience changed Davey Allison forever.

"Up to that point Davey had felt that the race car came before anything. He loved his wife and children but the race car still came first. It's hard to explain this to someone else, but that's what makes them the drivers they are. But after the crash, all that changed. Everything came second to me and the children and our family. From then on Davey felt there was nothing in the world more important than that. Not that he wasn't a wonderful husband and father before, but he had been very driven by what he was doing.

"Everything kind of became one for us. We shared. It's hard to put into words. We felt more. We just kind of became one. It's very hard to explain.

"Davey had another bad crash at Pocono in July. My big thing the whole year, he either won or he wrecked. There was no in between for him. I don't know why Pocono was so dangerous. It's where Bobby had ended his career. Judy, Davey's mom, told me, 'Good Lord, if I never go back to Pocono again, it will be a day too soon.' That wreck, which involved Darrell Waltrip, was a bad one. It was weird. It didn't look like much, but it turned into a lot. Davey fractured his skull. It was horrible, terrible. I was at home watching it on TV with strep throat. We chartered an airplane, got up there, and got there in time to see Davey being wheeled in for surgery. His head was huge. It was about four times the size of a normal head. I said to myself, Okay, this is it; you're not getting into a race car the rest of the year. After he regained consciousness, when I told him that, he never would say anything. In my heart I knew there was no way he would stop racing.

"The next day the swelling went down, and he told me, 'I'm racing on Sunday.' I told him right then, 'You're insane. You're in-sane. You are made out of something the rest of us don't understand.' And he was. Absolutely.

"He drove the first six laps at Talladega the next Sunday. That was a very emotional and difficult day for me, but at the same time it was also pretty amazing. I cried all the way out there. I was a crying idiot on pit road. I couldn't contain my feelings. I wanted to know, 'Why are you doing this? What are you trying to prove?' There was no answer. I knew the reason, of course. Davey was in the points lead. He felt he'd worked for this all his life, and by God, he was going to make this happen. The whole time they were putting him in the car, he was moaning and groaning, hollering out from the pain. They had to Velcro his hand to the stick shift, which I still can't believe NASCAR allowed him to do. He needed to drive until the first caution.

"Well, I just didn't see that there was going to be a caution for a long while. The sun was out, but after one lap, it started raining down in turn one. It was the weirdest thing. I thought to myself, Your guardian angel is looking out for you. Now you can get out of the car.

"Bobby Hillin filled in for him, and he did very well.

"Not only was Davey able to start and get the points, but Hillin finished third and kept him in the lead. The next week Davey went to Watkins Glen. I couldn't go because I had a sick child.

"Davey once again insisted on starting the race. I really wanted to tie him up, but at that point I gave up. I felt, If you're going to do this, I'm going to have to support you, because I married you, the race driver, and here we are. So if you're going to do it, what do I have to do to help you do this?

"Davey started, drove eighteen laps, and gave the car over to Dorsey Schroeder. [Schroeder finished twentieth, and Bill Elliott took over the points lead.]

"The next race was at Michigan. It was there that Davey's brother, Clifford, was killed during practice. Clifford was trying to make a name for himself, and he had not been able to get in there and do that yet. He hadn't had the opportunity, hadn't had the equipment, what a lot of race car drivers battle. Clifford was a funny little guy. He had a great personality. He and Davey were very different. Davey was real straitlaced, hardly drank anything. Clifford drank and smoked. They were just very different.

"They had the same brother thing every family has. They fought with each other, but they loved each other. I remember Davey telling me that Clifford had more born talent as a race car driver than he felt he had himself, but he just felt that Clifford hadn't gotten to the maturity level yet to put it into action. It frustrated Davey so much because he knew how capable Clifford was. And for a while Davey really battled with the question, Should I put him in my Busch car? That haunted him until the day he died.

"Clifford's death was terrible. We found out in the airplane flying up to Michigan. I remember sitting there thinking of the pain Davey was going through, and that I loved this man so much and could not take his pain away. I busied myself trying to help everybody else. I was trying to be Miss Fixit. I felt, Okay, we've got to go home. We've got to go home.

"We went to the hospital. Clifford's wife, Lisa, was there. One by one they all went home, and I kept waiting for Davey. I certainly wouldn't ask. At that point I wouldn't ask anything. I kept waiting for him to say, 'We're going home.' And he never said it. I thought, Are they going to have the funeral without us?

"Davey had a long talk with Mom and Dad on the Friday night. They told Davey to stay up at Michigan, to 'do what Clifford would have wanted you to do.' And Davey did. I don't know how the boy got through that weekend. I just don't know.

"It was just terrible. When he wasn't driving the car, he was sitting by the side of the truck crying. He truly had a strength that was unbelievable.

"And he drove that whole race at Michigan [and finished fifth]. And physically he was not on top of things by any means. He had several surgeries, which knocked him for a loop, and then to have this other thing happen. But he raced, made it through, we went home, and we buried Clifford the next day.

"Davey didn't know how to talk about it. He never dealt with Clifford's death. Never. No. He never went to the cemetery after the burial. He barely would talk about it. It was so painful for him that he chose to do everything but, and he went out of his way to do whatever he could to help Lisa and the kids and be a father to them. He gave Lisa a job as a secretary in his race shop. There was just a lot of unresolved stuff for him. Davey took all that upon himself.

"Davey went to Darlington. If he had won, he'd have won the Winston Million, and he led until the final six laps, and then it rained. That was very frustrating. For the most part I tried to stay really even-keeled at the races, because week in and week out you can't get so built up for everything, because you get let down more than built up. That was very frustrating. At that point, I was feeling the frustration of the whole year. I felt, 'Why is this guy having to go through so much? And then he doesn't get what he deserved.' It wasn't the money as it was the fact that he deserved the win, deserved the prestige and honor, and for it to start raining so they couldn't finish the race.

"Davey came in for gas, Darrell Waltrip took the lead, they were under caution, it started raining, and they didn't even get to finish the race. They called the race. So that was very frustrating, and I was more frustrated than he was.

"We went to Atlanta, and all Davey had to do to win the driving championship was to finish sixth. Lord only knows what happened that day. That is the most upsetting thing for me of Davey's whole racing career. I absolutely drove every lap with him. I felt, Lord, let this race be over. And then came the accident with Ernie Irvan. Ernie wasn't really well liked at that point anyway. He and Davey had had a few spats, a few things going on, so of all people to wreck him, Ernie Irvan, it was just beyond me. I thought, Jiminy crickets, everything that this man has been through this year, all the ups and downs, and to come in from Phoenix leading in the points and to lose the damn race now, it just doesn't seem fair.

"I was very angry. I was so angry. I just cried, and I felt so sorry for Davey. I wanted to hit Ernie. I wanted to choke Alan [Kulwicki, who won the title]. And when I got to the infield center, Davey was just as calm and peaceful as he could be, and I felt stupid for feeling the way I felt. I kept saying, 'I'm so sorry,' crying on and on, and Dave was trying to see if Ernie was okay. Davey was very disappointed, don't get me wrong. He just felt at that point that it just wasn't meant to be, that he had truly done everything in his power, the best of his ability to make it happen, and it just didn't happen.

"The off-season was a very special time. In January of '93 Davey and I renewed our vows. Both our children were in the wedding. So it was a great off-season.

"But then in early April of '93, Alan Kulwicki was killed in a plane crash. Alan was a great guy. I always really liked Alan. Alan, like Davey, was Catholic, and neither of them would miss Mass for anything. Davey would get me up at 5:30 in the morning before the race, and I'd be complaining all the way, but by golly, we were going. And Alan would always be there right with us. He was a great guy and very driven too. He was rather amazing. I found out about Alan's plane crash before Davey did. Davey was already up there. I was coming the next day. I called Davey and woke him up, and he was very shaken. He wouldn't even watch the TV to see any of the news. Davey told me, 'Now I know why I didn't win that championship. Alan won't have any other chances, and I'll have lots more.'

"What I wish Davey had said was, 'Alan crashed in his plane. Maybe we shouldn't be flying.' When he was in Charlotte he worked on his helicopter license. He would land in the parking lot of the turn-one condos at the track. Davey just thought that was the coolest thing in the world. He loved to fly, and then all of a sudden, he wanted to buy one. I was totally against it from the beginning. In '92 he bought a small helicopter. Lord, I don't know why.

"I flew with him one time. I don't like flying that much, and I certainly didn't like helicopters. I just felt it was one more big, expensive toy that was not needed. Then in June of '93 he traded in the little one for a turbo. He'd been taking lessons in it and had just gotten upgraded to fly it at the time of his accident. All the paperwork hadn't even been turned over.

"Davey used it to fly from the shop to the airport. That's it. I didn't want him to fly it. Neither did his family. But Davey was a hardheaded person. And so, I knew I was going to lose so I might as well be quiet about it.

"On July 12, Davey and Red Farmer flew to Talladega to watch David Bonnett, Neil's son, run. The odd thing about it was that Davey wasn't even running that day. I didn't even know he was going.

"I don't really know what happened. I really don't. I'm probably better off that way. People ask me how I handled a tragedy like that. By the grace of God. I mean, that is the truth. When you have children, you take your strength from them. You know you have to get up every day and make things work. I just truly believe that the Lord will not put you in a situation that you can't handle, and that you simply do what you have to do. What people see on the outside is not what is on the inside. So it's a long process, and when little ones are involved, it's even more detailed and confusing.

"I, of course, was not the only one devastated. Unfortunately for Davey's parents, his death tore them apart. Davey will be dead four years, and they have been separated for a year. They are waiting on a court date for their divorce. I'm sure they wouldn't mind me saying this, but as in any marriage Bobby and Judy had problems off and on, they had separated in the past, worked through the problems and got back together again, and this time I thought they would work through this and be fine. They have been through an awful lot. The two of them have been through more than any two people should have to go through. In situations like this, they either pull together or tear apart. For both of them, I know anger has been a real part of grief. They both have been eat up with it, and it just tore them apart. And I hate it for them. Hate it.

"I'm still very close to Judy and to both of Davey's sisters. I don't see Bobby quite as much. That's kind of a man thing. But I'm close to them, and I only want the best for them, and I do hate that they have had to go through more heartache.

"When Davey died, immediately afterward I questioned my faith in God. I remember telling someone, 'I prayed with all my heart, prayed on my hands and knees, prayed with everything I had, and Davey still died. And having little ones involved, holy cow, it's very hard to understand. It's hard enough to understand, but when you have little people involved, little hearts, it's even more difficult.

"I felt very angry with Davey. And I probably still do. It'll be four years this summer. I feel very angry because of the helicopter. 'Why in the heck did you have to have that helicopter, Davey? Why did you have to have these expensive toys?'

"I don't watch any racing at all. I'm very close to some of the families; Brett and Diane Bodine were our best friends at the track, and they are still my friends way beyond racing. And the Parsons, Phil and

Marcia, and families like that I am still close to. Marcia and I are tremendous friends. It goes way beyond racing. I don't even watch the races on TV. I don't know what anybody's doing.

"It's hard to understand those things, but I can say, as weird as it sounds, I am thankful that Davey and I had the two years we had before his death when Davey became a different man and dedicated his life to his family. Not that the years when we got engaged and married and first started our family weren't wonderful. But those last two years were really special, and because of what I brought away from that, I'm okay where I am now, and it has a lot to do with the way I raise our children.

"I want people to know that Davey was truly an exceptional person. He was a special person. No doubt people will remember his driving talent. That will be remembered forever, but I also want people to know the incredible man he had become in the last years of his life. It's what everybody should strive to be. That's how I want people to remember him: as a God-driven person with family number one in his heart and doing something he loved. Davey was a very blessed man."

42

A RACER'S SAD GOOD-BYE

IN 1988 LOU LAROSA JOINED THE Kenny Bernstein race team, building motors for Ricky Rudd. Immediately, LaRosa crossed swords with crew chief Larry McReynolds, who loudly accused LaRosa of hurting the team by building an engine low on horsepower. According to LaRosa, it was not his engine, but McReynolds's poor chassis design that slowed the car.

Despite the bitching and moaning from the fabricators, LaRosa's motors enabled Rudd to win at Sears Point and finish eighth in the points in 1989, and after Rudd left to go to Hendrick Motorsports, Brett Bodine replaced him. According to LaRosa, McReynolds instigated the ouster of Bodine—and of LaRosa as well. His enmity for McReynolds, the crew chief for Richard Childress beginning with the 1997 season, will be evident from his remarks.

Unable to stomach the politics, LaRosa left the Bernstein team and was hired by a new group, called Team Three. The team never got to the track because the team owner was a scam artist who ended up doing time for bankruptcy fraud.

LaRosa handled the sale of the Team Three equipment to Darrell Waltrip, then went to work for Waltrip as his engine builder. Instinct had told him not to take the job, but he accepted and as happened at Kenny Bernstein's shop, he found himself being pilloried by the managers and organization types who have recently come into racing to run race teams. When the team fared poorly in 1994, LaRosa was made the scapegoat. LaRosa left, gladly, happy to escape from men he says are the amateurs and ass-kissers who he contends have sabotaged Waltrip's efforts the past few years.

In 1994 Lou LaRosa walked away from racing, perhaps for good. He left behind the souvenir salesmen and the money guys, whom he refers to as the 'nitwit business managers in five-hundred-thousand-dollar motor homes.' He yearns for the days when winning was the priority, not the cash flow.

LOU LAROSA: "Ricky Rudd called in 1988 to ask if I'd build his motors, I said, 'Okay.' I've known Ricky over the years and liked him. He's a good driver who I figured could win.

"I went to Kenny Bernstein's place in Greenville, South Carolina, to see his operation. Bernstein drives drag cars, is a champion at it. The engine room was run inside a former smokehouse. The dyno was in what had once been a meat locker, where deer meat had been stored. It was filthy dirty, nasty. Bernstein had pumped big bucks into it, but it was the filthiest shop I've ever seen in my life.

"Bernstein made me a good financial offer, though I didn't leave Childress for money, because I was making a decent salary. Kenny made me certain promises about 'anything you want to do.' I told him, 'You can't run out of Greenville. We have to move near Charlotte.' It was like trying to run out of Daytona. There was nothing there; it wasn't centralized. Richard Childress was another one who didn't like being near Charlotte, where most of the teams are. His argument is that all the teams go out to eat together, and everyone is telling everyone else what they're doing, and one guy will leave for fifteen cents more, which is true. But it's also bullshit, because everybody sees everybody else at the racetrack. If a guy is going to stay, he's going to stay. If he's going to leave, he's going to leave.

"Kenny said he'd build me a new shop near Charlotte, and we did that in Huntersville, which is about fifteen miles north of Charlotte, and things went fair because it took the better part of a year to get organized. It was like starting a race team from scratch, and we didn't have the time.

"We started in November of 1988, and I had to order everything new. The first race was in February, and we had to move from Greenville *and* build everything from scratch.

"We started Daytona way down on power—*way* down. It was pathetic. I admit that. The year before Ricky had qualified great with an engine built by Ron Armstrong, a good guy who knew how to make good power. His expertise was in drag racing, and he was another guy who would run the motor, change the head, run the motor some more, make another change, and when you got all done, you might have gained two horsepower but the engines had no durability. Ricky would run like a son of a bitch half the race and blow up. His motors would run a short period of time and disintegrate.

"I took Ron's motor, the one they had qualified so good with the year before and dynoed it, and it was perfect, the same as before. They put the motor in the car, and they were nine miles an hour slower than what they ran the year before.

"Bernstein and our crew chief, Larry McReynolds, called up and they accused me of not having any horsepower. I said, 'Wait a minute. This is Ron Armstrong's motor, the same motor you qualified so good with last year. On the dyno it makes the exact same power, the same carburetor, same headers, same everything.' I said, 'It can't be that this is the same car.'

"Despite McReynolds's denials, the only thing the same about it was the name on it: Buick. When they had qualified the year before, they had narrowed up the car, and when it was on the track by itself it ran real good, but in traffic, it got squirrelly. So they brought the car back to the shop, and McReynolds cut the whole body off, put on what they call a table top, with quarterpanels on the back, and that car had so much downforce and drag, the car would drive itself through to China through the ground.

"But Larry told Bernstein it *was* the same car—until he was forced to tell the truth, that it *wasn't* the same car. Finally he admitted he had cut the car up and put a whole different body on it. And the whole time Larry was trying to throw off the blame on the motor.

"You'd a thought them sons a bitches would learn something as we went through the year, but the problem only got worse.

"A lot of the problem was that we were running a Buick. The car had a lot of down force. On a superspeedway it was a box. Nobody ran in that car. To make a car run you not only need low drag, you need to balance it with downforce. If the car isn't balanced, it will stick in the corners, but it won't go down the straightaway. Or else the car will go down the straightaway like a rocket, but it'll be unstable. The happy blend is a car that is not sucked to the ground and also isn't squirrelly.

"The Buick didn't run, and Larry McReynolds kept complaining about the motors, and I *know* we had decent horsepower. But we still couldn't run. The Buick was a slug. It ain't gonna outrun the other cars. So Bernstein had a brainstorm: he brought in another bullshit artist, Donald Seto, who made cylinder heads out in the Southwest. This was going to be a big thing for us. It took him three months to prepare his heads, which should have taken three or four days. He put them on, and this is the God's truth—it might have had fifteen more horsepower, but it was a high-rpm type of motor, long rods, short stroke, the wrong kind of motor for speedway racing. This is where the owner gets bullshitted. It shows more horsepower, but when you put the motor on the dyno, it wasn't there. I told them, 'This motor isn't going to run. It'll run at Bonneville, flat on the ground, where you don't have to lift and get back on the throttle.'

"We went to race, and it wouldn't run, qualified about dead last. We put another motor in, and we were running fast, but it was on the ragged edge. The cylinder head was really thin, close to the water jacket. Being a drag racer, Kenny kept insisting we needed a lot of horsepower. I told Kenny, 'You can't run this type of motor. Yes, it makes fifteen horsepower more, but you're going to blow it up, trying to tune it, tune it, tune it, making up for the car being a slug.' The next race we cracked the head in practice.

"'What are we going to do?' everyone wanted to know. I said, 'Put my race motor in.' 'How much difference is there in horsepower?' they wanted to know. I said, 'Don't worry about the freaking dyno sheet. Put the motor in.'

"The race motor was fifteen horsepower less, and was three-tenths faster on the racetrack! Kenny couldn't comprehend it. And neither could Larry McReynolds and the others who wanted to see the dyno sheet. I told them, 'Don't worry about the dyno sheet. I don't ask to see your results from the wind tunnel tests.'

"Ricky won a race at Sears Point and he finished eighth in the points, but at the end of the year he left us to go to Rick Hendrick, and for the '90 season Kenny brought in Brett Bodine. I didn't have a problem with Brett. He was straightforward and honest. Brett won the Wilkesboro race, the first race he ever won.

"But for another year the team was caught up in the Byzantine politics. McReynolds was the leader, always complaining: 'Get Bodine

out. He ain't doing this or that . . . ' And of course, they were campaigning for more horsepower, and it wasn't about horsepower. The
car was a slug. They had all the horsepower they needed.

"But I was working with a nitwit crew chief. We were running so
poorly in '89 that during the off-season Ray Smith, a representative
from Buick, told McReynolds what to do to make the car run faster,
but Larry was stubborn and wouldn't do it, so Buick went and had
people in Detroit called The Hammerworks put a body on the same
chassis, and they brought it down to Daytona to show Larry what they
did. The car wouldn't go 184 miles an hour. McReynolds told
Bernstein, 'If you put a gun to my head, I wouldn't know how to make
it go faster.' I told Larry, 'I have a lot of guns, and I'd like to have them
on your head.'

"After Brett ran approximately 184 miles an hour in Larry's car, we
pulled the motor out of the car, still steaming with the transmission
and all, and we dropped the son of a bitch in The Hammerworks' car,
and son of a bitch if Brett didn't run 193 miles an hour. I said to
myself right there, 'For him to sit there and . . . ' 'Cause all year long
McReynolds kept complaining over and over and over about 'Motor,
motor, motor, motor, motor.'

"And when that car went 194 miles an hour, that should have told
Bernstein something. If you look back, King Racing won three races
since Bernstein started running Winston Cup, and two of them were
with my motors.

"When you take a boy like that and they say, 'He's highly regarded,'
and at the same time they look down on Harry Hyde, who truly took
cars back in the sixties and seventies and with Buddy Baker ran over
200 miles an hour. Harry took Bobby Isaac to Bonneville and set all
sorts of records. Look at Robert Gee, a creative person, who really
knew how to make something. Larry never took the heat. And then
he comes with his bullshit.

"I'll tell you another story why I don't think much of Larry
Reynolds. We had a qualifying motor with titanium rods, which we
weren't supposed to run, but we ran them. One rod was maybe forty
grams lighter than the ordinary rod. Multiply that by the number of
rods, and our saving was maybe a half a pound total. You do it because
the rotating reciprocal weight when the motor is running makes
ounces mean a lot. So we ran the motor with Ricky twice in '89 and

did good. The third time we used the motor was at Rockingham in '90 with Brett Bodine. Qualifying wasn't that hot.

"I came down the next day. Larry and John Dangler, Bernstein's gopher, were running the motor and literally were going crazy. I said, 'What's wrong?' They said, 'You fucked us up. The nose weight of that race motor is thirty-five pounds heavier than the testing motor, and you screwed up the balance of that car.' I said, 'There isn't a half pound difference between the motors in total weight.' They said, 'Yeah, you fucked us up.'

"I said, 'I got a question. You practiced all morning. Now you are weighing the car in the afternoon. Did you put any gas in the car this morning?'

"And they just looked at me. I said, 'Push it down the scales.' They did, and they put six gallons of gas in the car. Gas weighs approximately six pounds a gallon. There was their 35 pounds. The car balanced right out again.

"I thought to myself, You stupid son of a bitch. And you're supposed to be smart.

"It's no wonder why I left Bernstein, because I did like Kenny. But Bernstein wouldn't leave Buick because he was committed to Buick, though he did promise to switch to Ford the next year, which he did. We'd sit in these meetings, and I'm not hot on meetings, but Bernstein would have these suck-asses who'd 'yes' him to death. It reminded me of the tale of the king with no clothes. 'You look beautiful with your clothes.' But you ain't got no clothes. And they would tell Kenny what he wanted to hear.

"Look, if my motor is screwed up, and you can show me I'm screwed up, I'll change. I'm not that hardheaded. But if you're saying generally that my motors don't have horsepower, I can tell you this: 'I know I've won a bunch of races.' I say this to Larry and these other idiots, 'I know I'm in the top five in engine building. But even if I'm in the top ten, why are we running fortieth? Are all the rest better engine builders? Am I thirty-ninth in engine building? There ain't no way.

"Sitting in the meetings and listening to Larry sucking ass and telling Bernstein what he wanted to hear—and in defense of Kenny, he was trying to run a drag car, trying to run an Indy car, trying to run a stock car; he's a smart man. But you have to be there all the time. He was getting scattered information.

"Finally, I left. I said to myself, 'This ain't going nowhere.' Bernstein paid me for the rest of the year. Everything that man said he'd do, he did. He always kept his word. But the man got bullshitted bad by these other people. They went and hired a bunch of new people, and they still ran like shit the rest of the year. And it wasn't because of the engines. With a Buick, with a Ford, with Bodine, without Bodine, they ran like shit so long as Larry McReynolds was there. Larry's true colors will come out some day. We'll see how Earnhardt runs with him as crew chief in '97. [Dale didn't win a single race in '97.]

"The hardest thing Larry did was leave Bernstein and go to Robert Yates. Larry and Robert supposedly had a love-match forever, ran well with Davey Allison, and then in '96 Ernie Irvan was having a mediocre year, and the prick jumps ship. I'll bet Ernie found out his true colors. If Larry really respected Ernie—he shed those crocodile tears when Ernie crashed and almost died—then he would have stuck with the man while he was recovering. I had stood with Earnhardt when he was hurt. And the other boys did too.

"I got a call from Barry Dodson, who I knew from my days at M. C. Anderson. Barry told me about two guys who wanted to start a new team, called Team Three, owned by Sam McMahon III, whose father was the first to own a Days Inn franchise in Charlotte and who was supposed to have a ton of money. I met with this guy, and he was smooth as silk. He was young, had monogrammed cuff links, had money up the yin-yang. He said he wanted to start a team and that he had hired a top architect, Dennis Yates, to build a state-of-the-art facility like what Hendrick has now, with a glass front, show cars in view like a dealership, and his driver was to be Mickey Gibbs. Barry was to be the crew chief, and I was the engine builder. Money was to be no object. I thought, What the hell. I'll try it. I wanted to get away from racing and go more into research and development, and this building was designed for that. It was what Sam wanted to do in '91. This was going to be my chance to go into R&D, like what Hendrick does now.

"In the beginning the checks were good, but then they started to bounce as the money dried up. We'd have to redeposit them, and it didn't take too long to see that this whole thing was a scam. Sam bought all this equipment, and it turned out he was skimming the money from the Days Inn franchise. His father, a rich man, not only owned the Days Inn hotel in Charlotte but Florida properties and a management company. They had limited investors and all this money, and they told the investors they were going to buy bankrupt properties for ten cents on the dollar, all these hotels worth hundreds of millions of dollars. When some of the investors took Sam to court, he was indicted for fraud, and he ended up having the largest bankruptcy fraud trial in the history of North Carolina. Sam was convicted and went to jail in 1996.

"Sam would always say, 'Money is no object. You can have anything you want,' which looking back is funny as shit. One day I said to him, 'The traffic is killing us after races. Wouldn't it be great to leave the track in a helicopter?' Sam ordered an Augusta helicopter costing several million dollars. Rick Hendrick had ordered it, but Sam offered an extra $60,000 just so he could have it. Sam had two airplanes. He had a beautiful summer house on Lake Norman. During the summer he catered a party for two hundred guests, put up a big tent, had some spread. It was a beautiful house, but he said he intended to tear it down because he also owned the lot next door, and the house wasn't centered. Crazy. He had a yacht that on Lake Norman looked like an ocean liner. 'Come on, let's go for a ride.' About thirty of us went with him. There was champagne and hors d'oeuvres. He was at the controls, holding up a champagne glass. 'To the team,' he said. I said to my wife, 'This is too good to be true.' And it was. Just joking, I said, 'I hope they didn't take fingerprints of everybody on that boat.'

"It was all a scam. Sam bled the companies dry. But he sure treated us good.

"At first it wasn't obvious it was a scam. Like all good con artists, he convinced you everything was on the up-and-up. He fired Mickey Gibbs and hired Kenny Wallace and brought in a sponsor, Dirt Devil, who came up with the big bucks. And then Sam skimmed millions from Dirt Devil. They gave him a big check at the end of year banquet, and he never did anything with it. So the whole operation folded, went into Chapter 11, and that was it.

"And this time I really intended to get out of racing when one of Darrell Waltrip's people told me he wanted to put in his own engine room. Darrell had left Rick Hendrick, started his own team but was renting motors from Hendrick. I had known Darrell from our DiGard days, so I helped him get a deal on the motors from Team Three, cause they were brand-new, the best of the best, and all paid for legally. After buying it, Sam had sold it to a lease company, and the lease company held the lien and wanted their money. So Darrell got a good price.

"Darrell called and asked if I would set up the equipment for him. From there he asked me to be his engine builder. I didn't want to, cause he's a person who's implacable, who has his own ideas and is stubborn, and it was on my mind to get out, but I said, Oh, hell, I'll go ahead and do it, and I set that equipment up and built an engine room.

"Darrell spent the money. He's not cheap. But all through his career Darrell and engine people and Darrell and crew chiefs don't get along too well. 'Cause it's never Darrell's fault. It's never him. It's *always* someone else.

"And the other problem Darrell has is that he's easily deceived by people. When I first went over there, Darrell said, 'Talk to Sam Conway.' I had never heard of this guy. At our first meeting Conway proceeded to tell me he had invented the heads Robert Yates was using. He said, 'We have all this equipment we bought.' He didn't know he had bought it through me. He said, 'We're going to send away to an outside company, and they're going to show us how to set up an engine room.'

"I said, 'Look, you bought the equipment from me. I've set up ten engine rooms. I don't need anyone to help me set it up.' And he got insulted.

"I came back the next day, and Conway apologized. He said, 'I didn't realize who you are. But you have to realize that two years ago I didn't know anything about Winston Cup racing.' Turns out Sam Conway had made false teeth in Lynchburg, Virginia, when he got involved with the church clique, and Darrell hired him to run his shop. Now a Christian race team is a good idea, or at least it was in Darrell's eyes. But this guy didn't know as much about racing as I did about making false teeth. He would tell you the most idiotic things. But that was Darrell. He liked having people around to feed his ego, the 'yes' people. So he's easily deceived when people kiss his ass.

"It took him until the end of the first year as things got worse and worse to discover that Sam Conway didn't know anything about racing—this is why I don't want to be in racing anymore—and he hired another bullshit artist by the name of Clyde Booth to blow Sam out. Clyde Booth's claim to fame was that he had been a manager for UPS up in Connecticut. He had worked for Rob Moroso, Dick's son, and Darrell said, 'Clyde is a very smart man.' Understand, everybody Darrell hires is a 'very smart man.' Well, this guy had no history or wins or championships either. Darrell ensconces him in an office, pays him big money, buys him a computer. At the same time Jeff

Hammond, an excellent crew chief, a guy who was supposed to be like a brother to Darrell, was forced out.

"We started the '94 season at Daytona with Barry Dodson as the crew chief, and I'm the engine builder, and we qualified tremendously well, in the top five. Darrell beat good cars like Kodak. Darrell was on top of the world, and he was praising Clyde Booth to the heavens. And Clyde was taking his bows and taking the credit.

"Lo and behold, we start the 125, and Darrell went right to the back. 'What's wrong, Clyde?' 'I don't know. I'm going to let Barry make that decision.' We were running on Hoosier tires, and we changed to Goodyears.

"We started the 500 and went right to the back. Darrell was getting lapped. He was going so slowly, he could sit there and smoke a cigarette. I said, 'Clyde, what are you going to do?' 'That's Barry's decision. I'm not going to interfere.' I thought to myself, You prick. You took the credit when we qualified. Now when we're running lousy, you're throwing off the problems on Barry.

"This went on all year as the car got worse and worse. Darrell kept saying, 'Clyde has a computer . . . ' Clyde was bullshitting Darrell with that Computer Aid Design. Like McReynolds, Clyde could talk the talk. Meanwhile, when Darrell wasn't there, Clyde was marketing parts for front ends, rear ends, parts to align the cars. The packaging said, 'Designed by Clyde Booth.' Now if you're a good team manager or crew chief or engine builder, you don't have time to go to the bathroom when you're racing. All you should be doing is working on the car. And he wasn't doing anything for Darrell as that car was running worse and worse. And he was another prick blaming the motors, blaming Barry.

"In July of '94 we went down to the Fourth of July race at Daytona, and we were as slow as shit. And this was with the same motor that had qualified so well for the 500. Clyde had gotten his hands on the car, and now we couldn't qualify in the top thirty-five, which means either that the driver isn't on the gas or the car is a slug. 'Cause it's the same motor. Clyde kept saying, 'The motor doesn't run. The motor doesn't run.' I saw the handwriting on the wall.

"I came in on Monday, and Mr. UPS said to me, 'I got bad news.' I said, 'What's that?' He said, 'Darrell said I'm going to have to let you go.' I said, 'Okay, now what's the bad news?'

"That dumb cluck just looked at me. I said, 'I'll get my toolbox and be out of here.' And when I left that place, I felt like someone had lifted twenty thousand pounds off my shoulder.

"Eight months later Darrell finally caught on and fired him, rolled his ass out the door, and he hired back Jeff Hammond and Waddell Wilson. But see, Darrell had hated Waddell. Darrell had hated Jeff. And it was all because Darrell has always been a follower, not a leader, not an innovative person. If Darrell had just stuck to driving—in his heyday he was a top driver. But even back when he was a youngster he was a follower, and you can't win races following what people do. If you copy someone, you can only be as good as they are. I've always said about building motors, 'It's not what they have, but how they got there.' How did they arrive at that? What logic led them to run a particular cam? What logic brought them to put the body on the car this way?

"Once you know how something works, you know how to change it. But the ones who copy people never see the whole picture. A friend of mine, Big John Simmons, would say about these people, 'They'd look at the picture, and they'd read the caption, but they never read the whole story so they only have a periphery view of it.'

"But Darrell was susceptible to that sort of person, the people who blew smoke up his ass. Every way the wind would blow, he would blow, because he believed them. And in my opinion it's because deep down he doesn't have faith. He says he does, but he has never had faith in his own people. Instead, he's always belittled them.

"And Darrell hasn't won since I left. I don't know how many Winston Cup champion provisionals he's taken to enter races, and then he'd run at the back of the field. His career is finished, but he won't admit it. Everybody's career comes to an end. And the same guys who in front of him are saying he's a great driver, behind his back are saying he can't drive. And he blames the motors, the cars, and they 'yes' him.

"I said to myself, Racing has turned into a commercial. It doesn't matter whether he wins anymore. All that matters is that he's a good spokesman for the sponsor. And Dale Earnhardt can deny it—they all can deny it—but the T-shirt sales and the souvenirs are more important than the race team. They'll say, 'We want to win.' Bullshit. Before, racing wasn't about money. It was about winning. All those nights you spent working on the car in the shop wasn't about money. You're not thinking about how much money you're making. You're not thinking about the glory. You're thinking, I have to get this done. Just like a good golfer who hits hundreds and hundreds of ball every day. Like the determination of a good boxer. It's about winning.

"These drivers now want to have chairmen of the boards, want to own sports companies, own magazines. They want to have something after racing, which is good, but where is the priority when you make four million racing and forty million selling souvenirs? They bring these nitwits in, these so-called business managers, and they feed these drivers a lot of shit about how good they are, and they are up in the suites sipping champagne while the guys in the shop and the pits are doing the work, and if the car doesn't run, they're sons of bitches. But if the car does win, the nitwits are the ones raking in the big bonuses while the workers are getting peanuts. What you're seeing now is a bunch of clowns, glory hounds, business people. These guys have $500,000 motor homes. What does the crew get?

"Is this bad? I don't know. It's certainly better to be making six figures rather than the hundred a week we used to make. But is it pure racing? Is it bad or good? I don't know. But for me, I've always considered myself a pure racer, and so when I walked out that day, I knew that was the end of it. I said to myself, the management-type of people—the Larry McReynolds and the Clyde Booths who blow smoke and bullshit—are coming into racing, and the guys who are getting pushed out are the racing people like Harry Hyde, Junior Johnson, Smokey Yunick, Jake Elder, myself. We're getting pushed to the side to make room for the bullshit people with computers.

"And I say to all you computer people, remember it's 3.1416, which if you know your math is pi. They are always trying to pi-R-square you. But the stupid sons of bitches don't know that pi are round. Cornbread is square. And they can take their computers and have a good time with them, because that ain't racing like it used to be."

43

HE (AND THE SPORT) SURVIVES AND FLOURISHES

IN 1985 BUDDY BAKER STARTED his own race team. He had several chances to win races, but failed. In '87 he did win the Winston Open, a contest held at the Charlotte Motor Speedway for race teams that had not won all year long.

Meanwhile, Baker watched Tim Richmond die of AIDS, and Alan Kulwicki and Davey Allison die in separate flying accidents. He saw the pall that hung over the sport. In 1988, in fact, he almost died himself, after a scary crash head-on into a wall at Charlotte. After suffering blackouts and dizziness, Baker went to see a neurologist who diagnosed him with an aneurysm. "My God, how are you alive?" he was asked. He underwent an operation and survived. He was told he was living on the bonus plan.

After the operation Baker sold the race team and turned to broadcasting, where he has become an outstanding color commentator on TNN and CBS. He still tire tests to keep his hand in.

Baker can attest to the fact that despite the terrible losses the sport has suffered in the last half dozen years, new blood is arriving to the scene to fill the void. You can't replace a Richmond or a Kulwicki or a Davey Allison, but exciting new talent will keep the fans coming to the races and attract millions more to their TV sets.

As one example, Baker witnessed Jeff Gordon's becoming a NASCAR star after the young ace enrolled at the Buck Baker Driving School. Today it is the Dale Earnhardt/Jeff Gordon dual that most excites race fans, as the Kid challenges the Legend.

Baker is confident that NASCAR, like he has himself, will survive and flourish despite all the tragedy.

BUDDY BAKER: "After twenty-five years in racing, I decided in 1985 to start my own racing team. I went in with Danny Schiff, a clothing manufacturer who makes Bullfrog Knits, high-class children's apparel. God, he loved racing better than anybody alive. He had a lot of money and was very passionate about our race team. I've heard people say, 'He's a hard guy to get to know,' but he was never anything but first-class around me.

"I hired the crew. When I picked Booby Harrington to be my crew chief, people said, 'Why are you doing that?' I said, 'He's in place. He has a garage. He's got all the parts to make this thing work, and he's a talented guy.' I had worked with him when we were at K&K Insurance with Harry Hyde. I hired Slick Johnson and a bunch of really good mechanics. Rick Hendrick has a lot of them working for him today.

"The first year we were putting it together. We had one race car to go to Daytona, and in our first race we finished fourth. I thought that was pretty good. I thought, Boy, we're ready to go here, but then reality set in. You can't take a team from ground zero and make it into a winner. You can buy a team that's been operating for eight or nine years and go to work, but this was a brand-new deal, and at the same time we were building a bigger race shop.

"We had success in some races. I lapped the field at the July Fourth race at Daytona in '86 in my own car. Dale Earnhardt was a lap down with just a few laps to go. Dale hadn't blown an engine in I don't know how long. I said to myself, God, I'm running side-by-side with Dale Earnhardt with a lap lead on the field. This is stupid. Let him go. And the minute I said that, *boom*, he lost his motor, went up against the wall, set off a huge wreck, and another driver came across the infield and knocked me into the wall. Tim Richmond went on to win.

"We had good race cars, and we were working toward something good. We didn't win, but it's hard to win. Look at Cale. Cale never won a race with his race team. He hasn't won one yet, has he? That tells you how tough it is to put everyone in place.

"But we should have won that race. I was in position. And one nice thing, we had a wonderful bunch of guys working for me. Last year, a bunch of them got together and came to see me during a race at Talladega. They walked up and said, 'Now that we've had time to reflect on it, it was the happiest time we ever had.' It was a family group, and we were working well, until I knocked my head a couple years later.

"Tim Richmond won a lot of races in '86. He was a teammate back in the eighties when I went with Hoss Ellington. He ran ARCA in another Hoss Ellington car, and I got to know him pretty well. I never saw his wild nights. There was such a big age difference between the two of us, and we were so different. I know he was quite a ladies' man and he had all the money he needed to be that. His lifestyle was totally different, alien to anything I had ever done or been around. 'Cause from the day I started racing until I quit, I didn't know what spending a weekend on a yacht was. I'm old school. I lived a different lifestyle.

"I will tell you this: Tim had the ability to get more out of shape and regain control of that race car again, very much the same as Earnhardt, and had he lived and not gotten himself into the problems he had, the battles that Dale and Davey Allison and Tim Richmond would have had . . . if you think the sport is big now, whew.

"In '87, I won the Winston Open. We had led at Darlington, had a chance to win there, but Davey had an engine problem and I got up a little too high, got into the oil that was down on the track, and I crashed. It was a series of things like that. But we did have seven top ten finishes, including a second and third, and when it's your stuff you are doubly proud to run in the top five all day long with people like Davey Allison and Alan Kulwicki.

"I knew Davey when he was a little boy running around in the garage area. He was into everything. He liked to get a joke on you if he could. I went through ninety percent of my racing career without anybody finding out I was ticklish. One time Davey walked up behind me and kind of scooched me on the back of the leg, and I kicked a guy in the seat of his pants, and from then on my life in the garage area was made crazy by Davey. He would see me and start grinning, and

he'd sneak around behind me and would tickle me. He knew I react-
ed strongly. I'd go straight up. To me he was like a little kid, a mis-
chievous guy who was fun to be around. We ran a lot of Legends races
all over the country, and we'd go together. I got to know him really
well. Those kinds of guys, you don't replace them. There might be
somebody else to come along who runs well. But Davey was a genuine
personality. And being from the Allison family, racing was his life.
There wasn't any football or basketball or baseball. It was racing.
There is something pure about that to someone like myself who was
brought up in racing. He was a friend before I really ever met him.

"Alan was another one. For the people who knew him, like Rusty
Wallace, came nothing but admiration for Alan from the time they
met him and for what he had done in the short period of time with
his own race team. The guys who worked for him would tell me stories about him. They would work up to the time to put the final setup
for qualifying the car, and he would send everyone home and do the
final touch-up himself.

"It was a combination that worked for him. He was an engineer. He
was very private. My wife and I went to the Speedway Club in
Charlotte one night, and Alan was sitting by himself. This was a holiday night, and Alan walked over, and I said, 'Sit down with us.' And
we had dinner together, and he was just a delightful guy. But he was
so private, it was almost like he acted mad at you, because he was so
in focus with what he was doing that some people didn't like him.
They didn't understand. A lot of people didn't take racing as seriously as Alan. That was the total focus of his life.

"You could tell how intense he was. I've watched his best friends
walk up and start a conversation, and he'd look up at the stars and
walk away. Alan wasn't just a driver, not by any means.

"We lost Tim Richmond, Alan, and Davey. That's star quality. See,
there is a huge pool out there, just like Jeff Gordon coming in. At one
time everybody said that Jeff Gordon was going to be the Indycar driver of the future. He was going to be your A. J. Foyt or Mario
Andretti. He went to my father's driving school, called his mom that
night, and said, 'Mom, I've made up my mind what I want to do the
rest of my life.' He wanted Winston Cup cars. Well, believe me, as far
as Indy racing goes, that was a kick in the pants for them no matter
what anybody says. 'Cause stars like him don't come along that often.

You never replace anybody, but the pool for Winston Cup right now is strong. It really is. It's a strong sport that's been able to survive the loss of three stars of that magnitude.

"My career as a competitive driver ended on May 29, 1988, at Charlotte, where I won my first major race. It was a time when there was a tire war between Goodyear and Hoosier, but that had nothing to do with it.

"The funny part about it, I was very, very careful about what I was doing that day. I was running just fast enough to stay in the top five. It got to the point where I could listen to a car near me and predict that he was going to have trouble, and that had happened two or three times. I thought I was really playing it cool, but then I looked up, and Eddie Bierschwale had spun around. Bobby Allison had run down to the bottom part of the track to avoid him and had gotten into the dirt, and he shot straight across the racetrack, and after he made contact with me, I went head-on into the wall. My head actually bent the roll cage that goes down to the right-front corner. I came out of the seat that far.

"I went to the hospital with a tremendous headache, and they thought maybe I had broken my neck. As they checked me over, I kept telling them, 'I'm not worried about my neck. My head hurts.'

"I was still in the top five in points, and I figured I'd try to make it to the end of the year. At night I started getting real bad headaches and started losing my balance walking. I was always a person who played a little hurt when I had to, and I convinced myself that everything was okay, that whatever I was going through would go away.

"I went to Talladega, where I finished tenth, and I was racing down to the very end with several cars when Benny Parsons checked up and I never saw him. I ran right into the back of him at 210 miles an hour and almost triggered a huge wreck. I said to myself, Geez, I saw that way back, but I just didn't react. I knew I had a problem.

"That next week I went to the road course at Watkins Glen, and I noticed that when I went through the corners, I felt good, but when I went down the straightaway, I felt lousy. And I didn't know why. I was going down the back straightaway at 160 miles an hour at Watkins Glen, and it was like somebody turned off the lights. I went, 'Whooooaaaa.' I went off the track, and when I came to, I was almost in the woods. I wrestled it back, slowed down and pulled off the race course. I thought, What in the world? I put it back in low gear and started back up the hill, and all of a sudden the racetrack looked like it was moving in front of me. I said, That's it.

"I went in, and I saw Dr. Jerry Punch standing there, and I said, 'I need to talk to you about something. I'm getting three-dimensional figures in my eyesight, and almost a sickness when I go to my right. And I blacked out going down the straightaway just now. I almost crashed.'

"Jerry said, 'You have an aneurysm. You have a real problem. Let me give you the name of a doctor. Get yourself home.'

"Along then I knew something was really bad. I wasn't able to talk myself out of it anymore. He gave me Dr. Jerry Petty's name in Charlotte. He's one of the best surgeons for neurology.

"Do you believe this: I drove my crew back from Watkins Glen to Charlotte that night. They laid down in the back of my van, and I drove all the way back.

"I went in to see Dr. Petty at his office for a CAT scan. He told me, 'My God, how are you alive?' I said, 'What are you talking about?' He said, 'You have a place up there as big as my fist where your skull was cracked and it bled into the outer part of your brain.' What was happening was that the pressure of the blood up there had pushed my brain off center, so when I'd go through the corner on a regular oval track, my brain would straighten up, go where it belonged. And when I went on a road course, the turns put double the pressure on it. After the operation and after he realized I was going to make it, Dr. Petty said, 'I don't know what's in store for you the rest of your life, but I can tell you that you are on a bonus plan. You should have been dead already.'

"For six months I was in la-la land. I tried to come back and run the race team, hired a couple drivers to run for me, and I realized it just wasn't the same. Owning the car wasn't enough for me. And at that time I wasn't convinced I couldn't come back.

"For a long time I did a dance with NASCAR, and looking back I'm glad they didn't say, 'You look okay.' Because I was really able to get well. I didn't mess around and have any aftereffects. I sat out all of '89, and then I wanted to run a limited schedule, but NASCAR said, 'You're going to need all kinds of tests,' and I said, 'If it's that much a concern to you guys, then maybe I'm not ready to come back anyhow.'

So that's why I stayed out as long as I did. Quite frankly, it was the blessing of all time. Because even though I was very competitive in '87, there's a time it means something extra special, and then comes a time when it's something to do.

"I came back, and the clincher came when I drove Derrick Close's car at Daytona in 1990. I finished eleventh in the race, and God, the crew came up and was hugging my neck. I thought, What? I would have burned a leg off to run that bad. I told myself, It is time for this old cat to think of something else to do.

"Quite frankly, I can run as good as anybody. But though I wanted to drive only a few races a year, I realized that the top-notch rides aren't available, and I went to work with my dad at the driving school. I still enjoy teaching.

"Then I started testing for teams, and that was the ultimate for me, to be able to go back to Daytona and Talladega, to go run well and still know a little more about what's going on out there than most of them.

"Then I began broadcasting with TNN, and they liked me enough to give me the time to go through the growing pains of going on national television and find out out what I was going to talk about. So all of a sudden, this was my passion and not driving. And it's been a challenge. Because I was brought up to be a race car driver. I was not brought up to be an announcer, not by a long shot. But to hear people say, 'Man, you do a good job at it,' for me that's like winning Daytona."

INDEX

Alexander, Mike, 372
Allen, Johnny, 73, 82
Allen, Loy, Jr., 346, 362
Allison, Bobby, xv, xvi,
    70–71, 104, 105,
    145, 148–49,
    169–70, 173–74,
    175, 176, 183, 193,
    199, 202, 205, 209,
    242, 249, 253, 254,
    271, 277, 280, 285,
    288, 295, 296, 304,
    319, 320, 369, 370,
    371, 372, 374, 375,
    376, 381, 399
Allison, Clifford, xv, 369,
    377–78
Allison, Davey, xv–xvi,
    xvii, 70, 169–70,
    176, 244, 251, 253,
    273, 281, 354, 355,
    356, 357, 363, 366,
    369–82, 389, 395,
    397, 398
Allison, Judy, xvi, 369,
    376, 381
Allison, Lisa, 378, 379
Allison, Liz, xviii, 369–82
Allison, Pam, 372
Allison, Pop, 375
All Pro circuit, 349
Amick, Bill, 27, 36, 117
Anderson, John, 281
Anderson, M.C., 285,

287–88, 289, 299,
    301–2, 309, 317,
    318, 319–20, 321,
    389
Andretti, John, 244
Andretti, Mario, 199, 201,
    202, 305, 398
Andrews, Paul 345–62
Armstrong, Ron, 385
Arrington, Tom, 8
Asheville-Weaverville
    track, 12
Atlanta, races at, 56, 359,
    379
Atlanta Motor Speedway,
    xviii, 2

Baerz, Richie, 250
Baker, Buck, 46, 63, 64,
    90, 100, 101, 102–3,
    107, 111, 118, 153,
    220, 260, 273, 278,
    285, 286, 293, 327
Baker, Cannonball, 4
Baker, Elzie Wylie
    "Buddy", xvii, xviii,
    44, 99–109, 164,
    168, 169, 170, 171,
    175, 176, 211–16,
    249–58, 265, 266,
    327, 340, 387,
    395–401
Ballard, Walter, 252
Beaty, Dick, 226, 352

Beauchamp, Johnny, 56, 58, 82, 117, 120
Bernstein, Kenny, 90, 383, 384, 385, 386, 387, 388, 389
Bickle, Rich, 187
Biederman, Don, 174
Bierschwale, Eddie, 399
Birmingham International Raceway (BIR), 372, 373
Bisher, Furman, 44
Bland, Sammy, 4, 142
Bodine, Brett, 362, 381, 383, 386, 387, 388, 389
Bodine, Diane, 381
Bodine, Geoff, 112, 275, 283–84, 312, 324, 346, 359, 362
Bodine, Kathy, 284
Bondy, Ned, 166–67
Bonnett, David, 366, 380
Bonnett, Neil, xvii, 145, 146, 149, 280, 284, 291, 296, 297, 302, 366, 372
Booth, Clyde, 391, 392
Bouchard, Ken, 325
Bowman-Gray Stadium, 66, 68, 69, 70, 241, 321, 332, 333
Bracken, J.D., 174
Brewer, Tim, 319, 327
Bristol, races at, 222, 324, 354, 355, 359, 361, 375
Brooks, Bob, 361–62
Brooks, Dick, 254
Brookstone Boulevard Speedway, 5
Bruner, Mary, 121
Brunner, John, Jr., 176
Burkelette, J.P., 200
Busch Clash, 290, 292, 308, 324, 325, 354
Byron, Red, 5, 15, 19

Campbell, Malcolm, 2
Carter, Bill, 321
Charles, Arnold, 67
Charlotte, races at, 5, 7, 9, 11, 13, 16, 17, 46, 47, 100, 120, 134, 135, 168, 182, 213, 214, 219, 252, 283, 303, 356, 373, 375
World 600, 57, 81, 168, 169, 182, 214, 252, 254, 255, 279, 281, 366
World Service Life 300, 303
Charlotte Motor Speedway, 2, 57, 83, 127, 141, 217–18, 221, 226, 234, 237, 259, 316
about, 141
Chevrolet, Louis, 3
Childress, Richard, xvi, 66, 70, 270, 273, 314, 317, 318, 320–29, 331–36, 383, 384
Christian, Sara, 5
Clemens, Crawford, 80, 153
Clems, Louis, 153
Close, Derrick, 401
Coca-Cola 600, 373
Colvin, Bob, 65
Concord Speedway, 70, 117–18
Conway, Sam, 391
Cox, Marion, 105
Cunningham, Briggs, 111, 122

Dangler, John, 388
Darlington, races at, 6, 10, 19, 22, 37, 54–55, 61, 65, 68, 71, 75, 81, 89, 90, 97, 103, 115, 121, 135, 140, 146, 167, 170, 191, 193, 196, 218, 250, 251, 254, 304, 313, 324, 333, 359, 365, 371, 379, 397
Rebel 400, 193, 251
Rebel 500, 196
Southern 500, 65, 71, 121, 123, 239, 242, 306, 308
David, Gus, 117
Davis, Stump, 246, 247
Days of Thunder, 339, 340
Daytona, races at, 2, 17, 18, 19, 21, 25, 33, 54, 62, 63, 116–17, 122, 127, 128, 134, 136, 140, 166,

215, 262–63, 295. *See also*
Daytona 500
Firecracker 250, 79
Firecracker 400, 123, 147, 194,
215, 255, 286, 295, 319
Firecracker 500, 120
Daytona 500, 6, 51, 55–56, 57, 80, 82,
83, 107, 111, 120, 123, 129, 155,
181, 201, 249, 251, 253, 284,
285, 286, 287, 288, 291, 292,
295, 297, 300, 312, 313, 320,
322, 354, 355, 359, 373, 374,
375, 385, 387, 392, 396, 401
1959, 55–56, 58
1960, 80
1961, 51, 55, 57, 82
1962, 180, 300
1963, 83
1964, 181
1965, 107
1972, 285
1976, 189, 195, 286
1978, 288
1980, 291, 292, 293
1983, 295
1988, 324–25
1991, 373
1992, 374–75
1993, 359
Daytona International Speedway, xviii,
2, 6, 11, 55–56, 78, 118–19, 120
Deiringer, Darel, 12
Deland, D. J., 283
Delaney, Jim, 299, 302, 303, 309
Dennis, Bradley, 80
DePaolo, Pete, 33–34, 35, 116, 117
Dieringer, Darel, 136, 147, 163, 206
Diffie, Joe, 369, 370
DiGard, 239, 242, 244, 245, 246, 247,
363, 364
Dodson, Barry, 389, 392
Dorton, Randy, 324
Dover, races at, 355, 359
Dunnaway, Glenn, 9–10, 17

Eargle, Maurice F. "Pop", 12
Earles, H. Clay, 229
Earnhardt, Dale, xvii, 45, 66, 70, 71,
91, 93, 104, 143, 169, 170, 199,
235, 243, 283, 292, 293, 297,
299–309, 311, 314, 317, 318,
319, 321–26, 328, 329, 331,
334, 335, 336, 354, 356, 361,
363, 364, 373, 374, 389, 393,
396, 397
emergence of, 299–309
Earnhardt, Ralph, xvii, 66, 82, 89, 91,
92–93, 98, 99, 104–5
Earnhardt, Teresa, 307
Economacki, Chris, 300
Elder, "Suitcase" Jake, xviii, 199–204,
208, 293, 299, 304, 305, 306,
308, 309, 363–67, 369, 394
Elkhart Lake, 64
Ellington, Hoss, 197, 286, 293, 294,
397
Elliott, Betty, 16
Elliott, Bill, 307, 324, 325, 326, 355,
356, 357, 358–59, 363, 365, 377
Elliott, Buddy, 16
Elliott, Harold, 319, 320
Epton, Joe, 129, 216
Eubanks, Joe, 9, 11, 153

Falcone, Cammy, 240
Falk, Betty, 129
Farmer, Red, 105, 380
Filmar Racing, 366
Firecracker 250, 79
Firecracker 400, 123, 147, 194, 215,
255, 286, 295, 319
Firecracker 500, 120
Fish, Robert, 33
Fishel, Herb, 67
Flagler, Henry, 3
Flock, Bob, 5, 6, 13, 14, 15, 16, 17,
19, 24, 54
Flock, Carl, 14, 15
Flock, Ethel, 5

Flock, Fonty, 5, 6, 13, 14, 15, 16, 54–55, 62, 65, 68, 75, 142, 218

Flock, Frances, 13, 23, 24, 44

Flock, Reo, 14–15

Flock, Tim, xviii, 5, 6, 13–26, 44, 54, 59–64, 65, 75, 90, 99, 100, 101, 116, 217–22, 223–24, 234–35, 237

Ford, Henry, 3

Fox, Ray, 107, 156, 157, 169, 211, 212, 213, 214

Fox, Ray, Jr., 277, 282

Foyt, A.J., 88, 107, 125, 285, 286, 348, 398

Fraisson, Nicki, 345, 348

France, Anne, 9

France, Bill, Jr., 3–4, 9, 66

France, Bill, Sr., xvii, 1–2, 3, 4–5, 6, 8, 9, 15, 16, 17, 18, 25, 33, 44, 60, 73, 75, 78, 80, 81, 82, 84, 119, 120, 122, 124, 125, 134, 139–41, 185, 217, 218, 219, 221, 234, 235, 255, 270, 271, 333

Frank, Larry, 76, 77–78, 121, 259, 265, 272

Frasson, Joe, 256

Freismuth, Donna, xv

Gahan, Ernie, 122

Ganat, Harry, 84

Gant, Harry, 303, 319

Gardner, Bill, 242, 245, 246, 364, 365

Gardner, Jim, 239, 242, 245, 246, 364

Gasoline Alley, 3

Gee, Robert, 242–46, 277, 278, 281, 282, 363, 387

Gibbs, Mickey, 389, 390

Gibson, Eddie, 282

Goings, A.C., 130

Gondolfo, Sonny, 74

Gondolfo, Vince, 74

Gordon, Jeff, xvii, 88, 235, 396, 398

Grady, Sandy, 43, 45

Granatelli, Andy, 73–74, 75, 80, 186

Grand American circuit, 269, 270, 331, 332

Grand National races, 5, 17, 18, 23, 27, 36, 46, 75, 89, 104, 213, 335

Greensboro, 55

Greenville-Pickens Speedway, 55, 89, 94, 154, 165, 175

Gurney, Dan, 123, 308

Gurrell, Bob, 327

Guthrie, Janet, 287

Hagan, Billy, 365, 366

Hall, Roy, 5, 15

Hamilton, Pete, 250

Hammond, Jeff, 391–92

Harbison, Tom, 115, 116

Hardtops, The, 114

Harrington, Booby, 396

Hawk, Don, 361

Hawkins, Alvin, 75

Hawkins, Joe, 75

Haygood, Tiny, 59–60

Hendrick, Rick, 275, 283, 284, 311, 314, 315, 316, 386, 389, 390, 396

Hendrick Motorsports, 316, 383

Hensley, Jimmy, 361–62

Hillin, Bobby, 282, 339, 377

Hoffa, Jimmy, 217–18, 220, 221

Hogg, Boss, 302, 321

Holloway, Lynn, 82

Holman, John, 27, 35–36, 79, 85, 114, 200, 201, 206, 207, 208. See also Holman-Moody

Holman-Moody, 8, 11, 27, 78–79, 116, 148, 159, 189, 191, 193, 199, 200, 202, 203, 205–10, 219, 247, 363, 364

demise of, 205–10

Hopkins, Ronnie, 162

Howard, Richard, 83, 130

Hunter, Jim, 266–67

Hurtubise, Jim, 83, 128

Hutcherson, Dick, 84, 165, 166, 175, 199, 200–201, 202, 203
Hyde, Harry, xvii, 249, 252, 253, 254, 275–84, 302, 311–16, 327, 339, 341–44, 363, 387, 394, 396
Hyde, Harry Lee, 277
Hylton, James, 254

Ifft, David, 244, 247–48, 287–88, 301, 302, 304, 317, 318, 319
Indianapolis, races at, 34, 128, 147, 161, 210
Inman, Dale, 179, 184
Irvan, Ernie, 83–84, 379, 389
Isaac, Bobby, xvii, 89, 91, 94, 98, 161, 166, 168, 169, 176, 177, 185, 191–92, 194, 201, 216, 252, 254, 275, 276, 278, 387

Jackson, Beryl, 115
Jarrett, Dale, xvii
Jarrett, Ned, 73, 82, 124, 130, 134, 142, 145–46, 158, 163, 165, 166
Johns, Bobby, 10
Johnson, Jimmy, 316
Johnson, Junior, 45, 62, 63, 64, 76, 79, 80, 83, 86–87, 119, 121, 140, 145–47, 155, 157, 163, 164, 165, 167, 175, 247, 290, 302, 319, 321, 322, 326, 327, 335, 341–42, 346, 351, 352–53, 359, 394
Johnson, Tommy, xviii, 275–84, 311–16, 339–44, 396
Jones, Buckshot, 198
Jones, Parnelli, 206

Kelly, Earl, 130
Kiekhaefer, Carl, 54, 59–64, 99, 100–101, 116
King, A.J., 168, 270
King, Clarence, 223, 224, 235
King Racing, 387
Kitts, Bill, 208

Krauskopf, Nord, 249, 254, 255, 275, 276, 278, 279, 283
Kulwicki, Alan, xv, xvii, 326, 345, 346, 349, 350–63, 365, 379, 380, 395, 397, 398
death of, 360–61, 380
Kulwicki, Jerry, 361–62
Kuralt, Charles, 44

Labonte, Terry, 112, 199, 294, 296, 326, 351, 363, 364, 365
LaJoie, Randy, 83
Lakewood Speedway, 56
Langhorne Speedway, 19–20, 56, 115
Langley, Elmo, 173, 175
LaRosa, Lou, xviii, 239–47, 289, 299–309, 317–29, 383–94
Latford, Bob, xviii, 1–6, 127–31, 145–49, 173–77
Laughlin, Mike, 200
LeMans, 125, 207
Little, Chad, 339, 340, 355
Littlejohn, Joe, 9, 156
Long, Bondy, 94, 96, 124, 166
Lorenzen, Fred, 47, 74, 80, 83, 85–88, 123, 124, 137, 145, 146, 157, 158, 163, 181, 201, 202, 205, 206, 208, 235, 290
Lowe, Ted, 147
Luftoe, Frank, 24
Lund, Chris, 271, 272
Lund, Tiny, xvii, 55, 66, 69, 77, 78, 79–80, 83, 89, 94, 95–96, 97, 98, 99, 104, 111, 113, 122, 123, 127, 128, 153, 161, 173, 174–75, 185, 190, 192–93, 257–73, 278, 370
death of, 78, 193, 257–58, 259, 270–72
Lund, Wanda, xviii, 259–74, 370

Makar, Jimmy, 281, 282
Mantz, Johnny, 306

Marcis, Dave, 279–80, 287, 288, 289,
    299, 301, 302, 321
Marlin, Sterling, 199, 293
Martin, John, 128
Martin, Mark, 356
Martinsville, races at, 87, 168, 275,
    284, 303, 311, 324, 326, 340, 356
Matthews, Banjo, 35, 67, 153, 209, 242
McDonald, David, 127, 128
McDuffie, J.D., 321
McMahon, Sam, III, 389, 390
McQuagg, Sam, 276
McReynolds, Larry, 373, 383, 385,
    386, 387, 388, 389, 392
Means, Jimmy, 321
Melling, Harry, 339, 340, 342
Memphis-Arkansas Speedway, 116
Meyer, Dick, 114
Michigan, races at, 374, 377, 378
Miller, Ed, 327
Millikan, Joe, 303
Milwaukee Speedway, 73
Minton, Turkey, 147
Moody, Mitsy, 28, 143
Moody, Ralph, xviii, 27–40, 47, 79,
    85–88, 112, 117, 133–37, 143,
    165, 200, 201, 202, 206, 207,
    223, 225–28
Moore, Paul "Little Bud", 89–98,
    161–71, 273
Moore, Walter "Bud", 7, 8–9, 12, 86,
    134, 137, 153, 155, 156, 157,
    192, 247, 248, 255, 269, 278,
    279, 285, 287, 288, 321, 332,
    334, 362
Moroso, Rob, 391
Muhlmann, Max, xviii, 41–49,
    139–43, 223, 224–25
Mundy, Frank, 64
Myers, Billy, xvii, 65, 66, 68, 69, 70,
    78, 331
    death of, 66, 69
Myers, Bobby, xvii, 20, 54–55, 65,
    66–70, 237, 331
    death of, 65, 68–69

Myers, Danny "Chocolate", xviii,
    66–71, 331–37
Myers, Gary, 70, 333
Myers, Lorraine, 67
Myers, Randy, 70
Myers, Richard "Pancho", 68

Nab, Herb, xvii, 79, 147, 215, 285,
    290, 291, 293, 304, 363
National Association of Stock Car
    Auto Racing (NASCAR)
    growth of popularity, 161
    organization of, 1
    origin of, 9
Negre, Norman, 282
Newman, Ducky, 247, 299, 301, 302,
    304, 317, 318, 320
Nichels, Ray, 158
Nolles, Sparky, 289
North Wilkesboro, races at, 75, 270,
    324, 356, 375

Olatta, Nick, 244
Oldfield, Barney, 3
Olds, Ransom, 3
Ongais, Danny, 246
Osiecki, Bob, 120, 121
Osterlund, Rod, 299, 301, 302, 304,
    308, 322, 324, 327, 363, 364
Ottinger, L.D., 270
Owens, Charles "Slick", xviii, 7–12,
    205–10
Owens, Cotton, 7, 8, 9, 10, 11, 12, 56,
    65, 75, 90, 153, 154, 155, 156,
    158, 159, 189, 206, 211, 212,
    214–15, 249, 250, 251

Pabst, Augie, 128
Panch, Betty, 111–12, 113, 118, 128
Panch, Marlette, 128
Panch, Marvin, xviii, 36, 82, 111–26,
    127–28, 130
Panch, Richie, 128
Pappas, Caron, 331
Pardue, Jimmy, 133, 136, 162, 182

Parker, Hank, 366
Parks, Raymond, 5, 15
Parrott, Buddy, 277, 282, 327
Parson, Marcia, 382
Parson, Phil, 381
Parsons, Benny, 146, 288, 294, 302,
    304, 316, 339, 340, 399
Paschal, Jim, 180, 182
Passano, Jacques, 201
Patterson, Bill, 328
Patterson, Raymond, 349
Pearson, David, xvii, xviii, 83, 91, 92,
    104, 124, 151–59, 161, 169,
    170, 177, 180, 183–84, 185,
    189–98, 199, 202, 203, 205,
    206–7, 249, 250, 253, 254, 255,
    256, 257, 277, 286, 294, 295,
    299, 302, 305–6, 319
Pearson, James "Bill", 152–53
Pearson, Larry, 198
Petrasek, Steve, 122–23
Petre, Joan, 108
Petree, Andy, 328
Petty, Jerry, 400
Petty, Julian "Julie", 115, 157
Petty, Lee, 17, 19, 25, 37–38, 45,
    51–56, 57, 58, 68, 78, 79, 82,
    100, 102, 108, 115, 119, 120,
    129, 140, 179, 181, 182, 184,
    185, 251, 267
Petty, Maurice, xviii, 51–58, 179–87
Petty, Richard, xvi, xvii, 13, 17, 38, 51,
    52, 55, 56–57, 61, 74, 80, 90,
    108, 112, 124, 125, 130, 151,
    158, 162, 168, 170–71, 176,
    179–80, 181, 182, 183, 185,
    186, 189, 190, 193–95, 200,
    201, 202–3, 206, 209, 213, 215,
    220–21, 234, 249, 250, 251,
    253, 255, 256, 257, 270, 280,
    286, 287, 288, 295, 302, 307,
    324, 341, 357, 370
Petty, Timmy, 187
Petty, Tiny, 55
Phoenix, races at, 351, 356, 357, 374

Pikes Peak, 177, 279
Pistone, Tom, 73–84, 153, 176
Pittman, Runt, 293
Pocono, races at, 324, 355, 376
Professional Drivers Association
    (PDA), 215, 216
Prudhomme, Don, 90
Punch, Jerry, 192, 400
Purser, Jack, 11
Putney, J.T., 124–25, 174

Quincy, Bob, 44

Rabon, Jerry, 122
Ragon, Lloyd, 114
Ranier, Harry, 285, 286, 289, 290,
    293, 294, 371
Rathmann, Jim, 73
Raymond Bealle, 282
Rebel 400, 193, 251
Rebel 500, 196
Reed, Jim, 75
Reeves, Carol, 233
Reeves, Don, 233
Regan, Larry, 282
Richardson, Jerry, 41
Richmond, Tim, 282, 311–16, 324,
    339, 341, 395, 396, 397, 398
    illness of, 311, 314–16
Riverside, races at, 134, 141, 157, 305,
    308, 314
Roberts, Doris, 129, 135
Roberts, Edward Glenn, Jr. "Fireball",
    xvii, 2, 6, 30, 33, 34–35, 36, 46,
    47, 60–61, 79, 81, 88, 96, 99,
    100, 102, 106–7, 117, 118–19,
    123, 124, 127, 128–29, 133,
    134–36, 139–43, 145, 146, 151,
    153, 155, 156, 157–58, 162,
    163, 180, 220, 300
    death of, 107, 124, 127, 129, 133,
    134–36, 139–43, 145, 162
Roberts, Tommy, 107, 352
Rockingham, races at, 221, 261, 277,
    324, 354, 356, 357, 359, 374, 388

Roper, Jim, 10, 17, 19
Rossi, Mario, 80, 242, 244, 246, 247,
    300
Rudd, Ricky, 70, 112, 317, 321, 322,
    327, 329, 362, 363, 365, 373,
    374, 383, 384, 385, 386, 387
Ruggles, Jim, 168
Runk, Joe, 11
Rutherford, Johnny, 88
Ruttman, Joe, 295, 321

Sabates, Felix, 104, 360, 361–62
Sachs, Eddie, 127, 128
Sanders, Ed, 208
Sauls, Bob, 33
Sawyer, Ralph, 154–55
Schiff, Danny, 396
Schrader, Ken, 339
Schroeder, Dorsey, 377
Scott, Billy, 105
Scott, Ramo, 253
Scott, Tighe, 281, 341
Scott, Wendell, 62, 175, 246, 265,
    321
Seagraves, Junior, 148
Seagraves, Ralph, 148
Sears Point, 383, 386
Seay, Lloyd, 15
Seto, Donald, 386
Setzer, Ned, 98
Shelby, Carol, 117, 143
Shelmerdine, Kirk, 325, 328
Shinn, George, 41
Shuman, Buddy, 31–32
Simmons, John, 393
Smith, Bruton, 81, 130, 131, 141,
    218, 222, 224–25, 234, 237,
    367
Smith, David, 328
Smith, Jack, 153, 156, 219
Smith, Louise, 5
Smith, Ray, 387
Snowball Derby, 348, 349, 372
Soldier Field, 74–75

Sommers, Sam, 301
Sonoma, xviii, 373
Southern 500, 65, 71, 121, 123, 239,
    242, 306, 308
Spartanburg Fairgrounds, 153
Spencer, G.C., 153, 163
Spencer, Jimmy, 83
Stacy, J.D., 275, 280, 281, 283, 302,
    321, 363, 364
Stacy, Nelson, 146
Stavola Brothers, 316, 339, 353
Stevens, Butch, 84
Stewart, Cliff, 348
Stricklin, Hut, 372, 374
Stroppe, Bill, 35, 64, 114–15, 206

Talladega, races at, 185, 193, 215–16,
    250, 254, 256, 257, 270,
    286–87, 289, 292, 293, 296,
    319, 335, 339, 377, 380, 397,
    399
Taus, Bill, 126
Teague, Marshall, 4, 6, 22, 129
Team Three, 383, 389, 390
Thomas, Herb, 23, 24–25, 54, 62, 64,
    75, 101
Thompson, Bruce, 16
Thompson, Speedy, 16, 33, 46, 54, 62,
    64, 116, 120–21
Thrap, Eddie, 319
Townsend, Jeff, 348
Trout, Kenny, 246
Turner, Bunny, xviii, 228, 229–35
Turner, Curtis, xvii, 8, 11–12, 19,
    20–21, 22, 23, 27, 35, 36–37,
    38–40, 45–47, 48–49, 53–54,
    55, 65, 66, 67, 76, 77, 78, 79,
    81, 86, 90, 99, 102, 103, 105–6,
    113, 117–18, 120, 129, 130,
    131, 135, 140, 141, 163, 210,
    212, 217–18, 219–20, 221,
    223–28, 229–30, 231–37,
    268
  death of, 223–28, 237

Ulrich, D. K., 282
Unser, Bobby, 268–69, 279
USAC circuit, 348
Vaughn, Linda, 122
Vernon, Tom, 119
Vogt, Red, 1, 5, 35, 36, 60

Wade, Billy, 133, 134, 136–37, 162
Wallace, Gary, 347
Wallace, Kenny, 363, 366, 390
Wallace, Russell, 347
Wallace, Rusty, 83, 220, 286, 325,
    345, 347, 348, 349, 398
Waltrip, Darrell, 146, 196, 199, 205,
    208–9, 243, 244, 246, 256, 286,
    288, 294, 304, 306, 307, 311,
    319, 322, 363–64, 365, 376,
    379, 383, 384, 391, 392, 393
Ward, Buddy, 343
Ward, Rodger, 206
Watkins Glen, xviii, 175, 313, 377,
    399
Watson, W.H., 11
Weatherly, Joe, xvi, xvii, 8, 11, 12, 22,
    23, 24, 27, 31, 35, 36, 37,
    38–39, 47–48, 49, 53–54, 55,
    56, 76–77, 86, 99, 105–6, 113,
    117, 118, 124, 127, 128, 133,
    134, 135, 141, 145, 146, 151,
    157, 162, 181, 225, 232–33, 305
  death of, 124, 133, 134, 141, 157,
    181, 305
Welborn, Bob, 80
Wheeler, Humpy, 162, 168, 302
Whitcomb, Bob, 325
White, Jack, 19
White, Rex, 57, 66, 153, 209
Whitford, John, 119
Whitney, Nat, 28
Widenhouse, Dink, 105
Wiley, Frank, 148, 215
Wilkesboro, 386
Williams, Peachtree, 14
Willyuh, Lee, 247

Wilson, Fred, 130
Wilson, Rick, 339, 340
Wilson, Waddell, 285, 290–91, 292,
    293, 393
Wimble, Bill, 122
Winston Cup, 269, 270, 284, 286,
    299, 307, 308, 309, 311, 332,
    334, 348, 349, 362, 387
Winston Million, 379
Winston Open, 397
Witners, Braddie, 29
Wlodyka, Roland, 299, 301, 302, 308,
    309
Wolf, Joe, 18, 32
Women drivers, about, 5, 287
Wood, Glen, 66, 121, 122, 128, 235,
    294
Wood, Leonard, 121, 122, 195, 197,
    207, 294, 295
Wood Brothers, 111, 120, 121, 123,
    125, 189, 193, 194, 195–96,
    197, 286, 294, 296, 302, 305
World Service Life 300, 303
World 600, 57, 81, 168, 169, 182,
    214, 252, 254, 255, 279, 281,
    366

Yarborough, Cale, xvii, 8, 9, 91, 104,
    164, 165, 169, 171, 205,
    209–10, 216, 249, 253, 254,
    256, 265, 266, 267, 271, 285,
    287, 289, 294, 295, 299, 302,
    305, 308, 317–19, 320, 365,
    396
Yarbrough, Eldon, 96
Yarbrough, LeeRoy, 89, 95, 96–97, 99,
    104, 105, 145, 147–48, 166,
    215, 264
Yates, Dennis, 389
Yates, Robert, 167, 184, 247, 248,
    363, 366, 371, 373, 389, 391
Yunick, Smokey, 36, 112, 119, 120,
    141, 142, 158, 180, 184, 186,
    299, 300–301, 394